PRIMATE SOCIOBIOLOGY

J. Patrick Gray

HRAF PRESS
New Haven, Connecticut
1985

ABOUT THE AUTHOR:

J. Patrick Gray (Ph.D., University of Colorado, 1976) is currently Assistant Professor of Anthropology at the University of Wisconsin—Milwaukee. In the past he has been a Lecturer at Xavier University, Cagayan de Oro City, Philippines; Assistant Professor of Anthropology at North Texas State University and a National Endowment for the Humanities Residential Fellow at Northwestern. His numerous publications on human and primate sociobiology, holocultural research, sexual behavior and related topics have appeared in *Ethos, American Anthropologist, Ethology and Sociobiology, American Journal of Physical Anthropology, The Humanist, Journal of Human Evolution, Journal of Social Psychology* and other scholarly journals and books.

Cover Design: Marylou Finch.

INTERNATIONAL STANDARD BOOK NUMBER: 0-87536-344-X
LIBRARY OF CONGRESS NUMBER: 85-60629
© 1985
HUMAN RELATIONS AREA FILES, INC.
NEW HAVEN, CONNECTICUT
ALL RIGHTS RESERVED
PRINTED IN THE UNITED STATES OF AMERICA

Acknowledgments

David Levinson of the Human Relations Area Files staff provided vital help on this project from the moment it was presented to HRAF. Elizabeth P. Swift's editing was invaluable.

Written or oral communications with the following individuals provided stimulation and help on specific matters: Cheryl Fosburgh, Kristin Griffin, John Hartung, William Irons, Donald Kurtz, Jerald Maiers, S. K. Nair, Roberta Newman, Joseph Roberts, Inger Wilkerson, and Patricia Zarafshar. Insights gained in two years of conversations with Jim Silverberg are frequently found in this volume. Linda Wolfe also contributed to my thinking on sociobiology.

Some of the research on this project was conducted while the author held a residential fellowship from the National Endowment for the Humanities. David Jorvasky and the members of the seminar group provoked much thought on the wider issues raised by sociobiology.

Finally, thanks to Lynne English for constant support.

Contents

CHAPTER 1

Defining Sociobiology

INTRODUCTION

This review monograph is the companion to *A Guide to Primate Sociobiological Theory and Research* (Gray 1984). The *Guide* contains profiles of 396 tests of hypotheses generated from within the sociobiological framework, as well as various indexes that permit researchers easy access to these profiles. In this volume, I examine the results of the hypothesis tests in more detail and review the progress of primate sociobiology from 1976 to the present.

The plan of the review monograph follows the divisions of sociobiological theory that are set out in the *Guide*. In the remainder of this chapter, I define the domain of primate sociobiology by discussing the hallmarks of general sociobiology. In Chapter Two, I examine what is at stake in the controversy over sociobiology and its application to the social sciences. I focus on anthropology and discuss what a sociobiologically-informed anthropology would look like and how it would differ from the discipline as currently constituted. I also explore the problems that some theorists see in applying sociobiological theory to human behavior.

Chapter Three reviews the theory and empirical research in primate ecological sociobiology. Chapters Four through Nine examine the results of hypothesis testing in each of the six main divisions of sociobiological theory as identified in the *Guide*. These are: nepotism theory, reciprocal altruism theory, parental investment theory, sexual selection theory, rank theory, and human reproductive strategy theory. Finally, an appendix reviews some recent tests of sociobiological theory.

This monograph can be utilized as an introduction to primate socio-biology. In each of the data review chapters, I discuss the major concepts that are relevant to the particular division of the theory under consideration. Although the main focus of the volume is the analysis of individual empirical studies, I indicate important directions of research which have not yet generated empirical work, and I provide references that allow a student to investigate them further.

DEFINING SOCIOBIOLOGY

Sociobiology is ". . . the systematic study of the biological basis of all social behavior" (Wilson 1975a:4). The discipline is the result of the recent convergence of three areas of biological investigation: evolutionary genetics, ecology, and ethology (Barlow 1980; Smith 1983). At present, interest in the evolutionary genetics component outweighs interest in the other two, and many people mistakenly believe that sociobiology is concerned only with evolutionary genetics. Although the ecological and ethological components are never forgotten in primate sociobiology, they are rarely given equal weight with the evolutionary genetics approach. In part this is because they are not as controversial; research into the ecological and ethological aspects of primate social behavior was already well advanced prior to the intro-duction of certain innovative and still controversial concepts from evolu-tionary genetics. It is these concepts that give sociobiology its new look, and consequently theorists are prone to emphasize them.

Emlen (1980) notes that sociobiology currently has two major research directions, which are not totally integrated. The first seeks to understand the evolution of social structure, while the second attempts to explain the evolution of individual behavioral strategies within different social struc-tures. Emlen labels the first research direction "ecological sociobiology." Some of the major topics in ecological sociobiology include (Emlen 1980:128): (1) the evolution of sociality (what ecological factors determine whether a species exhibits sociality); (2) the evolution of territoriality (what ecological factors determine whether and when members of a species defend resources, and what resources are defended); and (3) the evolution of mating systems (what ecological factors determine the types of breeding systems that are exhibited by a species). Although there are debates between specialists over concrete applications, the use of concepts from ecological sociobiology to explain primate social structure has not generated the controversy that is associated with the use of theory derived from the second direction of research.

Emlen does not provide a label for this second research direction. The label of "selfish gene theory" is suggested by Richard Dawkin's (1976) influential book, but such a label prejudges some of the issues still that are subject to debate among sociobiologists. In this volume, I use the phrase "strategic sociobiology" to describe this line of research. Emlen notes that strategic sociobiology attempts to provide evolutionary explanations of individual behavior within different social structures. Some of the topics in strategic sociobiology include: (1) resource gathering and distribution strategies; (2) mating strategies; (3) parental investment strategies; and (4) strategies of interaction with kin and strangers (Emlen 1980:126).

Although ecological and strategic sociobiology can be conceptually distinguished, and although most research is focused on either one or the other, the long-range goal of sociobiology is unification of the two. A mature sociobiology will demonstrate how the evolution of behavioral strategies is influenced by the factors that produce social structure and how the evolution of social structure is affected by the behaviors of individuals.

Wilson's (1975a) general definition of sociobiology and the distinction between ecological and strategic sociobiology do not adequately delimit the topics covered in this volume. Discussion of what I take to be four hallmarks of sociobiology will do so, however. For our purposes, current research in primate sociobiology can be roughly characterized as: (1) describing evolution by a strategy metaphor; (2) being concerned primarily with mechanisms of ultimate causation; (3) accepting the idea of group level selection only as a last resort; and (4) accepting Hamilton's concept of inclusive fitness.

Before discussing these features, two notes on terminology are in order. First, it seems that for various reasons many scientists whose research exhibits these hallmarks prefer that their work not be subsumed under the label of sociobiology. Instead, they use labels such as "behavioral biology," "evolutionary ecology," or "behavioral ecology." Although these researchers make strong cases for their preferences, and although there are subtle differences between these fields, in this volume I will subsume their work under the label of "sociobiology." I do so for three reasons. First, the term is already used by most social scientists to describe the type of research discussed in this volume. Second, Wilson's definition of sociobiology, as quoted at the head of this section, is sufficiently general to accommodate all of the research evaluated in the project. And finally, the adjective "socio-biological" is less cumbersome than the various alternatives.

Second, while I frequently make statements such as "sociobiologists state . . ." or "sociobiology holds . . . ," this type of statement is primarily a convenient form of shorthand and should not be taken to imply that all theorists whose work is reviewed would agree with each statement. Sociobiology is not a unified field, and there are major theoretical differences among sociobiologists.

THE HALLMARKS OF SOCIOBIOLOGY

1. The Strategy Metaphor

The first hallmark involves the metaphors that sociobiology employs to describe the processes of evolution. Darwin demonstrated that the two major forces of evolution were differential survival of animals varying in one or more traits (with differential reproductive success as an "accidental" outcome) and differential reproductive success among animals not exhibiting differential survival. A great deal of Darwin's work centered on the former process, demonstrating the role of the "hostile forces of nature" (predation, disease, lack of food, etc.) in creating differential survival. The process of intrapopulational competition over mates or resources, resulting in different degrees of reproductive success for animals with equal survival rates, was addressed by Darwin in his discussion of sexual selection, but it did not capture the attention of early evolutionists as did the idea of the survival of the fittest.

The image of evolution that is generated by focusing on differential survival is one of animals going about their lives while the hostile forces of nature remove those who possess less fit traits. This image contains two entities, the population of animals and the environment, with the latter seen as the active force in evolution. The population is characterized by the continual production of variability, but it is the environment that selects "for" or "against" particular traits. The unification of population genetics with Darwinian theory to produce the synthetic theory of evolution reinforced this metaphor by removing the basis for any Lamarckian interpretation of evolution. Mathematical formulas describing changes in gene frequency strengthened the image of the environment acting upon passive individuals, now conceived of as loci of alleles.

Sociobiology proposes a different metaphor to describe evolution; one more congenial with Darwin's discussion of sexual selection. In place of the image of a population of animals possessing traits with different fitness values being acted upon by the environment, sociobiology substitutes the images and vocabulary of optimization and game theory. Individuals are seen as actors whose goal is to maximize their reproductive success (actually, their inclusive fitness—see below). Behaviors are conceptualized as tactics resulting from strategies, and animals are said to gather resources and to make investments. Since resources are limited, competition is inevitable; animals compete against one another for access to the limited resources of mates, food, security, etc. Also, the various activities in which an animal might engage are said to compete for its time, energy, or other resources; time spent in feeding is time lost from mating or from developing social relationships leading to future matings.

This change in metaphors is one of the most controversial aspects of sociobiology. Sociobiologists argue that the switch is merely one of vocabulary, which has allowed them to see evolution in a new light by raising questions different from those suggested by the older image. However, processes described by one metaphor can always be translated into the terms of the other with no loss of information. For example, a typical research problem in sociobiology might consist of identifying the possible courses of action open to an animal, calculating the effect each would have on its inclusive fitness, and asking which course the animal should choose. This situation can be translated back into the images of traditional synthetic theory: assume two forms of behavior, X1 and X2; assume also that the differential propensity of animals in the population to engage in one or the other is partially or totally related to genetic differences between the animals. If animals engaging in X1 are more successful at resisting the hostile forces of nature or at obtaining mates, they will leave behind more offspring than those engaging in X2, and, all other things being equal, behavior X1 will be selected for and the genes relevant to its production will increase in future generations.

Critics have faulted sociobiology's use of the strategy metaphor on at least two counts. The less serious charge is that the metaphor works well as colorful shorthand, but tends to lead the unwary into the trap of attributing consciousness of goals and strategies to animals. This is especially troublesome when dealing with species that inhabit complex and/or unpredictable social or physical environments. Evolutionists agree that such species have been selected to be "flexible," meaning that a great deal of the behavioral variation within the species is the result of learning. In such cases, relating "strategies" to their genetic underpinnings becomes extraordinarily difficult. Even the statement that animals act so as to maximize their reproductive success generates a skeptical attitude in direct proportion to the number of behavioral options open to animals and the number of variables implicated in any particular decision. The solution to this problem is, no doubt, a stronger emphasis by sociobiologists on the metaphorical nature of their language.

The more serious charge against the strategy metaphor is that by using it, sociobiologists have fundamentally perverted Darwinian theory. A brief examination of Sahlins' (1976:74–91) version of this charge will highlight the issues involved. Sahlins identifies several differences between what he sees as the traditional view of natural selection and the sociobiological view of evolution. The former operates by examining relative fitness advantages among members of a population in a given environment. Sahlins notes that the traditional view says only that traits being positively selected for are "more or less" better than less fit traits. Thus, a trait could be selected for if its bearers produced fourteen offspring in a lifetime while animals without the trait produced only thirteen. This relative advantage view, Sahlins says, does not postulate maximization or optimization of any value or trait. A second difference suggested by Sahlins is that the expectation of maximization or

optimization is precluded in traditional natural selection theory, because
the theory implies that indeterminancy characterizes evolution. Environmental and genetic changes are more or less independent of each other, and
both are random with respect to prior adaptation. Sahlins argues that this
indeterminancy tends to prevent traits from being optimized in any given
population.

Sahlins suggests that sociobiologists who ignore the relative fitness view
and overlook the indeterminate nature of evolution to concentrate on
maximization of morphological features or behavioral traits fall victim to
teleology and end up viewing the organism (or population) as directing its
own evolution toward the goal of perfection. He also accuses sociobiologists
of engaging in the "fallacy of an a priori fitness course" (1976:82–83) when
they explain certain features of organisms in terms of an optimum response
to natural problems. For example, both Williams (1966:174) and Wilson
(1975a:97) argue that in semelparous (giving birth only once in a lifetime)
salmon, certain organic changes, such as atrophy of the digestive tract, have
evolved in order to maximize the number of eggs a female can produce.
Sahlins argues that this explanation illegitimately separates a currently
existing organism into an organism with prior (exhibiting semelparity)
traits, which create adaptive problems that create later (exhibiting atrophy
of the digestive tract) traits as responses. In the case of the salmon, Sahlins
argues that this procedure rules out other possible life histories for the
salmon (e.g., why not spawn twice?). Sahlins notes that there are few
guidelines to decide which trait should be taken as prior and which as later.

Sahlins does grant (1976:77–78) that sociobiologists frequently note that
animals are not perfectly adapted to their environment and often provide
reasons why perfect adaptation should not be expected. However, he rather
summarily dismisses such statements by noting: "To be *aware* of something,
however, to *recognize* it, is not the same thing as knowing the *concept* of it. It is
not to put it in its right theoretical place" (1976:78, emphasis in the original).

A possible interpretation of Sahlins' comment is that sociobiologists
should not become victims of their metaphors of maximization and
optimization. With this no one can disagree. However, I do not think that
Sahlins has a strong case in contending that merely thinking in terms of
maximization and optimization inherently perverts Darwinian theory. In
practice, the best sociobiological theorizing models the maximization of
traits or the optimum solution to an adaptive problem, examines the real
world to see whether or not the model is validated, and, if it is not, examines
the situation for factors preventing optimization or maximization. Among
such factors are precisely those of relative advantage and environmental
and genetic changes that are discussed by Sahlins. In this type of research,
the postulates of maximization or optimization play the role of guides to
thinking rather than being statements about reality.

Sahlins' discussion of the salmon is also not particularly convincing as a critique of the basic logic of sociobiology. It is true that when a single species is under examination, a large (but not infinite and not all equally probable) number of adaptive stories can be created to explain a particular trait. However, the sociobiological explanation of the salmon life history is not based just on the analysis of a single species. The explanation is generated with reference to a great deal of data that have not been discussed by Sahlins. For example, there are data on the congenerics of the salmon, some of which are not semelparous. There are data on the phylogenetic history of the salmon, which might allow a sorting of characteristics into primitive and derived, providing a check on any tendency to divide the salmon randomly into earlier and later traits. Further, there are data on the life histories of other animals that exhibit semelparity. With proper control for phylogenetic and other differences, this final set of data can provide a means of testing Wilson's and Williams' explanation of the salmon's life history. Finally, seen in isolation, the explanation offered by Williams and by Wilson does seem arbitrary, and in the nature of a "Just So" story. However, this is an illusion, created because Sahlins presents the explanation independently of its theoretical framework, which involves the evolution of senescence (Williams 1957). Within this framework, the explanation is definitely not arbitrary, and it becomes, furthermore, more amenable to testing.

The use of a strategy metaphor by sociobiologists will remain a point of contention. I suggest that the reader of any empirical study in sociobiology carefully examine how the author uses the metaphor and then decide whether or not the use is justified in the particular case under consideration.

2. Focus on Ultimate Causation

Biologists and social scientists agree that any behavior can be explained from different perspectives. Daly and Wilson (1978:8–13) identify four such perspectives (which they call "levels of explanation") commonly utilized in evolutionary biology: ultimate causation, proximate causation, ontogenetic causation, and phylogenetic causation. The display behavior of male Japanese macaques (Modahl and Eaton 1977; Wolfe 1981a) will be used to illustrate these perspectives.

Ultimate causation (sometimes called "distal causation") inquires as to the adaptive significance that branch shaking and other displays might have had in the evolutionary history of the species. A researcher interested in ultimate causation asks how the behavior was related to reproductive success in generations ancestral to the present one. Modahl and Eaton find that in their Oregon troop, the frequency of male display varies directly with the number of partners a male has in the breeding season. This suggests that one answer to the question of why male Japanese macaques display is that the males who displayed in the past achieved higher reproductive success than those who did not—perhaps because the former were more attractive to females.

Two features of ultimate causation explanations should be noted. First, such explanations focus on the evolutionary history of the species. If the population under consideration either has recently entered a new environment or has faced environmental change, behaviors that formerly maximized reproductive success may no longer do so. In other words, ultimate causation is always related to a species' environment of evolutionary adaptation. Second, the relationship between any behavior and reproductive success may be indirect and therefore difficult to identify. For example, in two troops of Japanese macaques, Wolfe finds that frequency of display is directly correlated with a male's dominance rank, but not with the number of partners he has in the breeding season. Some primatologists argue that high rank can increase reproductive success or inclusive fitness even if higher—ranking males do not mate more frequently or with more partners than lower-ranking males (see Fedigan 1983). For example, if higher-ranking males are more capable than lower-ranking males of protecting their offspring they may achieve greater reproductive success, even though there are no rank-related differences in the number of offspring sired. If this were true for the troops studied by Wolfe (there is, however, no evidence that it is), it could be argued that the ultimate cause of display behavior is its relationship to increased reproductive success, but through the indirect route of helping males establish or maintain their position in the dominance hierarchy, rather than the direct route of helping displayers sire more offspring than nondisplayers.

Proximate causation explanations discuss the physiological, psychological, or sociological stimuli that produce the behaviors under study. For example, Modahl and Eaton find that the percentage of males displaying and the frequency of display increase during the breeding season. Thus, a proximate explanation of display behavior might focus on hormonal changes between the breeding and nonbreeding seasons. If the start and the termination of the breeding season are related to environmental factors, such as resource availability or day length, these factors might also be included in a proximate explanation of display behavior. Finally, sociological factors may also be implicated. For example, if patterns of interactions between males change during the breeding season, social cues eliciting displays may increase, thereby increasing the frequency of displays. Wolfe notes that the troop she studied in Japan attracted solitary or migrant males during the breeding season. These males did not join the central core of the troop, and they made their presence known to females by displays. Troop membership thus might be relevant to a proximate explanation of display behavior in this setting.

Ontogenetic explanations describe how a behavior pattern develops over the course of an organism's lifetime. An ontogenetic explanation of Japanese macaque display behavior is not currently available, but the parameters of one are clear. For example, researchers might investigate the development of attention-getting strategies by infants, in the hope of relating these to the displays emitted by adults. Another focus of research would be on behaviors emitted in juvenile play groups. Finally, researchers would want to know whether the viewing of adult displays affects the occurrence of such behaviors in younger animals.

Finally, phylogenetic explanations adopt a broad perspective and explore the pre-existing morphological and behavioral structures out of which display behaviors might have evolved. Such explanations are not restricted to a single species, but rather trace a behavior back through the species ancestral to the species under study. There is not yet a phylogenetic explanation of display behavior, although the widespread existence of this trait in the primate order (Modahl and Eaton 1977) suggests that one is needed.

It is an often repeated truism that a complete explanation of any behavior requires answers from each of the four perspectives. In practice, however, researchers tend to restrict their attention to one perspective. Sociobiologists argue that since many biologists and social scientists attend only to the proximate and ontogenetic perspectives, they themselves are only redressing the balance by discussing ultimate causation.

The term "ultimate" has the unfortunate connotation of designating the most important or the most basic, and sociobiologists have been accused of writing in a manner suggesting that behavior can be explained "only" or "most adequately" as the outcome of the operation of natural selection. To the extent that such an impression is accurate, it is due to the attempts of some sociobiologists to define their field as a new and revolutionary discipline. In a public relations campaign of this sort, points are not made by emphasizing claims of moderation and the equal importance of all four perspectives (although such statements are usually present). Instead, explanations from the other perspectives are attacked as incorrect or incomplete and the new field introduced as the savior of biology or the social sciences.

I believe that the tendency of some sociobiologists to downplay the importance of alternative perspectives is not as serious as the failure of some social scientists to keep the perspectives separate. A frequent criticism of sociobiology is that it neglects this or that influence on behavior. The most common misunderstanding involves the role of learning, with many social scientists assuming that sociobiology explains only "innate" behaviors, those which are not learned. This stance confuses the ontogenetic, proximate, and ultimate causation perspectives and ignores the fact that what is learned and how it is learned may be related to the evolutionary past of a species and thus demand explanation from the ultimate perspective.

The language of the four levels of causation unfortunately leaves the impression that social scientists have the option of ignoring sociobiology by granting to it the study of ultimate causation but defining their own interests as being on the level of proximate causation. This tactic is especially attractive to social scientists who are interested in the applicability of their work to social problems. After all, we cannot change the evolutionary history of the species, but factors involved in the proximate causation of behavior can often be manipulated. Such an approach seriously underestimates the challenge of the sociobiological paradigm. The proximate factors involved in the production of behavior are related to the ultimate function of that behavior and have been shaped by natural selection. The stimuli an animal attends to, the threshold values of stimuli that are needed to generate particular behaviors, and the rules linking stimuli with other stimuli are all the outcome of evolution (see Shields and Shields 1983 for a more detailed discussion of this point). The full understanding of proximate causation must be predicated upon knowledge of ultimate causation. An implication of this fact for those seeking to apply social science to social problems is that knowledge of ultimate causation may often provide evidence on how effective the manipulation of different proximate factors might turn out to be. For example, Shields and Shields (1983) argue that the ultimate function of human rape is reproductive success and suggest that males will rape when the benefits of rape are seen to outweigh the costs. They evaluate various proposals to deal with rape in light of these considerations and suggest that the most effective course of action is to make the costs of rape both highly visible and appropriately large.

The translation of findings from an analysis of ultimate level causation to social policy is a dangerous task, one which requires continual sensitivity to possible cultural bias, to the innovative possibilities of human culture, and to the limitations of sociobiology (of course this is equally true of any translation of theory to practice). Although not all users of sociobiological concepts have exhibited such sensitivity, their failure to do so does not negate the fact that if the sociobiological paradigm is correct, social scientists cannot afford to ignore it by separating ultimate and proximate analyses and by underestimating the importance of the former.

3. The Lowest Level of Selection

The synthetic theory of evolution states that the traits that increase reproductive success are selected for, while those that result in fewer offspring are selected against. In the sociobiological metaphor, animals strive to maximize their reproductive success. Both of these views appear to be contradicted when animals are observed acting in ways which reduce their own reproductive success but increase that of conspecifics. The problem can be illustrated by imagining an unchanging environment with a population of animals exhibiting one of two strategies: altruists are willing to forego a percentage of the offspring they are capable of producing if by doing so they help conspecifics to reproduce; nonaltruists are unwilling to forego any reproduction, but will accept the aid of altruists to create additional offspring. We also assume that: (1) there are no other fitness differences between altruists and nonaltruists; (2) altruists randomly aid both other altruists and nonaltruists; and (3) there is a genetic component to the propensity to adopt either strategy. Over generations, the proportion of altruists in this population will decline, while that of nonaltruists will increase. Eventually, the propensity to adopt the altruistic strategy might be eliminated from the population.

Altruistic acts, then, are those that reduce the probability of the altruist's reproductive success to some degree while at the same time increasing that of a conspecific. Such acts remained a stumbling block in evolutionary theory until fairly recently (Hamilton 1964; Trivers 1971; Wilson 1975a). The need for an explanation of altruism was a major reason for the elaboration of group selection theory in evolutionary biology. Group selection theory (Wynne-Edwards 1962; Williams 1971; D. S. Wilson 1983) is a complex topic and will not be discussed in detail here. Its contribution to the present discussion is the idea that, in certain cases, selection for altruistic behavior may occur because of benefits to the group (deme, population, or species).

An extreme case wherein group selection theory seems to be required occurs when nonaltruistic actions by animals would lead to the extinction of the group. Imagine two groups of animals of the same species confronting a food shortage, one composed of altruists and the other of nonaltruists. Assume that overexploitation of food resources will result in the population having nothing to eat the following year. In the population of altruists, individuals forego a percentage of their reproductive potential either by producing fewer offspring than they are capable of producing or by not reproducing at all (we leave aside the proximal mechanisms determining who foregoes how much reproduction). These altruistic acts allow the conservation of enough food to ensure an adequate food supply in the following year. In contrast, in the population of nonaltruists, all animals fulfill their reproductive potential, and the extra mouths result in more food being consumed and the environment being overexploited. In the following year, the population has nothing to eat and becomes extinct. Group selection theory holds that differential extinction of groups could lead to the evolution and fixation of altruism in some populations.

From Wynne-Edwards' technical work on the evolution of reproductive restraint it is an easy step to assume that many animal behaviors can be explained by showing that they are "for the good of the group" or "good for the species." Many biologists never accepted group selection theory or the rather loose extensions of it implied in the "for the good of the group" argument. In 1966, G. C. Williams marshaled convincing arguments against group selection in his *Adaptation and Natural Selection*. He argued that most purported examples of group selection could be more parsimoniously explained as the outcome of individual selection. As a general orientation,

Williams argued, biologists should always assume that selection takes place at the lowest level of analysis. Thus, features of populations should first be examined as the summation of the behaviors of individuals seeking to maximize their reproductive success. Only after all possible explanations on lower levels are exhausted should we assume that a behavior has originated or is maintained by group selection.

Williams' volume did not disprove the possibility of group selection, and modern sociobiology does not rule out the possibility either. Several mathematical models of the process are available (Wade 1977, 1978, 1979; D. S. Wilson 1975, 1983), although they are controversial. The present consensus seems to be that group selection is possible, but that the conditions necessary for its operation are rarely realized in nature. Thus, group selection should be utilized only as an explanation of last resort.

The insistence on the priority of lower levels of selection at the expense of higher levels is one of the reasons sociobiology has encountered resistance among social scientists, who often speak of populations adapting to an environment and socializing individuals in manners that maintain such adaptation. These theorists often describe cases wherein individuals expend time and resources in behaviors which do not benefit the individual, but do reward others in the group. I will return to this point below.

4. Inclusive Fitness

The image of society as the summation of the behaviors of individuals seeking to maximize their reproductive success encounters the problem of altruism. If we rule out group selection, how can we explain situations where individuals act in manners that reduce their own reproductive success, while increasing that of others? The answer to this question depends upon going to a level of selection below that of the individual and introducing the concept of inclusive fitness (Dawkins 1976, 1982; Hamilton 1964; Trivers 1971, 1974).

Inclusive fitness theory holds that genes (however defined) are the true replicators upon which natural selection operates. Individuals can profitably be conceptualized as temporary collections of replicating genes. The individual organism will die, and the collection of genes within that body will disappear. If the individual has reproduced, however, replicas of individual genes will have been passed on to offspring and thus have the potential of replicating themselves in the future. A focus on the gene as the unit of selection suggests the image of the organism as the means by which individual genes protect and spread themselves. In the strategic metaphor of sociobiology, genes are seen as calculating entities, with the goal of maximizing the number of copies they add to the gene pool.

Hamilton notes that this focus on the gene as the entity maximizing reproductive success means that we must examine the fate of all copies of a given gene. This requires reconsidering the relationship between the individual and reproductive success. Under the synthetic theory of evolution, an individual's fitness is measured by the number of offspring he or she produces, relative to those produced by other individuals. Each offspring represents more of a parent's genes "projected" into the next generation. Hamilton suggests looking at the situation differently. Imagine a diploid, sexually reproducing species and visualize the fate of an allele A carried by a heterozygous female mating with a heterozygous male. Each time this female conceives, the probability is 0.5 that allele A is passed on to her offspring. If she has four offspring, the chances are even that two of them contain allele A. Hamilton notes that from the perspective of allele A in Ego, the sibling also receiving allele A may be a source through which the allele can project more copies into the next generation. If Ego can help this sibling reproduce, he or she should do so. Sometimes help should be provided even though Ego decreases his or her chances of reproductive success. This should be done only when the reduced reproductive success of allele A in Ego is more than offset by the increased reproductive success of allele A in the sibling benefiting from Ego's altruism.

Here we need to introduce some terminology relevant to a formal description of the situation sketched above. First is the concept of coefficient of relatedness (r). We can explore this concept by considering an Ego who is heterozygous for allele A. Assuming that both parents were heterozygotes at the loci in question, the probability that any one of Ego's siblings also contains allele A is 0.5. Now, suppose that one of Ego's siblings, Y, has a child, Z (assume no inbreeding). What is the probability that the allele A that X got from his or her mother is also present in Z? There are two cases to consider. First, if Y did not carry A, the probability that Z carries A is zero. On the other hand, if Y did carry A, the probability is 0.5 that he or she passed it on to Z. The average probability that any of Ego's siblings carries A is 0.5, and the probability that an average sibling of Ego passed on the allele to his or her offspring is also 0.5. The product of these probabilities is 0.25, the coefficient of relatedness between Ego and Z.

Barash notes there are two ways of defining r:

1. as the probability that a particular allele, present in one individual, is also present in the other individual because of descent from a common ancestor;
2. as the summed probabilities of all genes within an individual and, hence, the proportion of genotype in two individuals that are identical because of their common descent [Barash 1982:70].

There are subtle differences between these definitions (Blick 1977; Dawkins 1979), and for the present I will utilize only the first in this discussion. The r between various relatives, assuming no inbreeding and assuming that parents are correctly identified, are as follows: parents and offspring, full siblings, 0.5; half siblings, uncles/aunts and niece/nephews, 0.25; first cousins, 0.125.

This brings us to the concept of inclusive fitness and to Hamilton's solution to the evolution of altruism problem:

> Hamilton shows that natural selection will favor altruism between relatives whenever the "benefit" [B] (positive selective effect) to the recipient, weighted by the degree of relatedness between actor and recipient, is greater than the "cost" [C] (negative selective effect) to the actor, that is, rB > C [Kurland 1980:256].

This equation states that under certain conditions individuals should accept a reduction in their own reproductive success in order to increase the reproductive success of relatives. The information needed to specify these conditions includes the coefficient of relatedness between the two individuals, the costs to the donor, and the benefits to the recipient. As an example, let us return to the siblings Ego and Y and assume that a behavior by Ego will benefit Y but result in Ego's losing two potential offspring. Since $r = 0.5$ between parent and offspring, Ego will probably fail to place one copy of allele A in the following generation. However, let us assume that Ego's act permits Y to produce eight children who would not have been born without Ego's help. The r between Ego and any nephews/nieces is 0.25, meaning that of the eight children produced by Y, two will probably carry allele A. Under these conditions, more copies of allele A will enter the next generation if Ego helps Y than if Ego fails to help and produces two children (two copies versus one). In other words, from the perspective of allele A, an increase of two in Ego's reproductive success is not as beneficial as an increase of eight in Y's reproductive success.

The gene-level perspective requires a new measure of fitness, for number of offspring is not an adequate measure of the fitness of alleles. Hamilton used the term "inclusive fitness," defined as:

> the personal fitness which an individual actually expresses in its production of adult offspring [reproductive success] as it becomes after it has been first stripped and then augmented in a certain way. It is stripped of all components which can be considered as due to the individual's social environment, leaving the fitness which he would express if not exposed to any of the harms or benefits of that environment. This quantity is then augmented by certain fractions of the quantities of the harm and benefit which the individual himself causes to the fitnesses of his neighbours. The fractions in question are simply the coefficients of relationship appropriate to the neighbours whom he affects: unity for clonal individuals, one-half for sibs, one-quarter for half-sibs; one-eighth for cousins . . . and finally zero for all neighbours whose relationship can be considered negligibly small [Hamilton 1964:8].

Another way of phrasing the concept is that inclusive fitness measures the success that an allele has in projecting copies of itself into the next generation, regardless of where those copies reside. The central principle of sociobiology thus changes from the idea that individuals should behave so as to maximize their reproductive success to the statement that individuals should behave so as to maximize their inclusive fitness (Barash 1982:45).

Three comments on inclusive fitness theory are necessary. First, the theory operates on probabilities; it does not require that an individual somehow identify and direct altruistic behaviors to only those siblings that share a common allele with him or her (although mechanisms allowing such discrimination have been suggested). The calculations hold if Ego distributes altruistic acts equally to all of his or her siblings. Second, inclusive fitness theory utilizes a strategy metaphor, but does not suggest that animals consciously calculate coefficients of relatedness before acting. The proximate causation of altruistic behavior is an interesting and important topic, but one conceptually independent of the inclusive fitness concept. Finally, to illustrate inclusive fitness through consideration of a single gene greatly oversimplifies the real world situation. When we consider (1) the number of genes comprising the genotype of an animal; (2) the fact that it is the phenotype that relates to the environment; and (3) such phenomena as gene linkage (two or more genes which tend to be passed together), pleiotrophy (a single allele producing multiple effects upon the phenotype), or conflicts of interests among genes, then the situation becomes extremely complex. As with the other hallmarks, I am not dismissing these difficulties, but only want to point out that the acceptance of the inclusive fitness concept is one of the four hallmarks of sociobiology.

To summarize this chapter: the threads connecting most of the studies in this volume include concern with ultimate causation, preference for explanations based on individual or gene-level selection as opposed to those requiring group level selection, conceptualization of evolution with a strategy metaphor, and, finally, acceptance of inclusive fitness theory.

CHAPTER 2

Sociobiology and the Social Sciences

INTRODUCTION

Early presentations of sociobiology often cast the new discipline in the role of a savior of the social sciences and humanities—a claim that has naturally earned the antagonism of most social scientists and humanists. A brief examination of two key documents setting out the sociobiological program (Alexander 1975; Wilson 1975a) indicates why the discipline has generated such controversy. Wilson (1975a) writes that sociobiology will eventually subsume the social sciences and that such disciplines as anthropology, economics, and psychology are best seen as the study of the sociobiology of a single species. Many sociobiologists take it for granted that a complete social science must encompass *all* living forms. The implications of this view can be explored by examining the fate of a single discipline, economics, when the social sciences are conceptualized within the sociobiological framework. In such a conceptualization there will be three levels of economics. The first, and most parochial, is human economics as currently constituted. The second, more encompassing level (perhaps labeled comparative economics), will compare the "economic systems" (however defined) of different species. The generalizations or laws of human economics are species-specific examples of the propositions of comparative economics. Finally, both levels of economics will become subdivisions of a more general sociobiological project, when economic systems are linked to other comparative disciplines and tied to the processes of evolution.

To many sociobiologists, the hierarchy of sciences proposed by Wilson is merely the logical outcome of Darwin's removal of *Homo sapiens* from the pinnacle of creation; humans are only one species among many, and any law of human behavior must be related to more general biological laws. Many social scientists do not find this view of their discipline flattering, and they may reject Wilson's version of the importance of sociobiology. The most common response is the charge that sociobiologists are guilty of vulgar reductionism. I will paraphrase the argument for the case of economics. It is true that the processes of human economics are in some way related to the biological nature of human beings and to the processes of evolution. However, knowing the biological nature of human beings will tell us very little about human economics, because . . . Here the argument branches, with some social scientists arguing that there are emergent properties in complex systems, which cannot be predicted from knowledge of the elements of the system taken in isolation; others arguing that culture shapes human economic behavior in manners that are not predictable from a knowledge of human biology; and some arguing for both positions.

While I do not want to oversimplify the complex issues at stake in the imaginary Wilson vs. social scientist debate, one way to conceptualize the difference between the participants is to ask which viewpoint is most "cost effective" in producing knowledge about human economics. In other words, per unit of research effort, which research strategy will produce the greatest amount of knowledge about the phenomena under study? In one of the most important papers in sociobiology, Alexander (1975) formulates the relationship between sociobiology and the social sciences in roughly these terms. He argues that the behavioral sciences (including ethology) have failed to develop an adequate general theory, because there is no agreement on the basic units of behavior. In a complex discussion, Alexander notes that ". . . any and all events of natural selection can be viewed as basic units in the temporo-spatial structure of life" (1975:87). Alexander bases his claim for the priority of sociobiology on two implications of this view. First, he suggests that analyzing any behavior by relating it to the processes of natural selection is superior to current forms of analysis in the behavioral sciences, because this tactic produces more valuable information about the behavior than any other form of analysis (1975:88). In other words, the sociobiological position is the most cost effective strategy in studying human economics. Second, since natural selection is relevant to all life forms, viewing natural selection as the basic unit of behavior results in a concept that is capable of unifying the various behavioral sciences (1975:87). Sociobiology is therefore the most cost effective strategy in the overall study of behavior. If we return to the argument on vulgar reductionism paraphrased above, the implication of Alexander's view is that while knowledge of the evolutionary history of humans will not tell us everything about human economics, it will tell us more about it than any research strategy current in economics, and it will have the additional benefit of permitting us to relate knowledge of economics to other domains in the behavioral sciences.

Since he does not use the vocabulary of incorporation favored by Wilson, Alexander's position has not upset social scientists to the extent that Wilson's statements have. However, the implications of Alexander's position are just as radical as those of Wilson's. For both authors, the majority of work in the social sciences is seen as somehow fundamentally on the wrong track. It is not that the various disciplines have not produced some results, but rather that their findings are often unrelated to one another and that there is no progress toward a unified theory of human (or other animal) behavior. There are also specific theoretical orientations in the social sciences which both authors would see as highly improbable in the light of evolutionary theory. Thus, both Wilson and Alexander would suggest that theories arguing that humans often behave in manners detrimental to themselves but beneficial to the species or the population either are wrong or at least should be reanalyzed in terms of inclusive fitness striving.

The positions of Alexander and Wilson imply that sociobiology will revolutionize the social sciences. It is easy to state in the abstract the implications of such a revolution, but to understand them fully it is necessary to explore the practical results for each social science discipline. In the next section, I will examine some of the ways in which the adoption of the sociobiological research program would affect the discipline of anthropology. I focus on anthropology for two reasons. First, both anthropologists and sociobiologists agree that of all the social sciences, anthropology has the most immediate relevance to sociobiology. Although sociobiological studies have appeared in economics, psychology, sociology, and political science, the majority of studies have been firmly situated within an anthropological framework. Second, as an anthropologist, I am most familiar with this discipline and am naturally more interested in sociobiology's effect on it than on other disciplines.

SOCIOBIOLOGY AND ANTHROPOLOGY

There is debate within anthropology over sociobiology's claim to be able to revolutionize the discipline. Certain anthropologists have concluded that the gap between sociobiology and anthropology is not as wide as some believe. Silverberg (1980), for example, argues that sociobiology's claim to be a new synthesis, finally uniting the social and biological sciences, ignores the fact that from its beginnings anthropology has dealt with the interaction of biology and culture. He identifies anthropology as a science of human adaptation, one with the ultimate goal of integrating research into the cultural and biological factors that shape human behavior. Wolpoff (1981:8) also suggests that the introduction of sociobiology into anthropology is not as revolutionary as its proponents believe. He argues that most socio-biological theory could be taught as a part of physical anthropology.

One proponent of sociobiology who believes that the impact of behavioral biology on sociocultural anthropology would be significant, but not really revolutionary, is William Irons:

> The central and most widely agreed upon theoretical ideas in anthropology are the following: (a) human behavior varies widely between societies and is largely shaped by culture, i.e., things individuals learn as a result of growing up and living in a particular society; (b) cultures are integrated wholes, or at least institutions in the same culture are frequently functionally interrelated; (c) all value judgments are relative to the culture in which they are made; and (d) culture develops as a result of its own internal dynamics, not as a result of human input. Of these views, only the last is incompatible with behavioral biology [Irons 1979a:31–32].

Irons suggests that a sociobiologically-informed anthropology differs from traditional sociocultural anthropology on two main points: (1) the former rejects the notion of culture as a superorganic entity; and (2) sociobiological anthropology is based on the expectation that ". . . most forms of behavior will either be biologically adaptive, or will be expressions of evolved tendencies that were adaptive in the past (1979a:38)." He argues that the first point is not revolutionary, because many anthropologists had rejected the notion of the superorganic long before the advent of the sociobiological paradigm. Firth's (1964) distinction between social structure and social organization was a significant step in this direction, illustrating the fact that rule breaking can be a source of social structural change (see Bloch 1977). Culture conceptualized as the summation of decisions made by individuals has been emphasized by Barth (1966, 1967), Bailey (1969), and Goldschmidt (1966), among others. In a paper not widely cited in anthropology, Murdock (1972) also questions the notion of the super-organic:

> It now seems to me distressingly obvious that culture, social systems, and all comparable supraindividual concepts . . . are illusory conceptual abstrac-tions inferred from observations of the very real phenomena of individuals interacting with one another and with their natural environments. The circumstances of their interaction often lead to similarities in the behaviour of different individuals which we tend to reify under the name of culture, and they cause individuals to relate themselves to others in repetitive ways which we tend to reify as structures or systems. But culture and social structure are actually epiphenomena—derivative products of the social interaction of pluralities of individuals [Murdock 1972:19].

The rejection of the superorganic is often accompanied by a commitment to a closer relationship between anthropology and psychology. In the following passage, Murdock argues for a position similar to that advanced by many sociobiologists (see below):

> all human behaviour which is not biologically determined in the narrowest sense depends upon the interaction of two sets of factors. The first is a series of basically innate mechanisms such as those of perception, cognition, and learning through which all behaviour is mediated. The second consists of the specific conditions under which any behaviour occurs. The mechanisms, being fixed by heredity, are fundamentally identical for all mankind, and even to a remarkable extent throughout the mammalian order. The conditions, on the other hand, are almost infinitely variable over time and space. It is through the complex interaction of the constant mechanisms with the varying conditions that man's behaviour becomes adapted to his environmental circumstances [Murdock 1972:21].

For Murdock, psychology is the discipline that investigates the operation of the innate mechanisms of perception, cognition, and learning. To make Murdock's passage congruent with a sociobiological approach, it is only necessary to add: (1) that evolutionary biology is necessary to explain the ultimate causation of the cognitive, perceptual, and other skills that are characteristic of a species; and (2) that the interaction of these skills with the environment will, on the average, produce behaviors that serve to increase individual inclusive fitness.

Irons' point that anthropology's adoption of the sociobiological perspective would not be as radical as some have argued has merit. Still, it would be a mistake to underestimate the impact of such a step on anthropology. It would transform the conceptualization of the discipline and change the manner in which anthropological research is conducted. In a striking passage, Alexander (1981a) describes his vision of human sociobiology and discusses what is new about the discipline:

> I assume that some combinations of rates, kinds, timings, and accumulated numbers of social learning experiences determine the nature and intensity of human social interaction. This is nothing new. But it will be new to assume that the determining rates and kinds of social interactions among individuals have varied consistently and regularly with degrees of relatedness in genes identical by immediate descent; yet I think this assumption is necessary. It will be new to realize that the correlations of social experience with genetic relatedness can be an incidental consequence of geographic and social proximity and that such correlations can be imposed indirectly by those whose interests are served by creating them. It will be new to realize that the fragility of the correlation between social and genetic distance in a mobile, fluid society like our own can lead to multiple and complex surrogate social-genetic distance correlations, in the end understandable only from knowledge of long-term historical contingencies. It will be new to recognize that disruption of an individual's chances of establishing a pattern in his or her social interactions that reflects the long-term history of social-genetic contingency correlations may lead to that individual's social alienation, to

devastating confusion, to feelings of being orphaned, and perhaps even to suicide or outlandish searches for adoptive surrogates, including the substitute kin networks of intensely religious, political, or other support groups. It will be new to establish connections between the loss of the social experience of stable kin groups, or their surrogates, and broad-scale rise of concern with the effects of law and public activities of the so-called disadvantaged in every realm, whose vulnerability can be interpreted by even more individuals as paralleling their own. It will be new to hypothesize that variations in cultural patterns stem from variations in how ecological and other extrinsic events modify the social circumstances in which groups of genetic relatives have found themselves during the history of each separate society. It is new to attempt to explain such things as mother's brother, the asymmetrical treatment of cousins, the cloistering of women, the sizes of villages at fissioning, the abuse and neglect of children, clan exogamy, the distribution of male-biased inheritance, and the acceptance or rejection of harem polygyny as consequences of different patternings of social interactions among relatives that lead to outcomes predictable from inclusive-fitness-maximizing in different ecological circumstances and under different histories of cultural patterns and power distributions [Alexander 1981a:513–514].

Alexander's comments indicate that even if the introduction of socio-biology to anthropology would not be as radical an event as some have suggested, it would still transform the discipline. I will now briefly examine some of the more significant effects of such a transformation.

The human ecology approach of sociocultural anthropology could be subsumed easily under ecological sociobiology with two changes in orientation. First, the tendency of many human ecologists to think in terms of group advantage would be replaced by a research program dedicated to explaining adaptation as the outcome of processes that are operative on lower levels of selection. A topic discussed later, preferential female infanticide, provides an illustration of the difference. Chagnon et al. (1979) identify the Divale and Harris (1976) theory of the "male supremacist complex" as a group selection argument. Briefly, Divale and Harris argue that in certain ecological settings, a pattern of continual warfare serves to maintain population below the carrying capacity of the environment. As a strategy in this warfare, groups utilize preferential female infanticide to create as many male warriors as possible. Groups with more warriors are likely to be more successful than groups with fewer warriors, and once one group in a restricted area adopts the strategy of preferential female infanticide, the others are forced to follow suit. The death of each female infant results in the loss of her reproductive potential, serving to further reduce population growth.

Chagnon et al. reject the Divale and Harris model for a number of reasons. Here I note only their point that Divale and Harris explain infanticide as a trait benefiting the group and do not consider the possibility that the practice might occur because of the benefits it provides to individuals. In contrast, a sociobiological argument looks to the conditions under which it would benefit an individual's inclusive fitness to kill infants (Alexander 1974; Dickemann 1975, 1979a; Hrdy 1979). The sociobiological position does not rule out the possibility that the effects suggested by Divale and Harris exist, but sees them as epiphenomena of the attempts of individuals to maximize their inclusive fitness, and not as the direct subject of selective pressures.

The second major shift in cultural ecology would be a reconceptualization of the factors relevant to the genesis and operation of social structure. Currently, the main focuses of research on this topic are the influence of the distribution of food and other resources, geographic factors, and other social groups. A major interest is how social structures adjust societies to their environments and how this adjustment either changes or is maintained. Sociobiology would not ignore these topics, but would add others which have not received much attention. For example, research into environmental influences on the grouping of kin would seem to be an important topic. Do societies with groupings of close relatives function differently than those where relatives are more dispersed? Are the former characterized by more cooperation than the latter? What determines the distribution of kin? Another example involves the distribution of food and other resources. Sociobiologists would want to know how this factor influences the mating systems of human societies. It is generally agreed that polygyny, monogamy, and polyandry are found in different resource environments, but the implications of this distribution require more study. Exploration of mating systems will lead to questions on sex ratio and its adjustment, and so on.

Although the above questions have been phrased in terms of human cultural ecology, the same considerations apply to primatology. The role of resource distribution in shaping alloprimate social structure has long been studied, but such topics as the relative importance of individual selection and group selection and differences in the genetic relatedness among individuals in different social systems have been addressed only recently.

The introduction of strategic sociobiology to sociocultural anthropology and primatology has generated more controversy than has ecological sociobiology. Such introduction is occurring on several fronts, and I will briefly discuss only the more important of these.

A major task of strategic sociobiology would be a translation of the generalizations currently accepted by anthropologists into the language of individual or gene-level selection. An example of such translation involves the association between matrilineal descent and a man's property being inherited by his sister's children, rather than by the children of his wife (the avunculate). Many anthropologists view the inheritance rule as the logical outcome of the descent rule. Of course, these anthropologists agree that the question of why some societies have matrilineal descent must be answered by reference to ecological, social, or cultural factors. In articles discussed in the section on parental investment theory, sociobiologists (Alexander 1974; Flinn 1981a; Gaulin and Schlegel 1980; Hartung 1976, 1981, 1983; Kurland 1979) reinterpret the avunculate by suggesting that it results from males attempting to maximize inclusive fitness under conditions of low paternal certainty. Hartung (1983) takes the analysis one step further by identifying the conditions under which the avunculate benefits females.

Translation of anthropological generalizations into the language of strategic sociobiology will create a need for new types of data and new concepts of culture. For example, Chagnon's work on relatedness among the Yanomamo leads him to suggest that we need data on the distribution of genetic kin in different societies before we can conduct valid comparative studies on human social behavior (Chagnon 1982). The jural rules of kinship (descent rule, residence rule, kinship terminology, etc.) may be the same in two societies, and yet the distribution of genetic kin may be different. If sociobiology is valid, the different distributions of kin should be reflected in different behavioral and cultural patterns. Testing theories of strategic sociobiology thus requires data on both "sociological" and "genetic" kinship. Research along these lines is just beginning, but it promises to change the way in which anthropologists study kinship.

Examples of how strategic sociobiology might alter the concept of culture are provided by the works of Lumsden and Wilson (1981, 1983) and Alexander (1979). Lumsden and Wilson conceptualize culture as a series of traits ("culturgens") with alternative forms. Individuals continually choose between alternative forms, and the distribution of choices on all culturgens at a given point in time comprises the culture of a society. Following neurologically-based rules, various culturgens may be "lumped" together in the minds of individuals, creating the integration of culture so often remarked upon by anthropologists. Due to the population's past selective history, the distribution of choices among alternative forms of culturgens exhibits a predictable pattern. For example, the cost of inbreeding depression means that in every society the vast majority of people will choose the "not commit incest" alternative of the "incest" culturgen. In contrast, the distribution of choices among alternatives of the various "fashion" culturgens in Western societies exhibits much more diversity.

The view of culture advanced by Lumsden and Wilson has a number of implications for the way both fieldwork and cross-cultural research are conducted. The focus of fieldwork will be less on jural rules and people's descriptions of their behavior and more on the actual behavior of individuals. Comparative research will examine the distribution of choices between the alternatives of various culturgens in different cultures. Traditional tools of holocultural research, such as the *Ethnographic Atlas* (Murdock 1967), with its mixture of behavioral and jural data, will be inadequate for this type of research.

Alexander's view of culture is more traditional than that of Lumsden and Wilson, but it still requires anthropologists to rethink the concept. With Lumsden and Wilson, Alexander emphasizes that culture is the outcome of behaviors of individuals acting to increase inclusive fitness and that it must be studied by analyzing both actual behavior and jural rules. However, Alexander is also interested in the precise relationship between jural rules and behavior. He suggests that a major topic in a sociobiological anthropology will be research on how individuals utilize jural rules to further their reproductive interests. His discussion of socially-imposed monogamy in nation states (1979; also Alexander et al. 1979) should be compared to Cohen's (1969) discussion on state control of sexual behavior, to see what his view of culture offers to sociocultural anthropology.

The preceding discussion only hints at the changes in anthropology that would result from adoption of the sociobiological paradigm. Still to be answered is whether or not such a transformation would be necessary and worthwhile. Sociobiologists argue that it would be, for a number of reasons. The most important reason is that the evolutionary paradigm would bring some order into the way anthropology organizes its data. Separating questions of ultimate causation from those of proximate causation, and dealing with each on the appropriate level would reduce confusion within the field. Focus on behavior rather than jural rules would allow progress in explaining human behavior. Advances would occur even while the difficult problem of the relationship between rules and behavior continued to be studied. Further, sociobiological theory has already identified a number of primary topics relevant to social life (e.g., sex ratio, resource distribution, and predation pressure) and comparative sociocultural anthropology and primatology would progress at the fastest possible rate if researchers were to devote their greatest attention to these variables. A major advantage is that research on these variables among other species provides a source of testable hypotheses for sociobiologically-inclined anthropologists.

Another result of adding a sociobiological component to anthropology— that the data of the discipline would be included in the reductionistic program of science—is seen by sociobiologists as a great advance, but it is not assessed so kindly by some anthropologists. This topic will be discussed further in the next section.

One question related to reductionism is: How much, if any, of anthropology escapes the sociobiological research program? In the most general sense, the answer must be that none does. Everything humans do can be related back, directly or indirectly, to their biologically-based cognitive, perceptual, or motor skills, and the evolution of these skills is, of course, a topic for sociobiological research. In more practical terms, however, there are large areas of anthropology wherein sociobiology would seem to offer little except the noncontroversial point that if the species were different, things would not be the same. For example, sociobiology may have little to offer anthropologists who are interested in the analysis of meaning in cultural systems. Changes in the cultural content of specific societies over time may be analyzed fairly independently of sociobiological concerns. Sociobiology may suggest that Western artists innovate in order to gain the resources that allow maximization of inclusive fitness, but may have little to say about the *form* of innovation—e.g.: Why Warhol's soup cans or superrealism? However, even here it is probably too early to rule out totally the possibility of interesting contributions from sociobiology. An answer to "Why soup cans?" that suggests a grammar of art or a structural explanation postulating a human brain operating by means of binary oppositions opens the door to a sociobiological explanation of that grammar or the evolutionary origin of that type of brain.

This section has concentrated on the implications of sociobiology for anthropology. However, anthropology has a reciprocal influence on sociobiology. Up to the present time, this effect has mainly involved the popularization of the discipline and the problem of culture. Although E. O. Wilson is correct (1980:296) to note that the public errs in assuming that the validity of sociobiology depends upon successful application of the theory to human behavior, there is no doubt that sociobiological explanations of primate behavior are in large part responsible for the widespread interest in the discipline. Such topics as langur infanticide (Hrdy 1977), Yanomamo fierceness (Chagnon 1968), human incest rules, and dominance hierarchies among alloprimates have served to spark the interest of nonspecialists.

Another area of influence has been the "dual inheritance" problem (Wilson 1977:134) of how cultural evolution and genetic evolution interact in human social behavior. A number of models have been created to deal with this problem, and continued work in this area promises to influence both anthropology and sociobiology.

Wilson (1975b, 1977) identifies the areas of population biology that will be influenced by attempts to deal with anthropological data:

> In addition to the solution of the dual inheritance problem, there is a need for advances in the theory of group and kin selection to distinguish unilateral, "hard core" altruism from transactional, "soft core" altruism. Also, the complexity of human population structures presents unique challenges to biology. Population boundaries are seldom sharp, often being confused by discordant linguistic, cultural, and historical-political patterns. Groups also shift rapidly in their loyalties, forming alliances in one year and dividing into quarreling factions the next. The present theory of population genetics and ecology is entirely inadequate to handle such complications [Wilson 1977:134].

Silverberg (1980, 1984) points out that sociocultural anthropologists have long investigated the transmission of learned behavior and suggests that as sociobiologists begin to examine in more detail the role that learning and social transmission play in the life of some nonhuman species, anthropology will be an important source of concepts and models. Silverberg also notes that anthropologists can offer sociobiologists important insights into the problems of conceptualizing and studying intraspecies variability.

After this consideration of mutual influence, it is necessary to leave the topic of what sociobiology offers anthropology, and vice versa, and turn to an analysis of how sociobiology has been applied to human behavior and to some general objections raised by anthropologists to such applications.

THE APPLICATION OF
SOCIOBIOLOGICAL THEORY TO HUMAN BEHAVIOR

Insistence that the principles of evolutionary biology apply to human behavior is acceptable to almost all anthropologists. Problems arise when an exact characterization of the relationship is required. As the discussion in this section will illustrate, a number of positions have been advanced in the last few years. The alternatives indicate much disagreement among biologists and anthropologists on how the four hallmarks of sociobiological theory are to be utilized in the explanation of human social and cultural behavior. Examination of the alternatives illuminates the sources of disagreement and provides a framework within which to locate the empirical research discussed in succeeding chapters.

Wilson's discussion of three possible links between sociobiological theory and human social behavior is an excellent description of alternative positions:

> (a) During the rapid evolution of the human brain, natural selection exhausted the genetic variability of the species affecting social behavior, so that today virtually all human beings are identical with respect to behavioral potential. In addition, the brain has been "freed" from these genes in the sense that all outcomes are determined by culture. The genes, in other words, merely prescribe the capacity for culture. Or,
> (b) Genetic variability has been exhausted, as in (a). But the resulting uniform genotype predisposes psychological development toward certain outcomes as opposed to others. In an ethological sense, species-specific human traits exist and, as in animal repertories, they have a genetic foundation. Or,
> (c) Genetic variability still exists, and, as in (b), at least some human behavioral traits have a genetic foundation [Wilson 1980:296].

For the present, I will label alternative (a) the culturological thesis, alternative (b) the weak sociobiological thesis, and alternative (c) the strong sociobiological thesis.

The culturological thesis states that sociobiology has little to offer sociocultural anthropology. The principles of evolutionary biology are necessary to explain how *Homo sapiens* acquired the capacity for culture, and they will therefore be important for paleoanthropology. However, once we humans achieved the capacity for culture, we were for the most part "freed" from our biological heritage. The most important factor in creating patterns of human social behavior is culture, and the study of kin selection theory, sexual selection theory, etc. is irrelevant for explaining intersocietal variations in behavior. As Sahlins (1976) notes, humans live in culturally-created webs of meanings, and these meanings are the determinants of our behavior. A major portion of Sahlins' volume is devoted to arguing that cultural classifications of kin frequently result in behavioral patterns which would not be predicted by sociobiological principles. There is no need to describe the culturological position further at present, for it is the null hypothesis for many of the empirical tests in human sociobiology that will be discussed later in this volume. Instead, I will turn to the two socio-biological positions.

Most sociocultural anthropologists find the strong sociobiological thesis the least acceptable of the alternatives. The rejection of sociobiology by many theorists is too often based on a mistaken impression that all sociobiologists support this view. In fact, most hold the weaker thesis, and all empirical research in human sociobiology thus far can be utilized only to support the weaker thesis.

An argument based on the strong thesis must demonstrate that the behavioral trait under consideration varies among humans and that at least part of the cause of that variation is due to differences in the genome. Further, to be of interest to sociocultural anthropologists, it must also show that the behavioral variation found in different culture-bearing entities (societies, classes, castes, etc.) is related in some manner to variations in the genome of members of these entities. The charge that sociobiologists cannot demonstrate that genes "for" behavior vary between societies or classes holds that the conditions necessary to support arguments derived from the strong thesis have not been fulfilled.

It is difficult to find proponents of the strong sociobiological thesis. Although not exhibiting all the hallmarks of the sociobiological paradigm, the cross-cultural research on infant development conducted and inspired by Daniel Freedman (1974, 1979) illustrates the logic of the strong position. Freedman and his colleagues find that newborns from different gene pools exhibit significant differences in traits, such as level of activity, posture, and irritability. For example, infants born to Americans whose ancestors resided in China (Chinese-Americans) exhibit less reactivity when subjected to stimulation than infants of Americans whose ancestors resided in Europe (Caucasian-Americans). Infants born to parents claiming Navajo ethnic identity are even less reactive than Chinese-American infants. Such differences appear at birth or soon after, suggesting that they cannot be ascribed to cultural conditioning (although prenatal influences have not been totally ruled out). Therefore, Freedman argues, a genetic explanation of the differences is not implausible.

In a step of more interest to sociocultural anthropologists, Freedman suggests that these assumed genetic differences can partially explain cultural variation. Thus, the low reactivity of the Navaho infant may not be created by the cradleboard, but rather use of the cradleboard may be possible because of the low reactivity of the typical Navaho infant. Freedman notes that in one study, the higher reactivity level of Caucasian infants resulted in their mothers discontinuing use of the cradleboard earlier than Navajo mothers did. Freedman also speculates that differences in the ethos, religion, philosophy, and art of societies might be related to genetically-based differences in level of reactivity and other traits.

It is important to note some interpretations which cannot be derived from Freedman's work. First, Freedman does not postulate that gene pools differ in genes for specific cultural traits. Navajos do not carry an allele for use of cradleboards. Rather, there has been a past interaction between genome and cultural traits resulting in the reactivity level of Navaho infants being "fitted" to the cradleboard. It is theoretically possible that some cultural innovations have been accepted in part because they matched the reactivity level of the population, while others were rejected partly because they did not. Over time, the shape or tone of a culture could be influenced in the fashion suggested by Freedman. In a very real sense, then, the differences between the Caucasian and the Navaho genome can be said to be responsible for some differences between Navajo and various European cultures. However, the links are indirect and complex, and there is no hint of simple genetic determinism (as suggested by the slogan that "genes determine culture") in Freedman's position.

Second, Freedman's work does not imply that either individual behavior or culture cannot change. It does suggest, however, that the mechanisms of change might not be totally independent of genetic considerations. For example, infants of Americans whose ancestors resided in Japan show lower reactivity than Caucasian-American infants. However, a sample of infants of Japanese mothers whose families had resided in the United States for two generations emitted behavior at the same rate as Caucasian infants. This rate is achieved by the Japanese-American mother stimulating her infant at a much higher rate than the Caucasian mother. This finding suggests an addendum to the anthropological truism that any human infant is capable of learning any culture. Just as there are intrasocietal differences in the stress generated by socialization, there may be intersocietal differences in the stress created by imaginary cross-cultural fostering of infants. Such stresses would probably be minor and would not interfere with the average infant of one society being completely socialized into a second society. A sample of

Caucasian infants might exhibit a high level of dismay with extended use of the cradleboard, and a sample of Navajo infants might become upset by being overstimulated by Caucasian mothers, but all infants would become fully functioning adult members of the societies in which they were fostered.

Few claims for the strong thesis have been made by sociobiologists. The suggestion that the strong position must be considered as a possibility is provided by Lumsden and Wilson's discussion of the "coevolutionary circuit" (1981:297–300). The authors note that their model implies that under some conditions gene-culture coevolution can produce genetic diversity within a population. One such condition is "fitness suppression," a phenomenon occurring when the accumulation of resources beyond a certain level results in fitness reduction for the gatherer. Lumsden and Wilson argue that in complex societies, operation of the economic system requires an elaborate division of labor. They consider a possible outcome of this situation: "The result will be not just a spreading of economic and social roles, as expected from elementary economic theory, but a diversification of the genetic basis that underwrites the capacity to assume each role separately" (1981:298). However, the authors do not see different social roles as based on different genes:

> This result does not imply the partitioning of human-like societies into genetic castes. Rules of exogamy and the opportunities in most societies for some amount of socioeconomic mobility and occupation change militate against such an extreme phenomenon. Indeed, even the caste system of India, which is the strongest and most elaborate on earth and has been in existence over two thousand years, is maintained largely if not entirely by cultural conventions; members of different castes differ from one another only slightly in blood type and other measurable anatomical and physiological traits [Lumsden and Wilson 1981:298–300].

Wilson (1978) seems to argue that the strong version of the sociobiological thesis can be tested. In one passage (1978:21), he notes that surviving hunting-gathering populations do not differ genetically from populations in industrial societies, but later he writes:

> My overall impression of the existing information is that *Homo sapiens* is a conventional animal species with reference to the quality and magnitude of the genetic diversity affecting its behaviour. If the comparison is correct, the psychic unity of mankind has been reduced in status from a dogma to a testable hypothesis [Wilson 1978:21].

Once again, note that Wilson does not argue that specific genes determine specific behaviors:

> Thus it is possible, and in my judgment even probable, that the positions of genes having indirect effects on the most complex forms of behaviour will

soon be mapped on the human chromosomes. These genes are unlikely to prescribe particular patterns of behaviour; there will be no mutations for a particular sexual practice or mode of dress. The behaviour genes more probably influence the ranges of the forms and intensity of emotional responses, the threshold of arousal, the readiness to learn certain stimuli as opposed to others, and the pattern of sensitivity to additional environmental factors that point cultural evolution in one direction as opposed to another [Wilson 1978:22].

I now leave Wilson's ambiguous position on the strong sociobiological thesis and turn to the weak thesis that is argued by most researchers in primate sociobiology. The weak position holds that the genetic differences between human populations are not relevant to differences in cultural behavior, but that there are species-typical behavioral rules for humans. Intercultural and intracultural variations in behavior result when these behavioral rules confront different environments. An example of a frequent form of argument from this position is the idea that species-typical behavioral rules are "rules of thumb," which were selected in the past because following them led to greater inclusive fitness. One such rule of thumb might be "provide altruism to those who live in the same household (nest, etc.) with you." Theorists argue that such a rule might be favored by kin selection in species where proximity is highly correlated with genetic distance. Let us assume that at some point in a species' history there were two rules of thumb about the distribution of altruism: the one just cited and another which stated "provide altruism to all conspecifics." We must also assume that the propensity to follow either rule was in some way related to genetic factors. Kin selection theory demonstrates that the former rule would spread at the expense of the latter. In time, if the selection pressures were both consistent and intense enough, the genes relevant to the latter rule would be eliminated from the population. In this case the rule of thumb "provide altruism to those who live in the same household with you" would be followed by all members of a species and in most situations would produce a behavioral pattern which favored close kin over distant kin.

An interesting situation arises if environmental factors result in the movement of individuals such that households contain mixtures of near and distant relatives. In such a situation individuals would still follow the first rule of thumb, and we would have a case where the exhibited distribution of altruism would appear to run counter to the predictions of kin selection theory. Two considerations show that the proposed situation would not disprove kin selection theory. First, the rule of thumb itself was postulated to have arisen through the process of kin selection. Second, we assume that if a genetic mutation permitting discrimination of near and distant kin occurred in one of the groups where near and distant kin resided in the same household, it would also be selected for by kin selection.

The focus on rules of thumb means that cultural variation is not automatically assumed to arise from genetic differences within or between populations. The rules of thumb could be genetically fixed in all human populations, and differing environmental conditions would produce different patterns of social and cultural behavior. Irons outlines the logic of this position:

> The hypothesis that human behavioral propensities are adaptations shaped by natural selection does not imply that human behavior is not plastic or that differences in behavior among human populations are the result of genetic differences. The most reasonable hypothesis is that the behavioral differences exhibited by different populations are environmentally induced variations in the expression of basically similar genotypes, and that the ability and propensity to vary behavior in response to environmental differences is itself an adaptation [Irons 1979a:5].

An example of research in human sociobiology might help to clarify the distinction between the weak and strong positions. Hartung (1982a) assumes that humans have been selected to act in manners increasing their inclusive fitness. Parental investment theory suggests that when parents accumulate resources that can influence the reproductive success of their offspring, they should distribute them so as to maximize their own inclusive fitness. Gender is an important characteristic of offspring that is relevant to potential reproductive success. In societies permitting polygyny, a male might marry a large number of females, thereby achieving high reproductive success. If we assume that all females produce six children over the course of their lives, a male married to three wives can produce eighteen grand-children for his parents. In contrast, a daughter will produce only six grand-children. Thus, parents in polygynous societies should invest more resources in sons than in daughters (unless their sons would have little chance of finding mates, in which case investment in daughters might be more productive).

In societies with a jural rule of monogamy, the difference in the reproductive potential of the sexes is not as great as in societies with polygyny, although the possibility of extramarital sexual activity means that males will usually still have a higher potential. In societies with strict monogamy and no extramarital sexual activity, both sons and daughters have the potential to produce six grandchildren for their parents. Thus parents in monogamous societies will be more likely than parents in polygynous societies to provide inheritance to both sons and daughters.

With a holocultural sample, Hartung (1982a) demonstrates that in most polygynous societies, marriages involve bridewealth. Thus parents in these societies have the option of giving resources to sons, allowing them to pay bridewealth for additional wives. Hartung predicts that inheritance rules in polygynous societies will exhibit a masculine bias, while those in monogamous societies will exhibit no gender bias. A carefully designed holocultural study supports his prediction.

The difference between the weak and the strong sociobiological positions can be illustrated by imagining the next step in Hartung's research. The strong position might suggest demonstrating that populations in societies with inheritance rules favoring males differ genetically from those in societies without such rules. Hartung rejects this position, however, arguing that there is no intersocietal genetic variability that is relevant to inheritance practices. A possible next step in research guided by the weak thesis would be to search for ecological factors explaining why human groups exhibit monogamy or polygyny. A second possible step would be to examine the ethnographic record for cases of societies moving from one type of mating system to another, to see whether inheritance rules are also changing in manners predicted by Hartung's argument. According to the weak position, changes in investment strategies require no change in the gene pool of a society. Finally, a search for possible rules of thumb or proximate mechanisms related to differential treatment of the sexes might illuminate how parental decisions concerning inheritance are related to such factors as reproductive value of children, parent-offspring conflict, and so on.

An anthropological research program based on the weak sociobiological thesis would have two focuses. First, the principles of ecological sociobiology would be applied, to explain variability in human social groupings. Second, the principles of strategic sociobiology would be utilized, to explain how the behavior of individuals within particular social systems functions to maximize inclusive fitness. The majority of research reviewed in this volume flows from one or the other of these approaches. As previously noted, the hope is that eventually these two areas of investigation will merge and provide a more complete account of the variability in human socio-cultural behavior. At present, however, there are only a few signs of movement toward this goal.

When sociobiologically-oriented anthropologists attempt to convince skeptical colleagues of behavioral biology's value to anthropology, it is vital that they signify whether they are working with the strong or the weak version of the sociobiological thesis. As might be expected, the former generates much more resistance among sociocultural anthropologists. Most of the researchers whose work is reviewed in this volume clearly state that they are working with the weak position. There is an unfortunate tendency on the part of some sociocultural anthropologists to ignore the distinction between the two positions, to overlook explicit statements by researchers that they are not attempting to locate genes "for" cultural traits, and to reduce all work in sociobiology to claims for the genetic determination of behavior and culture. In fact, there are few sociobiologists whose work can be dismissed in this manner.

This brings us to the final topic in this section—a discussion of the more general objections that sociocultural anthropologists have to sociobiology. Each objection will be examined in more detail in succeeding chapters, and for the present I will identify them only briefly.

1. *Genetic Determinism.* This objection applies only to the strong socio-biological thesis. It states that the genes determining any human social and cultural behavior (more accurately, the differences in the genome of individuals or the genetic pool of societies that are relevant to differences in culture) have not been identified by sociobiologists. The objection is correct, but is irrelevant to the bulk of research conducted from within the weak sociobiological position, where the interaction between the genome and the environment is seen as responsible for behavior.

2. *Redundancy and Reductionism.* In a discussion between Edward Wilson and Marvin Harris, the former often argues from the weak sociobiological position. Harris' responses are common among sociocultural anthropologists. Here is an example:

> *Harris:* But my point is this: you seem to be admitting that to explain whether there will be polygyny or polyandry or monogamy or any of the other forms, one has to consider the sociocultural, demographic, technological and economic conditions which vary from one population to another ... The genes, then, permit in one instance polygyny and in another instance polyandry, but with no change in gene frequency [Harris and Wilson 1978:13].

In another passage, Harris details his objection to this type of argument:

> I think that when sociobiological principles are applied in a fashion which corresponds to the calculus of the "selfish gene" in order to explain various aspects of human life, such explanations are redundant with respect to a much more simple and, in a sense, more accessible explanation on a sociocultural, rather than a genetic level.... You reduced a phenomenon which is perfectly intelligible and explicable on a cultural level to a genetic level. Although there may be a correspondence between the two, it seems to me that if you are capable of giving an explanation for saving a drowning person or helping old people—or any of the behaviors which correspond to our moral codes—in purely cultural terms, you have a much more efficient system for explaining why people behave the way they do [Harris and Wilson 1978:15].

Harris identifies two interrelated objections to sociobiological explanations of human social and cultural behavior. The first might be called the redundancy problem. A sociocultural anthropologist hearing a sociobiologist explaining the distribution of human marriage systems by appeal to, say, the "demo-techno-econo-environmental" factors stressed by Harris (1979) finds the sociobiological explanation redundant in relation to the cultural materialistic explanation, and thus not convincing in its own right.

Why postulate the existence of inclusive fitness maximization considerations when they add nothing to the explanation of the phenomenon under study? In a slightly different version of the redundancy argument, some theorists see both sociobiological and nonsociobiological explanations of any particular trait as competing hypotheses and hold that when explanations are redundant, the nonsociobiological argument should be accepted since it requires no assumptions about the genetic foundations of social behavior.

The most general response of sociobiologists to the redundancy problem has been to note that often sociobiological and nonsociobiological explanations are not competing, but rather complementary. For example, showing that the inheritance decisions of a couple exhibit economic logic does not demonstrate that an explanation in terms of inclusive fitness maximization is either not valid or not necessary. In many cases, social or cultural determination of behavior can be seen as the operation of rules of thumb selected in the past. A second response to the redundancy problem is to note that in practice, the explanations offered by sociobiologists and nonsociobiologists frequently are not totally congruent. With some effort, it is usually possible to identify where the sociobiological and the sociocultural perspectives lead to different predictions concerning some aspects of the phenomenon under investigation.

The second problem identified by Harris is reductionism. Wilson (1975a) stresses the reductionistic orientation of sociobiology vis-à-vis the social sciences, and the hallmarks of sociobiology provide evidence of that discipline's commitment to reductionism. For many sociocultural anthropologists, a reductionistic orientation implies a desire to explain all behavior in terms of biological factors. As we have seen, this implication is not correct for sociobiologists working with the weak thesis. Focus on the ultimate causation of a behavior does not imply that the behavior can be explained totally by reference to differential reproductive success. Explanation is not complete until information on ontogenetic, proximate, and phylogenetic causation is provided.

Some anthropologists may accept the validity of a reductionistic orientation while questioning its utility. Anthropologists who are interested in the relevance of anthropological knowledge for social and cultural change are especially likely to take this stance. A sociocultural anthropologist who desires not to deal with sociobiology can argue that the weak sociobiological thesis suggests that research into such topics as the distribution of power, wealth, food, etc. can be fruitfully conducted independently of concern for ultimate causation. In contrast, sociobiologists, including those holding the weak thesis, are likely to claim that study of ultimate causation has important implications for the analysis of social and cultural change. For example, if human sociality evolved through kin selection, making people more likely to provide altruism to close relatives than toward nonrelatives (costs and benefits being equal), the operation of social institutions requiring extensive cooperation between nonrelatives will be affected by this state of affairs. Exploration of ultimate causation might provide knowledge of the mechanics, content, and limits of social change. It bears repeating that before sociobiological concepts are introduced into debates over social change, it is necessary to make sure that they are free of ethnocentrism and other forms of bias (a warning applicable to all social science concepts).

3. *Lack of Proximate Mechanisms.* Sociobiologists separate questions of ultimate and proximate causation and insist that knowledge of the latter is not necessary to verify ultimate causation explanations. However, information on proximate mechanisms may be necessary to decide between alternative ultimate causation explanations. This is especially true for sociobiologists working with the weak thesis, since they must identify the rules of thumb that are operative in behavior. Furthermore, information on proximate mechanisms may provide a check on more speculative interpretations generated by sociobiology's explicit hyperadaptationism (Gould and Lewontin 1979). Sociobiology examines each morphological and behavioral trait in hopes of finding an adaptive function for it. Theorists know that adaptive functions will often not be found, either because changes in the trait have resulted from selection operating on other characters or because the trait is not really adaptive. However, the first step is always to assume that an adaptive function can be found and to abandon the assumption only with great reluctance. In cases where function is hypothesized by appeal to animals acting as if they were making complex calculations of genetic relatedness, identification of proximate mechanisms is necessary to make the argument believable. Daly notes the importance of research into proximate mechanisms:

> How, mechanistically, are organisms constructed to attain the abstract goal of maximizing inclusive fitness? If, for example, natural selection has inclined human males to invest in wives' children in rough proportion to the culture-specific degree of paternity confidence, what is the nature of the evolved mechanisms that subserve the adaptive strategy? Furthermore, since every situation is unique, natural selection can only have equipped organisms to respond to abstractly categorical classes of situations that have occurred often enough to have selective significance. Therefore, organisms cannot always choose the best course of action for their genes' posterity, but only a course that works out on average. Just how finely categorized are choice situations, and how? Do organisms routinely integrate multiple information sources to optimize behavior, and, if so, how do these decision processes work [Daly 1978:103]?

The debate over exact and probabilistic coefficients of relatedness is an example of where knowledge of proximate mechanisms is important for guiding speculation (Barash et al. 1978; Dawkins 1982:133–155; Fagen

1976; Partridge and Nunney 1977). Recall that for full siblings, there is a 50 percent probability that an allele that Ego received from his or her mother is also found in a sibling. In a group of full siblings, Ego will have some siblings with the same allele and others without it. Would it not benefit Ego to be able to distinguish these two types of siblings, permitting altruism to be directed to the former, in preference to the latter? Fagen (1976) raises the same issue with reference to grandparental investment in grandchildren. This problem has been the subject of much debate, and, although the consensus currently seems to be that the difference between exact and probabilistic coefficients of relatedness is not of great importance, empirical work on proximate mechanisms affecting the distribution of altruism is necessary before the issue can be decided.

4. *Counterexamples.*   Some anthropologists have attempted to apply the ethnographic veto to generalizations suggested by sociobiologists. The strongest critique of sociobiology from this perspective is by Sahlins (1976). He argues that few, if any, human kinship systems are congruent with predictions generated from inclusive fitness theory. Sahlins notes that social categories of kinship organize human interaction and that near and far in these social categories does not parallel near and far in terms of genetic relatedness. Humans often provide altruism to terminologically close kin who are actually genetically distant or nonrelated, while denying aid to terminologically distant kin who are genetically closely related (see Alexander 1977, Etter 1978, and Hawkes 1983 for critiques of Sahlins' position). Sahlins also points to the frequency of adoption in Polynesia as an example of humans acting counter to the predictions of inclusive fitness theory (see Silk 1980a for a response).

Other potential counterexamples to sociobiological theory have been suggested by anthropologists: homosexuality, priestly celibacy, infanticide, polyandry, providing aid to nonrelatives, active measures to lower fertility, smaller family size in societies marked by the demographic transition, etc. In some cases, counterexamples are offered as if their very existence refutes the possibility that sociobiological theory might apply to humans. Counterexamples are often advanced without consideration for the sophistication of sociobiological theory. The theory does not state, for example, that all individuals will have as many offspring as possible. Sociobiologists have identified conditions in which fertility limitation is the key to maximizing inclusive fitness. Again, Hamilton's rule (1964) states neither that individuals will *never* aid a nonrelative nor that, when given a choice, individuals will *always* aid a relative in preference to a nonrelative. Rather, it holds that genetic relatedness is one factor in determining altruistic behavior. The ratio of donor costs to recipient benefits also enters into the equation and sometimes may lead individuals to favor nonrelatives over relatives.

I do not desire to leave the impression that the counterexamples advanced by anthropologists have all been satisfactorily addressed by sociobiologists; many of them have not, and some proffered explanations are not very convincing. What is important is that the counterexamples must be offered on the same level of theoretical sophistication that is characteristic of the sociobiological paradigm.

This brief review does not do justice to the various objections that anthropologists have raised to sociobiology. The more empirically oriented objections will be discussed in detail as specific sociobiological studies are examined. The more general objections are detailed in Harris (1979), Leacock (1980), Sahlins (1976), Silverberg (1980), and others. The brevity of this review of general objections should not be taken to mean that I dismiss their importance. Rather, its length reflects my belief that certain aspects of the debate over sociobiology can be settled on the basis of empirical research, and that the time is right to examine carefully the data that are advanced by sociobiologists in support of their claim to be able to revitalize the social sciences. The next chapter starts this process by examining the area of ecological sociobiology.

CHAPTER 3

Ecological Sociobiology

INTRODUCTION

All ecological research that examines the process of individuals and populations relating to their environments is of interest to sociobiologists, for this process creates patterns of gene frequencies which vary spatially and temporally. A complete review of primate sociobiology would of necessity discuss all the work in the ecology of the primates. In this chapter, I will not attempt this task. Instead, I will discuss several lines of ecological research that have been frequently addressed by sociobiologists. The chapter has two goals. First, by identifying major topics in primate ecological sociobiology, I hope to provide the reader with an idea of how sociobiological theory relates to more traditional ecological research. Second, I wish to introduce a number of concepts which will frequently be utilized in the chapters on strategic sociobiology. This chapter differs from succeeding ones in that comparatively few of the studies discussed in it involve the testing of hypotheses with empirical data.

Four general topics are covered in this chapter. The next section examines some general considerations relevant to use of the concept of adaptation in ecological sociobiology. This is followed by a brief review of various classifications of alloprimate and human social structure. The third topic involves the debate over whether distribution of food resources or predation pressure is the more important selective force in shaping the evolution of primate social structure. The final section discusses various models that have been advanced to explain the evolution of polygyny or monogamy among the primates. These are not the only topics of interest in primate ecological sociobiology, but they are the ones that have generated the most discussion and offer the best introduction to the field.

THE PROBLEM OF ADAPTATION

Emlen notes that the goal of ecological sociobiology is to "Understand and, ultimately, to predict the basic form and structure of a particular society" (1980:128). To go beyond this rather simple statement is to encounter a host of conceptual and methodological problems, some of which will be reviewed in this section.

A convenient way of introducing our topic is to construct a typical problem in ecological sociobiology. The primate order exhibits great variation in social forms; it contains solitary species, pair-bonded species, "harem-forming" species, multimale troop species, and so on. Given this variation, an ideal study in comparative primate ecological sociobiology might take the following form: (1) the social forms characteristic of the primate order can be explained as (2) adaptive outcomes of the interaction of (3) "primary" ecological factors, "secondary" ecological factors, and nonecological factors (e.g., phylogenetic inertia); and, when nonecological factors are controlled, comparative tests will demonstrate the covariation between social forms and, at least, the primary ecological factors. Although this problem is phrased in terms of intraorder variation in social forms, the same logic is applicable at lower taxonomic levels, and can be utilized to study intraspecific, or even intrademic, variation in social forms. Temporal variation in the social form of a specific population can also be studied from within this framework.

The numbers in the ideal problem just presented refer to some of the major theoretical and methodological problems confronting ecological sociobiology. In this section I will briefly mention the first and third problems, but will concentrate on the second problem, defining and measuring adaptiveness of social forms.

The first problem is the classification of social forms. Which features of social forms (group size, socionomic sex ratio, asymmetry in reproductive success, defense of territory, etc.) are to be taken as the dependent variables in tests of hypotheses? Since ecological sociobiology investigates the genetic bases of social behavior, theorists wish to identify features which are adaptive in the sense that their presence or absence and their exact configuration is, in some part, the result of selection for or against genes relevant to their production. Focus on nonadaptive (in the sense just given) features will probably result in a failure to find correlations with ecological factors. The problem of classifying primate social forms will be addressed in the following section.

The third issue in the ideal problem concerns the weighting of the ecological factors that are implicated in the evolution of social forms. For example, there is a major debate over the relative influence of predation pressure and distribution of food resources in the evolution of group living and in the production of variation in social forms. Because most studies in ecological sociobiology so far have been taxonomic in nature or, at best, have been analyses of associations between pairs of variables, the identification of primary and secondary ecological variables remains a major point of contention. Until better data permit multivariate analyses, such debates will no doubt continue. This problem will be examined in more detail in the last two sections of this chapter.

The second problem—defining and measuring the adaptiveness of social forms—has been addressed by both proponents and opponents of the ecological approach. One of the best summaries is presented by Rowell (1979). I discuss her argument in some detail, because she provides some useful concepts, such as the distinction between social structure and social organization, and because many of her points are as relevant to strategic sociobiology as to ecological sociobiology.

A basic problem in ecological sociobiology is to define what is meant by the statement that a given social form is adaptive (Williams 1966). In many alloprimate and human ecological studies, the statement means little more than that the population exhibiting this social form continued to exist during the period of investigation. In more sophisticated studies, adaptiveness is given a rough measure—such as the ability to maintain the population below the environment's hypothetical carrying capacity—and mechanisms presumed to maintain the adaptation are identified. In still more advanced studies, specific measures of adaptation (population growth rate, calorie flow, etc.) are postulated and measured in different social forms. However, the term "adaptive" has a stricter definition in ecological and strategic sociobiology, where the statement that the social form characteristic of a population or species is adaptive argues that the social form reflects a past selective history, during which alleles relevant to the production of that form were selected for, while those "producing" alternative forms were selected against. This definition of adaptation will be utilized in the remainder of this volume.

Sociobiological theorists confronted with intraorder or intraspecies variation in social forms usually attempt to devise adaptive hypotheses to account for such variation. Rowell notes that these theorists frequently neglect to formulate and test the null hypothesis that variation in social form is not adaptive. The bulk of her paper discusses the numerous ways in which such variation might *not* be the result of adaptation in the sociobiological sense.

Before exploring some of Rowell's examples, it is necessary to discuss her distinction between social structure and social organization. The former refers to the demographic features of a group, such as group size, population density, socionomic sex ratio, age pyramid, etc. Social organization is the pattern of interactions between group members and includes such items as dominance and affiliative interactions, food-getting strategies, defense against predators, etc. An important topic of investigation is the degree of freedom between social structure and social organization in primates. For example, the several primate species with unimale troop social structure exhibit widely different social organizations (see below). The degree of freedom between social structure and social organization might play an important confounding role in many interspecies studies in alloprimate sociobiology.

Rowell discusses numerous ways in which features of social structure or organization could arise without being the result of adaptation. For example, the feature might be an epiphenomenon; that is, the trait did not undergo selection itself, but was somehow linked with another trait which experienced positive selection in the past. Rowell illustrates this possibility by arguing that the tendency to behave aggressively toward conspecifics might be a by-product of selection for aggressive defense against predators. The former trait would thus not be adaptive, while the latter one would.

A second case where variation in social form might not be adaptive occurs when the variation is unrelated to either present or past genetic variation in the species. In this case, the variation may be explained fully as the outcome of environmental factors, and temporal and/or spatial transition from one form of the feature to another involves no change in gene frequencies.

The problem of local group size provides an illustration of how a feature of social structure may not be adaptive. Rowell argues that the overall population density in an area might be set by resource limitations and thus reflect adaptation. However, she reviews field studies suggesting that the number of troops in a given area may not be an adaptive response to the distribution of resources and conspecific competitors, but rather may result from social tradition. Rowell suggests that the null hypothesis that the number of social groups in an area is not an adaptation predicts that while average group size in an area is associated with population density, the variance in size is relatively large. The adaptive hypothesis would predict relatively low variance in group size.

Another feature of social structure commonly thought to be adaptive is the demography of the population. However, Rowell argues that demographic accidents, combined with other variables, make it unlikely that the demography discovered at any one particular study site is a fixed species characteristic created by adaptation (see also Dunbar 1979a). Her brief analysis of the fifteen-year reproductive histories of seven species of African monkeys housed in relatively stable conditions is an excellent example of the type of research that is needed to unravel the threads of adaptation, demographic accidents, and ecological adjustment.

Rowell also explores how variations in social organization may not be the result of adaptation. Some variations are the direct result of environmental factors, and social organization can change rapidly when these factors are altered. For example, the level of aggression within a troop might vary greatly with the availability of food in the environment. Other aspects of social organization may result from the social structure exhibited by a species or group. If this social structure changes, alteration in social organization may also be rapid and may not involve change in gene frequencies.

Finally, Rowell notes that while the requirement of behavioral predictability may be vital to the functioning of primate social groups and thus might be the result of adaptation, the exact rules of behavior creating predictability might not be affected by natural selection. Either intraspecies or interspecies variation in behavioral rules may be the result of random genetic or cultural drift. Rowell uses the case of paternal behavior among macaques to illustrate this problem. In some Japanese macaque troops, adult males behave protectively toward year-old juveniles displaced from the breast. A number of adaptive explanations for this behavior have been advanced (see Chapter Six). However, Itani (1959) finds that the juvenile survival rate in troops where males do not exhibit protective behavior is not lower than in troops with paternal care. He suggests that paternal care is an example of cultural drift, having no present adaptive significance, and Rowell argues that this null hypothesis will have to be tested against adaptive explanations for paternal care in other macaque and baboon species.

Rowell's article makes two important contributions to ecological sociobiology. First, her examples of nonadaptive variation in alloprimate social structure and her discussion of the factors responsible for such variation serve as warnings against the hyperadaptationism that is often the first step in the sociobiological approach to social behavior. The point is not that the adoption of hyperadaptationism as a working hypothesis is incorrect, only that the null hypothesis of nonadaptiveness must always be seriously considered and experimentally eliminated. Second, although not described in detail here, Rowell provides several examples of the type of research that is needed to distinguish between nonadaptive and adaptive explanations of the same phenomenon.

CLASSIFICATION OF SOCIAL FORMS

The classification of social forms is one of the most important steps in the testing of hypotheses in ecological sociobiology. Before examining some of the classifications of primate social forms that have been offered by theorists, I will briefly discuss three general problems: (1) Which features are utilized to classify social forms? (2) What is the role of classifications in hypothesis testing? and (3) How are classifications affected by intraspecies variability in social form?

There is no generally agreed upon classification of either alloprimate or human social forms. Wilson (1975a:16–19) notes that attempts to create essentialistic classifications of animal societies have failed largely because theorists cannot agree upon the features to be used in the classification. He identifies ten "qualities of sociality" that he believes can be quantified and utilized to compare different social systems: group size, demographic distribution, cohesiveness, amount and pattern of connectedness, permeability, compartmentalization, differentiation of roles, integration of behavior, information flow, and fraction of time devoted to social behavior. Wilson's hope is that in the future, either these or similar measures will be integrated into a complex model, allowing an unambiguous and useful classification of animal social forms. However, little progress has been made toward this goal so far. Instead, most authors classify primate social systems by the variable that most interests them. As noted below, most classifications involve the second of Wilson's measures, demographic distribution, usually operationalized as the number of males reproductively active in the group. However, other classifications are possible and may be more relevant to testing sociobiological predictions. Some of these are also reviewed below.

Researchers who use classifications of primate social forms in hypothesis testing are rarely searching for fixed species characteristics which will neatly sort all primates into mutually exclusive categories. Instead, classifications are seen as imperfect tools, permitting easy comparison of groups that vary in one or more features of interest to the researcher. A reader must continually be aware of the imperfection of the tool. For example, a key problem in ecological sociobiology is asymmetry in male reproductive success. In hypothesis testing, classification of primate social structure into monogamous pair bond, unimale troop, multimale troop, etc. is often utilized as a proxy measure for asymmetry in male reproductive success. These categories are assumed to exhibit gross differences on this variable, with monogamous pair-bonded species exhibiting less asymmetry than multimale troop species, which, in turn, exhibit less than unimale troop species. However, researchers acknowledge that the categories are not perfect indicators of asymmetry in male reproductive success. For example, the species placed in a single category may differ greatly on this variable. Thus, multimale troops exhibit great variation, with some reaching a level of asymmetry close to that achieved in unimale troops, and others exhibiting a low level more characteristic of monogamous pair bonds. Furthermore, species placed in different categories may actually exhibit the same level of asymmetry. And finally, intercategory variation in asymmetry may not always exhibit the neatness desired by researchers. Some unimale troops may exhibit less asymmetry than some multimale troops.

The "looseness" between classification categories and the actual state of the variable under study is unavoidable, but it is usually not fatal to the use of classifications in hypothesis testing. Errors due to intracategory and intercategory variability are viewed as "noise" or "measurement error" which result in the observed data not conforming precisely to the prediction derived from theory. Often the cases in a sample that do not conform to predictions can be explained by demonstrating that the category they have been placed in is not an accurate reflection of their score on the variable under study.

There is no doubt that the use of classifications as a shortcut in hypothesis testing is usually justified, especially in the first stages of theory testing. More direct measurements of variables, such as asymmetry in reproductive success, actual distribution of genetic kin, and so on, may not be available, and their collection might require resources which would not be worth the theoretical gains. However, readers should always be aware of the disjunction between the classifications and the actual measurements of the variable under consideration and realize that this disjunction may be worse for some variables than for others.

Another problem confronting classifications of social forms in primate ecological sociobiology is the flexibility of primates. In many of the studies discussed below, it is implicitly assumed that there exists a species-typical social structure, which can be explained by ecological factors. For some species, we know that this is not true: populations studied at one time or in one area exhibit one social structure (e.g., unimale troop) while those observed at another time or location exhibit a different structure (e.g., age-graded-male troop). For other species, observations have been conducted on only a few populations in similar ecological circumstances, and the result has been taken to be a species-typical trait. This problem does not mean that a primate ecological sociobiology is impossible. In fact, intraspecific variation in social structure is expected to be correlated with variation in resource distribution and predation pressure. Further, the degree of intraspecific flexibility in social structure should be predictable from ecological variables, with those species that have long inhabited temporally and/or spatially stable environments exhibiting less flexibility than those that have inhabited less stable environments. However, the fact of primate flexibility should alert the reader to the possibility that what is seen as a species-specific trait may, in fact, be variable. The reader should also realize that when classifications of social forms are utilized as proxy measures, primate flexibility may serve to increase the possibility of a significant disjunction between the categories of the classification and the actual values of the variable under study. It is necessary to examine the details of specific tests before deciding whether or not the disjunction invalidates the test.

With these three problems in mind, we can now discuss some of the classifications of primate social form that are utilized by ecological and strategic sociobiologists. In the following subsection, I discuss a number of classifications based on mating systems. These are frequently used in tests of sexual selection and reproductive strategy theory. This is followed by a subsection discussing classifications based on other criteria, including distribution of kin and the possibility for cooperation with nonkin. Such classifications are useful in tests of nepotism and reciprocal altruism theory.

Classification in Terms of Mating Structure

There are a large number of schemes that classify alloprimates according to their mating systems or the involvement of males in troop life (see especially Clutton-Brock and Harvey 1977; Crook and Gartlan 1966; Crook 1970, 1971). There is no need for a detailed discussion of each scheme, as an examination of one will serve to illustrate the importance of this approach in testing sociobiological theory. In a frequently cited article, Eisenberg et al. (1972) classify alloprimate social structure into five grades based on the role of males in social life: (1) solitary species (2) parental family species (3) unimale troop species (with minimal adult male tolerance of other adult males), (4) age-graded-male troop species (a single male of the dominant age class who exhibits moderate tolerance toward younger adult males) and (5) multimale troop species (more than one male in the dominant age class and higher tolerance of other adult males). The authors subdivide these grades by feeding ecologies. Thus, age-graded-male troops include arboreal folivores (*Presbytis entellus*), arboreal frugivores (*Ateles geoffroyi*), semi-terrestrial frugivore-omnivores (*Cercopithecus aethiops*), and terrestrial folivore-frugivores (*Gorilla gorilla*).

The importance of careful classification for hypothesis testing can be illustrated by Eisenberg et al.'s distinction between age-graded-male troops and multimale troops. This distinction was not commonly made in earlier classifications, and species exhibiting either of these social structures were placed in a single "multimale" or "polygynous" category. However, it is clear that asymmetry in male reproductive success may be quite different in these two structures. In an age-graded-male troop it is theoretically possible for the dominant male to monopolize all mating by preventing younger males from achieving what might be called "sociological puberty." In contrast, it is highly unlikely that such asymmetry could obtain in a multimale troop. A specific case where the distinction is of importance is Clutton-Brock and Harvey's (1977) use of socionomic sex ratio (number of adult females per adult male in the group) as a measure of intermale competition for mates. The socionomic sex ratio of an age-graded-male troop might be closer to that of multimale troops than to unimale troops, but the asymmetry in mating success in such a troop might more closely resemble that found in unimale troops.

Classification of alloprimate species in broad terms such as "monogamous/polygynous," "pair-bonded/unimale/multimale," etc. is the most frequently encountered scheme in ecological sociobiology. However, recent theoretical work suggests the importance of more refined classifications. For example, Kleiman (1977, 1981), makes an important distinction between facultative and obligate monogamy. In the former, the pair bond is weak or nonexistent outside of mating interactions, the male invests little in offspring beyond territorial defense, juveniles do not care for kin, and life history strategy involves early social weaning and early puberty, followed by dispersion induced by parental aggression. Such systems are likely when resources are not adequate to support two adult animals in close proximity and do not permit males to defend the home range of more than one female (although polygamy sometimes does occur). Obligate monogamy evolves in situations where male care is vital for infant survival and resembles the anthropological concept of the nuclear family. The pair bond is stable, and the activities of its members are coordinated. Juvenile, subadult, and nonbreeding adult animals may stay with the pair, forming an extended family. In these cases, alloparental behavior may be well developed. The life history strategy common to this social structure involves late social weaning and delayed puberty, with dispersion more often induced by sibling aggression than by parental aggression.

At first glance, the classification of mating structures seems to be further along for humans than it is for the alloprimates. However, major problems exist, which necessitate caution in using the most popular classifications, and these have generated calls for taxonomies more useful to sociobiologists. The interest of early anthropologists in the evolution of human marriage systems resulted in the identification of human societies as monogamous, polygynous, polyandrous, etc. Such classifications are usually based on normative rules of marriage, and the disjunction between the categories and the actual variance in male or female reproductive success may be great.

A much improved classification that is often employed to test sociobiological hypotheses is found in the *Ethnographic Atlas* (Murdock 1967), where societies are classified as exhibiting monogamy, polyandry, limited polygyny (when under 20 percent of marriages are polygynous), and common (general) polygyny. It should be noted that the scoring of societies in the *Atlas* and in other holocultural samples is not a perfect reflection of variance in male or female reproductive success. The quality and type of data used to score societies varies greatly. Sometimes the scores are derived from census data, at other times from normative rules, and at still other times from vague ethnographer statements on the type of marriage most common in a society. Furthermore, the scores do not take into account factors that serve to increase or decrease variance in reproductive success above or below the score given a particular society. These include the amount of extramarital sex, the proportion of each sex who never marry or never produce children, differences in the age of marriage, etc. As a result of such factors, some societies that were scored as monogamous may exhibit greater variance in male reproductive success than societies that were scored as exhibiting limited or common polygyny. In spite of these problems, Murdock's scores are probably a fairly accurate reflection of differences in the variance of at least male reproductive success. Considerations of convenience certainly justify their careful use in holocultural tests of sociobiological hypotheses.

A new classification of human societies based on variance in male reproductive success is suggested by Alexander et al. (1979). The authors contrast polygynous and monogamous societies and argue that the former exhibit more intense male-male competition over mates and greater variance in male reproductive success. However, they suggest that two different types of societies with different degrees of mate competition are incorrectly lumped together in the monogamy category. In the first type, resources are distributed so that males usually cannot provide for the offspring of more than a single female. Alexander et al. describe such groups as exhibiting ecologically imposed monogamy. There may be occasional instances of polygyny and/or polyandry, but by and large most males are married to a single female, and nonaccidental variance in male reproductive success is not as great as that found in polygynous societies. An interesting question is exactly how much variance does exist in these groups. Extramarital sexual activity and institutionalized "wife-lending" may create some variance, but since the latter is often reciprocal, and since we do not know whether some males are consistently more successful than others in the former, we cannot say how great this variance is.

In the second type of monogamous society, the distribution of resources permits males to support the offspring of more than a single wife, but polygyny is prevented by law. Alexander et al. designate such societies as exhibiting socially imposed monogamy. In these societies, male competition for mates is much higher than in societies with ecologically imposed monogamy and may equal or exceed the levels that are common in polygynous societies. Alexander et al. note that these societies frequently engage in warfare and suggest that male mortality in war increases the variance in male reproductive success. Furthermore, males may engage in casual extramarital sexual activity, and wealthier males may establish stable relationships with mistresses or concubines, providing economic aid to these women and their offspring. Other implications of the Alexander et al. classification are discussed later in this chapter. A sample of societies scored on this classification appears in the Alexander et al. (1979) article, and a larger sample is found in Low (1979).

There is no classification of alloprimate or human societies that is explicitly based on female mating strategies or variance in female reproductive success. The scoring of societies as monogamous, polygynous, etc.

does provide some information about female life chances, but more refined conceptualizations of female mating strategies are needed. Some of the classifications of alloprimate social structure discussed in the next sub-section may provide a start toward this goal. For humans, Irons' (1983) discussion of four female reproductive strategies (see below) may serve as a basis for classifying human social groups.

Classifications Based on Other Criteria

Classifications of mating structure are particularly valuable when testing hypotheses derived from sexual selection or reproductive strategy theory. For tests of hypotheses based on nepotism and parental investment theories, other classifications are often more appropriate. Recently several new ways of classifying alloprimate and human social forms have been suggested. These will be briefly reviewed in this section. Many of these schemes are so recent that it is still too early to judge their usefulness.

In a discussion of inbreeding and kin selection, Ted Wade (1979) implies that alloprimate societies can be profitably classified in terms of their genetic structure by examining the distribution of relatives. He notes that troops of bonnet macaques are more closed and inbred than troops of pigtail macaques and that behavioral differences between the species may be related to this factor. Compared to bonnets, pigtail behavior is more competitive and tends to be organized along the lines of matrilineal relatedness. The difference is illustrated in artificially formed captive groups, with bonnets tending to treat all group members as kin and pigtails tending to treat them as nonkin.

The importance of the distribution of relatives is evident in Hrdy and Hrdy's (1976) identification of three systems of hierarchy exhibited by alloprimate females. An age system exists when higher rank is achieved by older, and hence larger, females. This system is expected in societies where females are not closely related. A second type, the genealogical system, is found among some macaque species and operates by the ranking of matrilines. The rank of young females is closely correlated with the rank of their mothers, and in some species younger sisters outrank their older female siblings. The interaction between birth order and matrilineage affiliation means that neither age nor size is an accurate indicator of a female's rank. Finally, in the reproductive value system found among some langurs, younger females are dominant over older females. Hrdy and Hrdy argue that for old females with low reproductive value the most effective investment strategy is to aid younger matrilineal kin with high reproductive value. They suggest that such an "altruistic" system could evolve only in species where troop females are closely related. In a later paper, Hrdy (1981b) discusses the different roles played by older females among the "nepotistic" macaques and the "altruistic" langurs. In the former, older females are active participants in social life; while in the latter, they tend to avoid interacting with troopmates, but will take aggressive action on the behalf of younger females.

In his study of allomaternal behavior (see Chapter Six), McKenna (1979) discusses the different feeding strategies of the Colobines and the Cercopithecines, noting that the ability of the former to digest leaves and other "low quality" foods, which tend to be fairly evenly distributed, results in different types of interactions between females in the two subfamilies. Compared to most Cercopithecine species, Colobine groups exhibit high rates of social interaction and reduced rates intragroup competition. For example, female dominance interactions are not as important for Colobines as for Cercopithecines. As noted above, Hrdy (1981b) compared female behaviors in macaques and langurs, but thinks that the most important variable in explaining behavioral differences is the structure of genetic relatedness. Of course, McKenna's explanation is not necessarily opposed to Hrdy's, since the difference in feeding strategies may be a major cause of the structures of relatedness that are characteristic of each subfamily.

Classification of human groups in terms of structures of genetic relatedness has only recently attracted the interest of theorists. Distinguishing groups that exhibit local endogamy from those that are characterized by local exogamy might be a small first step toward a broad classification. Fraternal interest group theory (reviewed in Levinson and Malone 1980), with its distinction between societies that permit the cooperation of patrilineally related males and those where such cooperation is impossible, may also be viewed as a classification based on the distribution of relatives. However, the need for more refined classifications is brought out clearly in a series of papers in which Chagnon (1979a, 1980, 1981, 1982; Chagnon and Bugos 1979; Chagnon et al. 1979) explores the complex interaction between distribution of genetic and "terminological" kin and mate competition among the Yanomamo. Irons addresses similar concerns in his discussions of primary social allies (1979c) and lineage exogamy (1981).

A classification of social forms based on a different principle is suggested by Wrangham's (1982) examination of mutualism. He notes that animals sometimes confront situations where cooperation results in gains to the reproductive potential of two or more animals (e.g., joint hunting, defense against predation). These "mutualistic" relationships differ from both nepotistic and reciprocally altruistic relationships, in that none of the animals suffers a loss of reproductive or inclusive fitness potential. There are two types of mutualistic relations. In interference mutualism (IM), the gains achieved by acting cooperatively decrease the fitness of conspecifics; while in noninterference mutualism (NIM), conspecifics are not adversely affected when other animals cooperate. Both forms of mutualism result in partner preferences and travel in relatively stable groups. However, IM favors the selection of kin as mutualistic partners, while NIM neither favors nor disfavors kin.

Wrangham suggests that the stability of partner choice and the degree to which a group is "open" or "closed" may vary with the balance between IM and NIM in a species' social life. This balance, in turn, is related to environmental conditions of food type and distribution and predation pressure. Wrangham argues that in alloprimates, food distribution determines the balance between IM and NIM in female-female relationships and thus is the prime mover in the evolution of alloprimate social forms. This balance determines the grouping tendencies of females, which, in turn, dictate the reproductive strategies of males (Wrangham 1979, 1980; also see below).

There are a number of interesting suggestions in Wrangham's article. For example, he argues that intersexual IM might be important in the social structure of certain alloprimate species. Among gorillas, for example, several unrelated females may bond with a male but not develop strong ties among themselves. Another important suggestion is that the balance between NIM and IM in a group may modify the operation of reciprocal altruism or nepotism in manners that are not predictable from the original formulations of these concepts. Thus, in predominantly IM groups, the necessity of maintaining mutualistic relationships may result in the competition between allies being more inhibited than the competition between individuals who never cooperate. Further, "donation" of what Wrangham calls "passive altruism" may occur in mutualistic relationships but not between noncooperators (e.g., allies are not killed when defeated, but nonallies are). Another case arises when two unrelated individuals both attempt to create a mutualistic relationship with a third. This could lead to short-term altruism between the target and the competing animals. Wrangham notes that in this circumstance, IM could lead to the evolution of altruism without the involvement of kin selection or reciprocal altruism.

Wrangham's distinction between mutualism, kin selection, and reciprocal altruism will be of special interest to human sociobiologists, as many societies exhibit groups which seem to be based on mutualism. These groups may be short-lived—like those formed for the cooperative harvesting of a temporarily abundant, unpredictable resource (e.g., Shoshoni rabbit hunts)—or long-term, such as rotating credit associations. An interesting problem is how tendencies toward nepotism and reciprocal altruism constrain the formation and influence the operation of mutualism in humans. For example, if kin selection has been an important factor in human evolution, we might expect that mutualistic groups must constantly resist the tendencies of members to "cheat" by providing more benefits to near kin. On the other hand, we might expect family conflict over the decisions of family members to invest in nonfamilial mutualistic activities.

Another means of classifying social forms is Vehrencamp's (1983a,b) concept of skew. Skew is defined as the asymmetry in either resource harvesting or reproduction between dominant and subordinate group members. Theoretically, subordinates should leave the group when skew is too great and they have a chance of doing better elsewhere. Dominants should attempt to maximize skew without driving subordinates from the group. Calculation of the optimal skew in various primate societies is complicated by a host of factors. Thus, differing structures of relatedness will dictate different skews. In addition, the importance of subordinates to the group will vary from species to species and from group to group. Factors such as predation pressure, size of group, and food resources, among others, will determine the value of subordinates to the group. Alloprimate social structure has not yet been examined from this perspective, but the data on rank and mating behavior that are discussed in Chapter Eight provide a beginning for such an examination. The Alexander et al. (1979) article on socially imposed monogamy discussed below and Betzig's work (1982) on despotism informally make use of the concept of skew.

Many classifications of human societies that are used by sociocultural anthropologists have only limited potential for testing sociobiological hypotheses. For example, the frequently used classification in terms of access to political and economic resources (band, tribe, chiefdom, state) does not satisfy the needs of most human sociobiologists, and alternatives have been advanced. Van den Berghe (1979) sees societies as based on different mixtures of nepotism, reciprocal altruism, and coercion. Nepotism is the major force in band social life, while reciprocal altruism and coercion become more important as society becomes sociologically more complex. Barkow (1982) divides societies into non-complex and complex, arguing that in the latter, tendencies to restrict behavior to nepotistic and reciprocally altruistic relationships are counteracted by power blocs, such as elders or the state. He suggests that when these blocs are rendered powerless, society tends to return to a state of sociality defined only by nepotism and reciprocal altruism.

The approaches of van den Berghe and Barkow illustrate the types of variables that must be incorporated into a classification of human societies for it to be useful to human sociobiology. However, neither approach results in a simple classification of societies, and both exhibit problems that must be resolved before they can be utilized in research. For example, Barkow sees complex societies as transcending the limitations of nepotism and reciprocal altruism. In his article, he discusses the gerontocracy of the Migili of Nigeria as an example of a complex society. Yet he does not demonstrate that the elders themselves have transcended either nepotism or reciprocal altruism. The elders' command of the labor of younger age-graders might be profitably analyzed in terms of Vehrencamp's concept of skew, rather than as an example of humans "escaping ethology," as Barkow suggests.

Irons outlines two classifications of human societies which are potentially useful in the testing of sociobiological hypotheses. In a discussion of human female reproductive strategies, Irons (1983) describes four tactics that females employ to maximize their inclusive fitness: (1) using reciprocity to increase parental care; (2) family planning; (3) choosing fit mates; and (4) resisting male coercion. Different social systems permit or evolve from different mixes of these tactics. Irons compares and contrasts Plateua Tonga, Tiwi, and Yomut societies along these dimensions, illustrating the different mixture of tactics in each society. This type of close analysis will probably benefit the study of male and female reproductive strategies more than will broad classifications that group societies as exhibiting high or low paternal certainty or as matrilineal or patrilineal.

Irons (1979c) presents another means of classifying human societies based on the analysis of what he calls "primary social dyads." He argues that the environmental situation of a society may make it beneficial to stress some social dyads while ignoring others. For example, the traditional Nayar of India stressed the mother-son, mother-daughter, sister-sister, and brother-sister dyads; while downplaying the husband-wife, father-son, and father-daughter dyads. The Tiwi emphasized only the sister-sister and husband-wife dyads; the Yanomamo the father-son, brother-brother, husband-wife, and brother-sister dyads; and the Yomut the father-son, brother-brother, and husband-wife dyads. Irons' classification again promises to be of more use to human sociobiologists than the more traditional anthropological classifications that are focused on normative rules of descent and residence.

Other classifications of human societies are possible, and several others advanced by sociobiologists will be examined at various points in this volume. The above review is sufficient to illustrate the manner in which ecological sociobiology conceptualizes social groupings and how this conceptualization differs from classifications commonly used in primatology and sociocultural anthropology. The alternative classifications suggested by sociobiologists are still being developed, but enough research has been conducted linking social forms with ecological variables to indicate the potential theoretical power of ecological sociobiology. In the next two sections, I examine two areas of research where this is especially true: the debate over the primary ultimate determinant of social forms and the models advanced to account for mating strategies.

PREDATION OR FOOD DISTRIBUTION?

A major debate in primate ecological sociobiology is the relative influence of predation pressure and food distribvtion in shaping the evolution and operation of primate societies. In this section, I will review the two levels of this debate. The first level concerns the general theoretical analyses that seek to explain the evolution of sociality in any living form. The second level involves recent research on intraorder variation in primate social structure.

To sociocultural anthropologists and to primatologists studying social species, the general problem of identifying factors that select group living over solitary living does not seem particularly important. The social nature of their subjects is often taken as a given, and research proceeds from this baseline. However, the theoretical analyses of the evolution of sociality that are reviewed in this section suggest that social life has both costs and benefits and that the constantly shifting balance between these costs and benefits is a major factor in the functioning of social forms.

The most widely cited discussion of the evolution of sociality is Richard Alexander's 1974 article on "The Evolution of Social Behavior" (see also Wilson 1975a:32–62). Alexander notes that if animals seek to maximize inclusive fitness, we may hypothesize that group living is a possible means to this end. This view suggests that we examine the inclusive fitness benefits and costs that group living offers to individuals and assume that group living will evolve only when the benefits outweigh the costs.

Alexander identifies three general fitness costs which might be suffered by individuals in a group. The first two, increased competition for resources (including mates), and increased likelihood of disease and parasite transmission, are universal; while the third, increased conspicuousness, resulting in more vulnerability as prey or less effectiveness as predators, is relevant to many, but not all species. Alexander argues that there are only three general factors that make group living beneficial enough to offset these costs. First, the risk of predation may be lowered through group defense against predators, through group vigilance, or because an individual "hidden" in a group is less likely to be taken by a predator. Alexander cites savannah baboons as an example of the first possibility and herds of small ungulates for the second and third. A second advantage of group living is that the probability of obtaining food may be increased, either because catching the prey requires cooperative effort (wolves) or because the distribution of food resources is such that individuals have little chance of consistently locating food on their own. A third advantage of group living obtains if vital resources are extremely localized. Alexander cites the sleeping sites of hamadryas baboons and the breeding sites of some marine birds and mammals as examples of this situation.

Group living does not require complex social behavior. For example, if localization of resources is the only reason for grouping, complex social behavior may not evolve. Alexander (1974) identifies three reasons why more advanced forms of social behavior might be selected: (1) because it increases the original advantages of group living (e.g., better predation defense, more efficient food location); (2) because it reduces the probability of disease and parasite transmission (e.g., grooming); and (3) because it affects reproductive competition among group members (e.g., dominance interactions). Alexander notes that it is frequently difficult to identify the original selective force on a particular behavior, because the behavior may gain additional functions *after* it has evolved. For example, he hypothesizes that the original selective force for grooming among many alloprimate species was parasite removal, but that the behavior acquired the secondary function of creating and reinforcing social relationships. Similarly, he suggests that human incest taboos were selected for because they prevented inbreeding depression, but that once they were instituted, the resulting rules of exogamy acquired the additional function of creating and reinforcing political alliances between families, lineages, or higher order groups.

Alexander's discussion of the general factors that promote group living has not generated much interest among anthropologists. However, the implications of his argument are of vital concern to sociocultural anthropology. For example, Alexander argues that the only alternative position on this problem assumes that group living is the result of a "social instinct" and implies that sociality benefits all group members. From this perspective, the costs of group living are small, and the phenomenon of sociality needs no special explanation. Needless to say, this alternative is not acceptable to most sociobiologists, and there are probably few anthropologists who would defend it in regard to most animals. However, it is an often unexamined, implicit assumption in many discussions of human sociality.

The factors that Alexander identifies are also relevant to the operation of social groups within a species. Thus, the individuals within a social species are expected to attempt to maximize the benefits and minimize the costs of residing in a group. When the balance between costs and benefits becomes too unfavorable, individuals may leave the group to become solitary or to transfer into another group. This view of social groups focuses attention on factors that are frequently not addressed by sociocultural anthropologists or primatologists. It suggests, for example, that limitations upon the power of a dominant individual may result from the need to prevent the cost/benefit ratio of subordinates from becoming so unfavorable that they are willing to leave the group. The willingness of the dominant individual to provide benefits to subordinates should, in turn, result from the value of the subordinates to the reproductive success of the dominant, the genetic relatedness between subordinates and the dominant, and the potential costs and benefits to the subordinates of leaving the troop.

With this general theory in mind, we can turn to the debate over the relative roles played by predation pressure and resource distribution in the evolution of primate social forms. Before doing so, it should be noted that both of these variables are complex and that at present no study has managed to cope with them adequately. A glimpse of the problem is provided by Low and Noonan's (1983) discussion of the characteristics of resource distribution that are required in any model relating food resources to the evolution of social behavior and/or the present social behavior of a species. These characteristics include: predictability, richness, patchiness, temporal variation, degree of fluctuation over various temporal and spatial units, accessibility to individuals, and degree of risk or expense in locating, obtaining, and processing the resource. The description of predation pressure for comparative research faces just as many problems, with the only qualitative studies of the problem using the categories "predators absent" or "predators present." These problems do not mean that interesting work has not been done in primate ecological sociobiology, but they should serve to alert the reader to the limitations of any particular study.

Most classifications of alloprimate social structures take a position on the ultimate determinant of social form. For example, in their classification, Eisenberg et al. (1972) explore the interrelationships between phylogenetic inertia, feeding ecology, and predation pressure. They suggest that the solitary grade of social structure is favored in nocturnal alloprimates, while the unimale troop grade is found in most arboreal species, whether folivores or frugivores. They argue that the unimale troop grade is ancestral to both the age-graded-male and multimale troop grades and is not, as earlier suggestions indicated, a grade derived from the multimale grade (Crook 1970; Crook and Gartlan 1966). They suggest that the multimale troops of baboons and macaques may have arisen as an antipredation mechanism, but they note (1972:873) that there is little data on the predation pressure faced by most alloprimates.

A strong proponent of the position that the distribution of resources is the major determinant in the evolution of alloprimate social structure is Wrangham (1979, 1980). His work is an excellent attempt to combine ecological and strategic sociobiology into a single system of explanation. Discussion of both his papers is in order, especially since his analyses have been criticized recently by proponents of the predation defense model of social evolution.

In his paper on the evolution of ape social structure, Wrangham (1979) identifies intrasexual competition over limiting resources as the critical factor in the evolution of ape social systems. He suggests that an explanation of social evolution requires answers to three questions: (1) What resource limits female reproduction, and how do females compete for it? (2) What resource limits male reproduction, and how do males compete for it? and (3) When female and male reproductive strategies clash, what determines the shape of the compromise? Wrangham argues that the critical resource for male reproduction is females, and that the general shape of ape society is therefore determined by the distribution of females. The distribution of females is determined, Wrangham suggests, by the distribution of food resources and accordingly can be studied, in part, as a problem in optimal foraging theory.

As a first step, Wrangham suggests that we explore the question of whether females should travel alone or in the company of other females. He asserts that females are expected to forage alone to minimize feeding competition, and that, with the exception of gorillas, this seems to be the case for the apes. How a female reacts to other females depends upon the defensibility of resources. When day-ranges are long enough to allow a female to cover almost all of her core area each day, territorial defense is encouraged (e.g., siamangs and perhaps gibbons); while if the core area is not usually covered during the day, peaceful feeding at locally rich patches is encouraged (e.g., orangutans and chimpanzees).

When females are territorial, the male response is likely to result in the formation of monogamous pair-bonds. Once monogamy is achieved, males may "take over" the costs of territorial defense from the females, who may then divert resources into greater reproductive effort. When females do not defend a territory, considerations of feeding competition suggest that they should prefer to avoid males except during estrus, and there is evidence that orangutan and chimpanzee females do spend a great deal of time alone. However, male-male competition over access to females plays a major role in shaping the social structure of the great apes. Wrangham notes that such competition results in increased feeding competition for females and increases the risk of injury or death to females and their infants. Females therefore have an interest in limiting their exposure to male-male competition, and this leads to a preference for association with dominant males.

This preference works out differently among the three great apes. Gorillas eat a "low-quality" diet, and feeding competition is not a major problem for females. Therefore females travel with other, unrelated, females in the company of a dominant male. Presumably, the minimal costs of feeding competition experienced by gorilla females is more than offset by the benefits of belonging to a stable social unit, free of male-male competition. Wrangham notes that gorilla females rarely interact with one another, further evidence that it is the presence of the male that makes the group beneficial to females.

Orangutan social structure is similar to that of the gorilla, with the exception that dietary differences mean that feeding competition prevents the constant association of animals. However, females still prefer to mate with the most dominant male and may cluster around his core area. This preference may manifest itself in the tendency of some females to scream when younger males attempt to mate with them. Finally, chimpanzees differ from orangutans, in that lower locomotion costs allow communities of brothers to defend a core area containing the ranges of several females who spend most of their time alone. These fraternal communities often act aggressively against males from other communities. Once again, it is advantageous for females to be in the core range of a dominant group.

In his 1980 paper, Wrangham applies his perspective to the whole of the primate order. The key concept in this paper is the distinction between female-bonded (FB) and non-female-bonded (non-FB) groups. In FB groups, females stay together throughout their lives and breed within their natal troops. Females in such troops are closely related and bound together by ties of nepotism (although, of course, as group size increases, this level of relatedness declines). Males in FB species usually transfer to other troops upon puberty and confront distantly related or unrelated males and females, forcing them to resort to dominance relationships and reciprocal altruism as tactics in social interaction (Western and Strum 1983). Wrangham lists twenty-five FB species.

Only four non-FB species are listed by Wrangham: red colobus (*Colobus badius*), hamadryas baboon, mountain gorilla, and chimpanzee. In these species, females leave their natal troops to breed. For three of the four species, it is unclear whether males also transfer between groups. (It is known, however, that male chimpanzees do breed in their natal troops.) Female transfer means that, in contrast to FB species, adult females interact with distantly related and unrelated animals, and Wrangham notes that adult females in these species tend to avoid interacting with other females in their nonnatal troops. It is as if only the presence of the male(s) holds the group together.

Wrangham sees the evolution of FB groups as a paradox, since feeding competition is present in them, and the close genetic relationships between the females means that competition harms precisely those animals which inclusive fitness theory suggests an animal would avoid harming. The solution to the paradox rests in optimal foraging theory. Wrangham divides a species' diet into two components. The first consists of the preferred foods during periods of abundance. This "growth diet" usually consists of high-quality foods in nonuniformly distributed, nonpredictable, rich patches. During periods of scarcity, a species reverts to its "subsistence diet," which generally consists of low-quality food with a uniform distribution. Wrangham argues that FB species have evolved in response to competition over growth diets. A group of cooperating females may be better able than solitary individuals or noncooperating aggregations of animals to defend ranges or to displace other groups from resources. Thus, while a certain degree of intragroup feeding competition exists, the fitness costs are offset by the benefits created by success in intergroup competition over growth diet resources.

Wrangham sees the reproductive strategies of males as responses to the foraging strategies of females. For example, he argues that if the distribution of resources is such that an FB group can meet the requirements of its growth diet by defending a territory, there will be selection pressure against forming groups any larger than necessary for effective defense. Under these conditions, FB groups are expected to "accept" only one male and become unimale troops. In contrast, in nonterritorial FB groups, the major factor determining optimal group size is the size of neighboring groups. Groups need to attract males to provide aid in competitive bouts with neighboring groups and are therefore expected to exhibit a multimale structure. The number of males in a group will depend upon a number of factors: the number and age distribution of females in the group, male reproductive interests, the quality and nature of the food resources at stake, the number and size of neighboring groups, etc. Wrangham supports this analysis by noting a tendency for territorial FB groups to be unimale and nonterritorial ones to be multimale, although there are exceptions to this pattern (e.g., vervets and patas).

The remainder of Wrangham's paper contrasts social organization in FB and non-FB groups. He notes that female participation in intergroup interactions is high in FB species and low in non-FB ones. Females maintain high social contact, as measured by grooming, in FB species, but not in non-FB species. The reverse situation is true for males, with male-male grooming being more frequent than female-female grooming among red colobus and chimpanzees. Levels of aggression between troop males is higher in FB species than in non-FB species. Finally, females appear to play a major role in troop movement decisions in FB species but not in non-FB species.

Wrangham contrasts his food distribution model with the alternative hypothesis that alloprimate social evolution is best explained as a response to predation. He notes that the predation hypothesis does not explain why females disperse in some species and not in others. He also examines three lines of evidence often cited as support for the predation hypothesis and finds that they can be reinterpreted to support the food distribution hypothesis. First, the fact that terrestrial species tend to exhibit larger groups than arboreal species has been interpreted to mean that the former are under more predation pressure and that large groups make for more effective predator detection and defense. Wrangham offers the alternative suggestion that terrestrial species often exist in environments where rich food patches are likely to attract many animals, in which case larger group size would be favored by competition for these patches. Second, the fact that multimale troops are more common in terrestrial than in arboreal species is often interpreted to mean that terrestrial species attract more males to defend against predators. In contrast, Wrangham suggests that extra males are needed in interactions between nonterritorial FB species and notes that nonterritoriality is more common in terrestrial than in arboreal species. Finally, the fact that males in terrestrial species possess relatively larger canines than males in arboreal species, while often used as evidence for the predation hypothesis, could be interpreted as the result of intraspecific competition resulting from the dynamics outlined by Wrangham.

The position that predation pressure is the major ultimate causal factor in the evolution of alloprimate social structure has recently been examined in a series of papers by van Schaik and his colleagues. Van Schaik and van Hooff (1983) present a model of alloprimate evolution consisting of four categories: solitariness/polygyny, monogamous groups, single-male groups, and multimale groups. The authors argue that the solitariness/polygyny structure was the primitive primate social structure and was favored when primates were small, nocturnal animals, who responded to predation by hiding. Diurnal life demanded the evolution of group living in the form of single-male or multimale troops. The authors note that intragroup feeding competition results in a tendency for larger groups to break into monogamous groups or solitariness/polygyny, but that this tendency is counteracted by predation pressure. However, if there is no predation, if the species is immune to predation, or if predation is low but intragroup feeding competition is intense, the balance is tipped, and groups may become smaller. Thus, the twin forces of intragroup feeding competition (a factor influenced by the nature of food resources) and predation pressure are both implicated in the evolution of alloprimate social structure, but the latter is the primary factor.

Van Schaik and van Hooff argue that monogamous systems evolved in two different circumstances. Among New World alloprimates, the relatively high litter rates of females (including twinning) required male involvement in infant care, resulting in obligate monogamy. The authors briefly discuss an issue which illustrates the problem of explaining social groupings by a single factor. The small South American monogamous primates are vulnerable to predation from birds and therefore are predicted to live in large groups as a means of increasing the distance at which predators are detected (see below). However, female intolerance of sexually mature females may prevent attainment of a group size that is optimal for predator detection. A possible compromise structure is an analogue to the age-graded-male structure, in which adult offspring remain in the group as helpers and the breeding female suppresses the reproductive activity of mature females (see Epple 1977).

A second form of monogamy is found among the Old World primates, occurring when either the absence of predators or immunity from predation allows groups to reduce intragroup feeding competition by lowering group size. If the species inhabits an ecology that permits the defense of home ranges, monogamy will evolve (e.g., gibbons), but frugivores requiring larger home ranges may exhibit the solitariness/polygynous pattern (e.g., orangutans).

Surprisingly, given their emphasis on predation pressure, van Schaik and van Hooff reject the idea that multimale troops evolved through a mechanism of cooperative defense against predators (see Eisenberg et al. 1972). They question how common cooperative defense is in most multimale troops, citing cases where males run away from predators rather than defend females and infants. The authors suggest that, at most, such defense would be a consequence of a multimale social structure, not a factor in its evolution. They propose as an alternative hypothesis, that multimale troops evolve when males cannot monopolize breeding access to females.

The inability to monopolize females, in turn, results form distribution of food resources requiring scattered foraging by the group.

Van Schaik (1983) empirically tests the theory that predation is the ultimate causal factor in the evolution of alloprimate social structure [the predation-intragroup feeding competition (PFC) theory] against the distribution of food resources alternative [the intergroup feeding competition (IGFC) theory]. The latter is van Schaik's formalization of Wranghams's (1979) model of female-bonded primate groups. A number of tests appear in the article, but the major one concerns the relationship between group size and birth rate. Van Schaik interprets IGFC theory as predicting that as group size increases, the birth rate will also increase up to a certain point. This prediction follows from the idea that larger groups are more successful in defense of resources. However, some groups may grow beyond the size optimal for fitness, but, because of the existence of other groups, not be able to fission and still effectively compete for resources. In these groups, female fitness, as measured by the birth rate, may drop. Since PFC theory argues that larger group size always implies greater intragroup feeding competition, it predicts an inverse relationship between group size and the birth rate. This does not mean that females in large groups are outreproduced by those in small groups, for the higher risks of predation in smaller groups may result in females achieving a lower lifetime success than females in larger groups.

Van Schaik utilizes census data in a holospecies test and demonstrates that in twenty-two of twenty-seven samples, the slope between the number of females in a group (group size) and the number of infants per female (reproductive success) is negative. A binomial test, with the assumption that positive and negative slopes are equally probable, indicates that this result is significant. Van Schaik claims that the result supports PFC theory. However, there is some question about the strength of the test, since only three of the twenty-seven slopes are statistically significant. Van Schaik also discusses several species wherein the effect of population density upon birth rate seems to support PFC theory. Tests on the relationship between group size and mortality among immatures are too inconclusive to lend support to the PFC theory, although results are in the predicted direction.

In another empirical test of PFC theory, van Schaik, van Noorwijk, Warsono, and Suyriono (1983) use a sample of four forest alloprimate species in Indonesia to demonstrate that party size is positively related to the distance at which humans (and, presumably, other predators) are detected. This research also shows that small group size may be associated with utilization of certain niches. Thus, smaller groups of crab-eating macaques tend to remain higher in the canopy than larger groups. Finally, van Schaik, van Noordwijk, de Boer, and Tonkelaar (1983) demonstrate that in larger groups of crab-eating macaques, animals expend more energy to obtain food than in smaller groups. Further, tension is higher in larger groups, and tension reduction tactics, such as grooming, are less frequent. The authors see these patterns as evidence of more intense food competition in larger groups and note that they correlate with the lower rate of average female reproduction found in larger groups.

While the work of van Schaik and his colleagues is exciting and important for understanding the pressures faced by existing primates, it is not clear that the results can be applied directly to the problem of the evolution of alloprimate social structure. The currently observed configuration of predation pressure and food distribution may have little to do with the original forces shaping the evolution of a species' social structure. However, at present, the little empirical work that has been conducted seems to support the predation pressure hypothesis over the food distribution hypothesis.

The debate over the relative importance of the distribution of food resources and predation pressure also characterizes recent discussion in the evolution of human social structure. There are a number of papers which address the problem indirectly. Among the most important of these is Lovejoy's (1981) use of concepts from ecological sociobiological theory in his reconstruction of the social life of *Australopithecus afarensis*. He argues that the species exhibited monogamous pair bonds, which allowed reduced interbirth intervals and lower infant mortality rates. Males, given higher paternal certainty by monogamy, provisioned females, allowing females to divert resources into greater reproductive effort. It is not clear whether Lovejoy sees these monogamous units as isolated, territorial entities (similar to gibbon pair bonds) or as subdivisions within a multimale troop (similar to no known primate group). Although Lovejoy does not explicitly address the issue of food distribution versus predation pressure, his model is clearly relevant to this problem (for a criticism of Lovejoy based partly on principles of ecological sociobiology, see Allen et al. 1982).

The wide variety of opinion concerning early hominid social structure can be seen by contrasting Lovejoy's monogamous structure with two other recent interpretations. Baer and McEachron (1982; see also McEachron and Baer 1982) review "selected sociobiological principles" and conclude that early hominid social structure was probably polygynous and that monogamy became the rule for subordinate males only after the use of nonorganic weapons made it necessary to reduce the potential for intragroup aggression. In contrast, Hill (1982) reconstructs the role of hunting in human evolution and argues that in the earliest hominid groups, males traded food, especially meat, for copulations with estrous females, a system of promiscuity.

Alexander (1971, 1974, 1975, 1977, 1979, 1981a,b,c; Alexander et al. 1979; Flinn and Alexander 1982) is a strong proponent of the position that predation pressure played the main role in the evolution of early hominid social life. He notes that the hunting hypothesis, which sees large social groups evolving from the necessity for cooperative hunting of large game animals, is unrealistic, because the upper limit for group size would be reached fairly quickly. This limit would have been the point at which the incorporation of an additional individual into the group would not have resulted in an increase in food sufficient to offset the costs of maintaining that individual. Once this point was reached, it is assumed that, unless there were other factors that maintained larger group sizes, groups would fission. As hunting strategies improved and weapons became more efficient, the upper limit for group size would have fallen rapidly, resulting in a tendency toward smaller, not larger, groups. Since human societies have exhibited a long-term tendency to increase in size, the hunting hypothesis will not account for human social evolution.

Alexander's alternative to the hunting hypothesis is a "Balance of Power" hypothesis, focusing on interspecies and intraspecies predation:

> This hypothesis contends that at some early point in our history the actual function of human groups—their significance for their individual members—involved the competitive and predatory effects of other human groups and protection from them. The premise is that the necessary and sufficient forces to explain the maintenance of every kind and size of human group, extant today and throughout all but the earliest portions of human history, were (a) war, or intergroup competition and aggression, and (b) the maintenance of balances between such groups [Alexander 1981c:273].

Alexander hypothesizes three early stages of human sociality. In the first, small multimale bands stayed together for protection from large predators. These bands were polygynous in the sense that there was some variance in male reproductive success that was not explained by accidental factors. In the second stage, these small polygynous, multimale bands cooperated in aggressive defense against large predators and also cooperatively hunted large game. The third stage saw the evolution of larger polygynous, multimale bands, which stayed together mainly because of the threat from other human groups.

The necessity of intragroup cooperation created by the threat of war did no mean that there was not intraband competition for reproductive success and inclusive fitness. Human social evolution can be viewed as the outcome of a shifting balance between these two forces. The various classifications of social forms that were discussed in the previous section may be useful to the extent that they manage to distinguish between theoretically significant phases in the history of this balancing process. Vehrencamp's (1983a,b) analysis of skew and Chagnon's examination of war, nepotism, and mate competition among the Yanomamo are likely to be especially instructive in this regard.

Alexander sees human social evolution going in at least two different directions, once large polygynous bands formed. Groups that removed themselves or were pushed into marginal habitats found distribution of food resources to be more of a problem than protection against human predators. Such groups had a very low upper size limit and fissioned frequently. In the more extreme environments, no male could provide for the offspring of more than a single female, and facultative monogamy resulted. As noted above, Alexander labels such groups as exhibiting ecologically imposed monogamy.

The second direction of human social evolution occurred in those areas where kinship-based sociality was incapable of creating ties between enough people for adequate defense against other large and well-organized human groups. At this point we see the evolution of the nation state or empire. Alexander argues that from a sociobiological perspective, the unique feature of a nation state is the amount of social interaction that is conducted between the unrelated individuals within it. While this interaction may be responsible for a state's ability to meet the challenge of competitive societies, it also creates a host of internal problems. Since states are found in association with wealth differences, the problem of skew becomes prominent: how much asymmetry in reproductive success can exist before subordinates either withdraw from the society or seek to overthrow the existing arrangements? A related problem involves the role of kinship-based groups in state societies. Alexander argues that the vast majority of individuals within the state have a vested interest in preventing the formation of large kinship groups. Such groups may be tempted to resist state power in order to maximize their own power (to be utilized to increase the inclusive fitness of members). This could lead to feuds between strong kin groups, the cooperation of some kin groups with enemy groups, or to kin-poor subordinates perceiving cues indicative of too much skew in reproductive success. Any of these conditions would weaken the state's ability to meet the challenge of enemy groups.

Alexander suggests that a common response of states to the problem of kinship-based groups is socially imposed monogamy. As noted earlier, males in such states may engage in casual extramarital sexual activity or may establish more stable relationships with mistresses or concubines. However, since in most of these societies only the offspring of a man's wife are legally recognized, the interests of genetic half-brothers are usually opposed, preventing the formation of lineage-like kin groups. Of course, it is also in the interest of a man's wife to uphold the legal claims of her offspring against those of children her husband may produce outside of marriage.

Alexander makes a very strong case for his position that human social evolution can best be explained as the outcome of the balancing of intragroup struggles of individuals and kin groups to maximize inclusive fitness with the necessity of the group to maintain its position in a balance of power against competitive groups. However, it should be noted that sociocultural anthropology contains a number of possible alternatives to Alexander's position. Superorganic arguments would perhaps deny that either warfare or the distribution of food resources plays a major creative role in the evolution of human social groupings. Positions emphasizing the distribution of resources as a factor in the evolution of human social groups have been advanced by a number of theorists within the framework of human ecology, but few of these positions are general theories in the sense of Alexander's position. An exception is the "cultural materialism" position advanced by Marvin Harris (1979) and his colleagues. However, cultural materialists are often not clear as to the relative roles played by resource distribution and warfare in the evolution of human social forms. There is no doubt that the position, at least as sketched by Harris, frequently explains warfare as the outcome of competition over ecological resources, and this would seem to contrast with Alexander's emphasis on the primacy of warfare. On the other hand, Alexander's position does allow that competition over resources may be a major cause of warfare. Sometimes interpretations generated from a cultural materialist framework seem to require a type of group selection (e.g., food taboos as conservation), but in other cases interpretations require no such mechanism (e.g., the sacred cow complex in India). Further research is necessary to identify specific situations wherein these two theoretical positions generate contradictory predictions. Only then can empirical tests determine which is more adequate to the task of explaining the evolution of human social forms.

To summarize this section, we can say that ecological sociobiology holds that in their various combinations the three factors of predation pressure, the distribution of resources, and phylogenetic inertia determine whether a species will exhibit sociality. Within a social species, variation in these same factors (and perhaps others) determines the optimal social forms for specific environments. How close specific populations come to achieving the optimal social form will depend on numerous factors, including some of those identified by Rowell (1979) as accidental. The relative strength of the various factors on the evolution of social form is still a major topic of debate in ecological sociobiology, but empirical research on the question has started to clear up some of the issues.

MODELS OF MATING SYSTEMS

A major feature of social structure is the mating system (or systems) that is characteristic of a species. Numerous models of the evolution of mating systems have been advanced, and recent empirical work has examined the predictions of these models in the field. In this final section I will discuss some of the more popular models and examine several attempts to apply them to the primates.

First a word on the classification and measurement of mating systems is in order. This is one of the most confused areas in sociobiological thought

(Jenni 1974; Selander 1972). For example, primate species with unimale troops in which all females mate with a single male are often described as polygynous, but so are species with multimale troops in which females may mate with a number of different males. Age-graded troops are often seen as examples of multimale troops, but the pattern of male reproductive success in such groups often resembles the unimale troop situation.

Wilson (1975a:327) offers a classification of mating systems which I will follow in this volume, but many of the studies I examine do not make the distinctions suggested by Wilson, especially that between polygyny and promiscuity. *Monogamy* describes situations where the bond between a male and a female prevents either from mating with other animals during a given time period (usually a breeding season). In some species, the bond may last for a lifetime; while in others, new bonds may be formed each breeding season. *Polygamy* refers to a situation where an animal of one sex has bonds with a number of animals of the opposite sex during the breeding season. These bonds may be simultaneous or serial. *Polygyny* describes the situation where males are the sex with multiple bonds, and *polyandry* the situation where females possess multiple bonds. If neither sex forms bonds lasting the entire breeding season, the mating system is described by the unfortunate term *promiscuity*. A major problem in discussions of primate mating systems has been the tendency to describe unimale, multimale, and age-graded troops as exhibiting polygyny. Under the definitions given above, unimale troops would be polygynous (although females may sometimes "sneak" copulations with extra-troop males), as are age-graded troops. In contrast, most multimale troops exhibit promiscuity.

A major paper on the evolution of mating system is Emlen and Oring's (1977) attempt to relate ecological factors to sexual selection and mating systems. The authors argue that environmental features dictate whether an animal can economically defend a mate (e.g., prevent access by potential competitors), and, if so, how many mates can be defended. These factors are basically the ones discussed in the previous section, with the primary one being spatial and temporal dispersion of resources. The pattern of resource distribution determines what Emlen and Oring label the environmental potential for polygamy.

A species may inhabit an environment with a high polygamy potential and still not exhibit polygyny or polyandry. Some species may not be able to utilize the polygamy potential, because the time required for adequate defense of mates or resources would prevent individuals from engaging in other tasks necessary for successful reproduction. For example, a species where both parents must invest heavily in the care of infants may reside in an environment with a high potential for polygamy and still exhibit monogamy. The amount of parental investment required by most birds is often given as a major reason why monogamy is so frequent among these animals. The carrying of infants by fathers in many species of New World monkeys may result in many of these species being unable to take advantage of an environment's polygamy potential.

Emlen and Oring present an ecological classification of mating systems that contains eight categories. However, only a few of these are relevant to the primates. Monogamy exists when neither sex can defend more than a single member of the opposite sex. Polygyny can be divided into resource defense polygyny and female (or harem) defense polygyny. In the former, males control the resources that attract females to their territories. The location of females within a territory permits the defending male to achieve more or less exclusive mating access to these females. In harem defense polygyny, females are usually gregarious, and a male defend the harem itself rather than a particular territory. Polyandry is divided into resource defense polyandry and female access polyandry. The latter describes a situation where females compete with one another for access to males. Emlen and Oring do not include promiscuity in their classification, but this is obviously an important category for the study of primate mating systems.

Both resource defense polygyny and harem defense polygyny have been the subjects of model building by ecological sociobiologists. The most widely accepted analyses of resource defense polygyny fall under the heading of polygyny threshold models (S. Altmann et al. 1977; Orians 1969; Verner 1964; Verner and Willson 1966; Weatherhead and Robertson 1979; Wittenberger 1981a,b). These models identify factors that make it reproductively beneficial for a female to become the mate of an already mated male, rather than to mate with a male who is unmated at the time she makes her choice. The models agree that the major factors include: (1) variation in the quality of territories held by males, (2) the amount of resource competition a later-arriving female will face from females already located in a male's territory, (3) the nature of limiting resources (food or safety from predators), and (4) the role of the male in offspring care. For example, to mate with an already mated male holding a resource-rich territory may be more beneficial to a female than to pair bond with an unmated male holding a resource-poor territory.

Variations on polygyny threshold models have been advanced by many theorists. Weatherhead and Robertson (1979) offer a "sexy son hypothesis" to explain the fact that in red-wing blackbirds, harem size is not correlated with territory quality, as predicted by the Orians-Verner polygyny threshold model. They argue that if males possessing traits attractive to females do not necessarily hold the highest quality territories, females who mate with them may suffer a loss of fitness compared to that which they could have achieved by mating with a less attractive male on a higher quality territory. However, this loss may be restricted to the first descending generation. If females mating with attractive males produce male offspring who have inherited their fathers' attractive qualities, these sons may provide their mothers with large numbers of grandoffspring in the second descending generation. The probability of the sexy son effect spreading obviously depends upon the difference in reproductive success between holders of different quality territories, the difference in reproductive success between attractive and other males, the heritability of the attractive traits and the skills that are necessary to hold territory, and so on (see also Heisler 1981; Wittenberger 1981a). One implication of Weatherhead and Robertson's analysis is that models of polygyny cannot be tested adequately with data on reproductive success from a single breeding season or even from the lifetime of single animals. Multigenerational data on reproductive success, sex ratios of descendants, and so on are required to evaluate the relative success of different reproductive strategies. This requirement makes certain socio-biological theories difficult to test in long-lived species, such as the primates.

Stuart Altmann et al. (1977) offer an axiomatic treatment of two polygyny threshold models: a competitive female choice model and a cooperative female choice model. The former model is usually assumed by researchers who utilize the Orians-Verner approach and holds that the addition of a female to a territory reduces the fitness of females already on the territory. Altmann et al. argue that if larger group size produces increased fitness, additional females might increase the fitness of the already present females. Some possible benefits include predator detection or defense, division of labor, group foraging, and mutual raising of young. The benefits of larger group size may not have to be large for female cooperation to evolve if there are also factors reducing competition between females. Altmann et al. identify three such factors: (1) males play minor roles in the care of offspring; (2) the contributions that males do make to offspring are nondepreciable, in that a contribution to one mate does not lower the fitness of another; and (3) male contributions are depreciable, but the resources are so rich that the fitness of no female is adversely affected by a male's actions. The Altmann et al. model of female cooperation leading to polygyny has not been tested among primates, but at first glance, it does seem worthwhile to apply its logic to polygyny in certain human groups (see below).

The applicability of polygyny threshold models to primates has been questioned by Ralls (1977), who notes that many mammalian species do not meet the assumptions of the models. For example, the models assume female choice of mates, but in many primate species females have less than total freedom in mating. Further, the models assume that a female raises her offspring on the resources of her mate's territory. However, it is difficult to talk of the males in a multimale troop as possessing individual territories. Most importantly, the models developed for birds assume that male parental investment is the major force opposing the evolution of polygyny. However, Ralls notes that among mammals, low paternal investment is not a good predictor of polygyny. She suggests that in some mammalian species, the distribution of food resources may oppose the evolution of polygyny by creating a dispersal of females.

Models of harem defense polygyny are not as well developed as polygyny threshold models, but they may be more relevant to the primates. A formal treatment of such models is found in Wittenberger (1980), who argues that the mating system of a species depends upon how the environment selects for the distribution of females. The distribution of females, in turn, determines their defensibility, thus selecting male reproductive strategies. Wittenberger models the evolution of mating systems by exploring the interaction between optimal group size for females and male responses to this factor. Once female grouping is present, males should attempt to defend groups of females against other males, creating a unimale troop structure. However, as the optimal group size for females increases, the cost to males of excluding other males from the group also increases, until the benefits of such activity are not outweighed by the costs. At this point, multimale troops should occur.

Few of the models of the evolution of mating systems have been utilized to examine the primates. This chapter concludes with a discussion of the research that has been done so far, starting with the alloprimates and then turning to humans.

In a study of alloprimate obligate monogamy, Rutberg (1983) accepts the argument that the basic factor in the evolution of alloprimate social structure is female grouping. He views the intensity of predation as the primary factor selecting patterns of female sociality. However, the distribution of food may set an upper limit to group size, once sociality has been selected through predation pressure. In Rutberg's model, the hypothetical first step in the evolution of monogamy is female "choice" to live apart from other females. This choice may result from either of two conditions. First, the most effective response to predation may be a solitary lifestyle, featuring nocturnality and concealment. Second, patches of food may be scarce, small, and widely scattered, or they may be uniformly distributed but of low quality.

Once females choose a solitary lifestyle, males have three possible responses: (1) to be nonterritorial, range over a wide area searching for estrous females, and prevent other males access to any estrous female encountered; (2) to be monogamous and help defend the territory of the female against all intruders; and (3) to be territorial, excluding all males from a home range containing the areas of several females. Rutberg argues that the male response is determined by the defensibility of females (monogamy favored with a fairly even distribution of females) and the possibility that male parental investment might significantly contribute to infant survival (monogamy favored when such investment results in more reproductive success than could be achieved by seeking additional matings). He also notes that when a species evolves a system of reliable male parental investment, females might evolve so as to put more effort into reproduction, generating still more opportunity for male parental investment and further lowering the possibility of polygyny. He points to marmoset twinning as a possible example of this situation.

Rutberg tests his model with a sample of solitary and monogamous alloprimates. He predicts that monogamy will occur at intermediate relative population density, since low population densities will make territorial defense by males ineffective, and high densities will allow males to defend territories containing the home ranges of several females. This prediction is supported, although Rutberg's statistical methodology is questionable on several points. One confounding factor is the presence of small monogamous New World monkeys exhibiting monogamy at high population densities. Rutberg suggests that in these families (Callitrichidae and Cebidae), paternal investment in infants effectively prevents polygyny at *any* population density. A second confounding factor seems to be the prosimians in Rutberg's sample. Only one of twelve prosimian species exhibits obligate monogamy (the remainder are solitary), while seventeen of eighteen anthropoid species do so. Rutberg suggests that this might result from the fact that prosimian infants need less care than anthropoid infants and therefore provide less opportunity for effective male parental investment.

Popp (1983) introduces a harem defense model of polygamy in the context of a discussion of how environmental factors select for different individual life histories. The study of the evolution of life history can be seen as the analysis of the question: "Given this individual's (group's or species') environment, what pattern of reproductive effort will produce the maximum inclusive fitness?" For example, Popp argues that the optimal life history for well-fed baboon species involves high rates of reproduction with a short life span; whereas the optimal history for less well-nourished species involves low rates of reproduction and a long life span. Another variable aspect of life history is the amount of resources an individual expends in searching or defending mates, relative to the amount expended in parental investment.

Popp analyzes variation in the social forms of various baboon species and demonstrates that in rich environments (measured as high rainfall areas), males attempt to exclude other males from the troop, resulting in a unimale or age-graded-male troop structures. Sexual dimorphism is high in such species, male-male aggression is common, and females have little freedom in mate choice. In moderate rainfall areas, it is energetically too costly for males to exclude all other males from the group, and multimale troops evolve. Male-male aggression may be common as males compete over access to estrous females, and sexual dimorphism is moderate in these species. Females also have greater freedom in mate choice in these species. Finally, in species in low rainfall areas, males attempt to avoid other males, and small unimale troops are formed. Both sexual dimorphism and male-male aggression are low in these species, but female mate choice is very important.

A significant confounding factor in Popp's scheme is the plasticity of the multimale social structure. This structure may disguise more subtle forms of interaction between life histories and environmental factors. For example, Popp suggests that multimale troops in energy-poor environments may exhibit characteristics of male-male avoidance-based, unimale troops (lower levels of male-male aggression over females, a less skewed distribution of copulations, lower sexual dimorphism, etc.). Similarly, multimale troops in energy-rich habitats may exhibit the characteristics of male-male exclusion-based, unimale or age-graded troops. Popp's discussion is an excellent reminder that classifications of social structure may frequently disguise important variation in the variables of interest to a theorist.

The work by Wrangham and by van Schaik that was reviewed in the previous section may also be utilized to examine the evolution of alloprimate mating systems. Since the implications of that work for models of harem defense polygyny are so clear, there is no need to review it here.

Concepts from ecological sociobiology have been applied to the analysis of human mating and/or marriage systems. The most ambitious research is Ember and Ember's (1979) attempt to explain the institution of marriage. The authors note that the universality of marriage makes it difficult to choose between alternative hypotheses for its existence, since any other universal is perfectly correlated with it. Ember and Ember suggest the concept of male-female pair-bonding as a nonhuman animal analogue for marriage, and use a sample of 40 species of birds and mammals to test hypotheses relating pair-bonding to various factors. They demonstrate that length of infant dependency is not correlated with pair-bonding and suggest that theories relating human marriage to the long period of human dependency are not correct. Theories explaining marriage as a mechanism for reducing male competition over females are not supported by the finding that pair-bonding is not correlated with the length of female sexual receptivity or the presence or absence of a breeding season.

Ember and Ember's data suggest that pair-bonding is favored when maternal feeding requirements interfere with the care and protection of infants. The theory is supported in a sample of thirty-three species, including eight species of alloprimates. An interesting feature of this article is the authors' attempt to control for phylogenetic heritage in a manner similar to the way holocultural researchers attempt to control for Galton's Problem. A second feature is a discussion of why the pair-bonding of males and females is the optimal solution to the interference problem. Ember and Ember argue that bonds between two mothers, two fathers, or a group of nonbonded animals would result in lower reproductive success than that achieved by opposite sex pair-bonds.

In the same article, Ember and Ember also test the hypothesis that species with polygynous mating systems exhibit a sex ratio biased toward females, while monogamous species exhibit an equal sex ratio or one with a masculine bias. The three polygynous and eight monogamous species for which they have data support the hypothesis, with no exceptions to the predicted pattern. However, there were no alloprimate species in the test.

In another innovative holospecies study, Ember and Ember (1983) examine one of the most controversial problems in human evolution: human female sexual receptivity. Conceptualized as the "loss of estrus" or the "concealment of ovulation" problem, this topic has generated a great amount of debate among human sociobiologists. Some theorists see the concealment of ovulation as the key to the origin of human social structure, others view it as an adaptive response of females to early human social life, and still others see it as a nonadaptive epiphenomenon of physiological changes associated with bipedalism (these positions are reviewed in Gray and Wolfe 1983). In this flood of speculation, only Ember and Ember have produced empirical tests of propositions. They argue that human conceal-ment of ovulation should not be viewed as a unique phenomenon, but rather as one point on a continuum with the polar opposites of species with brief breeding seasons and those with continual sexual receptivity. If this view is adopted, data on the presence or absence of breeding seasons in other species can be used to test speculations on human female sexual patterns.

Ember and Ember hypothesize that the species that experience great seasonal variation in resources and climate will tend to exhibit breeding seasons as a means of assuring that most infants will be born during the most advantageous time of the year. They demonstrate that species in higher latitudes (an indirect measure of seasonality) tend to exhibit discrete breeding seasons. A second factor that Ember and Ember examine is the length of infant dependency, arguing that when dependency is longer than the season of optimal food supply, natural selection might favor a mechanism to distribute births randomly throughout the year. Their sample suggests that long dependency is precluded at higher latitudes and that year-round sexual activity is therefore confined to the tropical regions.

Ember and Ember's test has important implications for the study of human evolution. In their previous holospecies research, they argued that maternal feeding requirements played the major role in creating human pair-bonding. The present study implies that only *after* pair-bonding had been established, and the period of infant dependency consequently lengthened, would year-round sexual receptivity have been selected. Ember and Ember also address the problem of why human females did not evolve year-round asynchronous estrous periods, the more common primate mechanism for randomizing births. They argue that such a pattern would have caused frequent male competition for estrous females, resulting in constant group disruption and perhaps threatening the survival of infants.

Several studies of fertility and marriage form can be utilized to explore the applicability of polygyny threshold models to humans. Such models are often seen as supported if it is demonstrated that second-mated females in polygynous situations achieve reproductive success equal to or greater than that of monogamously mated females (see S. Altmann et al. 1977 for a criticism of this view). Although the models do not demand it, the reproductive success of the first-mated female in a polygynous situation may be greater than that of females entering the situation later.

In a study of Bedouins in southern Israel, Muhsam (1956) discovers that wives in polygynous marriages have fewer children than those in monogamous marriages, a result which holds when childlessness is controlled. In another study, Dorjahn (1958) finds that polygyny has a slight negative effect on female fertility among the Temne of Sierra Leone. However, there is a complex interaction of factors in this situation. Daly and Wilson (1978:93–95) note that Dorjahn's results show that the number of live births per female drops after a male has four wives. Dorjahn argues that this drop might result from lower coitus rate per female per year in polygynous marriages. He also suggests that polygynously married males may have more frequent intercourse than monogamously married males, lowering their sperm rate per emission. The combination of these two factors might explain the observed fertility differences. Another confounding factor is that the infant mortality rate is higher at all levels of polygyny than for monogamous marriages. Whatever the proximate causes, it is clear that the Temne results provide no support for a simple application of polygyny threshold models to humans.

Two studies of polygyny in Africa distinguish senior wives from junior wives in polygynous households. For populations in the Camerouns Clignet and Sween (1974) find that junior co-wives under the age of thirty-five averaged 1.95 children, while monogamously married females in the same age category averaged 2.49 children. However, senior co-wives in polygynous marriages averaged 2.81 children. These results agree with Isaac and Feinberg's (1982) finding that Mende senior co-wives were hyperfertile (mean excess of 1.28 live births), and junior co-wives were hypofertile (mean deficit of 1.47 live births), compared to monogamously married females. By demonstrating that infant survival to eighteen months is independent of marital situation, the Isaac and Feinberg findings eliminate the possibility that the presence of extra mother-surrogates in polygynous households might result in increased infant survival and reduce the gap in reproductive success between junior co-wives and monogamously mated females. The lower reproductive success of junior co-wives once again casts doubt on the extension of polygyny threshold model to humans.

None of the studies just reviewed was done with the purpose of testing polygyny threshold models, and it is questionable whether their results are adequate for this purpose. For example, none examines the marriage options open to females. Did junior co-wives have a choice between marrying monogamously or joining polygynous households? If they did, and chose the latter, the evidence for the short term is that they were acting counter to their reproductive interests. On the other hand, if the choice they faced was between joining polygynous households and either not marrying or marrying males who could provide few resources, the former choice would be in their interest.

Ralls (1977) notes that constraints on female mate choice violate an assumption of polygyny threshold models. Human females are often victims of the machinations of others seeking to maximize their own inclusive fitness. For example, both the Clignet and Sween and the Dorjahn studies demonstrate that males in polygynous households have higher reproductive success than those in monogamous households. In other words, polygyny is advantageous to males. Males might attempt to control the marital choices of females in order to increase their own inclusive fitness. The finding that senior co-wives are often hyperfertile raises the question of whether polygynous marriages somehow benefit these senior wives, who seek to arrange them for their own purposes. Finally, if daughters are "married off" for bridewealth, to permit sons to find wives, it is possible that parents achieve greater fitness by "trading" daughters to wealthy polygynists in return for bridewealth, thereby allowing sons to become polygynists. While the parents will lose some fitness because their daughters are hypofertile they will regain it if their sons head polygynous households. If the variance in reproductive success between the sexes is large enough, the female's loss of reproductive fitness may be offset by fraternally-produced gains to her inclusive fitness.

Mulder and Caro (1983) argue that a simple comparison between the average number of offspring produced in monogamous and polygynous households is not an adequate test of polygyny threshold models. Proper tests must control for the reproductive success of the primary female in a polygynous household prior to the arrival of other females and calculate the costs in reproductive success to the primary female after the arrival of other females. Still further, these figures must be corrected for loss of female reproductive value with age and possible decline or increase in male resource holding potential with age. Finally, if a society has experienced a decline in infant mortality rates, direct correlation between monogamy and higher female reproductive success might be the result of monogamous marriages being more recent than polygynous ones, and therefore less subject to higher infant mortality rates. Mulder and Caro's points indicate the necessity for more adequately analyzed data in testing the polygyny threshold model for both humans and animals.

A different model to explain intersocietal variation in polygyny is tested by Ember (1974). His holocultural sample of twenty-one societies demonstrates that polygyny is associated with a female-biased sex ratio. A sample of sixteen societies demonstrates that such sex ratios are found in societies with high male mortality in warfare. A final sample of forty-eight societies supports the logical conclusion that polygyny should be most often found in societies with high male mortality in warfare. Ember holds that natural selection favors maximization of reproductive rates and that when excess females are in a population, they will marry polygynously in order to achieve the highest reproductive rate under the circumstances. Here Ember utilizes a group selection mechanism, but in a later paper (1983), he provides an individual selection argument capable of explaining the same data.

In his more recent paper, Ember (1983) re-examines the problem of polygyny in light of a suggestion by Witkowski (1975) that a delayed age of first marriage for males is common in polygynous societies. Ember finds that the delayed age of marriage variable operates independently of male mortality in warfare and that a model incorporating both factors predicts intersocietal variation in polygyny better than models using either factor alone. Speculating on the logic of the delayed marriage factor, Ember suggests that in societies where spouses come from enemy villages, the groom's group would benefit by waiting until a male was no longer a warrior before allowing him to marry an enemy.

Van den Berghe (1979) argues that polygyny arises only when a society's resource base generates a surplus that permits a male to provide for multiple wives. He suggests that in many horticultural societies, the contribution of females to gardening means that extra wives are economic assets. He supports his case with a sample of 130 African societies, demonstrating that in 87 of 121 polygynous societies, females contribute as much or more productive labor than males, while this is true in only 1 of the 9 monogamous societies. A major weakness of van den Berghe's test is that it is restricted to a single region. Further, the percentage of labor contributed by the sexes does not provide evidence as to the ability of males to support multiple wives. Making use of a worldwide holocultural sample, Ember (1983) finds that polygyny is likely to be found in societies where males do more of the primary subsistence activity than females. However, when male mortality in warfare is controlled, the division of labor factor disappears, suggesting that van den Berghe's analysis is not correct.

There are other models of the evolution and intersocietal variation in human mating/marriage systems. However, enough have been reviewed to provide the reader with an idea of the possible contributions of ecological sociobiology to this problem. A major problem will be to decide whether human polygyny is best described by polygyny threshold or harem defense models. As the reactions to Hartung's (1982a) characterization of humans as exhibiting resource-defense polygyny indicate, this question requires considerable thought and research.

CHAPTER 4

Nepotism Theory

INTRODUCTION

In Chapter One, I noted that until recently the existence of behaviors lowering the reproductive potential of the performer while increasing that of a conspecific posed a major problem for evolutionary theory. Such behaviors, often labeled "altruistic," are not be expected to exist in a population when mutations might produce individuals who take advantage of the altruistic acts of others but cheat by not engaging in altruism themselves.

One solution to the paradox of altruism suggests that behaviors that appear to decrease the reproductive potential of the donor do so only on the level of the individual organism; they are actually beneficial to the altruist on the level of the genes. In other words, by engaging in the behavior, the donor increases, and does not decrease, the number of genes he or she will project into future generations. The excitement generated by sociobiology arises from its claim that in most cases the evolution of phenotypically detrimental, but genotypically beneficial, behaviors can be explained as the result of either kin selection or reciprocal altruism. As noted in Chapter One, the significance of this claim resides in its relationship to the possible role of group selection in the evolution of social life. Group selection explanations often suggest that phenotypically altruistic behaviors are also genotypically altruistic. That is, such behaviors do not serve to spread the alleles relevant to their production and, in fact, may aid the spread of alternative alleles. The relevance of sociobiology to students of social life lies in the possibility that societies where social behavior has evolved through, or is maintained by, the operation of kin selection or reciprocal altruism will function quite differently than societies where social behavior has evolved through group selection. These two perspectives often lead to different predictions about social behavior within a species or a group, and it is clear that knowing whether a particular behavior evolved through kin selection, selection for reciprocal altruism, or group selection will provide a great deal of useful information about the form, distribution, and constraints upon the behavior.

Of the two mechanisms advanced by sociobiologists to account for altruistic behavior, kin selection (Maynard Smith 1964), or nepotism theory, has generated the most interest. Recall that Hamilton (1963, 1964) argues that altruistic behaviors could evolve and become fixed in a population if the costs to a donor's reproductive success (i.e., a reduction in the number of offspring he or she will produce) is offset by the benefits to his or her inclusive fitness (i.e., an increase in the offspring produced by the donor's nondescendant kin). The claim that many forms of social behavior have evolved through the operation of nepotism is the cornerstone of recent sociobiology and has generated a great deal of research in sociocultural anthropology and primatology. It is probably not an overstatement to claim that the widespread acceptance and use of sociobiology in the social sciences ultimately depends upon convincing demonstrations of nepotism theory's power to explain the evolution and current operation of alloprimate and human social systems.

This chapter consists of four sections. In the following section, I examine aspects of nepotism theory that have been applied to the primates. I first discuss the logic of applying the theory to the primates and then detail some of the theoretical and methodological complexities that must be considered when evaluating propositions tested with primate data. This section is followed by a review and evaluation of studies of nepotism theory among the alloprimates. A review of the tests that use human data and a brief summary conclude the chapter.

THE LOGIC AND THE COMPLEXITIES OF APPLYING THE THEORY

Three Questions

Hamilton's rule is elegant in its simplicity and provides the promise of immediate utility in field research. Unfortunately, reality betrays that promise (see King's College Sociobiology Group 1982). The rule turns out to be difficult to apply in field research, and convincing empirical evidence of kin selection is surprisingly limited for a theory which is so widely accepted. The first step in detailing how existing empirical studies in primate social behavior relate to Hamilton's rule and other concepts in nepotism theory is to examine the types of questions posed by the theory and to indicate how empirical data can answer them. I believe that it is worthwhile to identify three separate questions. These vary in the complexity of the data that are needed to answer them, and we shall see that most research on primate nepotism is relevant to only the simplest question.

The question most frequently addressed by research on primates, and the one requiring the least information to answer, is: "In the most general terms, do primates act as if they follow Hamilton's rule?" I will refer to this query as the "interaction of relatives" question. For example, we might wish to demonstrate that behaviors assumed to be altruistic, such as grooming or defense in agonistic situations, occur more frequently between relatives than between nonrelatives, and more frequently between close relatives than between distant relatives. To demonstrate this point we do not attempt precise calculations of the costs and benefits of particular behaviors, but rather only deal with the interaction patterns between classes of animals. We also assume that the same behavior is equally valuable to all possible recipients and that the cost of the behavior does not differ for any of the possible donors. We know that these assumptions distort reality, but we hope that they do not do so in a systematic manner and that therefore they will not invalidate the test results.

If apparently altruistic behaviors occur more frequently between relatives than between nonrelatives, we have some evidence that nepotism theory might be applicable to the species in question. However, this type of evidence is not very strong. It is true that the null hypothesis that animals distribute altruistic acts randomly is discredited, but alternative explanations of the observed interaction patterns are still possible. For example, the distribution of altruism might be the outcome of the amounts of time that different classes of animals spend together, with near relatives associating more frequently than distant relatives. Another alternative hypothesis might be that the distribution of altruistic acts reflects ontogenetic learning processes and that interaction with relatives during the learning period is more frequent than interaction with nonrelatives. In this latter instance, nepotism theory is not supported unless it can be demonstrated that the factors selecting for the learning processes had some direct relationship with the differential favoring of kin.

Two other forms of evidence have been examined by researchers seeking to answer the interaction of relatives question. The reverse of the situation just discussed involves demonstrating that behaviors assumed to be "selfish" (i.e., where $B > rC$), such as agonism, are directed toward non-relatives more frequently than toward relatives. A third approach seeks to show that when several classes of relatives of varying degrees of relatedness are available, altruistic or selfish behaviors are distributed among them in proportions congruent with the level of relatedness (e.g., a mother provides more aid to her offspring than to her nephew, and more to her nephew than to her cousin). Both of these demonstrations also confront the problem of alternative explanations, and the third can fall victim to the gambler's fallacy (see below).

A positive answer to the second question, which I refer to as the "maximization question," provides stronger support for the hypothesis that nepotism theory is relevant to a particular species. This question may be phrased as: "When exact coefficients of relatedness are known, and the costs and benefits of particular behaviors are calculated, can animals be shown to act in manners that maximize their inclusive fitness?" The question assumes that the generation of animals observed by the researcher inhabits an environment which is similar to the species' environment of adaptation and that behaviors selected for in that environment will continue to lead to high inclusive fitness in the current generation. This type of research is especially effective when it identifies situations where the predictions derived from nepotism theory differ from those generated from alternative paradigms and demonstrates that the empirical data are congruent with the former. Of particular interest will be cases where cost/benefit ratios are such that nepotism theory predicts that Ego will donate aid to distant relatives or nonrelatives, rather than closer relatives, and alternative paradigms (e.g., proximity or learning perspectives) continue to predict favoritism toward near relatives.

The final question, the "evolution question," provides the strongest support for the assertion that nepotism theory is applicable to a given species: "Can it be demonstrated that there are genetic underpinnings to the tendency to favor kin (or to the proximate cues that result in the favoring of kin) in accordance with Hamilton's rule, and that these genes spread through kin selection?" This question suggests the kind of information that is needed for a fully convincing demonstration that kin selection is responsible for the evolution of a particular behavioral trait. It has not been addressed by any researcher working with primates, and it is mentioned here only to define the ideal against which answers to the first two questions must be evaluated.

I now turn to the complexities of nepotism theory. These are discussed in order to give the reader an indication of the problems of applying the theory to actual behavior and also to provide a guide against which readers should evaluate any research in primate sociobiology. Since primate socio-biologists have not yet attempted to demonstrate the genetic underpinnings of nepotism, I will ignore the many problems that face any attempt to answer the evolution question and will concentrate instead on the complexities creating difficulties for research on the two simpler questions.

The Proper Model
The first complexity results from the fact that Hamilton's original model contained a number of simplifying conditions (infinite population size,

panmixia, asexual reproduction, nonoverlapping generations, etc.) that obviously are violated by primate species. However, after the original papers were published, mathematical models examining the effects of relaxing one or more of these conditions have been advanced. Most of these models [many of which are reviewed in Michod (1982)] demonstrate that altering the conditions postulated in Hamilton's original presentation will have some effect on the specific predictions derived from the theory, but that the more general predictions will remain intact. Since research in primate nepotism is still at a fairly crude stage, these revised models have not been tested in any primate species. And since primates do violate so many of the conditions in Hamilton's original model, future research on this topic is imperative. Perhaps the most significant challenge to the applicability of sociobiology on this score is B. J. Williams' (1980) argument that kin selection works in species with certain demographic features (e.g., high fecundity), but that humans exhibit a demographic and life history pattern which makes it extremely unlikely that kin selection was an important factor in our evolution. Williams' criticisms demand a response from socio-biologists, and his proposed alternative model of human evolution requires further consideration.

The Measurement of Inclusive Fitness

A second major complexity involves the problem of measuring inclusive fitness. Grafen (1982) examines the measures of inclusive fitness that have been utilized by several researchers and discovers that a basic misunder-standing is often evidenced. He notes that researchers often incorrectly use a "simple weighted sum" (SWS) measure of inclusive fitness. This measure adds to the reproductive success of Ego the reproductive success of Ego's relatives, devalued by degree of relatedness. Grafen notes that we can never know all the relatives of an animal and that therefore SWS can never be calculated. He argues that the versions of SWS in which only certain close relatives are included in the calculation are also not congruent with Hamilton's definition of inclusive fitness, which requires that we make a number of difficult calculations before we can measure this variable. First, Ego's reproductive success must have deducted from it any component which is the result of the nepotistic acts of Ego's relatives. Then, any loss to Ego's theoretical reproductive success caused by the action of such relatives must be added back on to Ego's score. Next, we must separate the inclusive fitness of Ego's relatives into two components. First, there is the theoretical inclusive fitness of the relatives that is not influenced by Ego's actions. It is not proper to count this amount as part of Ego's inclusive fitness, since the relatives would have achieved it even if Ego had not existed. Second, there is the component of reproductive success of each relative that was created by the nepotistic acts of Ego. This component should be included in the calculation of Ego's inclusive fitness. Finally, if Ego's behavior served to reduce the inclusive fitness of these relatives, this amount must be subtracted from Ego's score to arrive at the final value of Ego's inclusive fitness.

It is clear that such calculations cannot be carried out for species with long life spans. Grafen suggests that for most field studies, the most appropriate measure of inclusive fitness will be the number of offspring produced by an animal, that is, the animal's reproductive success. This measure would seem to the most useful for field studies of the alloprimates. As of yet, no primatologist has attempted to measure the inclusive fitnesses of the animals in a population, and it is unlikely that this can be done for any free-ranging group. Although Grafen's suggestion is usually adopted in field studies, we should not overlook the rather unsatisfying nature of this tactic. The correlation between reproductive success and theoretical inclusive fitness will probably always be high, making it acceptable to use reproductive success as a proxy measure for inclusive fitness in hypotheses that test the interaction of relatives question. However, the less than perfect correlation between the two measures of fitness means that the use of the reproductive success measure in tests of either the maximization or the evolution questions may lead to incorrect conclsions.

Coefficients of Relatedness

A third conceptual and methodological problem concerns the measurement and interpretation of the coefficient of relatedness, r (see Michod and Hamilton 1980 for a review of this point). There are a number of different facets to this problem. For example, the measurement of r when inbreeding occurs becomes quite problematic (Harpending 1979; Kurland and Gaulin 1979; Michod 1979, 1982). More importantly, Kurland and Gaulin (1979) note that when pedigree-defined genealogies are utilized to calculate r, there is a danger that actual genetic relationships may be overlooked. This is especially true of the alloprimates, where researchers are usually forced to make use of genealogies tracing relationships only through females. An example of the potential difficulties created by this situation is found in Jeanne Altmann's (1979) discussion of paternal sibships among some alloprimate species. She notes that in troops where a single male or a small set of males sire most of the offspring in each breeding season, the offspring of different mothers may be paternal half-siblings. Further, in species with relatively long interbirth intervals and long postnatal dependency periods, members of these paternal sibships may have a greater chance to donate altruism to each other than to their maternal half-siblings. The genetic relationships between these paternal half-siblings will be overlooked in genealogies that are based on descent though females, creating a possible source of error when predictions derived from nepotism theory are tested.

With humans, the calculation of r from genealogies is even more difficult. One problem is that individuals may mislead the ethnographer about matters such as paternity or maternity. In some cases this may not be deliberate, as when a female does not know the genitor of a child and provides the ethnographer with the name of the pater. In other cases, a conscious falsehood is involved, as when a female knows that her husband is not the father of her child, but insists to the ethnographer that he is; or when people manipulate their genealogies for political ends. Whether, and to what extent, these problems significantly distort the calculation of r will vary from society to society. In societies exhibiting frequent extramarital sexual activity, genealogies may be of little use for calculating r. On the other hand, it is possible that in these societies the mistakes created by falsehoods and lack of knowledge do not systematically bias the data for or against nepotistic hypotheses, in which case the use of data from genealogies is an acceptable first step in testing such hypotheses.

A more significant problem with the use of human genealogies is discussed in detail by Sahlins (1976). He notes that systems of kinship terminology and their resultant genealogies are symbolic constructs, which often have little to do with actual genetic relationships. When ethnographers attempt to derive genetic relationships from genealogies, they assume that individuals sort "real" genetic relatives from putative relatives. It is often assumed that all languages permit this to be done. For example, an ethnographer faced with the statement that forty boys are all Ego's brothers may search for a query such as "from your mother's womb?" to distinguish actual genetic siblings from the others. The faith that such magic phrases can be found is based on the assumption that all people do indeed separate "real" and "terminological" kin. Sahlins presents examples from Polynesia indicating that this assumption is invalid. Although Sahlins makes a strong case for his position, I believe that the question is still open and that it requires more careful study of the political and other uses of kinship terminology. In any case, Sahlins' argument should be kept in mind when evaluating studies in human sociobiology which calculate r from genealogies; the reader should always ask how the genealogies were collected and whether or not the ethnographer attempted to control for manipulations of kinship terms.

A common response to the difficulties of calculating coefficients of relatedness has been to employ relative degrees of relatedness in tests of hypotheses. Thus, different classes of relatives may be compared upon the assumption that the mean level of relatedness between classes is an adequate proxy measure of relatedness. For example, a test in alloprimate sociobiology may compare Ego's behavior toward her maternal first-cousins with her behavior toward her maternal nephews and nieces. Paternal relationships, inbreeding, and other factors not reflected in the genealogies might mean that certain first cousins have a higher r with Ego than some of her nephews and nieces. However, the *class* of nephews and nieces will usually exhibit a higher mean level of r with Ego. The validity of using relative degrees of relatedness in proposition tests depends upon the number of factors that the genealogies overlook, the number of relatives in each class, and the exact proposition being tested. Relative degrees of relatedness are probably adequate to answer the interaction of relatives question, but not the maximization question.

Costs and Benefits

A fourth set of complexities applies mainly to studies seeking to answer the maximization question and involves the problem of specifying the costs and benefits of behaviors. These complexities might be summarized by the question: "What exact predictions are to be made in specific circumstances?" There are many aspects of this problem, and I shall only briefly identify some of the ones that are relevant to studies in primate sociobiology. These problems are particularly important because most of them have been ignored by studies that attempt to answer the interaction of relatives question. It is possible that, in some of these studies, the failure to examine such problems invalidates the results of the proposition test. This possibility is examined when specific studies are reviewed below.

The first complexity involves the cost and benefit components in Hamilton's equation for altruism. Hamilton's rule appears to predict that altruism will occur between close relatives. As Kurland (1980) notes, this interpretation has led researchers to focus on the r component in Hamilton's equation and to ignore the cost/benefit ratio component. Hamilton's rule actually holds that nepotism will occur between close relatives *only if* particular acts result in high fitness benefits to relatives and/or low fitness costs to Ego. The rule also implies that altruistic acts can occur between actors with low r if the cost/benefit ratio of the acts are of a certain magnitude (West-Eberhard 1975). In other words, theoretically we would expect to find nepotistic interactions with relatives at all different levels of relatedness. Exact predictions about what behaviors should be observed in the field depend upon precise measurements of the costs and benefits of specific behaviors.

Unfortunately, calculation of the fitness costs and benefits of specific behaviors is often a difficult task. A simple example relevant to alloprimates concerns grooming. Kurland (1977) argues that the distribution of grooming can be explained by Hamilton's rule, but his specification of the costs and benefits of this behavior is not very convincing. He argues that grooming costs time and energy, which Ego could use in other activities serving to increase his or her fitness. Risk of digestive tract pathology due to hair ingestion is seen as a second cost. Benefits of grooming include removal of ectoparasites from hard-to-reach areas of the body, increased peripheral blood circulation, and more efficient manufacture of vitamin D. However, other primatologists (Dunbar 1980, 1982a; Seyfarth 1977, 1980) have argued that grooming is an important element in coalition formation. If this is true, then grooming may serve to increase the personal fitness of the groomer and therefore need not be explained by nepotism theory, since the groomer does not suffer a fitness loss by his or her behavior. Of course, grooming could have originally evolved through kin selection, operating on the calculus of costs and benefits described by Kurland, and could later have obtained the secondary function of coalition formation (Alexander 1974). However, demonstration of this possibility requires that we answer the evolution question, and observation of a single troop of alloprimates cannot provide this answer.

Calculation of a behavior's effects on the fitness of Ego and Others is complicated by the fact that costs and benefits differ with life history factors of the actors (Charlesworth and Charnov 1980; Gadgil 1982; Milinski 1978; Rubenstein 1982; Schulman and Rubenstein 1983; Weigel 1981). Schulman and Rubenstein, for example, suggest that in addition to coefficients of relatedness, the following factors must be taken into account when calculating the costs and benefits of particular behaviors and predicting the optimum distribution of nepotism: the shape of the investment return curve for the behavior, the differing abilities of potential recipients to convert investment into reproductive success, whether or not the investment serves to increase survivorship of recipients or only affects their fecundity, and the location of potential recipients. By mathematically modeling these factors, they discover several situations where the optimum distribution of nepotism differs from the simple prediction that individuals will favor closer relatives over more distant relatives. Thus, one of their models indicates that under certain conditions, Ego's best strategy will be to provide kin with an r of 0.0625 with an investment equal to that given to kin with an r of 0.5 and to provide no investment to kin with r's of either 0.25 or 0.125. In a statement that summarizes the major problem with many of the studies reviewed in this chapter, Schulman and Rubenstein conclude that: "Merely demonstrating that the frequency of social interactions corresponds in a loose way with genetic relatedness does not demonstrate that kin selection is operating" (1983:785).

The life history factor that has received the most theoretical attention is the problem of age and reproductive value. Gadgil (1982) notes that a potential donor's reproductive value is a major factor in determining whether he or she should provide altruism to other animals and, if so, how much. Animals with high reproductive value should be unwilling to divert resources from themselves to others unless the potential rewards to inclusive fitness are extremely high. The reproductive value of potential recipients also must be examined. Schulman and Rubenstein (1983) note that reproductive value is an important component in a potential recipient's conversion efficiency (the ability of an animal to turn a given unit of aid into reproductive success). Donors are expected to be as concerned with conversion efficiency as they are with the coefficient of relatedness. There

may be frequent cases such that when the coefficients of relatedness to Ego
of two potential recipients are devalued by their conversion efficiencies, Ego
will maximize inclusive fitness by investing in the less closely related Other.

Life history models of nepotism seek to answer the question of how an
individual should distribute his or her resources so as to maximize lifetime
inclusive fitness. These models demonstrate that researchers predicting
behavior from knowledge of r alone will often be unable to identify which
option in a set of choices will maximize an animal's lifetime inclusive fitness.
The models often act as a source of alternative hypotheses, when animals fail
to behave as predictions based on knowledge of coefficients of relatedness
alone suggest that they should.

The relationship of maximization models to the general concerns of kin
selection theory is still quite unclear. Kin selection theory does not require
that all animals make perfect choices, which will result in their achieving a
theoretically defined maximum lifetime inclusive fitness. The theory does
suggest that any genetically implicated ability for making such choices will
be selected for, creating a tendency toward perfection and for the distribution of choices to match the specific predictions of life history models.
Sociobiologists do not expect animals to achieve perfection, and they
provide several theoretical reasons for this negative expectation (see Barash
1982:49–63).

Still remaining, however, is the problem of whether field studies should
be designed to test the weaker interaction of relatives hypothesis or the
stronger maximization question. At present, most studies seek to test the
former, but often resort to the latter when animals act in ways not predicted
by knowledge of r alone (e.g., by aiding more distant relatives to the
detriment of closer relatives). Although this tactic often does succeed in
clearing up apparent problems, it often leaves the impression that the
researcher is trying desperately to save a hypothesis which is not supported
by the data. The best way to avoid this problem is for researchers to clearly
state which question they are examining and to identify which parameters
are assumed to be relevant to that question. The identification of proximate
mechanisms is undoubtedly a major step in this process. To simplify
modeling life history and other maximization models often assume that
actors have perfect knowledge of all the factors that are relevant to the
calculation of costs and benefits of behaviors. In reality, the evolved rules of
thumb that are characteristic of a species substitute for perfect knowledge
and serve to prevent animals from making perfect choices, thereby creating
an unavoidable gap between the expectations of maximization models and
observed behavior. For example, in species where the rule of thumb is
"donate altruism to those you were raised with," the conversion efficiencies
of relatives reared in different locations will not affect an adult Ego's
behavior when confronted with a choice of investing in a childhood
associate with moderate conversion efficiency and the theoretically better

choice that Ego did not encounter until adulthood. Of course, if this type of situation occurs frequently, we would expect that any mutation creating a rule of thumb that permits discrimination based on conversion efficiency and coefficient of relatedness would spread rapidly through the population. However, such a mutation may never occur, and the species may forever exhibit a gap between the predictions of maximization models and observed behavior.

A final problem involving the prediction of which distribution of resources will maximize an animal's inclusive fitness is identified by Stuart Altmann (1979) as an example of the gambler's fallacy of distributing bets in proportion to odds. Let us assume that Ego has resources to invest and confronts three Others with equal reproductive value and conversion efficiency: a brother ($r = 0.5$), a niece ($r = 0.25$), and a first cousin ($r = 0.125$). The fallacy says that Ego will maximize his or her inclusive fitness by providing some aid to each individual, with the brother getting most and the first cousin getting least. Altmann argues that the proper choice is for Ego to invest *all* of his or her resources in the closest relative and to ignore more distant ones. However, he notes that several other factors, including those identified by life history models, may affect this strategy. For example, if nepotism reaches a point of diminishing returns, investment in other animals may be indicated (e.g., an animal needs only so much grooming). Interestingly enough, three studies of defense in alloprimate intratroop agonism (Kaplan 1978; Kurland 1977; Massey 1977) discover patterns of aid that make it appear as if animals were following the gambler's fallacy. This may have to do with the nature of this type of behavior or, as suggested by Richard and Schulman (1982), with considerations such as spreading risks. In any event, Altmann's conclusion that: "At present, the optimal allocation of altruism is unknown" (1979:958) summarizes the current state of maximization models.

This discussion has only touched upon a few of the complexities that confront a researcher who hopes to apply nepotism theory to the explanation of primate social behavior. Other problems were ignored, because they have no immediate relevance to the work that has been conducted in primate sociobiology up until the present. As proposition tests are reviewed, the reader should keep these complexities in mind as a standard against which to evaluate the methodology of each study. Results should be interpreted in the light of how well the researcher manages to cope with these difficulties.

PROPOSITIONS TESTING NEPOTISM THEORY AMONG ALLOPRIMATES

Studies testing nepotism theory among the alloprimates can be divided into two groups. Those in the first group examine specific populations to determine whether or not animals appear to be acting in accordance with Hamilton's rule. Up to the present time, such studies have not calculated costs and benefits of specific behaviors, and therefore their results can be utilized to answer only the "interaction of relatives" question. Studies in the second group examine the mechanisms of kin recognition among allo-primates and can be seen as exploring the proximate cues involved in the distribution of altruism.

Interaction of Relatives

Research on the interactions of relatives is best illustrated by describing the most ambitious study to date, Kurland's (1977) nine-month-long investi-gation of the provisioned Kaminyu troop of Japanese macaques. Kurland uses both census data collected by Japanese researchers and behavioral observations to construct matrilineal genealogies for most members of the troop. Relationships are traced only through females, because Japanese macaques mate promiscuously, making the assignment of paternity difficult in field studies. In several instances, relationships between animals are inferred from behavioral observations, a circumstance which probably leads to little error when assigning infants to mothers, but which may result in major errors when assumed mother-infant relationships are utilized to calculate more distant relationships, which are in turn used to assign dyads to relatedness categories. Altmann and Walters (n.d.:4) note that 91 percent of the dyads in Kurland's first-cousin category are inferred from six mother-infant relationships that were postulated on the basis of behavioral data.

Kurland uses his data to assign each possible dyad to one of six relatedness categories: F (individuals in different matrilines), C (cousins), A (aunts and nieces or nephews), G (grandmother and grandoffspring), S (siblings), or M (mother and offspring). Exact coefficients of relatedness cannot be calculated, due to lack of knowledge of both paternity and inbreeding. However, Kurland assumes that the F dyads have the lowest r, following in ascending order by C, A, G, S, and M. This ordering requires the assumption that if the paternal sibship effect described by Jeanne Altmann (1979) is present in this troop, its effects are masked by the operation of other factors.

Kurland's behavioral data are used to test hypotheses derived from nepotism theory. For example, he predicts that time spent near and interacting with individuals will increase as r increases. He finds very little interaction in F dyads but a lot in the S and M dyads, supporting his prediction. As noted previously, behaviors involving some time, energy, or risk on the part of the performer are assumed to lower Darwinian fitness, and, if such behaviors benefit other animals, nepotism theory predicts that individuals will perform them more frequently for animals with a higher r. Kurland demonstrates that both grooming and defense in agonistic situa-tions follow the predicted pattern. Although he does not attempt to measure the costs and benefits of these behaviors, he notes that they must be entered into Hamilton's equation before precise predictions of behavior can be made. For example, variables such as the reproductive values of dyad members (age and sex) and the rank relationship between attacker and potential defender (cost to the defender) must be included, along with information on r, before the pattern of defense expected in a troop can be predicted.

Kurland also tests the prediction that as r decreases, the frequency of agonism increases (he assumes that the costs and benefits of agonism are proportional to frequency). He finds agonistic behavior most frequent between the dyads with the highest r (M dyads) and the lowest r (F dyads). The other dyads do not differ from one another on frequency of aggression, exhibiting little. This finding seems at odds with nepotism theory. However, when all related dyads are grouped and contrasted with F dyads, and the time spent in association is controlled, Kurland finds that agonistic interactions are much more frequent in intermatriline dyads than between members of the same matriline. High scores for agonism in mother-offspring dyads merely reflect the amount of time animals in such dyads spend together. At any given moment, the probability of an agonistic episode between an interacting mother and offspring is low. In contrast, F dyads spend little time together, but at any moment in the interaction the probability of agonism is high.

To date, Kurland's research is the major study of nepotism in an alloprimate species. There are several aspects of his work that merit further discussion. An important methodological feature is the fact that Kurland usually tests hypotheses by employing different methods of controlling for the potentially confounding variables of the amount of time animals were observed and the amount of time two animals spend in association. In other words, he attempts to demonstrate that the pattern of positive interactions between kin is not merely the result of the fact that kin spend more time with one another than nonkin. For example, when he tests the hypothesis that grooming is more frequent among dyads with higher coefficients of relatedness he controls for observation time and association time in two ways: using "focal time" (dyadic allogrooming normalized by the amount of time each animal was observed) and "time together involved in allo-grooming" (allogrooming normalized by spatio-temporal association). In most cases, the results were not affected by the observation time and association time factors, but the example of the high scores for agonism between mothers and offspring illustrates the value of controlling these factors and of providing the reader with the results of all such tests.

The most detailed critique of Kurland's work is by Altmann and Walters (1978, n.d.; see also S. Altmann 1979). The authors' discussion of statistical problems should be reviewed by anyone who is interested in testing hypotheses with animal behavior data. Their more general points center on four issues. First, Kurland does not calculate the costs and benefits of specific behaviors. As noted earlier, for a behavior such as grooming, it is difficult to define any real costs and benefits. Second, Kurland frequently ignores the fact that alternative, nonnepotistic hypotheses can explain the observed distribution of behavior as well as a nepotistic hypothesis. When results are not consistent with a prediction from kin selection theory, Kurland often provides an alternative interpretation from within the same theoretical framework, rather than accepting a nonnepotistic interpretation of the outcome. However, it should be noted that Altmann and Walters do not indicate which general theory might explain as many of the details of Japanese macaque behavior as the theory championed by Kurland. Third, Kurland observed the animal mainly at the troop's provisioning site. The fact that the distribution of animals around food is frequently rank related, adds an unknown error element to Kurland's calculations. (Kurland 1977:35–37 discusses this point.) Finally, Altmann and Walters note that Kurland's use of correlation coefficients seems to commit him to the gambler's fallacy of expecting altruism to be distributed in proportion to degrees of relatedness. However, as S. Altmann (1979) notes, there are many factors that may result in a patterning of behavior which makes it appear as if animals were committing the gambler's fallacy. It should be noted that Kurland's charts graphing the distribution of altruism often exhibit a precipitous decline in nepotism beyond the two most closely related dyad classes.

In spite of its shortcomings, Kurland's research is still the strongest evidence for the operation of kin selection in an alloprimate species. However, an evaluation of this research must center on the fact that it provides only the weakest form of support for nepotism theory. Its major conclusions are that positive interactions tend to occur between relatives more frequently than between nonrelatives and more frequently between close relatives than distant relatives, and that the reverse is usually true for "selfish" interactions. Kurland does not demonstrate that positive actions, such as grooming, have significant fitness costs to donors and significant fitness benefits to recipients, much less than the costs to donors are offset by benefits to recipients, adjusted by the coefficient of relatedness. Without such a demonstration, it is possible to argue that grooming has no significant influence of the fitness of donors and recipients or that grooming serves to increase the fitness of the donor (Dunbar 1980, 1982a; Seyfarth 1977, 1980). Unless these alternatives can be eliminated, the hypotheses that grooming evolved through individual selection, mutualism, reciprocal altruism, or that it is a behavior which has not been a target of direct selection cannot be rejected. The same points can be made for the other behaviors examined by Kurland, including defense, interaction time, and so forth.

Other studies demonstrate that interaction patterns between group members correspond to predictions derived from nepotism theory. Most of these studies do not exhibit the methodological rigor of Kurland's research and are also subject to the criticism that costs and benefits of behaviors are not calculated. For example, in his study of the Yakushima-M troop of Japanese macaques, Furuichi (1983) finds that toleration for close spatial proximity is higher for female kin than for unrelated females. Not surprisingly, related females engage in more social grooming than un-related females. Dunbar (1979b) and Silk (1982) find patterns of grooming predicted by r for female geladas and bonnets, respectively. However, the situation among bonnets is complicated by considerations of rank. Silk finds that when the animals involved are of equal rank, females groom relatives more frequently than they groom nonrelated animals. However, females will also groom unrelated females who rank higher than themselves. Silk speculates that the grooming of unrelated, high-ranking females might be a tactic to gain protection from harassment by third parties (a protection hypothesis, suggesting that grooming is not altruistic, since it does not result in an overall lower fitness for the groomer) or might be a behavior that higher-ranking animals demand by threatening aggression (an extortion hypothesis, suggesting that the behavior is not altruistic, since the fitness costs of not grooming would be higher than those of grooming). Silk's study indicates once again the necessity of measuring the fitness effects of behaviors.

Silk (1979) discovers that the success of food solicitations by six captive immature chimpanzees varies with the degree of relatedness between the immature and the target of the appeal, with appeals to nonrelatives less likely to be successful than those to relatives. Solicitations of males are more successful than those directed toward unrelated adult females. This result may be explained by the unusual social structure of chimpanzees. Given female exogamy (see Ghiglieri 1984), the infant of one female is not likely to be related to adult females in the community. However, the infants in a chimpanzee community are likely to be the offspring of a group of closely related males, creating a high probability that a given infant will be related to any given adult male. However, Silk also notes that the success rate of appeals to unrelated females is higher than might be expected. She explores a number of possible explanations for this situation, including the idea that food sharing is a behavior with little cost to the donor, that reciprocal altruism in involved, and that immatures make the cost of not sharing food greater than the cost of sharing (Wrangham 1975). These hypotheses are not eliminated by Silk's data, and they remain as possible alternatives to an explanation based on kin selection.

In a study which is also relevant to the problem of kin recognition, Small and Smith (1981) demonstrate that interaction between infants and yearlings or juveniles in a captive rhesus troop can be predicted from knowledge of r. Paternity exclusion tests allow the authors to distinguish full siblings from paternal half-siblings and nonrelatives. The measure of nepotism was the attempts of individuals to interact with infants by touching, grabbing, or carrying them. The results demonstrate that full siblings engaged in more grabs than paternal half-siblings or nonrelatives, while these latter classes did not differ in number of attempted grabs. The authors suggest that this result is expected from the fact that full siblings maintain close proximity to the mother. The more interesting finding is that the grabs of paternal half-siblings were resisted by mothers less frequently than those of nonrelatives, suggesting that females might be able to recognize the unrelated offspring of males who have fathered offspring with them.

Close examination of Small and Smith's tables indicates that their conclusions are based on rather weak evidence. The major finding of the study is that females are more likely to resist grabs by nonrelatives than by paternal half-siblings. There are five cases of infants for whom both classes of animals made grabs. In three, the mothers resisted at least once a higher proportion of nonrelatives than paternal half-siblings (the number of resists per infant are reported, but the authors do not utilize these data in their analysis). In one case, infant 284, the mother resisted a higher proportion of paternal half-siblings than nonrelatives. In the final case, infant 857, Small and Smith's Table II lists the mother resisting grabs by more nonrelatives than Table I lists as attempting to grab the infant. In any case, infant 857 does not support the hypothesis, since its mother resisted at least once the grabs of *all* the animals, both relatives and nonrelatives, who attempted to take the infant. This means that in only three of five cases were a lower proportion of paternal half-siblings less likely to be resisted than nonrelatives, a distribution which might have easily occurred by chance.

Another shortcoming of the study is that the sex of the potential grabbers is not controlled. Small and Smith report that five of the sixteen immature males in the study participated in infant grabbing, but they do not provide a comparable figure for immature females. If females were either less or more likely to grab than males, and if some infants had a greater proportion of female or male siblings than others, the results could be seriously affected. These considerations suggest that Small and Smith's work needs to be replicated with a larger sample before their conclusions can be accepted.

Another behavior studied as an example of nepotism is coalition formation. When an animal not originally under attack intervenes in a fight on the side of one of the combatants, he or she may be risking some loss of fitness (how much depends on the rank relations between the animals involved). The possible fitness benefits to the animal being defended depend on a number of factors: whether a resource is at stake and whether the defendee ends up with it; how frequently escalated fights, resulting in serious injuries, result from defense; how effective two animals are against one; etc. Kurland (1977) finds that defensive bouts are fairly rare in the Kaminyu troop of Japanese macaques, occurring in only 7 percent of all agonistic interactions. As expected from nepotism theory, coalitions usually involve the defense of one matriline member by another (81 percent of all the cases). The nepotistic effect on defense is statistically significant, even after cases of mothers defending infants are eliminated from the sample. Kurland also explores the role of sex, age, and rank in the patterning of coalitions. His most significant finding is that defenders of kin rank lower than the aggressor they attack in 73 percent of the coalitions, but that this is true of only 25 percent of the coalitions between nonrelatives. It is probably safe to assume that defending against a higher-ranking animal incurs greater fitness costs than defending against equal-ranked or lower-ranked animals. Kurland also demonstrates that reproductive value plays a role in determining coalition formation, with older females of lower reproductive value being the most frequent defenders, and young females with high reproductive value being defended most often.

Massey (1977) shows that in a captive pigtail macaque group, aid in agonistic interactions is more common between members of the same matriline than between unrelated individuals. Furthermore, aid to relatives varies directly with r, with individuals of an r of 0.5 aiding one another at the greatest frequency, those with an r of 0.25 at moderate frequency, and those with an r of 0.125 at a low frequency (see Kurland and Gaulin 1979 for a criticism of Massey's calculation of coefficients of relatedness). Unfortunately, Massey does not control for time spent in proximity, and the alternative hypothesis that this variable is responsible for the observed distribution of aid cannot be ruled out. Massey also finds that older animals are more likely than younger animals to provide aid, a result that is congruent with considerations of reproductive value. Finally, the finding that females are more likely than males to aid others might be explained by the fact that male dispersal means that adult females are more likely than adult males to have relatives in the troop.

Kaplan (1978) examines fight interference in a Cayo Santiago troop of rhesus. An innovative aspect of his study is an attempt to calculate costs and benefits of interference by separating fights into serious (with biting) and nonserious categories. This division allows him to demonstrate that aiding is more frequent when the potential benefits to the recipient are high (i.e., during serious fights) than when they are low. Kaplan finds that both females and natal males interfere in fights involving relatives more often than those involving nonkin. The pattern of interference among kin also varies directly with the coefficient of relatedness, making it appear as if these animals, along with those studied by Kurland and Massey, are following the gambler's fallacy. Finally, Kaplan finds that females are less likely to enter coalitions to attack relatives than to attack nonrelatives.

Kaplan notes that while his data are congruent with nepotism theory, kin selection alone cannot explain fight interference behavior. For example, when females defend nonrelatives, it is usually during serious fights involving higher risk for the defender. Further, males tend to distribute aid more equally between relatives and nonrelatives than do females. Kaplan suggests that these patterns might result from the animals utilizing aid to create social bonds with unrelated animals and to ensure their membership in the troop. Kaplan's conclusion that "... the survival value and thus evolution of interference involves factors acting through both the social and genetic levels of organization" (1978:241) is difficult to interpret. Does this mean (1) that there are two sets of genetic factors involved in fight interference; (2) that there is a genetic component to kin-directed interference, but that nonkin-directed interference is the result of social factors and has no genetic component; or (3) that the original adaptive function of interference was nepotistic, but that the behavior has acquired the secondary function of creating social bonds and maintaining group membership?

Coalition formation in a troop of captive bonnet macaques is examined by Silk (1982), who finds that females are more likely to form coalitions to attack a third animal, or to defend against the attack of a third animal, with relatives than they are with nonrelatives. Once again, however, coalitions are frequently formed with unrelated animals, although these are usually of low cost to the defender, since the animal defended against usually ranks below the defender. In contrast, relatives are frequently defended, even though the aggressor outranks the defender.

Although often cited as evidence for the relevance of nepotism theory to the alloprimates, these four studies on coalition formation in different species of macaques do not provide clear support for the hypothesis that this behavior evolved through kin selection. Although each study demonstrates that relatives are more likely than nonrelatives to form coalitions, alternative explanations of the pattern (e.g., proximity, social support) have not been ruled out, and the high level of aid between nonrelatives exhibited by all four species is not predicted by nepotism theory. This does not mean that aid between nonrelatives disproves a kin selection argument, for, as noted above, this phenomenon can be related to the nepotistic argument in several ways. However, the situation is certainly more complex than a simple kin selection argument would suggest. Only more methodologically rigorous studies, involving precise calculations of costs and benefits and degrees of relatedness, will resolve the issues raised by these studies.

Another area of investigation relevant to nepotism theory involves the possible influence of brothers on transfer behavior in species where males leave their natal troops. Meikle and Vessey (1981) studied transfers in the La Cueva rhesus colony. They find that, given the option, young males prefer to transfer to a troop where a maternal (half-) brother already resides. This preference's strength is indicated by the fact that males frequently reject troops with more favorable adult-male-to-adult-female sex ratios to join their brothers in troops with less favorable ratios. In the new troops, brothers tend to interact with one another, rather than with unrelated males, and some of these interactions appear to be nepotistic. For example, brothers are more likely to form coalitions and less likely to interfere with one another's consortships.

Meikle and Vessey do not compare the reproductive success of males with brothers in their nonnatal troops to those without such relatives. However, they do find that the former achieve longer tenure in their nonnatal troops than the latter, and note that among rhesus, dominance rank is positively correlated with tenure length. They refer to laboratory studies of Duvall et al. (1976) and Smith (1980) which indicate a positive relationship between male dominance rank and reproductive success (see Chapter Eight) and suggest that males who transfer into troops containing brothers probably achieve a higher reproductive success than males who move into troops without such relatives.

Meikle and Vessey also speculate on the mechanism of kin recognition that is involved in transfer decisions. They identify attachment as a result of close common association with the mother as a major mechanism, noting that whenever a young male transferred into a troop containing a brother, the average age difference between the animals was 1.7 years. In contrast, when a young male avoided a troop containing a brother, the age difference was 2.6 years. In a study discussed below, Wu et al. (1980) suggest that infant pigtails may be able to distinguish unfamiliar paternal half-siblings from unrelated animals. It would be interesting to know whether rhesus have similar powers. If they do, it is possible that relationships traced through fathers also play a role in transfer decisions. This would greatly complicate the interpretation of Meikle and Vessey's results, but it might also explain why of thirty-one males who transferred, fourteen chose not to go to troops with their maternal brothers—perhaps they joined troops with paternal half-siblings.

A complex pattern of male transfer among free-ranging vervets is described by Cheney and Seyfarth (1983). The authors note that peers or brothers often transfer into new troops together. This may provide animals with related or familiar allies in their new troops—which would be a valuable commodity, since recent emigrants are often targets of attacks by resident males and females. In all six cases where a male transferred before reaching the size of an adult female, it was in the company of an older brother or peer. Cheney and Seyfarth note that transfer decisions may also be influenced by considerations of relatedness. When troops interact, those that have exchanged males in the past exhibit higher levels of affinitive behavior and lower levels of aggression than those that have not done so. Intertroop interactions may provide young males with vital information on the costs and benefits of transferring into particular troops. Cheney and Seyfarth identify other factors which play a role in determining the dispersal patterns of male vervets (the risk of inbreeding depression, the danger of predators when transferring, the chance that the animals have of bettering their rank positions, etc.). Although genetic relatedness is only one among these many factors, it clearly plays an important role in the dispersal pattern. Further research on transfer decisions obviously will be an important element in the analysis of nepotism among alloprimates.

Another major direction of research in alloprimate sociobiology is the influence of different levels of relatedness upon the operation of social structure and organization. As noted in Chapter Three, Ted Wade (1979) argues that behavioral differences between bonnet and pigtail macaques may be explained in part by the fact that the former species is more inbred than the latter, and Hrdy (1981b) examines the effect of patterns of relatedness on the behavior of older female macaques and langurs.

While the roles played by different levels and patternings of relatedness in alloprimate social structure have been the subject of much theoretical concern, so far only Chepko-Sade and Olivier (1979) have addressed the problem with empirical data. Their analysis of four rhesus troop fissions on Cayo Santiago demonstrates that groups are more likely to fission as the average level of relatedness drops. When r between all dyads in a matriline averaged less than 0.0514, lineages were certain to fission; while an average above 0.3349 guaranteed that there would be no split. The authors found that the average level of relatedness in both the daughter lineages produced by a fission was higher than in the original lineage. Interestingly, the average level of relatedness may be more important than either group or matriline size in predicting fissioning. Although the rank of a matriline is an important confounding variable in the fissioning process (Chepko-Sade and Sade 1979), Chepko-Sade and Olivier demonstrate that their conclusions hold when the influence of rank is considered. The authors conclude their study by noting that the results should not necessarily be taken as proof of kin selection, since they are also congruent with a group selection model. This research plays an important role in primate sociobiology, for it is congruent with the studies of fissioning among human groups, which will be discussed later in this chapter.

Not all tests of nepotism theory have obtained positive results. Kurland (1977) reports several cases where predictions derived from a straight-forward application of the theory were not supported by his data. He explains most of these cases by suggesting alternative predictions generated from within a sociobiological framework (unexamined costs and benefits of a behavior, the possible influence of reciprocal altruism, etc.). In a study of captive bonnet macaques, Silk, Samuels, and Rodman (1981) predict that aggression toward immatures will decrease with r, but they find no such pattern. They suggest, however, that severe aggression is rare between close relatives, but that it occurs more frequently between less related or unrelated animals. In contrast to the expectations of nepotism theory, females and natal males in one rhesus troop engage in high-risk intervention in agonistic episodes on behalf of nonrelatives more frequently than on the side of relatives (Kaplan 1978). Kaplan suggests that this pattern may result partly from females reinforcing social bonds with unrelated troop members.

A behavior exhibited in many species of birds and mammals—alarm calling—is often explained as the outcome of kin selection (see review in Barash 1982:83–86; also see Hoogland 1983; Sherman 1980). Cheney and Seyfarth's (1981) failure to find evidence for a nepotistic interpretation for vervet alarm calls is a significant negative result in alloprimate sociobiology. The authors argue that since vervet females do not disperse from their natal troops they will usually have more relatives in a given troop than males have. This argument suggests that the females should be more likely to give alarm calls, but this prediction is not supported in a free-ranging troop. The fact that callers give alarms to the predators to whom they themselves are most vulnerable, and not to those who create the most danger for infants and other relatives, also indicates that alarm calling is not nepotistic. Finally, the lack of correlation between the frequency of a female's calls and the number of offspring she has in the troop also challenges the nepotistic interpretation. Cheney and Seyfarth note that by giving alarms, individuals often benefit unrelated or distantly related competitors, perhaps lowering the fitness of closer relatives. However, they find no evidence that alarms increased the caller's chance of being taken by predators, suggesting that the behavior involves low costs to the donor, but may provide great benefits to the recipients. Benefits to unrelated competitors might be unavoidable costs for protection of close relatives. While the Cheney and Seyfarth study certainly does not eliminate the possibility that vervet alarm calls evolved through, or are maintained by, kin selection, it does suggest that a simple interpretation within the framework of nepotism theory is not likely.

The imbalance between the number of studies claiming to find support for nepotism theory among alloprimates and those reporting negative results should not be taken as an indication that kin selection has been demonstrated in one or more alloprimate species. It must be noted, first, that the results of these studies, positive or negative, usually bear only on the interaction of relatives question and are frequently open to alternative interpretations. Second, we must also take into account the understandable, but unfortunate, tendency of researchers (and probably of scientific journals as well) to report positive results and not to bother with publishing negative results. This tendency can give the illusion that theories have received more empirical support than they actually have. As sociobiology matures, we are beginning to see the promising sign of more studies reporting negative results. Such studies are vital not only in helping to decide whether or not nepotism theory is relevant to the alloprimates. They also serve to help refine the theory and indicate how it applies in concrete cases.

Kin Recognition and the Distribution of Altruism

At first glance, nepotism theory seems to require that before acting animals consciously distinguish relatives from nonrelatives and close relatives from distant relatives. As many writers have noted, however, consciousness need not enter the picture. If cues exist which provide fairly accurate estimates of coefficients of relatedness, and if they are incorporated into the proximate mechanisms involved in the distribution of aid, the pattern of altruism may reflect genetic relatedness without animals conciously calculating r statistics. Frequently, what some theorists label evolutionary rules of thumb operate so as to distribute altruism along the lines predicted by nepotism theory. If, for example, an animal grows up around close kin, a rule of thumb might be: "Donate aid to childhood associates and not to others." In primate troops divided into matrilines, such a rule would tend to produce a pattern where aid is most frequent between members of the same matriline.

Although knowledge of the proximate mechanisms involved in the distribution of altruism is interesting on its own terms, it is also vital for testing kin selection explanations of a species' behavior. Rules of thumb might result in a less than perfect match between coefficients of relatedness and altruistic behavior. In the case of a "childhood associate" rule, for example, perhaps some more distant relatives will not associate with Ego during childhood as frequently as some nonrelatives. Furthermore, older siblings might have left the troop prior to Ego's birth, and this would result in Ego treating them as nonrelatives, should they be encountered in later life. Such "mistakes" in aid donation are a source of error when observed behaviors are compared with predictions of nepotism theory. On the other hand, knowledge of proximate mechanisms may permit researchers to explain why empirical results sometimes do not match predictions. In the above example, a straightforward prediction from nepotism theory is that Ego will favor elder siblings over peers who are first cousins. However, the fact that the species has a childhood associate rule could explain what happened if we observed Ego donating aid to a first cousin in preference to his elder sibling.

The major research problem on the proximate mechanisms involved in the distribution of altruism is kin recognition: What cues allow animals to direct altruism toward kin? In a general review of the problem, Holmes and Sherman (1983) identify four possible mechanisms of kin recognition. *Spatial distribution* is a rule of thumb stating that you should behave nepotistically toward individuals in the community you grew up or reside in, but not toward strangers. *Association mechanisms* are also rules of thumb, one example of which is that you should behave nepotistically toward individuals with whom you frequently interacted during childhood. Another example is that you should donate aid to individuals whom you saw interacting with a party you had an altruistic relationship with (e.g., your mother). Both of these mechanisms are probably involved in the distribution

of altruism in many alloprimate species. A third mechanism, *phenotype matching*, can occur if there is a high correlation between coefficient of relatedness and phenotypic similarity on traits that actors use to distinguish individuals. A rule might be to donate nepotism to individuals resembling known kin (a spatial distribution or association mechanism might determine which individuals are seen as kin). Another rule involves self-matching: give altruism to individuals most resembling yourself. The final mechanism, *recognition alleles*, involves specific alleles creating phenotypic features that allow individuals with alleles identical by descent to distinguish each other, even from individuals with phenotypic resemblance on all traits except those coded by the recognition allele.

Exciting research has recently been conducted on mechanisms of kin recognition and on the proximate cues involved in the distribution of altruism in non-primates (Blaustein and O'Hara 1981, 1982; Getz and Smith 1983; Grass 1982; Holmes and Sherman 1982; Kareem and Bernard 1982; Klahn and Gamboa 1983; Lacy and Sherman 1983; Loekle et al. 1982). Two general preliminary conclusions from this work are: (1) that rules of thumb for distributing altruism vary greatly throughout the animal world and thus that variation is related to interspecies variation in ecology, rearing strategies, and dispersal patterns; and, (2) that although there are a few interesting studies concerning them, the existence of recognition alleles is doubtful.

Unfortunately, the ontogeny and operation of cues for distributing nepotism have not been investigated in detail in any alloprimate species. Rule of thumb mechanisms, especially childhood association and spatial distribution, would seem to be important for most species, but only studies designed to control a large number of variables will throw more light on the processes of nepotism distribution in various species. Cheney and Seyfarth (1980) make a start in this direction with their study of the ability of vervet females to recognize juvenile screams. They predict that mothers will be able to distinguish the screams of their own offspring from those of other juveniles in the troop. Using tape recordings of screams in playback experiments, the authors find their prediction supported: females exposed to the recorded screams of their offspring responded to the hidden loudspeaker more rapidly and with more intensity than other females hearing the same screams. Of some interest is the finding that other females appear to identify the source of the screams as an individual associated with a specific female; females would often glance at the mother of the infant whose scream was being broadcast.

Cheney and Seyfarth's study does not demonstrate that nepotism in vervets is based on recognition of relatedness. They note that the ability to distinguish individuals in a troop (and perhaps in other troops, see Cheney and Seyfarth 1983) might have evolved for various reasons. For example, reciprocal altruism might select for recognition of individuals, as might a high level of agonism in social groups. Animals may learn to recognize which infants belong to which females as a means of avoiding harassment by more dominant mothers. Evidence that the ability to recognize animals is involved with altruism in this species will require further investigation. An interesting experiment would be to play the screams of specific juveniles and study the reactions of females of differing degrees of relatedness.

At present, Wu et al.'s (1980) study on the ability of infant pigtail macaques to recognize previously unfamiliar kin is the most important work on kin recognition in primatology. Subjects are placed in a mechanism that allows them to view and to enter one of three cages. One is empty, and each of the others contains a young animal. The amount of time the subject spends looking at each cage and the amount of entry time to each cage are recorded. When given a choice between two previously unknown infants, subjects spend more time with (and more time gazing at) a paternal half-sibling than with an unrelated infant. When subjects are presented with a choice between a previously unknown paternal half-sibling and a previously preferred unrelated infant, there is a statistically nonsignificant tendency for them to prefer the former.

The results of this study have been the subject of much debate. Beyond noting that visual cues probably play a very important role, Wu et al. do not speculate on the proximal cues allowing a pigtail to detect relatives in the absence of prior association. Blaustein (1983) notes that as yet the possibility of recognition alleles cannot be ruled out for this species. Holmes and Sherman (1983) suggest that the mechanism involved is phenotype matching:

> Under this mechanism, an individual learns its own phenotype or those of its familiar kin by association. When first encountering an unfamiliar conspecific, it matches the unfamiliar phenotype against the template it has learned. Such matching may parallel a process psychologists term "stimulus generalization" . . . in which the response to an unfamiliar stimulus depends on its similarity to a familiar stimulus [Holmes and Sherman 1983:48].

Holmes and Sherman argue that the subjects in the Wu et al. study derived their templates from their own phenotypes, although there is little evidence for this conclusion.

Two authors have suggested that the results of the pigtail experiments provide evidence concerning mating preference, but not kin recognition. Bateson (1978, 1980, 1982, 1983) has demonstrated that the mating preferences of Japanese quail are affected by early social experience. These birds prefer to mate with individuals who have phenotypes slightly different from those of the individuals with which they were reared. Since the latter are usually close kin, this preference may be the result of selection to optimize the balance between inbreeding and outbreeding. Bekoff (1983) argues that the same process may explain the outcome of the Wu et al. study.

The subjects were reared with unrelated peers whose phenotypes provided the background against which they judged novelty. Since the phenotypes of close kin were not seen by the subjects during rearing, these might have been the most novel stimuli the experimenters could have presented to the subjects, and a mating preference for novel phenotypes would have produced the results obtained by the researchers. Bateson (1983:263–264) adds more evidence for the operation of a mating preference mechanism when he notes that Wu et al.'s attempt to control for age-correlated differences in mobility hid an association between age and kin preference. The eight oldest subjects exhibited a much stronger preference for the kin choice than the eight youngest monkeys. With a kin recognition hypothesis, there is no reason to predict a developmental sequence for kin recognition, while a mating preference hypothesis might require such a sequence.

A simple experiment could decide between the kin recognition and the mating preference hypotheses. If infants reared with relatives prefer nonrelatives over previously unknown relatives during choice tests, the mating preference hypothesis would appear to be the more likely explanation for Wu et al.'s results. As of yet, this experiment has not been reported in the literature.

If the kin recognition hypothesis is supported, it will be necessary to find out whether pigtails utilize the ability to recognize kin in the absence of prior association in making decisions on the distribution of aid. One immediate consideration is suggested by the fact that the recognition involved paternal half-siblings. In many alloprimate species, such siblings will be raised in different matrilines, and under a childhood association rule of thumb would not be expected to engage in nepotistic interactions. However, in the case of males emigrating to other troops, identification of paternal siblings might be advantageous. As noted earlier, Meikle and Vessey (1981) did not explore the possibility of paternal half-sibling recognition in their study of rhesus transfers.

The Wu et al. study is clearly a major paper in alloprimate sociobiology. It demonstrates some of the difficulties encountered in trying to discover which proximate cues govern the distribution of altruism among allo-primates. Unfortunately, the experiment has not been replicated for pigtails, nor has its methodology been applied to study other species. Until both these tasks have been accomplished, the proximate cues for nepotism among alloprimates remain unclear. This lack of information, in turn, means that most tests of nepotism theory will be less than convincing to skeptics.

TESTS OF NEPOTISM THEORY AMONG HUMANS

The most exciting work in human sociobiology is in the area of nepotism theory. The central role of kinship in cultural anthropology has resulted in sociobiologists and cultural anthropologists clashing over this issue more than any other topic. Kinship is seen by one cultural anthropologist (Sahlins 1976) as the key discussion in the dialogue between evolutionary biology and the social sciences, especially cultural anthropology. Sahlins claims that kinship is unique to human society and that human kinship systems cannot be explained by kin selection theory. He also argues that the anthropological perspective on kinship might serve to discredit the entire project of a human sociobiology:

> An effective anthropological criticism of kin selection, therefore, would do great damage to the thesis and interdisciplinary objectives of sociobiology. If kinship is not ordered by individual reproductive success, and if kinship is admittedly central to human social behavior, then the project of an encompassing sociobiology collapses. The issue between sociobiology and social anthropology is decisively joined on the field of kinship [Sahlins 1976:18].

Sahlins here incorrectly reduces sociobiology to the theory of kin selection, overlooking the importance of reciprocal altruism, sexual selection, and so on. However, his point that the theory of kin selection must be validated for humans before sociobiology will be widely accepted in the social sciences is correct. It is convenient to conceptualize the studies reviewed in this section as responses to the challenges Sahlins makes to sociobiologists. I will therefore first examine his position that anthropological studies of kinship demonstrate that kin selection theory does not apply to humans, and then discuss how specific studies in human sociobiology relate to this argument.

Sahlins argues that the anthropological study of kinship has demonstrated that:

> no system of human kinship relations is organized in accord with the genetic coefficients of relationship as known to sociobiologists. Each consists from this point of view of arbitrary rules of marriage, residence, and descent, from which are generated distinctive arrangements of kinship groups and status, and determination of kinship distance that violate the natural specifications of genealogy. Each kinship order has accordingly its own theory of heredity or shared substance, which is never the genetic theory of modern biology, and a corresponding pattern of sociability. Such human *conceptions* of kinship may be so far from biology as to exclude all but a small fraction of a person's genealogical connections from the category of "close kin"; while, at the same time, including in that category, as sharing common blood very distantly related people or even complete strangers. Among those strangers (genetically) may be one's own children (culturally) [Sahlins 1976:57].

Sahlins identifies at least two separate problems in this passage. The first might be labeled the "absent near relative" problem. In most societies, Ego is surrounded by Others who have a low r with him, while many Others who have a high r with Ego live elsewhere. Further, Ego often classifies these coresident distant genetic relatives as close kin, while classifying the nonresident near genetic relatives as nonkin. For example, in a society with patrilocal residence, Ego's sisters reside in their husbands' villages, and their offspring may be classified as distant relatives. However, the offspring of in-marrying women may be classified by Ego as close kin even though they may be genetically distantly related. There is no human society, in other words, in which all of Ego's relatives with an r of 0.5 live closest to him or her, and where relatives with an r of 0.25 interact with him or her less frequently than those with an r of 0.5, but more frequently than those with an r of 0.125, and so on. Marriage, residence, and descent rules result in great intersocietal variation in the classification of genetic relatives, but they always result in the absent near relative problem.

The absent near relative problem is not unique to humans, for it also exists in those alloprimate species where members of one sex disperse at puberty. In both cases, Ego is born into a group composed of close genetic relatives, distant relatives, and perhaps unrelated individuals. In other groups will be relatives who share a higher r with Ego than some members of Ego's group (e.g., offspring of Ego's older siblings). For humans, Sahlins argues that this results in a classification of relatives into the categories of near and distant, which has nothing to do with the actual r shared between two individuals. However, this is also true of the alloprimate situation. Ego might, for example, combine with distantly related animals to defend the troop against a troop containing individuals who were closely related to Ego. Unless some sort of recognition allele or phenotype matching mechanism operates, Ego might act selfishly when the degree of relatedness between him or her and animals in the other troop would theoretically dictate acting nepotistically. This would not mean that kin selection does not operate among allo-primates, only that it operates within the constraints imposed by the use of proximate mechanisms, which, in turn, are determined by ecological, psychological, and other factors. Sociobiologists argue that testing nepotism theory does not require demonstrating that individuals somehow magically distribute their resources in a manner allowing them to achieve a theoreti-cally calculated maximum inclusive fitness. Instead, the prediction to be tested is that when cost and benefit ratios are equal, Ego should favor close genetic relatives within his or her group over nonrelated individuals within the same group (note that the fact that a close genetic relative resides in a different group might make the cost of donating aid so high as to rule out the expectation of nepotism).

Sahlins' second point is that a society's kinship terminology may group genetically distant relatives or strangers under a category label that requires Ego to provide aid to these people. On the other hand, genetically close relatives may be placed in a category that Ego regards as having no right to his or her aid. Thus, even for coresidents, conceptions of kinship may act so as to cause Ego to distribute aid in a pattern that is not predicted from kin selection theory. Sahlins makes this point as follows:

> as the culturally constituted kinship relations govern the real processes of cooperation in production, property, mutual aid, and marital exchange, the human systems ordering reproductive success have an entirely different calculus than that predicted by kin selection and *sequitur est*, by an egotistically conceived natural selection [Sahlins 1976:57].

Sahlins here argues that cultural concepts of kinship are not mere facades or mystifications (1976:25), concealing people who are actually behaving so as to maximize their inclusive fitness. He rejects the idea that when Ego, a member of lineage A, calls a second cousin in lineage B by a kinship term we translate as "distant relative" and a fourth cousin in lineage A by a term we translate as "brother," he or she "really knows" that the second cousin has a higher r value and therefore will be more willing to treat the second cousin than the fourth cousin nepotistically, all things being equal. Sahlins argues that to Ego, the fourth cousin actually is a closer relative than the second cousin, and that Ego will be more willing to cooperate with or donate aid to the former. In other words, there is no calculus of kinship independent of cultural concepts that will allow individuals to perceive actual genetic relatedness and to act accordingly.

Sahlins supports his case by describing societies where kinship classifications are based on principles which act so as to erase any link between residence, terminological category, and genetic relatedness. There is no need to review these cases here, for any anthropologist can provide his or her own illustration. However, I do want to mention a major methodological issue raised by Sahlins' review of these cases. The review strikingly illustrates the fact that genealogies are cultural constructs and may often bear little relationship to the facts of "genetic" history. The importance of this issue goes beyond the simple case of two individuals who are called "daughter" by a woman, even though everyone recognizes that one is actually the woman's sister's daughter and can give the anthropologist this datum if he or she phrases genealogical inquiries correctly (e.g., "Is X the product of Y's womb?"). Sahlins raises the troubling possibility that such "actual" relationships are not part of the knowledge of individuals and that there is no magic question which will permit sociobiologists to get "beneath" cultural conceptions of kinship to discover the genetic facts.

How frequently this situation occurs, and its relevance to human sociobiology, seem to me to be questions requiring a great deal of empirical research. Anthropologists are very good at collecting genealogies and at distinguishing "classifactory" kin from "real" kin. Furthermore, it is possible that the mistakes created by calculating coefficients of relatedness from less than perfect genealogies will not be systematic and therefore will not bias the data for or against specific hypotheses. However, Sahlins' point does illustrate the necessity for investigators who use genealogies in this manner to detail how the data were collected and to describe the steps that were taken to deal with this problem. Unfortunately, few of the studies reviewed below provide such information.

As noted above, we may view studies of human nepotism as responses to Sahlins' critique. These responses take a number of forms. Some researchers attempt to demonstrate that features of human social life commonly seen as cultural products (e.g., rules concerning marriage, residence, inheritance of property, etc.) manifest the logic of kin selection and that their intersocietal variation can be explained as the interaction of the "constant" of kin-selection-evolved nepotism with environmental variation. Other workers study single societies and demonstrate that patterns of social interaction or aid donation follow the logic of nepotism theory. Finally, there are several studies which do not fall into either of these categories.

Cultural Forms and Nepotism Theory

The major research on this topic is Flinn's (1981a) holocultural study relating the flow of altruism within a society to rules of residence and marriage. Flow of altruism is a vague concept, but Flinn seems to have in mind any donation of economic or social aid from one person to another. For reasons which Flinn does not discuss, but which presumably involve ecological and historical factors, different societies exhibit different patternings in the flow of altruism (one factor identified by Flinn is paternal certainty). In some societies, the majority of individuals expect to receive more inheritance, economic aid, etc. from their mothers' brothers and other uterine kin than from their fathers or other agnatic kin, creating a uterine flow of altruism. In societies with an agnatic flow of altruism, an individual's father and other patrilateral kin are the major sources of economic and social aid. Finally, some societies exhibit a more even balance of aid, and both uterine and agnatic kin contribute to the success of an individual.

Flinn predicts that the flow of altruism in a society is related to its residence rules. Thus, if the main source of a male's wealth or social support is his uterine kin, residence would be avunculocal rather than virilocal. If the flow of altruism varies over the lifetime of an individual, his or her residence may also change to reflect this. Flinn notes, for example, that in societies with avunculocal residence, children often stay with their parents until such time as the aid of their mothers' brothers becomes important.

To test his prediction, Flinn examined ethnographies of over 300 societies and scored each on a variable he calls "source of altruism." Categories of this measure were: (1) father and agnatic kin; (2) mixed, with father the major source; (3) mixed; (4) mixed, with mother's brother the major source; and (5) mother's brother and uterine kin. When source of altruism was cross-tabulated with rule of primary marital residence, Flinn's prediction was strongly supported. Of 19 societies with an avunculocal residence rule, 16 are in category 4 and none is in category 1 or 2. There are 174 societies with a patrilocal residence rule, and 153 of them fall into categories 1 and 2, while only 1 falls into category 4 or 5. Societies with matrilocal residence fall mainly into categories 2 and 3.

While Flinn's results demonstrate that residence rules and flow of altruism tend to be congruent, some considerations cast doubt upon his conclusions. First, as noted by Flinn, correlation does not prove causation, and it is possible that the flow of altruism within a society is determined by its residence rules, and not vice versa. This admission need not be particularly damaging to Flinn's arguments, since his results do suggest that kin selection could operate in human societies, regardless of the direction of causation. A second problem involves the independence of the two measures Flinn uses in his test. Is it possible that Flinn's scoring on the source of altruism variable was influenced by the type of residence rule that a society has? Flinn does not indicate that he was unaware of the hypotheses under consideration when he coded societies on his various measures. Furthermore, he writes that he spent only about an hour coding each society on a large number of variables. Although he did not have another coder replicate a portion of his sample, he does not indicate whether or not he discussed the independence of measures with the second coder. These considerations suggest that Flinn's results should be treated with caution.

Flinn also examines the relationship between cultural rules governing marriage of cousins and sources of nepotism. He argues, for example, that preferential father's brother's daughter (FBD) marriage should occur in societies where the father and agnatic kin are the main sources of nepotism and where the pooling of inheritance from father and father's brother is profitable. Of the 14 societies in his sample exhibiting this form of cousin marriage, 11 fall into category 1 and 3 fall into category 2. This result strongly supports Flinn's prediction.

Circumstances conducive to a preference for mother's brother's daughter's (MBD) marriage are not as clear. Flinn suggests that MBD marriage should not occur in societies with low paternal certainty, because a male cannot be sure that his putative daughters are actually his offspring, and he would not attempt therefore to increase his inclusive fitness by arranging marriages favorable to them with a sister's son. Flinn demonstrates that in his sample, paternal certainty is low in societies with strong uterine flows of nepotism, and he predicts that MBD marriage will not be favored in these societies. Forty-nine societies in the sample exhibit a preference for MBD marriage, and only 5 of them fall into categories 4 and 5, a result supporting Flinn's argument. In contrast, 39 fall into categories 1 and 2. Flinn suggests that in societies with agnatic flows of nepotism, a man's agnates may be his major social competitors, and that a mother's brother may be an important alternative source of altruism, which may be "harvested" if by means of MBD marriage.

Flinn's results on cousin marriage are not as clear-cut as those on residence rules, and the case of MBD marriage seems to require special pleading. For example, it can be argued that even if a male from a low-paternity certainty society could not be sure of the paternity of his wife's daughter and would not waste resources attempting to increase these daughters' reproductive success, he would still be wise to increase the reproductive success of his sisters' sons by providing them his putative daughters as wives. In so doing, he would be increasing his own inclusive fitness, as his sisters' son have an r of 0.25 with him. Alternative explanations can also be suggested for some of Flinn's other results. However, the results are interesting, in that they do provide evidence for a congruence between flow of nepotism, paternal certainty, and cultural institutions such as marriage and residence rules. An important feature of Flinn's article, which makes further research on these topics possible, is the fact that he published his scores for paternal certainty and altruism flow in an appendix to the paper. These scores can thus be examined by researchers and utilized in other holocultural tests. Unfortunately, the editing of Flinn's paper is poor and raises some questions about the scores. Thus, on page 459 there is a list of fourteen societies with preferential FBD marriage, and each of them has a different score for cousin marriage rule than is listed for it in the appendix. One of the societies is not listed in the appendix, and seven of the remaining thirteen have scores on variables other than the cousin marriage rule which differ from the scores listed in the appendix. It is not possible to tell whether the mistakes are in the appendix or in the listings in the text (mistakes also appear in the list on page 461). A published revision of Flinn's codes would be welcome.

Van den Berghe (1979) has also conducted holocultural tests relating cultural forms to patterns of nepotism. He argues that sisters who are co-wives can increase their inclusive fitness if they aid one another. This leads him to predict that in societies with perferential sororal polygyny, co-wives should share residences. The Standard Cross-Cultural Sample (SCCS) provides statistical support for this prediction, with co-wives sharing residences more frequently in such societies than in societies where polygyny is nonsororal.

A second holocultural study reported in van den Berghe (1979) indirectly relates to the absent near relative problem raised by Sahlins. Van den Berghe argues that the size of groups based only on the operation of nepotism is limited, because coefficients of relatedness drop off rapidly beyond the first cousin relationship and because only full siblings have identical sets of relatives. These facts mean that societies that are organized through bilateral kinship tend to break apart when they grow too large (i.e., when the average level of r declines below an unspecified threshold), due to conflicts of interest over the donation of altruism. Bilateral kinship is thus expected to occur either in small-scale societies or in large industrial societies, where reciprocity and coercion have replaced nepotism as the basis of social life. Van den Berghe argues that unilineal descent rules will most often occur in societies of moderate size and complexity, which are under competitive pressure from other groups. This pressure creates the need for cooperative groups larger than those which can be maintained through the operation of nepotism alone. The solution to this problem is the creation of unilineal descent groups, where the loss of opportunities to invest in those relatives "lost" to other kinship units is offset by the greater level of cohesion gained by reducing the potential for conflicts of interest in donating nepotism. Van den Berghe makes use of Murdock's (1957) "World Ethnographic Sample" to demonstrate that bilateral descent is most frequently found in hunting and gathering societies, and unilineal descent in societies based on horticulture, pastoralism, or plow agriculture. However, his test is rather weak, since he does not demonstrate that societies in the latter category are under competitive pressure from other societies, nor does he eliminate any possible alternative, nonsociobiological explanations for the association. Finally, his discussion of how a unilineal kinship group works seems more of a stereotype of this social form than an analysis of how it operates in reality. For example, the great differences between societies with unilineal descent rules in Africa and New Guinea (Barnes 1962) are ignored in van den Berghe's analysis.

The most sophisticated research on coefficients of relatedness and cultural concepts of kinship in a single society is Hawkes' (1983) study of the Binumarien of New Guinea. She finds that social kinship (as determined by domestic affiliation) accurately predicts the donation of gardening aid; while genetic kinship (derived from genealogies) does not. This finding supports Sahlins' position that it is the cultural constructs of kinship, and not some ability to distinguish close from distant genetic relatives, that determines social interaction. However, when Hawkes examines the relationship between social kinship and genetic kinship, she finds that the two are highly, although not perfectly, correlated. In other words, genetic distance and social distance track one another fairly closely in this society. It is true that the Binumarien use the latter as the proximate cue for the distribution of nepotism, and in doing so sometimes donate aid to more distant genetic kin while ignoring closer genetic kin. However, since the *average* level of r between Ego and Others in close social categories is higher than the *average* level between Ego and Others in distant social categories, the effects of such mistakes will be overshadowed by the large number of "correct" aid donations that are created when social categories do indeed provide an accurate assessment of genetic relatedness.

Hawkes speculates on why the Binumarien use social distance as the proximate cue for distributing garden aid, rather than tracking genetic distance more accurately. She suggests that this might be explained either: (1) by the existence of unidentified (as of yet) benefits that are created by interacting on the basis of social cues; or (2) by the fact that tracking genetic distance would be too costly in terms of fitness. She also suggests that the degree to which societies use social cues rather than genetic distance in organizing sociality might be a trait under natural selection.

The importance of Hawkes' paper as a response to Sahlins' critique of kin selection theory is clear. She demonstrates that, for at least one ethnographic case, the fact that individuals donate garden aid (and, we assume, other altruistic acts) on the basis of cultural conceptions of kinship rather than on cues of actual genetic relatedness does not result in a situation which violates the logic of Hamilton's rule. Of course, Hawkes does not demonstrate that the fitness costs to individuals who make "mistakes" in donations because they make use of social cues are offset by fitness gains created by the number of "correct" donations made by such individuals. Such a demonstration would require data on the costs and benefits of specific behaviors. Many other societies need to be subjected to the type of analysis suggested by Hawkes before a final judgment on the validity of Sahlins' position can be made.

Patterns of Social Interaction and Coefficients of Relatedness

The major sociobiological response to Sahlins' arguments has been to ignore the question of how cultural classification of kin track genetic relatedness and to concentrate on demonstrating that in specific societies the calculus of r orders social interaction in a manner predicted by Hamilton's rule. As Morgan notes, "the present issue is not whether the terms humans use to describe social kinship precisely reflect their biological relationships, but whether the structure of human activities is such that kin selection might in fact operate" (1979:83).

Morgan's contribution to this effort is the suggestion that Yupik Eskimo whaling crews are organized in terms of genetic kinship, even though the verbal rules of recruitment emphasize social classifications. Morgan demonstrates that in nine crews, the average r of crew members ranged from 0.03 to 0.44. Unfortunately, he lacks data on several other crews, and he does not report the average level of r between all clan members or between all the dyads that could be included in a crew. This lack makes it impossible to judge the statistical significance of the averages he reports, and consequently the meaning of his results is not clear. He notes that his evidence does not prove that the Eskimos' preference for working with close kin evolved through kin selection, only that kin selection could operate in such a situation, especially since whaling is a dangerous activity.

Two of the more interesting studies seeking to demonstrate that behavioral interaction varies directly with degree of genetic relatedness apply a technique that is common in primatology—scan sampling—to discover the frequency of interaction between all possible dyads in a group. A common technique is for a researcher to follow a prescribed path through a village at random times and record the identity of all the people whom he or she sees interacting. The type of interaction may also be recorded. Once the genealogies of all village members are collected and r values for all possible dyads are calculated, these can be correlated with the data on frequency of social interaction. Studies among the Ye'kwana Indians of Venezuela (Hames 1979) and in a Trinidadian village (Flinn 1981b) have shown that frequency of interaction varies directly with degree of genetic relatedness, as determined by genealogical information.

Hames (1979) discusses how his results relate to Sahlins' position on sociobiology:

> Sahlins argues that since most people do not consciously calculate kinship distances in terms of genealogical (or biological) principles of descent but rather by idiosyncratic cultural principles that vary from culture to culture, kin selection is useless as a broad generalizing theory. Sahlins' critique is off the mark largely because he confounds two levels of analysis. Kin selection does not pretend to account for how humans conceive of, or mentally order, relatedness. The theory simply states that, *ceteris paribus*, behavioral patterns of interaction (such as nepotism and reciprocity) vary according to the amount of relatedness shared by the individuals interacting. Therefore, if kin selection in humans is to be disconfirmed, one must do so with behavioral data and not with data on ideological systems [Hames 1979:247–248].

In light of the previous discussion, it is clear that Hames partially misrepresents Sahlins' ideas. Sahlins does not argue that kin selection fails because it cannot explain the cultural classification of relatives; his point is that such classifications are an important causal factor in human behavior, and that because they often do not accurately track genetic relatedness, much human behavior will not correspond to the predictions of kin selection theory. Sahlins would certainly agree with Hames that the data needed to settle the issue must be behavioral, not ideological. Given this agreement, do Hames' results meet the challenge issued by Sahlins? This is not an easy question to answer. The data of both Hames and Flinn are restricted to single villages, and they do demonstrate that within each village, genetic relatedness (assuming the accuracy of genealogies) and frequency of interaction covary. This result would seem to meet the predictions of nepotism theory. However, neither researcher measures the cost and benefits of interactions, which means that their research cannot answer the maximization question. And, as both Flinn and Hames note, the covariation they find might be produced by factors other than kin selection. For example, Hames notes that frequency of interaction can also be explained as the outcome of residential propinquity. However, he suggests viewing propinquity as a proximate mechanism for determining interaction patterns and seeing kin selection as the ultimate explanation for why these patterns are adaptive. Hames also shows that propinquity cannot be the only proximate mechanism determining interaction patterns, by demonstrating that when Ego resides in a household containing Others related by differing levels of r, he or she interacts most frequently with Others who have a greater r value.

Finally, Hames argues that the kin selection position is supported by the fact that although the Ye'kwana have a generational kinship terminology, when distributing social interactions they apparently use genetic distance to distinguish between people classed in the same kin category. It is unclear how this relates to Sahlins' discussion. Sahlins does not suggest that people treat all members of a kin category the same; he allows that individuals might distinguish between members of the same terminological category, using any number of criteria (e.g., propinquity, distinctions between actual and classificatory kin, etc.). The vital question is whether these criteria track genetic relatedness in a manner that permits the operation of kin selection. Hames' data suggest that they do, but further research on this question is required.

The most serious response to Sahlins' challenge has been a series of studies on the Yanomamo Indians of Venezuela by Chagnon and his colleagues. The methodology of these studies involved the collection of genealogical data for individuals in numerous villages (for complete details, see Chagnon 1974, 1975, 1979a,b). Chagnon uses a modification of Wright's Inbreeding Coefficient to produce a Coefficient of Genealogical Relatedness (Fg) score for every possible dyad in his sample. This coefficient is an estimate of the r value that is used in Hamilton's rule. Chagnon's data allow him to find the average level of Fg between populations, villages, lineages, or any other subset of individuals. The data also permit him to calculate the degree of relatedness of individuals due to kinship links in past generations. It should be noted that the information he obtains is probably far more detailed and accurate than the information that individual Yanomamo utilize in making behavioral decisions (Chagnon and Bugos 1979:224–225).

Chagnon's work is subject to all of the previously discussed problems of deriving genetic relatedness from genealogies. In fact, certain features of Yanomamo society make Chagnon's task uncommonly difficult. The problems of collecting geneologies from people who dislike uttering the names of the dead are described in Chagnon's account of his fieldwork (1974). Furthermore, extramarital sexual activity among the Yanomamo is fairly frequent, and we do not know how this affected Chagnon's data. He notes (1979a:98) that paternity exclusion tests indicate a nonpaternity level of about 10 percent for the Yanomamo. It is not clear whether this means that only 10 percent of the time a male claiming paternity was definitely ruled out as a possible genitor or whether the male claiming paternity was definitely established as the genitor in all but 10 percent of the cases. If the former is the case, the level of paternal uncertainty could still be quite high in this group. The misattribution of paternity is potentially critical for

Chagnon's work, because Fg is calculated through multiple genealogical pathways, and an incorrect identification affects the calculations for numerous individuals. Although these potential problems are significant, it should be noted that there is no reason for believing that either incomplete genealogies or paternal uncertainty systematically biases Chagnon's data toward support for predictions derived from nepotism theory.

A related methodological problem is how seriously one should take Chagnon's Fg statistics. In calculating them, Chagnon examines all possible links between individuals and ignores sex and age data (e.g., whether two individuals could have produced a child). How such stastistics relate to the probability of alleles being identical by descent, a probability that falls off rapidly after a couple of generations, is not clear at present. It seems best to treat the differing values of Fg as ordinal rather than interval data. Chagnon is somewhat inconsistent on this point, often testing hypotheses by examining the mean Fg value between two groups, for example, but not conducting tests of the statistical significance of such differences. The absence of a method for deciding whether or not differences between two means are statistically significant is especially unfortunate, because it is not clear that the mean is the appropriate statistic to report when dealing with (untransformed) probabilities.

From the perspective of nepotism theory, perhaps the most interesting of the Yanomamo studies involves an ax fight filmed by the ethnographers (Chagnon and Bugos 1979). A small group of visitors formerly belonging to the host village fought with a number of men of the host village. Chagnon and Bugos have used data on the relatedness between individuals to demonstrate a number of points. First, members of the two fighting teams were, on the average, more closely related among themselves than to members of the opposing team. Second, the fighters of the host team were more closely related among themselves than they were to the village at large. Third, the fighters of the visiting team were more closely related among themselves than they were to members of the host village. And finally, the followers of a major fight leader were more closely related to that individual than to the fight leader of the opposing team.

These results are presented as a disconfirmation of Sahlins' suggestion that genetic relatedness plays a minor role in the patterning of human social behavior. Genetic relatedness, as measured by the Fg statistic, does appear to have played a major role in the individual choice of which side of the fight to join. Furthermore, several members of the host village joined the visitors' team, suggesting that, at least in this case, genetic relatedness may have taken priority over residence as a factor in nepotistic behavior. However, Chagnon and Bugos note that because the village fission was fairly recent, the moving of residences back and forth was fairly common and members of the host village who joined the visitors' team might have resided among the visitors in the recent past.

Although Chagnon and Bugos' analysis of this ax fight is convincing, there are some major problems in interpreting the results. As noted above, it is unclear how the Fg statistic and the "number of loops in a dyadic relationship" statistic relate to the "probability of alleles being identical by descent" measure that is necessary for testing predictions derived from nepotism theory. If the first two are highly correlated with the last, there is probably no difficulty in assuming that Fg is a good proxy measure. Another problem in interpreting the results arises from the lack of information on the statistical significance between the mean levels of Fg that were reported by the authors. This problem is further complicated by the gambler's fallacy as discussed by Stuart Altmann (1979). It is possible, for example, for Ego to have a single close relative on one team and a large number of distant relatives on the other. When the Fg figures for the distant relatives are summed up, the result might be larger than the Fg that Ego shares with his close relative. A prediction as to which side Ego will join is difficult to make. Chagnon and Bugos' analysis suggests that Ego should ally himself with the numerous, but distant, relatives; while Altmann's discussion indicates that aid to the close relative would be Ego's most profitable course of action. Unfortunately, the data presented by Chagnon and Bugos do not allow us to estimate how frequent and significant this type of problem is in their sample.

The fact that, as Chagnon and Bugos note, degree of relatedness is not the only factor influencing individual decisions is made clear when it is demonstrated that some individuals joined the side to which they were less closely related. This fact is clearly demonstrated in the chart on the genealogical distances between fighters that was produced by Faux and Miller (1984:28). These authors utilize metric multidimensional scaling to summarize the relationships between fighters and find that, although Chagnon and Bugos' general conclusions seem to be validated, there are several anomalies. For example, the main fighter of the hosts, Uuwa, and two other host fighters (individuals 1109 and 1062) appear to be more closely related to the visitors than to the hosts. Uuwa, for example, is more closely related to Mohesiwa, the main fighter of the visitor team, than he is to Kebowa, Yoinakuwa, or Sinabimi, all major figures on the host team. Individuals 2513 and 0789 appear to be closely related to one another and distantly related to all other fighters, yet they joined opposite sides. As mentioned earlier, such anomalies do not necessarily discredit the conclusions of Chagnon and Bugos, for there may be a number of factors making it more rewarding for Ego to join a team of less related individuals. The authors identify both residence and marital alliances as such complicating factors. However, it is clear that the influence of such factors makes the interpretation of results difficult and limits the value of any single case involving so few people.

A final problem with the Chagnon and Bugos study is the lack of discussion of the proximate cues that individuals used in deciding which fighting team to join. This lack results in an unintended, but unfortunate, impression that individuals somehow magically discern slight differences in degrees of relatedness, independently of the cues of kinship terminology, past association, etc. Although the possibility of recognition alleles or phenotype matching has not been disproven for humans, there is no strong theoretical rationale, and no empirical evidence, that such abilities exist, and Chagnon and Bugos' article would have been significantly strengthened by a detailed discussion of this problem.

Chagnon's other studies of the Yanomamo have also documented the possible role of nepotism in their social life. Chagnon (1979a) demonstrates that villages with a high average level of relatedness tend to grow larger before fissioning than villages with lower levels of relatedness. As noted above, Chepko-Sade and Olivier (1979) discovered the same situation in their study of rhesus macaque matrilines. Chagnon suggests that mean level of relatedness might be an adequate proxy measure for the often utilized, but rarely operationalized, concept of social cohesion. Chagnon (1981) indicates that when a village fissions, the average level of relatedness in the daughter villages is usually higher than the level that characterized the parent village before the fission. This article is especially important for Chagnon's discussion of how individual responses to village fissions are influenced, not only by degrees of relatedness but also by such considerations as mate procurement. He finds that although individuals tend to remain with closely related genetic kin, the Yanomamo marriage system results in males being more successful at this than females. He demonstrates, for example, that males prefer to remain with closely related (high Fg) individuals in the terminological category of consanguineal kin, but tend to separate from distantly related (low Fg) members of that terminological category. Distant consanguineal kin often compete with Ego or with Ego's children for mates, and by separating from these relatives a male may greatly increase his chances of achieving high reproductive success or inclusive fitness.

The importance of both genetic and social relatives to a man's chances of finding a mate is discussed further in Chagnon (1982). Chagnon demonstrates that single males have fewer matrilineal relatives in their population bloc than married men have. Furthermore, males with more genetic kin in the first ascending generation have a better chance of finding mates than males with fewer kin. Also, there is a positive correlation between the probability of marriage and the number of genetic relatives that a male has in his own generation.

Chagnon's analysis of the possible role of nepotism in Yanomamo social life is both detailed and complex, and it cannot be summarized further here. One of his most interesting and important conclusions is that, at least for groups like the Yanomamo, sexual selection theory may be more relevant to the explanation of social behavior than kin selection theory, although both are obviously important. The possible role of sexual selection in Yanomamo life will be discussed in Chapter Nine. Chagnon argues further that the cultural classification of relatives adds a dimension to the explanation of Yanomamo social behavior which cannot be gained through examining only the operation of nepotism and sexual selection. For example, he writes: "While kin selection theory predicts that the males should align themselves with close kin to form successful coalitions, social anthropology theory predicts that those close kin will be selected from particular structural types, and not simply on the basis of closeness of kinship alone" (1981:507). In this passage, Chagnon agrees with Sahlins' point that cultural conceptions of kinship play an important role in the shaping of human behavior. However, in contrast to Sahlins' position, Chagnon's data do suggest that considerations of genetic relatedness are not irrelevant in shaping this behavior. His results indicate the potential value of examining the influence of both these factors in any given situation.

Research on degree of relatedness and fissioning choices using a methodology similar to that utilized in the Yanomamo study, has been conducted in a quite different context by Hurd (1981), who demonstrates that when churches fission among the Nebraska Amish of Pennsylvania, close kin tend to separate from more distant kin. Hurd also shows that males are more likely than females to maintain association with close kin. In the Amish case, the reason for this sex difference has more to do with the distribution of valuable economic resources (farms) than with competition for mates.

A very interesting study, with direct bearing on the interaction between genetic relatedness and cultural concepts of kinship, is Fredlund's (1981) research among the Shitari Yanomamo. He notes that every society has rules for judging marriages as legitimate or incestuous and that these rules are frequently manipulated by individuals. It is possible that a person's willingness to accept such manipulations is conditioned in part by the degree of relatedness between that person and the manipulator. Fredlund analyzed the logic of the Shitari kinship terminology and marriage rules and judged existing marriages as either legitimate or incestuous by this logic. These judgments he called structural designations. He then had four closely related (genetically) informants judge the legitimacy of a sample of marriages. These judgments he called labeled designations. He finds that in most cases the two designations matched, illustrating that people are usually constrained by their rules. However, in some cases the two designations did not match. When this happened, it appears that the informants biased their judgments according to the degree of relatedness between themselves and the participants in the marriage. Thus when the informants labeled a structurally legitimate marriage as incestuous, the Fg between the judges and the male involved in the marriage averaged 0.101. In contrast, the average Fg was 0.165 when informants labeled a structurally incestuous

marriage as legitimate. Fredlund also finds that his informants under-
estimated the amount of incest in villages where males were closely related
to them and overestimated it in villages where males were less closely
related. Fredlund notes that these judgments are not examples of nepotism,
but argues that they might serve as indirect indicators of the willingness of
informants to interact nepotistically with the individuals involved in the
marriages.

Other studies indicating that humans behave in accordance with the logic
of nepotism theory include: (1) Essock-Vitale and McGuire's (1980) review
of gift giving and loans in several societies; (2) Daly and Wilson's (1982b)
finding that maternal kin respond to a postcard questionnaire about a
newborn more frequently than paternal kin (parental certainty is higher for
maternal relatives); (3) Flinn's (1981b) study of a Trinidadian village,
indicating that nepotism is directed toward biological children rather than
step-children when a choice between the two exists; (4) Hames' (1981)
demonstration that garden labor exchange among the Ye'kwana varies
directly with average Fg between households, and that closely related
households are more willing to tolerate an imbalance in labor exchange than
less closely related households; and (5) Faux and Miller's (1984) finding
that in the central hierarchy of the early Church of Jesus Christ of Latter-Day
Saints (Mormons), the members who were related to founder Joseph Smith
were more likely to have been polygynists and to have received more wives,
but less likely to have been excommunicated, than members who were not
related to Smith. Each of these studies is interesting in its own right, and the
only reason I am not reviewing them here is lack of space. In general, each
supports the prediction of nepotism theory that the distribution of aid
among humans is strongly influenced by genetic relatedness.

Two Apparent Counterexamples

Human sociobiologists have also responded to Sahlins' challenge by
showing that some of the behaviors that apparently violate the predictions
of nepotism theory actually support, or at least do not contradict, the theory.
Silk's (1980a) study of adoption in Oceania and Daly and Wilson's (1982a)
analysis of homicides in Detroit are examples of this strategy.

Silk's article may be seen as a response to a specific challenge by Sahlins
(1976:48–49), who cites adoption in Polynesia as an example of the freedom
of human kinship from biological considerations. In several societies,
individuals adopt unrelated or distantly related children and treat them as if
they were their own children. Of course, the willingness of individuals to
give up their own biological children to adoption does not seem to support
nepotism theory either. Silk reviews empirical studies of adoption in eleven
communities in Oceania and shows that frequency of adoption varies
directly with relatedness (although there are few adoptions between dyads

related by 0.5). Further, she demonstrates that parents favor biological children over adopted children with regard to inheritance. Finally, she shows that the biological parents of an adopted child still retain some jural rights over the child. In other words, adopted children are not accepted on an equal footing with biological children, and parents do not totally "give up" a relationship with their offspring because other people adopt them. Silk argues that adoption in Oceania is a means of adjusting family sizes in an adaptive manner. She notes that a completely successful study of adoption would demonstrate that the families who are involved in adoption are actually increasing their inclusive fitness by their actions, but she herself does not have data on this issue. However, she does claim that her results indicate that, contrary to Sahlins' claim, adoption does not "violate the moral logic of kin selection" (Sahlins 1976:48).

The fact that most homicides in the United States occur in the domestic realm seems at first glance to contradict nepotism theory. Daly and Wilson (1982a) explore the influence of kinship on homicide by examining data on 98 homicide cases in Detroit during 1972 in which the victim and the offender were cohabitants in a household. They find that consanguineal kin are at a very low relative risk of being murdered, while both spouses and nonrelatives are at a high relative risk. Interestingly, spouses are at the same risk level as nonrelatives. Of course, the killing of a spouse is not a good way to increase reproductive success, but Daly and Wilson suggest that in many of these cases the spouse may have given evidence of a lack of commitment to the pair bond (adultery, children by another mate, etc.) Unfortunately, the data do not allow the authors to verify this suggestion.

In the same article, Daly and Wilson also examine the relatedness between members of triads involved in collaborative homicides in eight societies. In each case, the co-offenders are usually more closely related than either of the killers is to the victim, a result that is to be expected from nepotism theory.

Daly and Wilson are not arguing that murder of spouses or nonrelatives is an evolved adaptive trait. They suggest that most homicides probably have an adverse effect on the killer's inclusive fitness and should be viewed as "mistakes." Such mistakes might arise from the fact that the credible threat of violence is a common tactic in human social interaction. The willingness of individuals to turn the threat into action depends upon a number of factors, including costs and benefits of "winning" or "losing" a particular interaction. However, there may be proximate cues, which act to lower the possibility of violence between close relatives, and these cues may not have time to develop or may not operate with spouses or with nonrelatives. The result may be that in relationships with nonrelatives, neither the killer nor the victim is accurately communicating or evaluating the threats of violence, a situation that serves to increase the probability that violence will actually occur. The statistical outcome of this process demonstrates that "... even where a murder is a 'mistake' ... the underlying passions manifest the adaptive logic of nepotistic self-interest" (Daly and Wilson 1982a:377).

Miscellaneous Studies

Two other studies illustrate the wide range of behavior to which nepotism theory can be applied. Werner (1979) attempts to test Wilson's (1975a) hypothesis that although exclusive homosexuals have low reproductive success, they may increase their inclusive fitness by nepotistically aiding relatives. He suggests that if Wilson is correct, homosexuality should be most frequent in societies where kin do not disperse. Using precoded data for the societies in the SCCS, Werner demonstrates that homosexual behavior is rated as more common in societies with extended rather than nuclear families, and in societies with a rule of patrilocal residence rather than with other postmarital residence rules. However, in contrast to Wilson's position, homosexual behavior is rated as more common in societies with exogamy than in those with endogamy. Werner concludes that his results provide only marginal support for Wilson's position, and suggests that a cultural materialistic explanation, relating homosexual behavior to population control, better explains intersocietal variation in the frequency of this behavior.

Finally, Barkow's (1982) study of farm labor exchange among the Migili of Nigeria is an interesting case, demonstrating the relevance of nepotism theory to the analysis of social change. Barkow notes that in the past, the Migili were an example of a "complex" society, with age-grades organized and run by a gerontocracy. He argues that in this system, nepotism and reciprocal altruism had been suppressed by the operation of the age-grade system. Members of the younger age-grades labored on all the farms and were not reciprocated for their labor until they became elders.

In 1967, the authority of the elders was overthrown in a revolution and the age-grade system destroyed. Barkow argues that once the system was destroyed, there was a "return to ethology," and the principles of reciprocal altruism and nepotism once again became the basis of social life. His data show that currently people tend to donate aid to kin, but to demand reciprocity from nonkin. Barkow unfortunately does not have data on nepotism and reciprocity in the system prior to the revolution, but his argument that, at least in the area of farm labor, these principles had been suppressed by the age-grade system seems convincing. Of interest, too, is his finding that the return to nepotism and reciprocity has not been complete—a large amount of aid is still donated to nonkin. Barkow attributes this to a sort of cultural lag, arguing that the old norms of helping the elderly and ill are still alive.

With Barkow's work we reach the study of history and politics. A possible response to Sahlins' challenge would be to demonstrate that social change is related in a predictable manner to changes in the operation of nepotistic and reciprocally altruistic strategies. Barkow's Migili study is an excellent first step toward such a demonstration. As Alexander (1979) notes, the study of history could profit greatly from the realization that people in earlier times may have been operating under a different mixture of nepotistic and reciprocally altruistic strategies than the mixture that is relevant to individuals in modern nation states.

A Negative Result
As of yet, no studies utilizing data from humans to falsify a prediction derived from nepotism theory have been published. In part this is because opponents of sociobiology have dismissed the theory on theoretical grounds and concluded that empirical tests are not required to discredit it. Another partial cause is that identification of the specific predictions that are to be generated from nepotism theory is difficult. Hypotheses involving the interaction of relatives question suffer from the redundancy problem, since results conforming to the prediction can often be interpreted from other theoretical frameworks. Until costs and benefits of particular acts are measured, placed into life history parameters, and associated with proximate cues, tests of the maximization question cannot be conducted. And until a genetic substrate can be associated with behavioral alternatives, the evolution question remains beyond our reach. Given these circumstances, it is difficult to see what kind of negative evidence would serve to eliminate the possibility that nepotism theory is applicable to human social behavior.

As noted earlier, B. J. Williams (1980) has argued that early human social structure and our life history parameters provide little support for the hypothesis that kin selection was responsible for the evolution of altruistic behavior among humans. As Williams puts it:

> in a low fecundity species such as *Homo sapiens* the "index of potential selection" cannot achieve the levels possible in a high fecundity species such as salmon or the social insects. This means that the potential for benefit from being a recipient can never be as great, per individual, in the low fecundity species. This makes kin selection less feasible in the low fecundity species. An alternative is to have a large number of recipients benefiting from the act of fitness altruism. Our data indicate that large numbers of recipients are not available in the demographic and social structures which typify human prehistory. [Williams 1980:577–578].

The data referred to by Williams demonstrate that in !Kung and Bihor bands of hunter-gatherers, the average number of adult siblings per individual is less than one. For the Bihor, the mean number of first cousins is only 1.26 per individual (there are no data for the !Kung).

It should be noted that Williams does not totally rule out kin selection as a mechanism in human evolution. Instead, his point is that given the demographic situation of early humans, alternative models not involving kin selection might be more appropriate to the explanation of human evolution. At present, the validity of these alternatives, and the significance of Williams' data on the number of close relatives in band society, are still open questions. However, by questioning the applicability of kin selection models to early humans and by providing mathematically-based alternative models of helping, his work does serve to discredit the idea that the only possible way humans could have evolved helping behaviors is through kin selection.

CONCLUSIONS

I suggested earlier that the widespread acceptance and use of sociobiology in the social sciences probably depends upon convincing demonstrations that nepotism theory is relevant to primate social behavior. My major conclusion after reviewing the studies cited above is that, although several interesting studies have been made, no such demonstration exists at the present time. Of the three questions that must be answered to provide such a demonstration (concerning interaction of relatives, maximization, and evolution), current research addresses only the first, and the results obtained so far are marred by the redundancy problem, which is created when alternative explanations that are adequate to explain the results are advanced from a nonsociobiological framework. As long as research is restricted to the interaction of relatives problem, the standoff between sociobiologically-oriented and nonsociobiologically-oriented social scientists will continue. Although sociobiologists may continue to demonstrate the plausibility of kin-selection-generated interaction patterns in situation after situation, these additional cases will probably not convince skeptics. Such demonstrations will, however, become more convincing if sociobiological researchers identify the proximate mechanisms that guide the distribution of altruism, overcome the problems of calculating degrees of relatedness from genealogies, and provide measures of the costs and benefits of specific behaviors (within the context of life history models). Whether these problems can be overcome, and whether nepotism theory will be found to be supported if they are, are still open questions.

I do not mean to leave the impression that the empirical work on primate nepotism provides little support for the sociobiological position. In fact, several of the studies strongly support the discipline's claim of relevance to the explanation of primate social behavior. The studies of Chagnon, Chagnon and Bugos, Fredlund, and Hawkes on the complex interaction between cultural classifications of relatives and genetic relatedness, whatever their individual weaknesses, do appear to meet Sahlins' challenges, and hold out the possibility that genetic relatedness may play an important role in the shaping of human social behavior. Of course, this research must be refined and replicated in other societies before a final judgment on its validity can be rendered. The research on alloprimate behavioral interactions has also strongly supported sociobiological predictions, and it should be remembered that although alternative, nonsociobiological, hypotheses can be advanced to explain these data, such hypotheses are still just alternatives—they do not automatically discredit sociobiological interpretations.

As serious empirical research on the applicability of nepotism theory to the primates enters a second decade, I believe that it is only just beginning to identify the central problems that confront the sociobiological program. Future research will evidence more concern with the formulation and testing of precise predictions—predictions which will contain statements on the operation of proximate mechanisms, costs and benefits of behavioral options, life history factors, and so on. Also, researchers will more frequently identify situations wherein predictions from nepotism theory oppose predictions from alternative explanatory frameworks. We can hope that enough of these situations will be discovered to eventually permit a judgment on the plausibility of nepotism theory's claim to be a necessary component in any explanation of human and alloprimate social life.

CHAPTER 5

Reciprocal Altruism

INTRODUCTION

The theory of kin selection explains situations wherein Ego engages in phenotypically altruistic behaviors benefiting Others who share with him genes identical that are by descent. Observation of humans and of many species of alloprimates soon reveals that animals often donate phenotypically altruistic behaviors to individuals who are unrelated, or very distantly related, to them. At first glance, this appears difficult to explain without adopting a group selectionist model; due to Ego's decreased reproductive success (and perhaps to additional decrements in other components of his her inclusive fitness), the gene(s) implicated in the production of the behavior will suffer a reduced probability of being placed in the next generation. At the same time, because the coefficient of relatedness is very low or zero, this loss will not be offset by the reproductive success of the recipients. However, the donation of aid that decreases Ego's reproductive success and increases that of unrelated individuals is placed firmly within a gene-level selection framework by the subject matter of this chapter, i.e., by Trivers' (1971) controversial concept of reciprocal altruism.

Trivers' article on reciprocal altruism is one of the most widely cited papers in sociobiology, and I will discuss it in detail in this section. I will then examine some of the theoretical and methodological problems that surround the concept and its use in empirical research.

Trivers begins by modeling a population containing both altruists and nonaltruists, the difference between these individuals being in part genetically based. Under some conditions, altruists are willing to engage in altruistic behavior, which Trivers defines as: "... behavior that benefits another organism, not closely related, while being apparently detrimental to the organism performing the behavior, benefit and detriment being defined in terms of contribution to inclusive fitness" (1971:35). Nonaltruists do not engage in altruism. Trivers then examines three rules which might guide altruists in the distribution of aid. The first is for altruists to randomly distribute aid to both altruists and nonaltruists. Trivers notes that this rule would result in the genes "for" altruism being selected against and eventually eliminated from the population.

The second rule is for altruists to dispense aid by reference to kinship (i.e., coefficients of relatedness). There is a semantic problem here, since the phrase "not closely related" in Trivers' definition of altruistic behavior seems to eliminate this rule, but perhaps the problem is only that Trivers does not define what he means by "not closely related." In any event, Trivers argues that this situation is successfully modeled by Hamilton's equation and could lead to the evolution of altruism (or better, nepotism).

The third rule, which Trivers labels reciprocal altruism, is for altruists to distribute aid according to the altruistic tendencies of the recipients. In other words, Ego utilizes proximate cues to identify unrelated individuals who are willing to donate aid to Ego (repay their "debts"). Under this rule, altruists will not donate aid to nonaltruists (assuming that the proximate cues allow accurate assessment of behavioral tendencies). The paradigm case of reciprocal altruism occurs when the donor and recipient in a situation involving an altruistic act change roles at some future time. The result is that, although Ego, as donor, lowers his reproductive success (or inclusive fitness) by original action, he regains this, or more, when he receives altruism in the future interaction. In this manner, both parties are assumed to achieve greater reproductive success or inclusive fitness than either would have attained if the interactions had not occurred. Trivers argues that if the altruists in his model followed this rule, the genes for altruism could spread throughout the population.

The difference between kin selection and reciprocal altruism is most dramatically indicated by Trivers' point that reciprocal altruism:

> ... does not depend on all altruistic acts being controlled by the same allele at the same locus. Each altruist could be motivated by a different allele at a different locus .... The argument will therefore apply, unlike Hamilton's (1964), to altruistic acts exchanged between members of different species. It is the *exchange* that favors such altruism, not the fact that the allele in question sometimes or often directly benefits its duplicate in another organism [Trivers 1971:37].

Trivers examines several cases of cleaning symbioses in fish as examples of interspecific reciprocal altruism. For our purposes, the vital point in this passage is that, because the allele does not aid copies of itself in other organisms, alleles "for" reciprocal altruism can spread only when the donor himself (or a close relative?) achieves gains which offset the original fitness costs created by his altruistic behavior. Unlike nepotism, the gains to the recipient's fitness are irrelevant to the donor's fitness. This means that systems of reciprocal altruism face a problem that is not present in systems of nepotism, i.e., "cheating" (the failure to repay donated aid).

Trivers speculates on the life history features which might be associated with a species' development of reciprocal altruism (the remainder of this discussion will ignore interspecific reciprocal altruism since there has been no work done on it among primates), and identifies three. First, the members of the species must live long enough for them to experience many situations in which the donation of altruism is an appropriate response. Thus, long-lived species are more likely to exhibit reciprocal altruism than short-lived ones (see, however, Western and Strum 1983). Second, animals must interact with the same small number of individuals for extended periods of time. There are two aspects of this feature. First, long association permits individuals to monitor the willingness of others to repay "debts." It is possible that in some species the readiness of individuals to pay debts serves as a proximate cue for the distribution of altruism. Second, repeated interaction increases the probability that a donor will experience a situation wherein he or she requires aid from someone he or she had aided to in the past. Trivers suggests that species with low dispersal rates will be more likely to exhibit reciprocal altruism than those with a rapid turnover of group members. Finally, reciprocal altruism is more likely to evolve when pairs of individuals are capable of rendering roughly equal benefits to one another. Trivers notes, for example, that in species with strict linear dominance hierarchies, reciprocity has little chance to evolve between individuals of widely disparate ranks, because subordinates can rarely offer dominant individuals equivalent benefits. However, he points out that aid in agonistic interactions may be a special case, since subordinates may tip the balance when two animals of equally high rank are fighting.

As noted above, systems of reciprocal altruism are always confronted with the problem of cheating. Such cheating may take gross forms, with individuals attempting to evade *any* repayment of debts, or it may be more subtle, as when individuals repay with less aid than is justified by the donor's original costs. Trivers implies that members of a species do not differ because some are altruists and others are cheaters; rather they differ in the degree of altruism they demonstrate, in their response thresholds to proximate cues of altruistic tendencies, and in the circumstances under which they will cheat.

Trivers' discussion of reciprocal altruism and cheating indicates that such systems may create more selective pressure than kin selection does toward the evolution of complex forms of social interaction. For example, the possibility of cheating may lead to the evolution of psychological and sociological tactics that serve to detect tendencies toward cheating. In turn, behaviors making cheating more difficult to detect are selected for, which only increases the selection pressure on behaviors permitting more accurate detection of the tendency to cheat. The complexity of these processes is indicated by the list of psychological traits that Trivers argues are relevant to the operation of reciprocal altruism among humans: choosing friends according to their willingness to be altruistic, moralistic aggression against cheaters, gauging gratitude responses to the costs and benefits of Others's actions, sympathy, guilt, and interest in gossip.

The concepts embodied in reciprocal altruism theory are much richer than this brief summary can illustrate. For our purposes, the key point is that the theory explains phenotypically altruistic interactions between unrelated animals without resorting to a group selection model. However, as in the case of kin selection, this simple model confronts major theoretical and methodological problems when it is applied to reality. The problems that are most relevant to the study of reciprocal altruism among the primates are discussed in the following section.

THE COMPLEXITIES OF APPLYING THE THEORY

The first major problem in reciprocal altruism theory is simply a matter of definition. Some biologists object to Trivers' definition of altruism; while others note the necessity for distinguishing between mutualism, altruism, cooperation, sharing, and other such terms. A second problem, closely related to the first, is the old difficulty of measuring the costs and benefits of behaviors. Finally, there are some questions as to how a system of reciprocal altruism could evolve in the first place. Each problem will be discussed briefly in this section.

Altruism, Reciprocity, and Other Behaviors

Although the concept of altruism is widely utilized in sociobiology, there is little agreement on its definition. Some of this disagreement is relevant to Trivers' attempt to define reciprocal altruism. In one of the best discussions of this problem, Bertram (1982) reviews numerous definitions of altruism and finds little agreement on the concept. Bertram offers his own definition:

> Altruism in biology is defined as behaviour which is likely to increase the reproductive output of another member of the same species who is not a descendant of the actor, and which at least in the short term is likely also to reduce the number of the actor's own descendants [Bertram 1982:252].

It should be noted that Bertram's definition explicitly rules out the possibility of altruism between members of different species. Thus he does not view cleaning symbioses in fish as examples of altruism.

A contrast to Bertram's rejection of the term altruism to describe interaction between members of different species, is Rothstein's (1980) suggestion that "pure" reciprocal altruism occurs only in the context of interspecific relationships. Rothstein argues that individuals within a population exhibiting reciprocal altruism and strategies for detection of cheating probably share genes that are "coding" for these strategies. He concludes that purported cases of reciprocal altruism between members of the same species are acutally examples of kin selection, relevant to these shared genes. Discussion in the previous section suggests that Trivers would not accept Rothstein's argument. Trivers' definition of reciprocal altruism does not really help here, however, for although he emphasizes that the relationship must be between individuals who are not "closely related," he does not define what he means by closely related. Obviously, the separation of the behaviors that evolved and are maintained by reciprocal altruism from the ones that evolved by kin selection is a serious theoretical problem for sociobiology—one which must be resolved before empirical work can advance (see West-Eberhard 1975; Western and Strum 1983).

The problem is complicated by the fact that in some places Trivers suggests that humans and some other animals might engage in both reciprocally altruistic and neopotistic relationships with the same individual, a suggestion also advanced by Alexander (1974, 1979). Furthermore, in some cases a single behavior may be viewed as either nepotism or reciprocity, depending on whether or not the recipient repays the debt. The problem of distinguishing between nepotism and reciprocity in specific situations often makes the testing of reciprocal altruism theory difficult. Also, it is possible that the interaction between nepotism and reciprocal altruism may create behavioral patterns which cannot be predicted from knowledge of either alone. For example, while considerations of reciprocity might be important for relationships even with relatives, it is possible that there is a lower demand for reciprocity from kin and that the strength of the demand varies inversely with the degree of genetic relatedness. As Alexander notes, if a relative does not repay a debt created by Ego's altruism, the loss to Ego's reproductive success might still be offset by the gains to his inclusive fitness that were created when the altruistic act increased the relative's reproductive success. In contrast, if a nonrelative fails to repay Ego, there are no indirect gains to offset Ego's loss of reproductive success. Thus we can predict that Ego will usually be less willing to engage in repeated altruism without repayment with nonrelatives than with close relatives (Irons 1979a:26).

Before leaving definitional problems, it should be noted that not all cooperative behaviors between unrelated animals need to be analyzed as examples of altruism. Wrangham (1982), among others, notes that mutualistic relationships can often be explained independently of nepotism or reciprocal altruism theory. In mutualistic relationships, no individual suffers a decrement to reproductive success which increases the reproductive success of others. In a mutualistic hunting relationship, where two animals are needed to discover or to kill prey, for example, both members risk fitness losses in hunting, and both obtain fitness gains if the prey is won.

Other theorists note that we must distinguish situations where a semblance of cooperation is created because other animals make it too costly for Ego not to cooperate from those where Ego "freely" donates altruism to Others. As discussed below, Blurton Jones (1984) and Moore (1984) argue that food sharing among chimpanzees is not an example of reciprocal altruism, but rather of sharing due to pressure from conspecifics. Both note that the form of aid is a crucial factor in determining the type of situation that evolves. Resources which can be shared, or those which Ego attains in amounts which cannot be easily defended against determined opponents and/or cannot be used entirely by Ego (and cannot be stored for future use), may lead to the development of cooperation without reciprocal altruism. In contrast, aid such as support in agonistic encounters cannot be forced from Ego and may be more likely to have evolved through reciprocal altruism.

Costs and Benefits

Empirical studies of reciprocal altruism face all the problems of measuring the fitness costs and benefits of behaviors that were discussed in the chapter on nepotism theory. However, there are some significant differences in the problems that confront empirical tests of the two theories. On the one hand, studies of reciprocal altruism do not need to devalue the benefits of behaviors by the coefficient of relatedness, which eliminates many of the problems that were detailed in Chapter Four. In fact, the major concern of field studies of reciprocal altruism has been to eliminate the possibility that two or more animals are related. On the other hand, reciprocal altruism's focus on the repayment of debts creates new measurement problems that are not found in field studies of nepotism theory. In this section, I will note some of these unique problems. As in the case of nepotism theory, studies of reciprocal altruism among primates have not addressed most of these difficulties, and I therefore present them as ideals against which to evaluate the studies that will be reviewed.

A key measurement problem is whether the behavior that Other uses to repay Ego must be identical to that performed by Ego, or whether complementary behaviors resulting in equal or greater benefits to Ego may be counted as repayment. While many of Trivers' intraspecific examples concern identical behaviors (e.g., Ego rescues Other from drowning, and Other returns the favor at a later date), most of his interspecific examples involve complementary behavior (e.g., cleaning fish trading parasite removal for safe access to food). Focus on complementary behavior means that reciprocal altruism might be more widespread in the animal world than originally suggested by Trivers (Western and Strum 1983), but it makes calculations of costs and benefits extremely difficult. To date, most studies in primate reciprocal altruism have adopted the assumption that repayment must involve behaviors that are similar in form and cost to the original donation of aid. The problem with this assumption is that primates would seem to be the types of animals for whom systems of repayment utilizing complementary behaviors are most likely to evolve.

A second factor that complicates calculations of costs and benefits is the time delay between the two acts of altruism. Trivers notes that this delay means that costs and benefits must be adjusted for the changing reproductive value to the two actors. He speculates that humans, for example, might routinely demand that fitness "interest" be added to behaviors repaying donations of aid performed much earlier in time, in order to offset the decline in Ego's reproductive value over the life of the debt. So far, studies of reciprocal altruism among alloprimates are of such short duration that the time factor does not enter into play, while the time factor has been ignored in studies among humans.

A third problem is whether the fitness gains received by Ego when he is repaid must equal the fitness gains created for Other by Ego's original act. Sahlins (1976:83–88) seems to assume that this condition is part of reciprocal altruism theory, but Trivers does not discuss the problem in detail. Is it possible for reciprocal altruism to evolve if Other pays Ego back with a behavior which offsets Ego's original fitness loss (adjusted for the passage of time), but does not create fitness benefits equal to those enjoyed by Other? The mathematics of such a case have not been described in the literature up to the present time. If this possibility exists, it raises the issue of skews in benefits based on differences in social power or resource control among individuals in a group. Could a dominant Ego gain "surplus" fitness benefits by "extracting" from subordinates altruistic behaviors which greatly increase his reproductive success and repaying with behaviors which only barely offset the subordinates' original costs? In such a situation the calculation of costs and benefits would be complex.

Another difficulty in the study of reciprocal altruism is the question of reproductive success versus inclusive fitness: Can repayments of altruistic acts be directed to the close kin of the donor, rather than to the original donor? In such cases of "indirect reciprocity" (Irons 1979a:26), the tallying of costs and benefits would be complicated. For example, the fitness benefits to the original donor's kin would have to be devalued by the coefficient of relatedness before they were added to his inclusive fitness. Furthermore, the time factor becomes difficult to handle in calculating the effects of repayments. Finally, the study time necessary to observe intergenerational transfers of reciprocal altruism is greatly increased. Again, no primate study has dealt with this problem.

Bertram (1982:264) raises another possible complication in calculating costs and benefits when he inquires whether the repayment of altruism must be a positive action. Might not an animal lower its reproductive success and increase that of another animal by *failing* to act in a certain manner? Bertram points to the example of an animal that wounds rather than kills an opponent. If this allows the opponent to continue to compete with the winner or the winner's relatives, such an act can be seen as altruistic. Silk's (1982) finding that higher-ranking female bonnet macaques refrain from attacking lower-ranking females who are grooming them might be interpreted in this way. If Bertram's question is answered affirmatively, the problems of measuring the fitness effects of altruism obviously become much greater, for now costs and benefits must be calculated also for behaviors which do *not* occur.

The methodological problems just reviewed bring us to the topic of which questions empirical research among primates might seek to answer about reciprocal altruism. As with nepotism theory, three questions are possible: they concern interaction, maximization, and evolution. And, also as in the case of nepotism theory, only the first of these questions has been addressed so far. With few exceptions, empirical research on reciprocal altruism has focused on behaviors between animals assumed to be nonrelatives, has not adjusted for reproductive value or otherwise measured actual costs and benefits of behaviors, and has examined identical rather than complementary behaviors. Thus, the results of the studies reviewed below provide evidence that at times animals appear to be acting as if they were following the logic of Trivers' analysis. The existence of alternative explanations for these results means that only the weakest support is given for reciprocal altruism theory.

The Problem of Start-up
Boorman and Levitt (1973, 1980), among others, notes that a major theoretical problem is accounting for the initial spread of reciprocal altruism in a population of nonaltruists. A lone altruist in such a population will be at a disadvantage, because his donation of aid will not be repaid, and he will achieve lower relative reproductive success than other members of his group. Trivers' argument that altruists provide aid only to those animals who exhibit proximate cues evidencing altruistic tendencies does not solve this problem, for now we must account for the origin of the genes that create altruistic tendencies in two unrelated animals. Many writers suggest that some form of genetic drift or kin selection is necessary to explain the initial evolution of reciprocal altruism. Thus, accidental demographic or genetic changes in a system of aid donations to relatives (nepotism) might have somehow "opened up" the system to nonrelatives. As Moore (1984:5) points out, this requires postulating the rapid evolution of a second set of adaptations relevant to the discovery of and discrimination against nonrelatives who failed to pay debts.

Mathematical modeling of the start-up of reciprocal altruism is just beginning, but it has already produced some interesting results. Axelrod and Hamilton (1981) use game theory to model the evolution of cooperation. They discover that a simple "TIT FOR TAT" strategy—where Ego's response to an opportunity to donate altruism is dictated by the last interaction he had with Other—is the most effective response in a tournament of strategies in a "Prisoners' Dilemma" game wherein Ego and Other interact more than once. Although Axelrod and Hamilton speculate on how this strategy, arising in a population of nonaltruists, might start a species toward the evolution of reciprocal altruism, the relationship between reciprocal altruism and cooperation still needs to be clarified.

Other models for the evolution of cooperation and/or reciprocal altruism have recently been suggested, but have not been developed. Thus, Rubenstein (1982) suggests that low-ranking animals might provide altruism to higher-ranking, nonrelated animals as part of a risky strategy of inclusive fitness maximization. And, as noted above, Blurton Jones (1984) and Moore (1984) suggest that models of the evolution of cooperation or sharing must take into account the nature of the aid or resources that are involved in the interaction. Both emphasize the distinction between resources that can be shared and those that cannot.

The start-up problem is far from being settled, but some of the theoretical work that has been applied toward its solution might also be applicable to the empirical study of reciprocal altruism among alloprimates. This is especially true of Blurton Jones' and Moore's point that the nature of the resource at stake must always be analyzed in any test of the theory.

TESTS OF RECIPROCAL ALTRUISM THEORY AMONG ALLOPRIMATES

The strongest case for the existence of reciprocal altruism in an alloprimate species is Packer's (1977) study of solicitations of aid during agonistic interactions by male olive baboons at Gombe. His three-troop sample contains 140 instances where one male solicited the aid of another against a third. In 97 cases, the solicited male joined in a coalition against the third. On 20 of these 97 occasions, the opponent was consorting with an estrous female at the start of the interaction, and in 6 of these cases, he lost the female to the male who solicited aid. On these occasions, the soliciting male ceased fighting and left with the female, leaving the solicited male still fighting with the opponent. In none of these 6 cases did Packer later observe the solicited male in the company of the estrous female after the fight. This last datum suggests that the behavior in question is a possible example of altruism, rather than cooperation (behavior increasing the reproductive success for both solicitor and solicited).

Packer finds a strong correlation between a male's willingness to join in coalitions when solicited and his success in obtaining aid when he solicits other males. He also notes that pairs of males tend to develop aid relationships such that they solicit aid from and provide aid to one another more frequently than they do with other males. Packer further discovers that males most often direct aid solicitations to members of the age and sex classes most likely to provide effective help in future encounters, and that they are less likely to respond positively to solicitations from members of age and sex classes who would be of little help in agonistic encounters. Taken together, these results suggest that coalition formation among olive baboons operates by means of reciprocal altruism.

Packer's work indicates some of the problems that are encountered in studying reciprocal altruism in free-ranging alloprimate populations. For example, he notes that since males join troops singly, and their original troops are often unknown, it is difficult to rule out the possibility that some coalitions were formed by related individuals. If this were the case, the behavior under study might be the outcome of kin selection and not reciprocal altruism. However, Packer provides evidence for assuming that at least five out of the thirteen reciprocating pairs he studied were not close relatives.

A second problem is the calculation of costs and benefits. Packer notes that he cannot say whether or not the fitness benefits received by the solicitor offset the fitness costs of the males who joined a coalition. In the cases where the solicitor obtained an estrous female, the benefits might have been quite high. However, this occurred in only 6 of 97 coalitions. Packer does note that the costs incurred by the solicited male may be low if the opponent elects not to fight when confronted by two individuals. If this is often the case, the benefits to the solicitor need not be too high for the behavior to be selected. In order to calculate costs and benefits, it is necessary to know the outcome of interactions when a male solicits aid and does not receive it. Does he cease interacting with the opponent, thus encountering no costs? Or does he continue the interaction, perhaps suffering an injury? Also, information is needed on the balance of costs and benefits over time for any reciprocating dyad. If male A solicits aid from male B and ends up with an estrous female on two occasions, his responses to male B's solicitations on other occasions should result in male B obtaining access to females in estrus, for a balance to be maintained. Parker does not provide evidence for such a balance.

An ingenious study of reciprocal altruism among free-ranging vervets by Seyfarth and Cheney (1984) addresses the problem of distinguishing nepotism from reciprocal altruism and also raises the issue of whether repayment may be in complementary or identical behaviors. The study involved tape recording the aid solicitation vocalizations of a number of individuals (vocalizers). These individuals were then observed, and their grooming interactions noted. When a vocalizer was out of the sight of the subject, experimenters broadcast the tape of the vocalizer's aid solicitations and observed the behavior of the subject. The dependent variable was the number of seconds the subject spent looking in the direction of the hidden speaker. This variable might be seen as an indirect measure of an animal's willingness to join a coalition with the vocalizer. The tests were run twice for each vocalizer-subject pair. In the experimental condition, the vocalizer had groomed the subject between 30 and 90 minutes prior to the test. In the control condition, the pair had not been engaged in grooming for at least two hours prior to the test.

In agreement with nepotism theory, Seyfarth and Cheney find that a subject's responses to the vocalizations of kin (as determined by matrilineal genealogies) are stronger than their responses to the calls of nonkin, although the difference does not reach statistical significance. The key finding relevant to reciprocal altruism is that a subject's response to the calls of kin did not vary with whether or not the vocalizer had recently groomed the subject; apparently kin manifest a willingness to defend one another regardless of how recently an affiliative interaction has occurred. In contrast, the intensity of a subject's responses to the calls of nonkin varied directly with the probability that the vocalizer had recently groomed the subject. In fact, subjects often gave stronger responses to an unrelated vocalizer who had recently groomed them than to a related vocalizer.

Seyfarth and Cheney's article is an exciting contribution to the study of reciprocal altruism. It addresses some major methodological problems confronting this type of research. For example, separate analyses of responses of kin and nonkin should be standard practice in the study of reciprocal altruism. However, there are a number of theoretical and methodological problems which deserve mention. First, of course, is the problem of unknown genetic relationships through males; this unknown factor throws the distinction between relatives and nonrelatives into question. Second, we have no idea of how the costs/benefits of grooming relate to the costs/benefits of joining an alliance. They do not appear to be commensurate, raising the question of whether grooming/alliance partners switch roles in other situations. Unfortunately, Seyfarth and Cheney's data do not permit an answer to this question. There is also the problem of the time factor involved in the repayment of grooming aid. The data suggest that beyond two hours, a grooming interaction between nonkin has little ability to generate an alliance response. With such a rapid temporal decay in the effect of grooming, it seems that a great deal of grooming must go "unrewarded" unless either agonistic interactions or grooming interactions between nonrelatives are fairly frequent in vervets. Data on these topics are not presented in the article. Finally, there are alternative explanations of Seyfarth and Cheney's results. Is it possible, for example, that responses to solicitations reflect selfish reactions to individual danger, rather than altruism? This might occur if the time elapsed after a grooming bout were strongly inversely correlated with the probability that the vocalizer would be in the vicinity of the subject. The call of a recent grooming partner might thus indicate to Ego that there was danger nearby, and Ego's glances toward the cry would be a first step in identifying and responding to it.

Although not as sophisticated as Packer's (1977) or Seyfarth and Cheney's (1984), three other studies have found little support for the idea that aid in agonistic interactions is organized by reciprocal altruism: studies by Kaplan (1978) on rhesus macaques, by Massey (1977) on pigtail macaques, and by Silk (1982) on bonnet macaques. In each case, the hypothesis that aid to nonrelatives would be reciprocated is not supported. Massey finds that of 47 interfamily aids, only 10 were reciprocated, while Silk finds only 2 reciprocal coalitions out of 44 coalitions between unrelated females of similar ranks. Trivers' suggestion that aid to nonrelatives will have low fitness costs to donors and will be reciprocated is not supported by Kaplan's finding that among rhesus, aid between nonrelatives tends to involve higher fitness costs (e.g., is more likely to involve serious fights, with biting) and is less likely to be reciprocated than aid to relatives. Thus, these three studies fail to find support for reciprocal altruism theory. Future research will have to determine whether the differences between these studies and Packer's and Seyfarth and Cheney's results reflect species differences or differences in research methodology.

Grooming as a possible example of reciprocal altruism has been explored by Kurland (1977) for Japanese macaques and by Silk (1982) for bonnet macaques. Kurland finds that grooming relationships between nonrelatives tend to be reciprocal, while those between relatives usually are not. In contrast, in Silk's study only 20 of 157 grooming relationships between unrelated females of similar ranks are reciprocal. It is unclear at present whether the variant results of these studies are due to species differences in reciprocal altruism, to differences in the cost/benefit calculus of grooming in these species, to the failure of the authors to consider complementary behaviors, or to differences in research methodology.

Silk (1982) also points out that when females of different ranks groom there is frequently an imbalance, with higher-ranking animals receiving more grooming than they provide. In an attempt to explain the behavior of lower-ranking animals, Silk notes that they are often immune from attack while grooming higher-ranking females. She advances an extortion hypothesis, which suggests that higher-ranking females harass, or threaten to harass, lower-ranking females into grooming them. However, as noted above, if Bertram (1982) is correct in accepting restraint from action as a form of altruism, this situation could be interpreted as a case of reciprocal altruism. Thus, by not harassing the lower-ranking female, the dominant female increases the reproductive success of the latter, while adding to the competition that her own daughters will face in the future. Of course, if lower-ranking females tend to produce male offspring, restraint by the dominant female does not necessarily increase the competition her daughters will face (see Chapter Six). A difficulty with this restraint hypothesis is that grooming of high-ranking females apparently does not reduce the likelihood of aggression outside the context of grooming.

Chimpanzee sharing of meat with unrelated animals is analyzed by Blurton Jones (1984) and by Moore (1984), who suggest that what appears to be an example of reciprocal altruism is actually something more complex. As noted earlier, both authors argue that a distinction be made between donations of aid involving resources that can be shared and aid involving helping. For resources that can be shared, two conditions make it beneficial for Ego to share. First, if Ego is sated and cannot gain further fitness by eating or storing the resource, he could utilize the remainder to forge or strengthen social bonds. Second, if Ego cannot easily defend the resource, sharing may occur at the point where defense costs overwhelm the costs of sharing. In either of these conditions, sharing may result in little or no fitness loss to Ego and therefore would not constitute altruism. In contrast, helping behavior (defense, grooming, etc.) always involves some fitness costs to Ego, and animals can almost never be coerced into helping if they do not desire to do so.

The point of the distinction made by Blurton Jones and by Moore is that systems of resource sharing can arise without reciprocal altruism or kin selection being involved. Both authors suggest that sharing among early humans might have developed out of a system of meat-sharing (or "tolerated theft"), and Blurton Jones further argues that such a system would permit the evolution of reciprocal altruism.

Moore's argument is strengthened by his analysis of meat-sharing among chimpanzees. He notes that individuals who have meat might suffer attack from group members who desire this resource. Sharing therefore might be a way of avoiding such attacks. Moore suggests that if the loss of meat to others is a foregone conclusion, an animal should incorporate the distribution of meat into its strategy for obtaining status within the group. Moore provides some indirect evidence relevant to these speculations by analyzing Wrangham's (1975) data on the success rates of obtaining meat by eight male chimpanzees at Gombe. Moore argues that if animals share to avoid being attacked or to gain social status, the animals most likely to attack and those high-ranking animals who can "award" social status will be the most successful solicitors of meat that is held by others. The results are congruent with Moore's argument, with the older and higher-ranking males being most successful.

TESTS OF RECIPROCAL ALTRUISM THEORY AMONG HUMANS

In his original article, Trivers (1971) argues that human behavior represents the best-documented case of reciprocal altruism. He discusses early human evolution in light of reciprocal altruism theory, and analyzes the complex psychological and sociological tactics he sees developing out of the operation of human reciprocal altruism. Unfortunately, very little empirical work that is specifically focused on reciprocal altruism has been conducted with humans. There is a massive literature in economics and social psychology, which touches on many of the issues raised by reciprocal altruism theory, but it cannot be reviewed here. However, it is my impression that a great deal of it would support many of the points made by Trivers. One of the major future tasks of human sociobiology will be the translation of this literature into the vocabularies of nepotism and reciprocal altruism theories.

Trivers provides a list of five behaviors, which he states would be on any complete list of human altruism:

(1) helping in times of danger (e.g., accidents, predation, intraspecific aggression);
(2) sharing food;
(3) helping the sick, the wounded, or the very young and old;
(4) sharing implements; and
(5) sharing knowledge [1971:45]

What is of interest in this list is the fact that few of the behaviors supposedly exemplifying human reciprocal altruism involve actions that lower the inclusive fitness of the donor. It is difficult to see how sharing knowledge and implements reduces Ego's reproductive success. As Moore (1984) notes, sharing of food might not result from reciprocal altruism, but rather from selfish motives. Only the care of the physically incompetent and helping in times of danger, when done for unrelated individuals, unambiguously qualify as examples of reciprocal altruism, in that they definitely do have fitness costs for the donor. The confusing aspects of this list illustrate the necessity for remembering that not *all* examples of cooperative behavior need to be explained from the perspective of reciprocal altruism theory.

The most interesting use of reciprocal altruism theory to explain human behavior is Thompson's (1980) analysis of several studies in social psychology. Thompson's article is also noteworthy for its discussion of reductionism and the redundancy problem. He argues the strong reductionist position that:

> If existing social science theories are to avoid reduction to simple evolutionary biology they must show that simple natural selection either makes false predictions about human behaviour or that it makes fewer predictions about human behaviour than its alternatives. If this cannot be done, all superorganic theories will be superceded [sic] by, that is, reduced to, the theory of evolution by natural selection [Thompson 1980:344].

Thompson takes Trivers' theory of reciprocal altruism as an experimental hypothesis and counterposes it to what he calls the null hypothesis—that human altruism cannot be explained as a simple biological adaptation. This null hypothesis he sees as held by theorists who advance superorganic views of human culture. He later contrasts the two hypotheses by arguing that the experimental hypothesis predicts that the equation for reciprocal altruism will be a human universal, while the null hypothesis holds that there is no universal equation for human reciprocal altruism. Finally, he pairs the hypotheses again by deriving three predictions from the equation for reciprocal altruism. The experimental hypothesis predicts that: (1) altruism varies directly with the cost/benefit ratio of the action; (2) altruism varies directly with the probability of situation reversal; and (3) altruism by the donor varies directly with altruism by the recipient. Thompson argues that superorganic theories predict no consistent correlation between the two terms of each prediction.

Thompson reviews several studies which support the experimental hypothesis. An example is the association between architecture in housing projects and an indirect measure of reciprocal altruism, the reporting of crime:

> ... as building height and corridor length increase, the number of inter-actions between any two people taken at random from those that share a common entrance decreases. This lowers the variable p, which is the probability of situation reversal between donor and recipient altruists. The lower value of p results in less reciprocal altruism, including witness rates per crime committed, which, in turn, results in more crimes committed. The greater number of crimes committed ultimately express themselves [sic] in higher rates of reported crime, though the increase in unreported crime is probably even greater [Thompson 1980:360].

Thompson compares crime rates for two New York public housing projects, which are located across a road from one another. The projects are evenly matched on important variables (population, racial composition, average income, number of minors, etc.) but vary on the physical features that are relevant to probability of interaction. As predicted, the project with features that serve to reduce the probability of situation reversal exhibits a higher reported crime rate.

Thompson makes use of reciprocal altruism theory to reinterpret several of the studies on helping behavior that are reported in Latane and Darley (1970). In one experiment, for example, students asked passersby for one of four types of aid: the time, directions to Times Square, change for a quarter, or a dime. This sequence of requests becomes increasingly expensive for the passerby, and the rates of positive response were 85 percent, 84 percent, 73 percent, and 34 percent, respectively. Thompson interprets this as indicating that as the cost of the altruism increased, the probability of its occurrence declined. A second study showed that the number of people who were willing to give a dime varied with a recipient's statement about the value of the donation. Thirty-four percent responded positively when merely asked for a dime with no reason given, but 64 percent responded when the phrase "I need to make a telephone call" was added, and this increased to 72 percent when the statement that "my wallet has been stolen" was added. This indicates to Thompson that as the benefit to the recipient of an action increases, the probability of altruism rises.

Thompson's interpretations of the Latane and Darley studies are interesting and lend support to the idea that reciprocal altruism theory is relevant to understanding some kinds of human behavior. However, his attempts to pit superorganic and biological theories against one another are frequently unconvincing. For example, he cites an experiment in which forty theological students read either the parable of the Good Samaritan or information on jobs for seminary students before being sent to a recording studio by a route which would take them by a confederate who was lying in a doorway and acting as if he were in pain. The dependent variable was the number of students who offered aid to the confederate. Thompson argues that this is a test of a prediction of the superorganic theory that human behavior can be directed into areas that have a random relationship with biological adaptation. Yet not all nonsociobiological theories of human behavior would argue that merely reading a parable would result in an immediate increase in helping behaviors to strangers. Other predictions that Thompson derives from the superorganic hypothesis seem equally unrealistic.

Another article that takes existing data and analyzes them from the perspective of reciprocal altruism theory is Essock-Vitale and McGuire's (1980) survey of the sociobiological predictions they find to be supported in the anthropological literature. Six studies relevant to the prediction that the flow of economic aid in friendships will be reciprocal are reviewed and found to support the prediction. These studies (among Bantu tribesmen, Brazilian sharecroppers, Urban Coast Salish, Japanese Americans, and West Indians) employed standardized questionnaires to obtain data on the normative rules governing friendships. Unfortunately, the value of such studies for testing reciprocal altruism theory is limited, for the actual flow of economic resources in friendships may bear little relationship to normative statements.

Although Hames' (1981) study of garden labor exchange among the Ye'kwana was mentioned in the chapter on nepotism, his finding that closely related households tolerate more imbalance in labor exchange than unrelated households supports Trivers' and Alexander's suggestion that individuals may demand less reciprocity from kin than from nonkin.

A final empirical examination of reciprocal altruism among humans is Ginsberg and Miller's (1981) test of Trivers' suggestion that in societies with strong linear dominance hierachies, the amount of reciprocity between individuals who occupy widely disparate ranks will be low. They analyze a linear hierarchy among boys in grades three to five in an elementary school and find that boys who intervene in playground fights were not repaid by the beneficiaries of their aid in either the immediate context or in subsequent fights. The authors raise the question of complementary behaviors, by suggesting that recipients might repay their debts in a different domain of sociality, such as loyalty or economic rewards. A major problem with this study is that we cannot be sure that the intervention of high-ranking males in fights is an act of altruism directed toward one of the fighters. A plausible alternative is that such intervention is the way high-ranking males and maintain their positions in the hierarchy. If this alternative is correct, the benefits to the recipient are epiphenomena which need not be repaid.

CONCLUSIONS

It is obvious that the concept of reciprocal altruism is a vital topic in primate sociobiology. To sociobiologists, it is necessary to explain the many examples of animals donating phenotypically altruistic behavior to unrelated animals. However, to many critics of sociobiology, the concept seems to be an evasion: an alternative thrown into the argument to save the sociobiological approach when any particular case cannot be explained by either individual or kin selection. Unfortunately, the confusion surrounding the concept is so great that its validity and usefulness is still unclear.

The concept clearly needs a serious rethinking before it can be applied successfully and convincingly to human and alloprimate data. This rethinking must focus on a number of the issues discussed above. First, theorists will need to define clearly how reciprocal altruism differs from mutualism, cooperation, "tolerated sharing," and other social interactions wherein two or more unrelated animals act in concert or donate aid to each other. Second, the problem of complementary versus identical behaviors as repayments for altruism needs to be carefully examined. If complementary behaviors are accepted as possible repayments, researchers studying reciprocal altruism among primates will have to identify the possible repayment alternatives before seeking to identify certain relationships as being based on reciprocal altruism. Third, a clear statement on how the interaction between reciprocal altruism and nepotism affects empirical research is desirable. Until such issues are clarified, social scientists perhaps cannot be faulted for finding the concept of reciprocal altruism to be a smokescreen covering the limitations of sociobiology.

The empirical work in primate reciprocal altruism is rather limited and, given the theoretical and methodological problems with this topic, does not provide strong support for the position that reciprocal altruism is an important component in primate social life. None of the published tests utilizing human data are particularly convincing. The situation with the alloprimates is a little better, with both the Packer (1977) and the Seyfarth and Cheney (1984) studies providing some exciting results. However, even these studies need to resolve several methodological problems and to be replicated before their significance is clear. Until that time, reciprocal altruism theory will remain the weakest component in primate sociobiology.

CHAPTER 6

Parental Investment Theory

INTRODUCTION

The sociobiological approach to the parent-offspring relationship is examined in this chapter under the heading of "parental investment theory." As Dawkins (1979) notes, the parent-offspring relationship can be treated as an example of nepotism, once it is realized that offspring are only one pathway for placing alleles into descending generations. However, the great amount of theoretical and empirical work on this topic requires that it be examined in a chapter separate from the one on nepotism theory.

The difference between classical Darwinian theory and sociobiology is most strikingly manifested in the treatment of the relationship between parents and offspring. In the classical theory, individuals produce offspring and the hostile forces of nature eliminate those who are less fit. In this treatment, the reproductive interests of parents and offspring are congruent, and there is little room for conflict. In contrast, the gene selectionist approach and strategy metaphor that are characteristic of sociobiology suggest that individuals are not blind reproducers, but rather that they have been selected to act over their lifetimes as if they were making a series of choices with the goal of maximizing their inclusive fitness. Sociobiological theory notes that offspring may or may not be a component in an individual's inclusive fitness strategy. If offspring are produced, inclusive fitness strategies may differ on when during a lifetime this is done and on how much care is provided to those who are born. Sociobiology further suggests that the hostile forces of nature are not the only factors that select between an individual's offspring; in an effort to maximize inclusive fitness, parents may often take on this role themselves.

Two major concepts form the core of parental investment theory. The first is *parental investment*, which Trivers defines as "... any investment by the parent in an individual offspring that increases the offspring's chance of surviving (and hence reproductive success) at the cost of the parent's ability to invest in other offspring" (1972:139). Parental investment takes many forms beyond initial investment in egg or sperm. Maternal investment by alloprimates may include gestation, lactation, transport, protection, grooming, defense, or other caretaking behaviors. Paternal investment by alloprimates may involve transport, protection, play, grooming, toleration, etc. Among humans, transmission of property to children is often seen as a form of parental investment.

The other major concept is *parental certainty*, the probability that the individual in whom Ego invests is his actual genetic offspring. Maternal certainty for primates is usually assumed to be perfect, 1.0. In contrast, internal fertilization means that paternal certainty for alloprimates is usually less than perfect and varies with the types of breeding system and other factors.

As noted earlier, parental investment theory argues that animals have been selected to invest resources in a manner allowing them to achieve maximum lifetime inclusive fitness. Tests of the theory will require that we identify: (1) the types of investment decisions an animal must make during its lifetime; and (2) the factors relevant to these decisions. At least five types of decisions have been discussed by sociobiologists. First, at any given time, a potential parent has the option of producing its first offspring or investing resources in itself in the hope of achieving greater reproductive success by delaying parenthood. Such decisions are usually discussed under the heading of reproductive strategy or life history theory. Second, at any given time, potential parents have the choice of producing their own offspring or giving investment to nondescendant relatives. Third, at any given time, parents may invest additional resources in their existing offspring or provide that investment to other nondescendant relatives. The second and third decisions are usually discussed under the heading of nepotism theory. Fourth, at any given time, parents may face the choice of giving investment to an existing offspring or utilizing their resources to create a new offspring (e.g., by diverting the resources to mating effort). Finally, at any given time, parents may have to decide how to divide their resources most effectively among their existing offspring. These last two problems are the main concern of parental investment theory.

Sociobiologists have identified numerous factors that affect parental investment decisions. Among them are: (1) the quality and quantity of resources held by a parent at any given time; (2) the parent's ability to gather more resources if he or she invests them at a given time; (3) the opportunities for alternative investments; (4) the resource costs of rearing various types of offspring, and (5) the potential reproductive success of different types of offspring. These factors will be explored in more detail when specific components of parental investment theory are reviewed.

Discussion thus far has concerned only the parental side of the parent-offspring dyad. The sociobiological argument, however, holds that offspring seek to maximize their own lifetime inclusive fitness and that manipulation of parents may be a component in this program. Robert Trivers (1974) notes that the investment strategies of parents and offspring may sometimes conflict, with offspring demanding more investment than parents are willing to give and resisting parental demands to accept less than is optimal for the offsprings' inclusive fitness. The theoretical possibility of a genetic basis to parent-offspring conflict suggests that the relationship between parents and offspring is a bit more problematic than is indicated by formal treatments of Darwinian theory.

This chapter reviews the empirical research on six topics that are relevant to parental investment theory. These topics are interrelated and are separated only for ease of discussion. The reader should bear in mind that a number of the topics may be relevant in a particular situation. Thus, parent-offspring conflict will influence the amount of positive investment provided by a parent and will also affect the willingness of parents to engage in child abuse or infanticide. At the same time, each of these factors may relate to the sex of the child and the sex ratio strategy of the parents.

The first topic involves positive investment strategies among alloprimates. Subjects under this heading include the cost of offspring to mothers and the role of males in child care. The second topic concerns positive investment strategies among humans and includes maternal and paternal child-care and inheritance practices. The third topic, infanticide and child abuse, may be seen as the reverse of positive investment strategies or as the outcome of parental investment practices favoring offspring other than the victims of abuse. The fourth topic, sex ratio theory, examines how the costs and benefits of rearing offspring of different sexes are related to parental investment practices. Parent-offspring conflict, the fifth topic, explores the theory that the investment strategy of the parents will not always coincide with the demands of the offspring. The final topic, allomaternal or "helping" behavior, could have been placed under a number of different subject headings (e.g., nepotism theory, reproductive strategy theory), but since many authors discuss it in the context of parental investment, I include it in this chapter.

I will not discuss difficulties with the general theory of parental investment at the start of this chapter, as I have done in previous chapters. Instead, I will mention such difficulties at the start of each component topic.

TESTS OF POSITIVE PARENTAL INVESTMENT
AMONG ALLOPRIMATES

Thus far, no studies of parental investment have been designed to answer the maximization question (can it be demonstrated that a given set of investment choices maximizes an individual's lifetime inclusive fitness?) or the evolution question (can a given set of investment choices be related in a direct manner to genotype?). The studies that do exist seek for general matches between the broadest predictions of the theory and observed social behavior. For example, the majority of studies in this section seek to demonstrate a relationship between male parental investment and paternal certainty. As noted earlier, the studies that find a general congruence between the theory and the empirical world provide the weakest form of support for the sociobiological paradigm. With this point in mind, I now review studies of positive paternal and maternal investment by alloprimates.

Male Parental Investment

Interaction between adult males and infants or juveniles varies greatly among the alloprimates. (Although parents may invest in adult offspring, this is probably rare for male alloprimates and will be ignored here.) In some species (e.g., tamarins and marmosets), males carry infants and may expend almost as much energy as females in child care. In other species, males interact little with infants and exhibit few caretaking behaviors (however, such males may care for infants when housed with them in the absence of females; see Redican 1978). Kleiman and Malcolm (1981) review paternal behavior among mammals; while reviews of adult male-infant interaction among alloprimates include Mitchell (1969), Mitchell and Brandt (1972), Parke and Suomi (1981), Redican (1976), and Snowdon and Suomi (1982).

The major problem in formulating tests of paternal investment theory among alloprimates lies in identifying behaviors which qualify as paternal investment and then quantifying their fitness costs and benefits. Snowdon and Suomi (1982) address the identification problem with their suggestion that male care of infants may take two forms. *Substitutive behaviors* are actions that are also engaged in by females (e.g., transport, grooming, play, etc.); while *complementary behaviors* are those not usually exhibited by females (e.g., defense against predators or hostile conspecifics). Either form of behavior creates measurement problems. For example, complementary behaviors, such as troop defense, may protect a male's mates or his nondescendant relatives as well as his offspring. Should species exhibiting this behavior be scored as "paternal care present" in holospecies tests of hypotheses? Or should the costs/benefits of the behavior be divided up, with a percentage apportioned to mate defense, another to nondescendant relatives, and the remainder to paternal investment? Or, perhaps most reasonably, should we seek to identify the primary and secondary functions of troop defense?

Measurement of costs/benefits is not any easier in the case of substitutive behaviors, for many of these actions may not significantly reduce a male's ability to invest in other offspring. For some behaviors, the costs seem trivial (e.g., grooming or toleration). Also, a species' mating system may prevent males from siring other offspring even if they do not engage in infant care. For seasonal breeders, interaction with infants outside the breeding season seems to generate few, if any, costs (unless the time spent with infants might be used to create bonds with females that could be activated in the next breeding season—an untested hypothesis and one which opens the possibility that infant care is only a tactic in male mating strategies).

The majority of empirical work on paternal investment among allopri-mates concerns the relationship between paternal certainty and investment. The logic of this research was discussed in Chapter Three: a male's willingness to invest in a female's offspring will vary directly with his certainty that they are the result of his matings with her, all else being equal. This research has taken two directions. First, some investigators apply a holospecies approach to demonstrate that males in species that are characterized by breeding systems conducive to high paternal certainty exhibit more paternal investment than males of species with breeding systems that create lower paternal certainty. The second approach is to examine single groups of alloprimates and demonstrate that classes of males with higher paternal certainty (e.g., frequent copulators) interact with infants and juveniles differently than classes of males that are assumed to have less paternal certainty. A variation of this approach concerns itself with groups where most males exhibit paternal behavior. Such an approach seeks to discover whether males in multimale troops preferentially direct attention or aid to those infants or juveniles which they are most likely to have sired.

Several systematic reviews of paternal behavior support the hypothesis that species with breeding systems conducive to high paternal certainty will exhibit the highest degree of male substitutive behavior. Thus, monogamous species show the greatest amount of male care for infants, and Redican (1976) notes that monogamy, when combined with the territoriality of many monogamous species, produces the highest paternal certainty among the alloprimates.

Males of species that are characterized by unimale troops, or "harems," have higher paternal certainty than males of species with multimale troops and are predicted to provide more infant care. However, unimale troops exhibit great variability in adult male-infant interaction, making comparison with multimale troops difficult. For example, while patas males rarely interact with infants, they may risk their lives protecting their troop against predators. Langur males have been observed to play with infants, but this is uncommon. However, they do tolerate and protect infants.

Multimale troops theoretically produce the lowest paternal certainty and, as is to be expected, Redican (1976) rates species with this social system as exhibiting little adult male-infant interaction. However, once again there is great variation. Adult rhesus males rarely interact with infants, while adult male Barbary macaques handle infants more frequently than males in most of the species characterized by unimale troops. Although some Barbary macaque males use infants to prevent attacks by other males (i.e., agonistic buffering; see Deag 1980; Deag and Crook 1971), there appears to be much substitutive care in this species. Furthermore, adoption of infants by adult males has been reported in species with multimale troops (Berman, cited in Snowden and Suomi 1982:76 for rhesus; Wolfe 1981b, for Japanese macaques).

Redican (1976) notes that a major confounding variable in the holospecies study of paternal investment is interspecific variation in maternal style. He rates six species of macaques and baboons on maternal restrictiveness and adult male-infant interaction and finds an inverse correlation between these variables. The meaning of this result is not clear. It might be that an evolved pattern of restrictive maternal style serves to block the development of adult male-infant interaction in some species where paternal certainty would predict much interaction. On the other hand, it could be argued that the style of mothering that is characteristic of a species responds to the evolution of paternal investment patterns. Or, both variables may be related to an unidentified third factor. In any case, Redican's argument should be kept in mind when we examine the tests of paternal investment theory in single troops, since the restrictive style of some mothers may prevent all males, including fathers, from interacting with infants. A corrective for this problem is to control for maternal style in all tests, a method which has not been utilized in any of the studies reviewed below.

Snowden and Suomi (1982) also review the literature on paternal care in the alloprimates and conclude that paternal certainty does not account for much of the interspecific variance in adult male-infant interaction patterns. They note that monogamy does not always predict high rates of interaction, citing the case of the monogamous de Brazza monkey (Gautier-Hion and Gautier 1978), among whom males in captivity do not interact with infants. (This is not a strong example, however, since monogamy in this species may be a recent result of human disturbance; see Hrdy 1981a). Snowden and Suomi (1982) also note that recent fieldwork indicates that paternal certainty in some of the monogamous New World monkeys may not be as high as previously thought, and yet males still care for infants among these species. Finally, the authors note that many species with breeding systems conducive to high paternal certainty exhibit less paternal interaction with infants than would be predicted from a paternal certainty hypothesis. To explain the interspecific variation of paternal care among the alloprimates, Snowden and Suomi propose an alternative to the paternal certainty hypothesis. Their theory implicates the need for helpers in raising infants in some species and the necessity for defense against predators in others. Up to now, their hypothesis has not been empirically tested against the paternal certainty argument.

The only empirical holospecies test of the relationship between paternal certainty and paternal care is the one made by Bales (1980). He constructs a five-point Guttman scale of paternalistic behavior (tolerate, protect, play, groom, nurture) and finds that species closer to a monogamic breeding system score higher on the scale than species nearer the polygamic end of the continuum. Unfortunately, Bales' study is weak, since he provides no operational definition of breeding systems and fails to report any statistics to validate his conclusion. A further weakness is that his scale does not include complementary paternal behaviors.

We find mixed results of empirical tests investigating whether males of species with promiscuous mating can direct investment toward the infants they have sired. Packer (1980) shows that the adult male olive baboons that are present in a troop prior to the birth of an infant (i.e., potential fathers) are more likely to interact with and care for the infant than the males who join the troop after the infant's birth. However, a search for a mechanism permitting more precise targeting of parental investment obtains only negative results. Packer argues that a male has higher paternal certainty if he has: (1) exhibited a strong consort preference with a particular female; (2) mated with a female during her conception cycle; and (3) mated with a female on the third day prior to detumscence (i.e., D-3, when matings are most likely to lead to conception; see Hendrickx and Kraemer 1969), in her conception cycle. He finds that none of these measures correlates with adult male-infant interaction, however, suggesting that males cannot recognize the offspring they might have sired. The results obtained by Packer do not rule out the possibility that male association with infants has nothing to do with paternal investment, but is merely the outcome of the attitude of the mother or her infant toward the male.

Packer's findings are confounded by male use of infants for agonistic buffering; a practice sometimes resulting in infants being injured. Parental investment theory suggests that given this risk, males would not use their possible offspring in such encounters. A predicted pattern would be for males who could not have sired an infant to use it in bufferings against males who might be the infant's father. However, Packer finds that infants are most frequently used by males who are present in the troop prior to their birth, and not by males who enter afterward. On the surface, this result contradicts parental investment theory. However, without information on the fitness benefits to the adult male of buffering, and on the fitness costs to the infant, we cannot say whether or not these males are acting counter to their reproductive interests.

Paternity recognition by yellow baboons is suggested by Stein and Stacey's (1981) field study, which shows that probability of paternity (measured by whether a male mated with the mother on days D-4 to D-1) is positively correlated with three measures of adult male-infant proximity and interaction. The findings that infants suffer less harassment from other animals and that they may forage on partially processed food when they are close to adult males suggest possible benefits of such associations for infants.

The Stein and Stacey study is notable for its discussion of the influence of demography on the amount and type of adult male-infant interaction. Observations made upon a troop containing a single adult male and a lone infant were compared with those made in a multimale troop containing several infants. The latter observations distinguished between the behaviors of the potential fathers of an infant and those of other adult males. The behavior directed toward the infant by the male in the unimale group resembled that of potential fathers on some measures, but matched that of nonfathers on others. Stein and Stacey suggest that much of the interaction between adult males and infants may fall into the functional category of helping infants cope with the social environment, and that differences in the demography of unimale and multimale troops may mean that infants in each type of troop may face significantly different social environments. For example, in multimale troops, adult males may position themselves near, or interact with, infants to insure that they will have access to them in situations requiring agonistic buffering. In contrast, since agonistic buffering does not occur in unimale troops, this consideration does not affect the behavior of an adult male in such a troop.

A major problem with both the Packer and the Stein and Stacey studies is that probable paternity is measured by observed sexual activity between a male and an infant's mother. As will be discussed in the chapter on rank theory, this measure may not be an accurate indicator of paternity. It may incorrectly eliminate many potential fathers who mated with the mother, unobserved by the researcher. Studies by Drickamer (1974a) and by Stern and Smith (1984) suggest that this is a major problem confronting studies that use behavioral measures of paternity. Unfortunately, whether, and to what extent, this problem affected the findings of Packer and of Stein and Stacey is not known.

This problem is minimized in a study using paternity exclusion techniques to assign probable paternity in a laboratory group of rhesus (Berenstain et al. 1981). The authors find that paternity accounts for only about five percent of the variance in adult male-infant spatial relationships. Adult males are more likely to be in close proximity with their offspring than with other infants. Although congruent with the theory, paternal investment is not strongly implicated in this finding. First, proximity is not a good measure of investment, since we are not sure of costs and benefits. Second, further analysis suggests that spatial proximity is not a result of positive action on the part of fathers. Infants approach their father more often than they do other males, but fathers do not preferentially approach their offspring. Nor are fathers more tolerant of their offspring or more likely to support them in agonistic episodes. Berenstain et al. demonstrate that while an infant maintains proximity to its father independently of the presence or absence of its mother, it is the relationship between the mother and the father that first establishes the contact between the infant and the male. In other words, unless the mother has a relationship with the father, the infant and its father will not form a close relationship. The authors conclude that male rhesus do not recognize their offspring and do not use matings as proximate cues to identify infants they may have sired.

In another test of paternal investment theory, Judge and Rodman (1976) investigate spatial relationships between central males, females with new infants, and pregnant females in a colony of bonnet macaques. They argue that if a male's presence serves to prevent aggression toward animals near him, then his association with females outside of the breeding season might be a form of paternal investment. Since females with new infants are a more certain investment than females who might miscarry or produce stillborn infants, males should prefer to associate with the former. Results support the prediction, but the authors note that the data can also be interpreted as the outcome of female competition for proximity to males.

To summarize, several reviews of the alloprimate literature lend impressionistic support to a predicted association between paternal certainty and paternal investment, but there are many exceptions to the expected pattern. More detailed study awaits an adequate definition of paternal investment that will permit interspecific comparisons on this variable. To date, most studies have used spatial proximity and other interaction patterns between adult males and infants as indirect measures of paternal investment. However, unless it can be shown that the interactions lower the adult male's ability to produce additional offspring, they do not qualify as parental investment in Trivers' sense. In other words, costs and benefits of these interactions must be calculated before they are utilized in tests of parental investment theory. An indication of the importance of this requirement is Werren et al.'s (1980) theoretical argument that paternal certainty will affect the evolution of paternal investment only in the case of strict monogamy, since only in monogamous breeding systems is a male's investment in one offspring likely to prevent him from producing additional offspring.

The results of studies of species with multimale troops are mixed as to whether or not males have the ability to identify their offspring and preferentially direct care toward them. At present, there is no clear demonstration that males have such abilities. However, the methodological

problem of using indirect measures of both paternity and paternal investment has muddied the picture.

Female Parental Investment

Sociobiologists argue that different problems determine the parental
investment strategies of males and females. For males, sperm are considered
cheap (but see Dewsbury 1982; Small 1983), and paternal investment
strategy is mainly a response to the probability of obtaining matings. In
contrast, for alloprimate females, lifetime reproductive success is limited by
the heavy physiological demands of gestation and, in some species,
lactation. Maternal investment strategies are in large part responses to this
problem. So far, the major sociobiological topic in positive maternal
investment theory involves the modeling of optimum reproductive life
histories. Sociobiological theory predicts that females should distribute
maternal investment so as to maximize their lifetime reproductive success.
The first step in testing this prediction is to discover how the production and
care of infants affect a female's reproductive potential and how these effects
change over her lifetime. The second step is to identify the behavioral and
physiological variables that might be affected as a species undergoes
selection for a particular optimal life history distribution of maternal
investment. Examples of questions raised by this topic include: (1) the
relationship between female reproductive effort and age (see Clutton-Brock
1984; Clutton-Brock et al. 1983; Pugesek 1983); (2) the relationship
between rank and investment strategies (see Chapter Eight); (3) the relationship between resources and reproductive effort (see below); and (4)
whether "style" of mothering is a component in maternal investment
strategies.

As just noted, the first step in testing theories of maternal investment is to
measure the fitness costs of producing and caring for offspring. Clutton-
Brock (1984) indicates the complexities of making such measurements
when he notes four ways in which an offspring imposes costs on its mother:
(1) costs serving to reduce her probability of survival; (2) costs serving to
reduce her future fertility; (3) costs to her lifetime reproductive success
through the negative effects that a new infant may have on the potential for
reproductive success of her existing offspring (e.g., the necessity to wean the
older child before the optimal time); and (4) costs to her lifetime
reproductive success through the negative effects that an infant may have on
the potential for reproductive success of her future offspring (e.g., a
demanding infant causing such physiological stress on the mother that later
offspring are born smaller than if the original infant had been less
demanding). Although no researcher so far has calculated these costs for an
alloprimate species, some interesting preliminary investigations have been
made.

One of the most intriguing questions in maternal investment theory is whether, and how, maternal "style" may relate to investment strategies. Studies by Altmann et al. (1978), Simpson et al. (1981) and Wilson et al. (1983) provide evidence on this question. Altmann et al. (1978; see also J. Altmann 1978, 1980) identify two maternal styles in a free-ranging troop of savanna baboons. Restrictive mothers attempt to maintain constant physical contact with their infants, while nonrestrictive mothers permit infants earlier and greater independence. Nonrestrictive mothers also exhibit higher rejection rates for infant contact attempts and wean their offspring earlier than the restrictive mothers do. The authors' analysis of sexual behavior indicates that nonrestrictive mothers experience shorter periods of postpartum amenorrhea than restrictive mothers. A number of possible reasons for such an effect have been suggested (as reviewed in Wilson et al. 1983). The one most frequently advanced is that lactation suppresses ovulation (lactational anovulation), and that the two styles of mothering create different patterns of nursing.

This study would appear to lead to the conclusion that nonrestrictive mothers have a lifetime reproductive advantage over restrictive mothers. However, Altmann et al. (1978) demonstrate that although the former start cycling before the latter, they also undergo more cycles before conceiving. Thus, the interbirth interval of the two maternal styles is equal. The authors speculate that the potential advantage of nonrestrictive mothers may be realized only when resources are abundant, which was not the case during the period of this study.

Simpson et al. (1981) examine maternal style and reproduction over two breeding seasons in a laboratory group of rhesus macaques. They compare "quick" mothers (those producing infants both years) with "slow" mothers (those producing an infant only in the first year) and find three major differences between them: (1) the first-year infants produced by the quick mothers were more likely to be males; (2) first-year infants of quick mothers were more active during their first twelve weeks of life; and (3) quick mothers more frequently rejected contact attempts of their first-year infants. The authors suggest that rhesus females may attempt to shorten interbirth intervals by promoting independent behavior in their infants, perhaps by rejecting contact attempts. Again, the proximate mechanism implicated may involve differences in nursing behavior. Why certain mothers persist in promoting the independence of their infants is not clear, but this behavior may be influenced by factors such as resource availability or the social rank of the female.

The finding that there is a tendency for the first-year infant of a quick mother to be a male is somewhat surprising, given that males are slightly heavier at birth and would seem to place a greater physiological burden on mothers than female infants (for red deer, see Clutton-Brock et al. 1983). There is a slight sexual dimorphism in infant activity level at two weeks of age, but this disappears after that time and seems unlikely to account for the finding. The authors note that long-term studies in free-ranging rhesus groups do not replicate the association between sex of infant and probability of conception in the following breeding season and suggest that the phenomenon may be a result of captivity.

The previous studies suggest that maternal style may be an important component of female investment strategies. A study of first pregnancies in a group of laboratory rhesus (Wilson et al. 1983) suggests that physiological factors affecting age at first pregnancy may interact with behavioral variables to create a complex investment strategy. The authors compare early-maturing females (first birth at thirty-six months) with typically-maturing females (first birth at forty-eight months) and find that the former are less likely to give birth the year following their first parturition than the latter. This means that, although early-maturers have a reproductive "head start," over a lifetime the early-maturing and typically-maturing females produce about the same number of offspring. Wilson et al. speculate that early-maturers might still obtain a reproductive advantage, since their offspring enter the breeding pool a year or two earlier than the offspring of typically-maturing females, but there is no evidence on this point.

Behavior enters this picture in at least two ways. First, rank is related to early-maturation, with females of high-ranking matrilines more likely to be early maturers than those of low-ranking matrilines (however, only about half the females of high-ranking matrilines are early maturers). Wilson et al. (1983) cite van Wagenen and Catchpole's (1956) finding, that early-maturing rhesus females are heavier at birth than typically-maturing females, and suggest that if high rank leads to priority of access to food, maternal rank may indirectly be a cause of early parturition. Such an effect might be of major importance in troops facing limited food resources. The authors note that there are no data available on the association between birth weight and rank in rhesus, but suggest that Small's (1981) finding in a laboratory group that high-ranking rhesus females are heavier than low-ranking females, and Riopelle et al.'s (1976) discovery that heavier rhesus females tend to produce heavier infants provide some evidence for the likelihood of such an association.

Behavioral patterns may also partially account for the sterile year following a first birth. Both early-maturing and typically-maturing females experience a reduced probability of a live birth in the second year, but the reduction is much greater for the former. Wilson et al. (1983) speculate that primiparous mothers may exhibit a more restrictive maternal style than multiparous females, which could lengthen their period of lactational anovulation. It is possible that early-maturing females might be even more restrictive than typically-maturing primipara. Further, early maturers may not be able to cope with the physiological stress of lactation as well as females who mature later. The combination of these factors could result in early-maturers suffering a greater reduction in live births in the year following the first birth. Unfortunately, Wilson et al. do not have data on the maternal styles of early-maturing and typically-maturing females, but they do note that other studies of rhesus have demonstrated that primiparous and multiparous rhesus interact differently with their infants (Mitchell et al. 1966; Seay 1966).

Wilson et al. (1983) also find that the sex of the first infant produced does not influence the probability of a live birth in the second year for either early-maturing or typically-maturing females. Analysis of females who gave birth in the year following first parturition reveals that the interbirth interval was not affected by the sex of the infant produced in the first year. Both these findings run counter to the expectations created by Simpson et al.'s (1981) previously discussed results. Since both studies utilized laboratory groups, the reasons for the different results are not clear. It may be that the sex-of-infant effect discussed by Simpson et al. does not come into play until late in a female's reproductive career; a reanalysis of the results of both studies, controlling for birth order and maturity, might clarify this problem.

A final study that is relevant to the patterning of maternal investment is Small's (1983) work on the mating behavior of sexually mature females who did not give birth the previous breeding season. For laboratory groups of bonnet and rhesus macaques, she finds that such females cycle earlier in the season and more actively seek out males for sexual activity than females who produced infants in the prior year. Small suggests that some females with infants may experience lactation-induced amenorrhea during the breeding season, while for others the presence of an infant lowers frequency of sexual activity. She suggests that delaying a new pregnancy, or even foregoing reproduction in the year following a birth, may be part of an optimal spacing of births in these macaque species. The early cycling and pursuit of males by the females without recent infants is seen as an attempt to insure that a pregnancy results in the breeding season. Small suggests that we question the prevailing view that sperm is an unlimited resource and argues that females may compete for sperm to insure conception. The amount of competition will vary with the number of sexually active males in a troop, providing an example of the potential of demographic factors to affect behavioral strategies.

Further studies of maternal investment strategies will be reviewed in the discussion of sex ratio theory and rank theory. It should be noted that there is a massive literature on mother-offspring interaction among the allopri-mates and that much of it can be analyzed within the framework of maternal investment theory. Unfortunately, though, until the costs and benefits of maternal behaviors are measured it will be difficult to use the data in this literature in empirical tests of propositions. The studies that are reviewed in this section do illustrate that offspring affect a female's reproductive potential. Surprisingly, both the Altmann et al. (1978) and the Wilson et al. (1983) studies provide examples in which the expectation that females adopting different patterns of maternal investment will exhibit differential fitness benefits is not vindicated. Of course, these two negative results cannot be taken as permitting the rejection of maternal investment theory, but they do indicate the need for further long-term research and caution against the all-too-common practice of judging the adaptiveness of a behavior on the basis of an analysis of costs and benefits derived from short periods of observation.

TESTS OF POSITIVE PARENTAL INVESTMENT AMONG HUMANS

Empirical studies of parental investment theory among humans have been concerned either with the relationship between paternal certainty and paternal investment or with the analysis of rules of inheritance as forms of parental investment. At present, there are no proposition tests involving maternal investment, although some sociobiologists have examined inheritance rules as a form of cooperative investment by a male and female pair. Important theoretical analyses of some of the components of human female maternal investment strategies are found in Hartung's (1983) analysis of matrilineal inheritance and in Irons' (1983) discussion of reproductive strategies. Let us hope that these preliminary statements will soon generate more empirical research on this vital topic.

A brief discussion of two theoretical points must precede a review of the studies on human parental investment strategies. The first concerns the relationship between genes and investment strategies and can be illustrated by considering the logic of many of the studies reviewed below. One hypothesis that is examined by a number of authors is that paternal certainty (p) is directly correlated with the willingness of males to invest in the children produced by females. This hypothesis can be tested within a single society by showing that males with different levels of p exhibit different investment strategies. Or, it can be tested holoculturally by showing that the societies that are characterized by mating systems creating low p exhibit different property inheritance rules or different degrees of father-child contact than societies with mating systems generating high paternal certainty. If either of these tests supports the hypothesis, a major question will be whether males adopting different strategies also carry different alleles relevant to paternal investment. In other words, are there "genes" for matrilineal inheritance, and does, for example, the population of the matrilineal Trobriand Islands exhibit a greater percentage of these than the population of the patrilineal Kimam Island society? Most of the sociobiologists whose work is reviewed in this section reject the idea of either intrasocietal or intersocietal variation in the genes that are relevant to paternal investment strategies. Hartung is most explicit:

It is assumed that the behaviours relevant to this analysis [inheritance practices] have little heritability across same-sex individuals within a society, and negligible heritability by sex across societies—that is, it is presumed that differences in individual behaviour are phenotypic responses to different conditions, that the behaviours in question have been too important for too long for there to be much genetic variance left, and that extant within-sex genetic variance is an irrelevant variable [Hartung 1981:654].

In other words, the relationship between p and investment tendencies is genetically based, but it is a human constant; the interaction of this constant with environmental conditions produces the phenotypic variation in paternal investment that is observed in the ethnographic record. The problem with this argument is that it makes it impossible to test decisively the sociobiological position against nonsociobiological hypotheses that are redundant with it. To demonstrate a genetic influence upon a phenotypic trait, geneticists must first partition phenotypic variation into environmentally-produced variance and genotypically-produced variance. If there is no variance in the genotype, the total variation in the phenotype is usually assumed to be caused by environmental conditions. This does not mean that the sociobiological argument is incorrect, only that it is impossible to demonstrate a genetic influence upon parental investment strategies. Sociobiologists at this point must resort to plausibility arguments to suggest why their hypothesis is superior to redundant nonsociobiological arguments. As noted earlier, these might include the arguments that: (1) the relationship between p and degree of paternal investment among humans is similar to the relationship found in other animals; (2) the sociobiological explanation directs attention to factors previously overlooked in the explanation of inheritance rules, and these factors are better predictors of a wider range of behavior than those implicated in nonsociobiological theories; or (3) the evolution of humans can be interpreted only in such a manner as to demand the relationship between p and paternal investment that is hypothesized by sociobiologists.

The second theoretical point demonstrates the gap between sociobiological and cultural approaches to the problem of cultural rules. Even if sociobiologists convincingly demonstrate that different levels of paternal certainty dictate different paternal investment strategies, we are still left with the problem of explaining how—and why—a society elevates one particular strategy into a normative rule. Sociocultural anthropologists have pointed out that the explanation of the latter problem may relate to cultural factors which have nothing to do with the investment strategies of individuals within a society (e.g., the symbolic integration of culture). On the other hand, some sociobiologists (see especially Alexander 1979) argue that to ignore such strategies is to overlook the fact that many normative rules are advanced and enforced by individuals seeking to maximize their inclusive fitness. How closely the normative rule of inheritance tracks actual conditions of paternal certainty may also be an important factor in how smoothly a society operates. For example, if circumstances begin to create high levels of paternal certainty in a matrilineal society, a sociobiologist would expect to see many males attempt to circumvent the normative inheritance rule and to provide resources to their spouses' offspring. This situation would, in turn, create tension as individuals sought to force recalcitrant males to honor their obligations to matrilineal relatives. This gap between the cultural and sociobiological approaches to inheritance rules (and to other cultural rules) can be closed only when we have clear conceptualizations of the relationships between evolved behavioral tendencies, proximate cues relevant to these tendencies, and the ontological status, operation, and evolution of cultural rules. Unfortunately, such conceptualizations are in the future. For the present, I suggest that the reader keep in mind that, although many of the studies reviewed below find evidence of a relationship between paternal certainty and rules of inheritance, it is unclear how investment behaviors relate to the origin or operation of cultural rules.

Male Parental Investment

The major research topic in this subject area is the relationship between paternal certainty and measures of paternal investment, especially father-child contact and rules of inheritance. As in the case of the alloprimates, the main prediction is that in societies with high paternal certainty, males will tend to invest in the offspring of their spouses, while they will tend to invest elsewhere in societies with low paternal certainty.

An indirect measure of paternal investment is the amount of contact between a male and his presumed offspring. Gray and Wolfe (1982b) conduct a holocultural test of the hypothesis (Kleiman 1977) that societies characterized by monogamy (presumably with high p) exhibit higher levels of father-child contact (Barry and Paxson 1971) than societies scored as exhibiting either limited or general polygyny (Murdock 1967). The societies in the SCCS support the prediction, but the association is weak. A problem with this test is the assumption that polygynous societies exhibit a lower level of paternal certainty than monogamous societies. Unlike the alloprimates, where polygyny often describes a mating system with both sexes having multiple partners, in polygynous human societies often only males have multiple spouses. Since a female may be restricted to a single mate, paternal certainty may actually be quite high in these societies. To cope with this problem, Gray and Wolfe use Broude and Greene's (1976) SCCS codes on the level of female extramarital sexual activity as an indirect measure of paternal certainty. This test reveals no association between extramarital sex and level of father-child contact, failing to support the hypothesis that paternal investment declines with lower paternal certainty.

West and Konner (1976) also use the SCCS to explore father-child contact and find a complex system of relations indicating that ". . . high contribution of women [to subsistence] increases male parental investment unless the male's role prevents it: where the contribution of women is high fathers are close except where there is polygyny" (1976:206). The authors conclude that their results support the utility of parental investment theory in explaining father-child contact. However, the cell sizes in tests of their model are frequently so small that it is difficult to interpret the significance of many of their findings. West and Konner's use of a multivariate analysis is an advance over Gray and Wolfe's (1982b) more simplistic test of the relationship between paternal certainty and father-child contact, but the model requires clarification and further testing before its significance becomes evident.

Rule of inheritance is the most frequently utilized indirect measure of human paternal investment in holocultural studies of the hypothesis that paternal certainty is directly correlated with paternal investment. The simplest prediction is that in societies with low paternal certainty, rules of inheritance concerning Ego's property will favor individuals other than the offspring of Ego's wife. This prediction is usually tested by contrasting rules of patrilineal inheritance against rules of matrilineal inheritance. There have been at least five holocultural tests of this prediction.

(1) Hartung (1976): Societal attitude toward female premarital sexual activity is used as an indirect measure of paternal certainty. The twelve societies in the sample with matrilineal descent rules do tend to exhibit a permissive attitude toward such activity. However, Hartung does not demonstrate that societies with other descent rules exhibit more restrictive attitudes.

(2) Van den Berghe (1979): The prediction is tested three times, employing three indirect measures of p that were coded by Broude and Greene (1976) for the SCCS (frequency of rape, level of female extramarital sex, and the presence of culturally sanctioned wife-sharing). In each test, societies scored as exhibiting low p tend to have nonpatrilineal descent rules.

(3) Gaulin (1980): For the SCCS, Gaulin constructs a measure of male parental certainty, utilizing scores on three variables rated by Broude and Greene (1976): presence or absence of a double standard concerning extramarital sexual activity, level of female extramarital sexual activity, and culturally sanctioned wife-sharing. With this measure, he tests the hypothesis that agricultural societies are characterized by high p, while hunting-gathering societies exhibit low p. The logic of this prediction is that agricultural work allows males to monitor their mates more effectively than is possible in hunting-gathering societies. Although the distribution of cases falls into the predicted pattern, the results do not reach statistical significance. Gaulin then tests the correlation between subsistence regime and

rules of inheritance, demonstrating that inheritance rules favor the offspring of a man's spouse in agricultural societies (assumed high p), but not in hunting-gathering societies (assumed low p).

Gray and Wolfe (1981) note that some of Gaulin's coding decisions invalidate his test results. For example, societies scored as having no property to be inherited, usually hunting-gathering groups, were rated as having inheritance rules favoring individuals other than spouse's offspring. With these societies eliminated from the sample, no association between subsistence regime and inheritance rules is evident, and that sociobiological hypothesis is not supported.

(4) Gaulin and Schlegel (1980): Tests with the SCCS indicate that low p (measured by the scale applied in Gaulin 1980) is associated with the following conditons: (1) inheritance rules that do not favor wife's offspring; (2) rules of succession to headmanship that do not favor patrilineal relatives; (3) residence rules which are likely to be mother-centered or mother's brother-centered; and (4) descent rules oriented toward female lines. Each of these associations is offered as support for the validity of parental investment theory.

Wolfe and Gray (1981) criticize this study on methodological grounds. For example, there are few societies in the SCCS with data on all three of the variables comprising Gaulin's measure of male paternal certainty, and it is impossible to derive accurately the missing data when scores for only one or two variables are present. Gaulin's decision on how to handle the missing data rendered the scores on the independent variable invalid. When tests were redone, making use of only those societies for which there were complete data, none of the hypotheses was supported.

(5) Flinn (1981a): In the study that was discussed in Chapter Four, Flinn demonstrates that societies with low scores on his "confidence of paternity" variable tend to exhibit a uterine flow of altruism. Rules of inheritance are included in Flinn's flow of altruism variable.

Although these studies do seem to provide impressive support for the sociobiological position, I believe that methodological and theoretical problems undermine this support. The most important methodological problem is the use of indirect measures of paternal certainty and investment. Thus, it is not clear that the Barry and Paxson (1971) codes on father-child contact provide an adequate measure of paternal investment. Alcorta's (1982) finding that degree of contact varies inversely with population density suggests that father-child contact may be an artifact of the number of alternative places where a male may spend his time. In low-density societies (usually hunting-gathering groups, see Murdock and Wilson 1972), there are few alternatives to the campsite, and males may be in contact with many children, not just their own. Since this contact does not prevent males from investing in other offspring, it is doubtful that father-child contact as coded by Barry and Paxson is a good measure of paternal investment. The measure may be made more useful by controlling for the number of alternative places where a male may spend time, but this has not yet been done.

Use of inheritance rules as a measure of parental investment is also not without difficulty. Individuals may circumvent rules by distributing resources, especially movable property, before death. Males in matrilineal societies may provide their sons and daughters with resources that should go to their sisters' offspring. (Question: Have these males achieved high paternal certainty?) Also, the value of inherited property for the fitness of individuals may vary from society to society; receiving songs and spells from one's maternal uncle may not have the same fitness effects as receiving a few cattle from a father's herd.

Finally, the indirect measures of paternal certainty that are used in most holocultural tests are also not very satisfying. Frequency of rape, attitude toward female premarital sexual activity, marriage form (monogamy versus polygyny), and presence of culturally sanctioned wife-sharing do not appear to be adequate measures of the general level of p in a society. Level of female extramarital sexual activity is probably a better indicator, as long as we realize that most ethnographers provide only the most impressionistic data on this topic.

The need for adequate measures of p is related to the major theoretical difficulty with the material under review. The basic argument is that if paternal certainty is low, males investing in the offspring of their spouses will, on average, achieve lower inclusive fitness than those investing in children produced by a relative (usually a sister). For example, assuming they are full siblings, a male is related to the offspring of his sister by at least 0.25, while his relatedness to his wife's children may range from zero to 0.50, depending on paternal certainty. A major question is how low paternal certainty must become before a male should divert resources to individuals other than his spouse's offspring.

Sociobiologists have addressed this problem mathematically with reference to the "mother's brother phenomenon" of matrilineal inheritance. Depending upon the assumptions of the model, it is worthwhile for males to adopt a strategy of investing in their sisters' children in preference to their wives' children when paternal certainty falls below 0.268 (Greene 1978; Hartung 1981) or 0.333 (Flinn 1981a). How often is this low level reached in the ethnographic record? Hartung notes that at these levels of p males will achieve twice as much reproductive success with the wives of other men as they will with their own wives. Such a situation is unlikely. In fact, Flinn (1981a) rates only three societies (Nayar, Minangkabau, Toda) out of over three hundred as exhibiting paternal certainty under 0.333. With reference to the indirect measures of paternal certainty utilized in holocultural tests, it is unlikely that many of the societies in the SCCS would fail to reach the 0.333 level of p that is required for investment in wife's offspring to be the most productive investment strategy.

The fact that it is extremely unlikely that many human societies will exhibit a p below 0.333 (or even 0.5) has prompted some sociobiologists to search for alternative explanations of the mother's brother phenomenon. Flinn (1981a:447–450) argues that pressure from uterine kin and competition among agnatic kin may create the phenomenon, even if p is greater than one-third. Several authors (Flinn 1981a; Hartung 1981, 1983; Kurland 1979) argue that high divorce rates may favor investment in uterine kin even when p is high. Flinn (1981a) tests this in his sample and finds the prediction to be supported.

The most interesting analysis of the mother's brother phenomenon is found in two papers by Hartung (1981, 1983). Hartung (1981) argues that the 0.268 level of paternal certainty is important only if we restrict our attention to the generation immediately following the male in question. If additional descending generations are included, the picture changes. He calculates that with an intergenerationally stable paternal certainty of 0.725, a man will share more genes that are identical by descent with his third-generation matrilineal heir than with his wife's putative son's son. However, in a later paper, Hartung (1983) retracts this analysis, noting that computer simulations indicate that, on the average, the inclusive fitness advantages that accrue in later generations to males with moderate paternal certainty who invest in their sisters' children will never offset the fitness losses suffered by the failure of these males to invest in their wives' offspring in the first descending generation.

Hartung's later paper (1983) contains an analysis of the fitness benefits of the mother's brother phenomenon to females. He demonstrates that whenever paternal certainty falls below 1.0, females should favor matrilineal inheritance. Inheritance passed through males may be "wasted" on spouses' offspring who are not descendants of the original female; a problem that can be avoided by tracing inheritance through females. Hartung's argument implies that matrilineal inheritance should be more widespread than is indicated by a focus on the 0.268 or 0.333 figures for paternal certainty. In fact, his analysis raises the question of why matrilineal inheritance is not more common in the ethnographic record, since it is always beneficial to females. Of course, it is only beneficial to males when p is very low. Future research should be directed toward discovering conflicts between the investment strategies of males and females and identifying the factors that determine which sex wins such conflicts.

Hartung has also analyzed how patrilineal societies might cope with the problem of low paternal certainty. He suggests (1981) that in some of these societies, brother inheritance may be a coping mechanism. In this system, the eldest in a group of brothers passes property on to his younger brother, who then passes it on to a still younger brother, and so on, until the last brother in the generational set is reached. At that point, the property returns to the eldest son of the eldest brother. Hartung argues that when p is less than 1.0, a male shares more genes identical by descent with his brothers than with any other potential male heir and thus would benefit in terms of inclusive fitness by investing in his brothers.

A possible objection to this logic is anticipated by Hartung when he notes that the average level of p rarely reaches 1.0 in any society, and that we therefore would expect patrilineal brother inheritance in all societies without matrilineal descent. He rejects this argument by noting that at the time of an average father's death his son may be near his reproductive prime, while the father's next oldest sibling is probably past his prime. The son's higher reproductive value will bring greater inclusive fitness benefits to the father in societies where p is not too much less than 1.0, and therefore property will be passed on to the son, and not to the brother (note that this explanation does not explain why Ego could not pass his property on to younger brothers, who were closer to their reproductive prime).

Hartung argues that in holocultural tests of the relationship between p and inheritance practices, societies with patrilineal brother inheritance should be grouped with societies with matrilineal inheritance rules to comprise the category of societies with inheritance rules predicted by low paternal certainty. A careful holocultural test, utilizing twenty-two societies in the SCCS, shows that low p is indeed associated with this category.

Gray and Wolfe (1982a) criticize Hartung's article on the grounds that his test does not control for the influence of mode of descent. In a revised sample of thirty-one societies, they find that only two societies exhibited brother inheritance, while eight nonmatrilineal societies with low levels of p did not exhibit this practice. The authors suggest that Hartung's test actually reveals only that matrilineal societies tend to be characterized by low p, while nonmatrilineal societies pass property on to "wife's offspring," even in the face of high paternal uncertainty.

Hartung (1983) presents another test of the association between p and inheritance practices. The author notes that an alternative means by which patrilineal societies may cope with low paternal certainty is to pass on inheritance to both sons and daughters. He suggests that the fairest test of the hypothesis that high p is correlated with inheritance directed toward wife's offspring is to contrast societies with matrilineal inheritance against only those societies where inheritance goes solely to a male's sons. Hartung uses Flinn's (1981a) confidence of paternity codings and finds that out of twenty-two societies with moderate or lower confidence ($p < 0.80$), seventeen exhibit matrilineal inheritance; while forty-five of the forty-eight societies with high or very high confidence provide inheritance only to sons. While the limitations of Flinn's codes should be kept in mind when these results are interpreted, they provide strong support for Hartung's argument.

Investment Strategies of Couples
A second topic in positive human parental investment concerns the married couple as a source of investment. Some researchers explore conflicts over investment strategies within the couple, while others raise the issue of how a

couple might optimally distribute resources. Two studies by Hartung (1976, 1982a) illustrate the latter topic. In the earlier article, he suggests that two factors combine to make greater investment in sons than in daughters rewarding for both members of a couple. In the first place, in most societies variance in reproductive success is greater for males than for females. This will create a masculine bias in investment under two conditions. First, if sons and daughters have equal chances of finding mates prior to the distribution of parental wealth, and if resources can be used in mating effort, then the fact that males can increase their reproductive success through additional matings, while females generally cannot, means that both parents are better off investing in sons. The second condition occurs, if the sexes differ in mating opportunity prior to the distribution of parental wealth, their daughters are usually more likely to find mates, regardless of resources; while access to parental resources may be the difference between finding a mate or not for sons. Again, both parents are better off investing in the sons.

The second factor discussed by Hartung is the male's certainty that the Y chromosome possessed by his genetic son is identical by descent to his own (as is that of his grandson, etc., as long as paternal certainty is 1.0). This means that a male gains a little "extra" benefit by investing in sons rather than in daughters. Hartung argues that his analysis is supported by the fact that the societies in the *Ethnographic Atlas* exhibit a male bias in inheritance more frequently than would be expected by chance.

Hartung (1982a) examines the relationship between variance in reproductive success and inheritance rules. A holocultural test demonstrates that marriage in polygynous societies usually requires bridewealth. Since male variance in reproductive success is highest in polygynous societies, parents benefit if they provide the resources that allow sons to obtain wives. Hartung predicts that polygynous societies will exhibit a male bias in inheritance, while monogamous societies (usually lacking bridewealth) will exhibit no sex bias. The prediction is supported in an excellent holocultural study that makes use of both the *Ethnographic Atlas* and the SCCS.

Studies of conflict over parental investment have been conducted with samples in the United States and Canada. Van den Berghe (1979) shows (1) that as pair bonds become less stable, the number of children who live in households with only one parent increases, and (2) that the major investing parent is usually the mother. Itzkowitz and Nyby (1981) note that the age of the child is a major factor in child custody suits. They argue that when children are young, maternal investment is important, and that therefore the interests of the father and mother coincide. However, as the child ages, maternal investment becomes less vital, and fathers are expected to sue more often for custody. Analysis of 176 child-custody suits in Pennsylvania and of U.S. Census data shows that the likelihood of a male being the head of a single-parent household increases with the age of the child, supporting the authors' argument.

In an innovative study, Daly and Wilson (1982b) relate paternal certainty to child-naming practices and to judgments on the resemblance of infants to adults. They viewed videotapes of 111 births and found that people more often assert infant resemblance to father than to mother. Mothers assert paternal resemblance more often than fathers. These findings are interpreted as attempts by mothers to increase the level of male paternal certainty, thereby guaranteeing paternal investment. A questionnaire study in Canada replicates these results and indicates that child-naming practices may be viewed in the same light, with the mother and her relatives more likely than the father and his relatives to favor a paternal name for the child. The authors also suggest that maternal concern over paternal investment is greatest at the birth of the first child, and they predict that maternal relatives will assert paternal resemblance more frequently for first-born than later-born children. This prediction is supported by the questionnaire responses.

The studies reviewed in this section are clearly preliminary and are perhaps too slight to be convincing. However, they do suggest interesting new areas of research in human social behavior. Hartung's work is especially important, for it demonstrates that the reproductive potential of offspring is an important component in the parental investment strategies of couples. Since this potential is influenced by demographic and life history factors, Hartung's work also indicates the complexity of testing precise predictions regarding parental investment. The work on conflict over investment also identifies a major complication in testing such predictions. Recognition that the fitness interests of females do not always coincide with those of their mates when it comes to the distribution of family property should generate more research on maternal investment strategies and thus serve to correct the existing overemphasis on paternal strategies.

TESTS OF INFANTICIDE AND CHILD ABUSE

The sociobiological approach to infanticide and child abuse argues that the inclusive fitness interests of the perpetrator is the key to understanding these behaviors. When an individual kills a child who is not his offspring, the situation is usually explained as a tactic in the reproductive strategy of the killer. In contrast, when parents kill offspring, the explanation usually centers on the problem of the optimal distribution of parental investment. Although infanticide by nonparents could be discussed in the chapter on reproductive strategy, I am reviewing it in this section because it is most frequently discussed in the context of parental care and adult male-infant interaction.

Infanticide by Nonparents
The most important work on nonparental infanticide is Hrdy's analysis of male langur infanticide as a reproductive strategy (1974, 1977, 1979, 1981a,

1982). There were scattered reports of infanticide in the alloprimate literature prior to her work (see Angst and Thommen 1977; Hrdy 1979; and Itani 1982 for reviews), but her analysis sparked interest in the topic and has resulted in more frequent reporting of infanticide (Butynski 1982; Goodall 1977; Harcourt, Fossey, and Sabater-Pi 1981; Nishida et al. 1979; Rijksen 1981; Timmermans et al. 1981).

Hrdy sees infanticide by langur males as an evolved adaptive behavior. In the troop she observed at Abu, the takeover of a harem by a male was often followed with the deaths of infants in the days after the ouster of the previous holder. Hrdy observed males attempting to take infants from their mothers in the days prior to the infants' deaths. She argues that two facts can explain the evolutionary logic of this pattern. First, a male who takes possession of a unimale troop may have only a limited time to achieve reproductive success, since he may soon be ousted by another male. Any behavior allowing a male to maximize reproductive success during his tenure might therefore be selected. Second, in many alloprimates, nursing prevents ovulation, and females who are lactating when a new male gains a troop are reproductively unavailable to him until their infants are weaned. A male who allows infants sired by the previous holder to mature faces the possibility of being ousted before impregnating the mothers of those infants—"wasting" his tenure. In some species, however, the death of a nursing infant will cause the mother to resume cycling. In these species, infanticide might allow a male to impregnate such females early in his tenure. Since the victims were sired by the previous holder, the infanticides have no costs for the killer (unless females defend the infants, or unless the previous holder is related to the new holder).

Many factors are implicated in Hrdy's explanation of langur infanticide. These include the average tenure length of males (which may vary inversely with population density), how fast females resume ovulating after losing their infants (which may relate to resource availability), the willingness of females to defend infants, and so on. Chapman and Hausfater (1979) model some of these factors in computer simulations and they find that infanticidal males always have a reproductive advantage in populations where the majority of males are noninfanticidal. While the infanticidal strategy is not optimal at all tenure lengths in populations where most males kill infants, it is greatly advantageous at most; and when it is disadvantageous, it is only slightly so. The simulations thus suggest that under the proper conditions, a reproductive strategy with an infanticidal component could spread in a langur population.

Hrdy's analysis has been rejected by a number of authors (Boggess 1980; Curtain 1977; Curtain and Dolhinow 1978, 1979; Dolhinow 1977; Laws and Laws 1984; Schubert 1982; see also Fedigan 1982; Wheatley 1982). A common response notes that infant killings have rarely been observed by primatologists, and that therefore the identity of the perpetrator must usually be inferred. A second response is to point out that not all langur populations exhibit the social structure observed by Hrdy at Abu. For example, Laws and Laws (1984) find little aggression between males of bisexual and all-male troops and no infanticide among langurs at Rajaji. The literature cited earlier in this paragraph describes several other populations where troop takeover patterns differ from those at Abu. Of course, the meaning of this variation is open to different interpretations. It may be that the genes that are relevant to the infanticidal strategy are not present in troops where infant killing has not been observed. This would not invalidate Hrdy's argument that the behavior is an evolved adaptive strategy in the populations where it does occur. It could also be argued that there are no interpopulational variation in the genes that are relevant to infanticide, but that the practice is a facultative trait, and that troops where infant killing has not been observed do not generate the proximate cues necessary to elicit its expression.

A third response to Hrdy's argument is the alternative explanation that infanticide is not an evolved adaptive trait, but rather only an epiphenomenon of the social chaos that is created when langurs are subjected to stress, especially the destruction of their habitat by humans. Hrdy (1979) notes that this social pathology hypothesis does not explain why only the infants at the time of a takeover are victims of infanticide. In an attempt to test the two hypotheses, she examines studies of langurs at ten sites and finds that troop takeovers with infanticide are not correlated with a measure of human disturbance of habitat, but are positively correlated with population density. She argues that this result does not support the social pathology hypothesis, but is congruent with the reproductive strategy analysis, since higher population density is probably associated with shorter male tenure.

The reproductive strategy theory of infanticide raises some interesting questions. One is how infanticidal males manage to avoid harming their own relatives. Curtain and Dolhinow (1978) note that langur males sometimes take over troops where they have previously sired offspring and thus might accidentally kill relatives. Hrdy (1979) discusses evidence that among alloprimate males, familiarity with females may act as a proximate cue to prevent infanticide. Experimental studies of infanticide in mice (e.g., Huck et al. 1982; Jakubowski and Terkel 1982) also support the hypothesis that infanticide is prevented when males are familiar with the mothers of infants.

A second question is that of female counterstrategies to male infanticidal tendencies. Hrdy (1979, 1981a) describes several such strategies that are exhibited by langurs. For example, if an infant has a potential reproductive value greater than the costs of defending it against a determined infanticidal male, its mother may choose to fight the male. In some troops, older females have been observed to defend infants against males, a behavior which can be explained through nepotism theory, as the infants are probably closely related to these females. Hrdy also suggests that females who are pregnant when a takeover occurs may exhibit "sham-estrus" and copulate with the new male. If prior association or sexual contact with a female is a proximate cue preventing infanticide, sham-estrus may result in the female's infant not being harassed by the new holder.

Research with nonprimates has identified female counterstrategies which further investigation might reveal as existing in some species of allo-primates. Packer and Pusey (1983a,b) note that after a takeover, female lions exhibit great sexual activity with the new males, initiating copulations more frequently and copulating with more of the holders than they did with the previous males. In spite of this sexual activity, however, females exhibit a period of infertility after a takeover. Packer and Pusey suggest that the females may be testing the ability of a particular coalition to hold the pride for the time that is required for a set of cubs to mature. The increased sexual activity may incite competition between male coalitions (see Cox and LeBoeuf 1977), resulting in the "best" coalition (i.e., the one with the greatest probability for long tenure) finally gaining the pride. Such a pattern has not been described for an alloprimate species, but we have very few data on the reactions of females to takeovers. Butynski (1982) argues that for many alloprimates, the length of male tenure is the critical determinant of female, as well as male, inclusive fitness. This argument suggests that a search for the mechanisms that allow females to judge a male's ability to achieve a lengthy tenure and for the processes by which females influence male tenure might provide some interesting results.

A final example of female counterstrategies is induced abortions. Berger (1983) has described this pattern for wild horses, and Pereira (1983) observed three miscarriages after the immigration of an adult male into a troop of savanna baboons.

While the reproductive strategy and social pathology hypotheses have been studied most thoroughly as explanations of infanticide, Hrdy (1979) notes that the killing of infants by nonparents is widespread among animals and that it probably does not have a unitary explanation. She discusses two other hypotheses which may be relevant to some cases of alloprimate infanticide. The exploitation hypothesis argues that the death of infants may be the direct or indirect result of their value as resources to others. In the case of cannibalism to obtain food, the infant's death is obviously a direct goal of the killer (Goodall 1977). In contrast, when infants are utilized as "buffers" in agonistic encounters, the death of the infant may be an accidental by-product of the situation. In cases where a female "aunts" an infant to death, either by abusing it or by allowing it to starve through preventing the mother from retrieving it, it is difficult to say whether the death was "intended" or not and also to judge whether or not the behavior is a tactic in a strategy to maximize inclusive fitness (Wasser and Barash 1981).

The resource competition hypothesis holds that the killing of unrelated or distantly related infants may lower competition for resources that are needed by the killer and/or his relatives. It is frequently difficult to identify the resources that might be at stake, but food, territory, mates, and parental investment have been suggested in various cases. A resource competition hypothesis may explain either intragroup infanticide or the "xenophobic" killing of infants belonging to other groups (Itani 1982).

The explanation of nonparental infanticide among alloprimates as an evolved adaptive behavior is one of the most widely cited examples of sociobiological theory. Although the nature of the behavior means that the empirical data will continue to be rather limited, the sociobiological interpretation seems to be gaining ground among researchers. One reason for this gain is the number of reports of infanticide that have been published since Hrdy's original contribution. Many of these seem to validate the suggestion that males tend to kill infants they could not have sired. Especially important here is Butynski's (1982) report of takeover-associated infanticide among blue monkeys in Kibale Forest, Uganda. Since population density is not extremely high and human habitat disturbance is almost nil, the social pathology hypothesis does not seem to apply to this case. However, while unsystematic reviews of infanticide do support the reproductive strategy hypothesis, it should be noted that a demonstration of the ability of infanticide to increase the reproductive success of males requires long term data, and these are not available for any troop at present.

Infanticide and Child Abuse by Parents

Although it seems impossible that infanticide by parents could be an adaptive strategy, Alexander (1974) argues that there are at least four situations in which such behavior might be selected: (1) when the environment constantly and rapidly changes, creating the possibility that offspring produced at one time cannot all survive a period of lower resource availability; (2) when children are malformed or otherwise defective (i.e., have low reproductive value); (3) when limited resources force parents to space children; and (4) when parents utilize infanticide to adjust the sex ratio of their offspring. Although each of these factors has been implicated in primate infanticide, none has been the subject of empirical tests. The major sociobiological contribution to this topic concerns sex ratio theory, which will be discussed below under that heading.

The alloprimate literature does contain examples of mothers abusing their infants, and it is possible that some of these cases might be explained by parental investment theory. Thus, if as suggested earlier, mothers in some species attempt to foster independence in their infants, their behavior may result in situations which an observer would describe as abusive. However, this topic is fraught with both methodological and theoretical difficulties. What appears as a case of abuse may be an evolved behavioral strategy on the part of the mother, but it may also be the result of a female's inexperience with infants or her failure to develop adequate maternal skills. At present, no study has empirically tested a sociobiological hypothesis for offspring abuse among alloprimates.

Data on child abuse and neglect in the United States and other industrial countries are applied to test parental investment theory by Daly and Wilson (1981), Lenington (1981), and Lightcap et al. (1982). These studies generally support the hypothesis that considerations of paternal certainty, reproductive value of children, and extent of parental resources are involved in child abuse and neglect.

Daly and Wilson (1981) analyze statistics on child abuse in several countries and find that households with parent substitutes (stepparents or foster parents) are more likely to exhibit child abuse than households composed of biological parents. Further, male substitutes are especially likely to abuse children. Both results are consistent with parental investment theory's argument that individuals will be less likely to invest in offspring produced by nonrelatives.

Daly and Wilson also find an inverse relationship between family income and risk of abuse. It may be that poorer families must limit distribution of resources to the reproductively most valuable children, and that the abuse of other children is the outcome of this situation. Finally, the authors show that in Australia, England, and the United States, children with congenital handicaps are at a greater risk of abuse than other children. Presumably, the former have lower reproductive value.

The proximate mechanisms of child abuse and neglect interest Daly and Wilson, who argue that at least some of the variance in these behaviors can be explained as a result of the lack or disruption of a parent-offspring attachment process. For example, due to medical problems, children with congenital handicaps often do not interact with their parents immediately after birth. Stepparents may not meet the children of their mates until the children are quite old, and the bonding process may be weak or absent. Although disruption of an attachment process is certainly a plausible hypothesis for abuse, it should be noted that the hypothesis of a critical period for human attachment has recently been subjected to numerous critiques (see Lamb 1983).

Lenington's (1981) review of the child abuse literature replicates many of Daly and Wilson's results. She also examines the relationship between reproductive value and child abuse by investigating the factors of birth order and age. She argues that as a child ages, his reproductive value increases, making it less likely that parents will abuse him. Her prediction that younger children are at greater risk of abuse is supported in a number of the studies she reviews. Also supported by several studies of child abuse cases in southern states is Lenington's argument that since the reproductive value of children born later in the birth order is lower than that of their earlier-born siblings, the former will be at greater risk of abuse. Lenington notes that the lower reproductive value of later-borns may result from the association between either high birth order and physical defects or large family size and low family income.

Finally, Lenington finds that males are at greater risk of abuse during childhood, but that during adolescence, females run greater risks. She argues that this finding supports the Trivers and Willard (1973) suggestion that in economic circumstances where parental investment in all children is not possible, daughters are a surer investment than sons (see below). Unfortunately, Lenington does not examine the correlation between sex of child and abuse risk when controlling for socioeconomic status. The Trivers and Willard argument leads us to expect that middle-class and upper-class families will exhibit a different pattern of abuse than lower-class families.

Lightcap et al. (1982) utilize a sample of twenty-four rural Pennsylvania, two-parent households, in each of which there was at least one victim of child abuse, and replicate most of the results of the two previous studies. They find that stepchildren are at higher abuse risk than natural children, and that when an abusive parent has both natural children and stepchildren available, he or she almost always abuses the latter. In line with parental certainty theory, males are more likely than females to be abusers; a finding which holds even when the stepchild versus natural child factor is controlled. Handicapped children are more likely to be abused than children without handicaps. Finally, males are at higher risk than females, although the difference does not reach statistical significance.

A result of the Lightcap et al. (1982) study contradicts Lenington's (1981) finding that younger children are at greater risk of abuse than older children. Lightcap et al. find the opposite situation in their sample. They explain this result with Trivers' (1974) parent-offspring conflict model (see below), suggesting that older offspring may object when parents start investing in newly born children. The authors do not reject Lenington's reproductive value model, but rather note that risk of abuse exhibits a trimodal distribution, with peaks at early infancy, at two years of age, and again around puberty. They suggest that their interpretation is relevant to the last peak.

While these three studies of child abuse support parental investment theory, there are problems with each. First, the data exhibit numerous shortcomings. Is abuse really less common in higher-income families, or just more subtle and/or easier to hide from authorities? Are daughters really abused less than sons, or are they less likely to report abuse to outside agencies? Second, sociobiologists themselves have raised the redundancy problem. Lenington (1981) suggests that her results can be explained by postulating that humans seek to maximize economic resources. While an inclusive fitness and an economic interpretation are not mutually exclusive

(Irons 1979b), Lenington asks why we should accept the former if the economic alternative is convincing. She sees this as an important question, because:

> ... although it is possible to present very plausible arguments for the adaptive significance of child abuse, it has not been possible, and it would be extraordinarily difficult to show that individuals who abuse their children are, in fact, increasing their reproductive success. The entire sociobiological argument, in this case, rests on plausibility [Lenington 1981:26].

As a way of answering this criticism, Lenington lists seven predictions on the patterning of abuse, all of which are logical deductions from an evolutionary explanation, but are not predicted by an economic model. As of yet, these predictions have not been tested.

Lightcap et al. (1982) are also concerned with the redundancy problem and argue that sociobiological theory makes two predictions which non-evolutionary models of child abuse do not make: (1) that males are abusers and victims more frequently than females; and (2) that individuals do not indiscriminately abuse all of the children in a household. Neither example is particularly convincing. For example, a Freudian interpretation centered on the Oedipal aspects of parent-child relations predicts both a male bias in abusers and victims and parental discrimination in abuse. Lightcap et al. also disagree with Lenington on the necessity of demonstrating that child abuse increases the inclusive fitness of abusers:

> Genetic relatedness and benefits and costs to both parents therefore importantly *condition* parental behavior. It is not reasonable to conclude, however, that child abuse (or neglect) is "adaptive". It may be that even when social interactions break down the resulting patterns still exhibit some aspects of an evolutionary logic that ordinarily underlies the organism's more adaptive behavior [Lightcap et al. 1982:66].

The contrasting views of Lenington and Lightcap et al. illustrate the confusion that surrounds the topic of child abuse. The confusion is magnified by the fact that it is not clear just what must be explained. Parental investment theory might explain how evolved patterns of parental investment could result in the failure of parents to invest in certain children (i.e., through infanticide or neglect). However, the theory does not explain why parents would abuse the children in whom they are investing resources, especially given the risks of the activity. Although the possibility cannot be ruled out, it is unlikely that active abuse is merely the result of "deflected" infanticidal tendencies. It is possible that future research on the life history consequences of child abuse may clear up this problem:—e.g., Do abused children leave home earlier than nonabused children, or do they fail to claim inheritance rights? Focus on the proximate causes of child abuse might help to clarify the problem. Until such research is conducted, we are left only with the finding that patterns of child abuse do appear to be congruent with the predictions of parental investment theory.

TESTS OF PARENT-OFFSPRING CONFLICT

The idea of a genetic basis for parent-offspring conflict appears to be paradoxical. Offspring are the parents' pathways to reproductive success, and it seems logical that the interests of the offspring will overlap with those of the parents, making conflict minimal. Where conflicts do occur, they are usually seen as the results of the naiveté of the offspring being corrected by the wisdom of the parents. For example, a conflict may arise over dependency, since the naive infant may desire to remain dependent upon the parents; but the latter, knowing the facts of life, force independence upon the child. In a groundbreaking paper, Trivers (1974) uses inclusive fitness theory to question this image of the parent-offspring relationship and to suggest that conflict between parents and offspring may be genetically based in that it results from each party seeking to maximize its inclusive fitness. He argues that parents often attempt to coerce offspring to behave in manners that are detrimental to the offsprings' inclusive fitness, but beneficial to that of the parents. Similarly, offspring may seek to engage in behaviors that increase their own inclusive fitness but reduce that of their parents.

The core of parent-offspring conflict theory is that Ego is related to her parents and full siblings by an r of 0.5, but to herself by an r of 1.0. She will be related to her own offspring by 0.5 and to those of her siblings by 0.25 (assuming paternal certainty of 1.0). These figures are contrasted with an r of 0.5 by which a parent is related to each of its offspring. Trivers argues that parents will frequently desire to invest resources to create additional offspring. These siblings can provide Ego with nephews and nieces who are related to her by 0.25. However, if Ego can convince her parents to invest these resources in herself, rather than in potential siblings, Ego can produce offspring related to her by 0.5. As long as Ego's actions bring her at least twice the extra fitness lost by a (potential) sibling who would have received the resources, Ego is expected to "selfishly" demand parental investment. Trivers notes that conflict is therefore inevitable:

> As long as one imagines that the benefit/cost ratio of a parental act changes continuously from some large number to some very small number near zero, than there must occur a period of time during which $\frac{1}{2} < B/C < 1$. This period is one of expected conflict between mother and offspring, in the sense that natural selection working on the mother favors her halting parental investment while natural selection acting on the offspring favors his eliciting the parental investment [Trivers 1974:251].

Several factors determine the form of parent-offspring conflict that is found in a species. Trivers notes that there may be several different types of conflict: actors may differ over intensity of investment (e.g., how often an infant nurses), over when investment is terminated (e.g., when weaning occurs), or over behavioral tendencies (e.g., parents may attempt to socialize offspring to act more nepotistically than is optimal for the offspring's inclusive fitness). A second factor is the effect that time has on costs and benefits of behaviors. Behaviors that are vital to an infant become less important as it ages. Behaviors that cost the mother little when the offspring is young increase in cost without providing offsetting benefits as time passes (e.g., carrying behaviors). The life history stage of the mother also influences the course of conflict. Younger females may be less tolerant of demands for additional benefits, while older females with little chance for future reproduction may be more indulgent. A final factor involves the tactics that the participants employ in conflicts. Since parents control resources, it might appear that they would always win. However, Trivers notes that infants and children do have some weapons, especially psychological tactics. Timing, type of conflict, and the cost/benefit ratio all interact to determine the type and effectiveness of the tactics by the actors.

Breeding structure also plays a role in the genesis and intensity of parent-offspring conflict. In the example above, it is assumed that Ego can predict that her future siblings will be full siblings. If, however, they will be half-siblings, Ego should demand investment until the costs to these half-siblings exceed four times the benefits to herself. An interesting study would be to determine whether weaning conflict in alloprimates with monogamous or unimale breeding structures (assuming low rates of male replacement) is less intense or of shorter duration than that observed in species with promiscuous mating.

Before turning to primate studies of parent-offspring conflict, we should take note of a question which will probably stimulate more empirical research in the future. Under the heading of parental manipulation of offspring, Alexander (1974) raises many of the issues that were addressed by Trivers. In this paper, he opens the still controversial question of whether offspring might ever "win" parent-offspring conflicts and force their parents to provide investments which decrease the inclusive fitness of the parents. Alexander does not see this happening:

> The parent-offspring interaction is unlike most other kin selection situations for several reasons. First, the parent is usually bigger and stronger than the offspring, hence in a better position to impose its will. Second, the offspring is always in a position of benefiting from parental attention, and in some circumstances is wholly dependent upon the parent even for survival. Third, the entire parent-offspring interaction has evolved because it benefited one of the two individuals—the parent. No organism can evolve

parental behavior, or extend its parental care, unless its own reproduction is thereby enhanced. As a result, when a parental benefit is used by an offspring to increase its own inclusive fitness at the expense of that of the parent, selection will favor either retraction of the benefit or elimination of the "misuse" [Alexander 1974:340].

Alexander notes that an allele causing a child to increase its inclusive fitness at the expense of its parents would work against that child when she became a parent and therefore would not spread in a population. This does not mean that a child may not sometimes win behavioral conflicts with parents, only that victories by the child cannot occur at the genetic level. However, Alexander notes (1974:345) that offspring may win conflicts if they are better able than their parents to select behaviors that increase the parents' inclusive fitness. Mate selection in unpredictable environments might be an example of such a situation.

Alexander's contention that parents will always win parent-offspring conflicts has been rejected by a number of theorists (Blick 1977; Dawkins 1976, 1982; Parker and MacNair 1978; Stamps and Metcalf 1980; Stamps et al. 1978). Several mathematical models that demonstrate the spread of a "selfish offspring" allele in a population have been advanced. There is no need to discuss these models, but I will briefly examine their logic as exemplified in Blick's argument. Blick models a situation wherein parents produce a brood containing one selfish individual and a number of altruistic individuals. The gathering of additional parental investment by the selfish child increases his probability of survival to adulthood (PSA), while reducing that of the altruistic children. Blick writes:

> ... the allele who bearers have the greater average PSA will be the one to spread in a population. In this case (assuming random mating), the average PSA of selfish offspring is higher than that of altruistic offspring. This results in a greater proportion of altruists dying off between birth and reproductive maturity. Since we have assumed no other fitness effects, and because there is no difference in the number of children initially produced, the result is a spreading of the selfish trait [Blick 1977:598].

As noted by Kurland (1979), the fact that this situation may ultimately result in the extinction of the lineage bearing the selfish allele is irrelevant to the spread of the allele through the population. Both Blick and Kurland point out that the spread of a selfish allele is an excellent illustration of the difference between thinking on the level of the gene and on the level of the individual phenotype. While the trait in question is being selected against on the level of the individual, it is being selected for at the genetic level.

At present, the argument over the possibility of selfish offspring seems to be settled in favor of Alexander's critics, but the exact parameters of the problem and its relevance to the natural world remain unclear.

Studies Among Alloprimates

Little empirical work has been conducted on alloprimate parent-offspring conflict. There are, however, some literature surveys supporting certain components of the theory. Thus, Trivers (1974) argues that results of rhesus mother-infant separation studies (Hinde and Davies 1972a,b; Hinde and Spencer-Booth 1971) support the hypothesis that infants are alert to the investment tendencies of their mothers. When a mother who has been removed from her infant and the social group for six days is returned to the group, her infant spends more time on her than it did prior to the separation, even if the experiment occurs during a period when infants become increasingly independent of their mothers. Trivers suggests that the infant interprets the absence of its mother as an event over which she had control and one which could happen again; a possibility that the infant seeks to prevent by staying close to her. This suggestion is supported by two other findings of the separation studies. First, infants of mothers who were rejecting prior to separation spent more time with their mothers after re-union than infants whose mothers were not rejecting. Second, when infants are removed from their mothers and the group, they exhibit less distress and spend more time off the mothers after reunion. This result may be due to the fact that the experiment does not raise the issue of maternal investment intentions. Trivers argues that this type of complex psychological monitoring system may be the outcome of a selective history of parent-offspring conflict.

Tutin (1979) notes that copulation interference by juvenile chimpanzees is particularly intense when their mothers first resume sexual activity; a situation that Barash (1982:332) sees as congruent with parent-offspring conflict theory. However, the fact that female juveniles restrict interference to copulations of related individuals, while males also interfere with those of unrleated animals (Tutin and McGinnis 1981) clouds this picture. Barash also discusses Nash's (1978) study of maternal rejection by baboons in the light of parent-offspring conflict theory. Nash finds that conflict over rejection intensifies when the mother resumes sexual activity. Further, older mothers (with lower reproductive potential) are slower to reject infants than younger mothers. Finally, Alexander (1974) cites Lawick-Goodall (1967) on the absence of weaning conflict among chimpanzees as an apparent contradiction to the prediction that such conflict will be more intense in species that exhibit promiscuous mating.

The most detailed examination of parent-offspring conflict theory among alloprimates is Altmann's (1980) study of yellow baboon mothers and infants. She finds evidence for weaning conflict, including "tantrums," between the ages of four to six months. However, she questions whether the conflict model is relevant to her data, noting that birth patterns in many alloprimate species do not correspond to the model's assumptions. Sibships are small, and the sequential pattern of single births reduces the overlap between siblings. Models have been proposed to cope with this type of life history, but their validity has not yet been established with field data.

Altmann's most important question deals with the possible costs and benefits of behavior. She notes that any act that costs the mother inclusive fitness will do so in one, or both, of two ways. First, an act may increase the mother's risk of death, as might be the case if she foraged away from the group in order to gain enough nourishment to feed a demanding infant. Second, the act may delay the mother's return to sexual activity and/or her date of conception. Altmann points out that it is necessary to detail which behaviors the mother could change so as to provide extra parental care for offspring. For example, if the infant demands more care or nourishment, the mother might have to reduce her own feeding time to supply it. Extra care may require that the mother reduce her attention to the environment, thereby increasing her exposure to predation. Finally, if the mother reduces her transport time to care for an infant, she may lose contact with the group, again increasing her chances of death. Altmann concludes that each of these behaviors will also tend to result in harm to the infant and argues that behaviors with self-inflicted costs will not be demanded by the infant. She concludes:

> These immediately detrimental effects of any attempt by an infant to demand more of its mother, combined with an infant's increasing abilities to care for itself, abilities whose development is crucial to the infant's eventual independence, suggest that parent-offpsring genetic conflict of interest may arise infrequently as a relevant variable in many real-life situations [Altmann 1980:182].

Altmann also poses the question of whether genetic conflicts of interest will inevitably result in conflicts at the behavioral level and concludes that the answer is negative. She argues that in many cases, nonconflicting strategies may be more successful in obtaining extra investment. She suggests that the abilities to cooperate and compromise that are learned through finding peaceful solutions to parent-offspring conflicts may serve as a developmental basis for adult social interaction. Her speculations suggest that resolution of conflicts of interest through behavioral conflict might be more common in solitary and territorial alloprimates.

Undoubtedly, Altmann is correct in her observations on compromise and cooperation. However, there is a semantic problem here, which may trap the unwary. Trivers (1974) does focus on behaviors such as temper tantrums when he describes examples of parent-offspring conflicts of interest, but there is no reason why genetic conflicts cannot be resolved in favor of one party by behavioral sequences which observers would label as conflict-free. A child who uses smiles to obtain investment that parents should have directed elsewhere might have been in conflict with his parents on the genetic level and won, even though at the behavioral level no conflict occurs. Altmann notes the reverse situation when she points out that not all behavioral conflicts can be traced back to a conflict at the genetic level.

Altmann does not reject the possibility that parent-offspring conflict theory might be applicable to alloprimates. She is pointing out that we need more information on the costs and benefits of acts to the various participants and on the alternative behaviors between which animals may choose, as well as models with assumptions more closely in line with primate breeding systems, before any judgment can be made.

Horrocks and Hunte (1983) use a form of parent-offspring conflict theory to explain the acquisition of rank by female vervets. Vervet sisters exhibit an inverse correlation between birth order and rank, with the younger females usually outranking their older sisters. Schulman and Chapais (1980) argue that this phenomenon ("ascendency of the youngest") can be explained in terms of reproductive value. Mothers who seek to maximize the inclusive fitness returns for maternal investment should support the daughter with the greatest reproductive value at any given time. For macaque and vervet females, reproductive value is low at birth, rises until just prior to first parturition, and declines slowly thereafter. Schulman and Chapais argue that when the reproductive value of a younger female exceeds that of a slightly older sibling, a rank reversal occurs, with the mother supporting the younger female.

Horrocks and Hunte reject this interpretation, noting that rank reversals often occur before reversals in reproductive value. In fact, mothers often support younger females from birth, even before they obtain high reproductive value. The authors argue that if we view female offspring as potential competitors of the mother, the ascendency of the youngest may be seen as the result of a strategy whereby a mother prevents her daughters from forming coalitions and surpassing her in rank. By supporting younger daughters, the mother ensures that they will have little to gain by joining a coalition with their elder siblings. This strategy may also implicate nepotism theory, for in multimale troops and in unimale troops with short male tenure, each one of a female's daughters may have a different father.

Horrocks and Hunte (1983) support their position with data from a study of maternal aggression in vervet troops on Barbados. When mothers direct aggression toward their own offspring, the targets are usually (71.6 percent) daughters. Since males in this species disperse, they compete with their mothers for only a brief period of time. In contrast, daughters will be competitors for as long as their mothers stay in the troop. A second finding is that for pairs of sisters, older sisters receive more maternal aggression than their younger siblings. The authors also cite preliminary data which indicate that when mothers lack young daughters they often fall below their mature daughters in rank. Finally, when mothers are not present to support their younger daughters or are already outranked by their older daughters, the younger daughters frequently do not dominate their elder sisters.

Further work with vervets and with other species exhibiting the ascendency of the youngest is required before a judgment can be made on the relative validity of the reproductive value and the parent-offspring conflict hypotheses of this phenomenon. For the present, I will merely note that this is an instance where investigation of proximate mechanisms, in this case those of rank acquisition, is probably necessary to decide between two ultimate explanations of the same situation.

In summary, the evidence for the relevance of parent-offspring conflict theory to alloprimate social behavior is very weak. There are no holospecies studies of this topic, and the studies within single species have been less than convincing.

Studies Among Humans

Few studies of parent-offspring conflict among humans have been conducted, even though Trivers (1974) identifies the temper tantrums of two-year-olds as a tactic in such conflict, and although much of his discussion of the psychology of conflict concerns human behavior. As noted above, Lightcap et al. (1982) explain their finding that older children are frequently abused in spite of their greater reproductive value by arguing that these children may conflict with parents over the investment being directed toward younger siblings.

Hartung (1977) suggests that because Ego has the same r with a full sibling as with an offspring (0.5), parent-offspring conflict should not occur in species with mating systems which ensure that siblings are full siblings. He concludes that since humans manifest parent-offspring conflict, we could not have been functionally monogamous or polygynous for very long. Hartung cites some holocultural evidence for his position. For example, he predicts that as the probability that Ego's siblings are full siblings decreases, Ego will be less willing to aid them. In a very indirect test of this prediction, he notes Textor's (1967) finding that as the acceptibility of wife-lending in a society increases, the degree of diffusion among an infant's nurturant agents decreases.

In a later paper, Hartung (1980) retracts his theoretical discussion, noting that parent-offspring conflict will occur even in situations where all siblings are full siblings (see also Robinson 1980). For Ego, the investment of parental resources is not a choice between having full siblings or offspring, both with an r of 0.5. Rather, the real choice is between the investment going to Ego to produce offspring with an r of 0.5 or going to her full siblings to help them produce offspring with an r of only 0.25 with Ego. It should be noted that this retraction does not affect the prediction that Hartung tested with Textor's data.

One of the more interesting attempts to apply parent-offspring conflict theory to humans is Rubin et al.'s (1979) study on parental wealth and control of children. The core idea is that:

> We may distinguish three major forms in which individuals can hold their productive wealth—human capital (primarily investment in education), financial capital (stocks and bonds) and real capital (personally owned farms and businesses). As the form in which parents hold their wealth changes, there will be implications for intrafamily behavior. As more wealth is held in the form of human capital rather than in other forms of capital, parents have less wealth to leave as an estate for children. This implies that the control which parents can exert over children (through the possibility of disinheritance) falls [Rubin et al. 1979:54].

This argument is subjected to two tests. First, the authors predict that as the proportion of human wealth to total wealth increases, families should produce fewer children. As the threat of disinheritance as a means of controlling children declines in effectiveness, parents must spend more time with each child, inculcating values which will make them easier to control in later life. This additional time is gained by having fewer children. The prediction is tested with data from the National Longitudinal Surveys on households of American males from age forty-five to fifty-nine. The test shows that the husband's, wife's, and child's educational levels are each negatively correlated with the number of children in a family.

In the second test, Rubin et al. (1979) argue that when the proportion of human capital to total wealth rises, parents must more often provide for their own care through pension plans. Data from the United States between 1930 and 1970 indicate that as the proportion of high school graduates in the population increased, the number of people participating in private pension plans increased. As expected from the compulsory nature of the program, this relationship does not hold for the number of people participating in the Social Security System.

The results of the Rubin et al. study are interesting, although a large number of alternative explanations could be advanced to explain them. The model of parental manipulation of children through wealth suggests a number of tests that could be made in preindustrial societies. For example: Are signs of conflict less common in societies where inheritance rules are standardized (e.g., primogeniture) than in societies where parents have a free hand in distributing inheritance? How do the forms and intensity of conflict differ in societies with much heritable wealth and in those with little?

As with the alloprimates, the theory of parent-offspring conflict has the appearance of being relevant to many aspects of human social life, but the empirical support for the theory is very weak. Perhaps more than any other aspect of parental investment theory, this component requires precise measures of the cost/benefits of behaviors. An adequate test of the theory must demonstrate that conflict occurs when the fitness benefits to Ego of gathering additional parental investment are less than twice the fitness costs to his full siblings. A convincing test would show that once the costs to siblings exceeded twice the fitness gains obtained by Ego, conflict would cease, and Ego would demand no further parental investment. So far, no study among the primates has attempted this type of demonstration.

TESTS OF SEX RATIO THEORY

Introduction

Sex ratio theory is one of the most controversial topics in evolutionary biology (see Burley 1982; Charnov 1983; Clutton-Brock 1982; Clutton-Brock and Albon 1982; and Williams 1979 for reviews). Several models are available for the evolution of the population sex ratio and of the facultative adjustment of sex ratio by parents. I will deal only with the three that have been applied to primates: Fisher's model, the local resource competition model, and the Trivers-Willard model.

Fisher's (1930) model examines the evolution of the population sex ratio. It distinguishes cases where the sexes are equally costly to raise (in terms of parental investment) from those where one sex is more expensive. In the former case, Fisher demonstrates that the population sex ratio will be 50:50. If there is an imbalance, parents producing offspring of the rarer sex will achieve higher average reproductive success than those raising members of the more common sex. The greater success of the former will tend to make the rarer sex more common, until the 50:50 balance is reached. This is the ratio most commonly observed in nature.

When one sex requires greater parental investment, Fisher argues that the total amount of parental effort should be balanced, resulting in a population sex ratio favoring the "cheaper" sex. For example, differential mortality of the sexes during the period of parental investment is a factor that influences the expenditure of parental effort. Thus, in humans, males usually have a higher mortality rate during the period from conception to social adulthood (I leave aside the very real problem of when parental investment ceases for humans). If total investment in the sexes is to be equal, more males than females must be started, a prediction supported by the 105:100 sex ratio assumed to be characteristic of humans. Fisher's theory can be linked to sexual selection theory at this point, for in many species mortality due to mate competition characterizes the sex with the greater variance in reproductive success.

The local resource competition model is advanced by Clark (1978) to explain her finding that *Galago crassicaudatus* exhibits a sex ratio strongly biased toward males. Resources necessary for female survival (gum-producing trees and insect-attracting bushes) are both scarce and patchy. Further, during late pregnancy and early postpartum, female mobility is restricted. Clark suggests that females who produce daughters will compete with them for these resources. This is not true of females who produce sons, since males disperse from their natal area and are more mobile than females. Clark argues that Fisher's model does not apply in this case, because there is no high juvenile male mortality. However, Hoogland (1981) subsumes Clark's model under Fisher's by considering maternal investment in daughters after sons disperse. He suggests that mothers continue investing in daughters through nonreciprocal grooming, sharing knowledge of feeding and sleeping sites, and resource sharing. Presumably, this heavy investment in a few resident daughters equals the light investment in many dispersed sons.

The Trivers-Willard (1973) model deals with intrapopulational variation in sex ratio and applies to species where: (1) the reproductive success of one sex is more dependent than that of the other sex on a particular resource; and (2) individuals differ in their ability to provide this resource to their offspring. To explore the model, we can imagine a species with the following characteristics: (1) high variance in male reproductive success; (2) male reproductive success directly correlated with physical strength; (3) male physical strength directly correlated with maternal physical condition at conception; and (4) female reproductive success correlated with neither physical strength nor maternal condition. The Trivers-Willard model predicts that in this species, females in good physical condition will specialize in producing sons, while those in poor condition will produce daughters. These choices are explained by the potential reproductive success of the offspring. Mothers in poor condition will produce weak sons, with little chance of reproductive success. However, the physical state of the mothers in poor condition does not affect the reproductive potential of daughters; meaning that investment in females is more likely than investment in males to result in grandoffspring. In contrast, mothers in good condition who produce daughters are assured of grandoffspring, but on average receive no more than mothers in poor condition who produce daughters. Because sons of mothers in good condition are strong, however, they will have a high probability of obtaining mates and achieving great reproductive success. If variance in male reproductive success is large, mothers in good condition who produce sons obtain many more grandoffspring than those who invest in daughters.

Two factors complicate attempts to make predictions from the Trivers-Willard model. First, tendencies toward altruism may influence the probability of reproductive success. When members of one sex perform more acts benefiting kin of the opposite sex than vice versa, parents should invest more heavily in the altruistic sex. Second, Clutton-Brock and Albon (1982:224) emphasize the model's point that parental investment strategy depends upon whether or not the resources to be invested influence the reproductive potential of the sexes. When males exhibit great variance in reproductive success, but parental investment can only affect the reproductive fate of daughters, investment will be biased toward the females.

The possibility of intrapopulational regulation of sex ratio raises the problem of proximate mechanisms. Several have been suggested for primates. The one most under parental control is sex-biased infanticide. This appears to be a wasteful approach, because parents lose the investment that they have made up to the time of death. However, it is important to avoid the Concorde Fallacy (Dawkins and Brockmann 1980; Dawkins and Carlisle 1976): the decision to commit infanticide must be evaluated in light of its effects on the future inclusive fitness of the parents and not on the amount of past investment. Thus, if we return to the species previously discussed and add the condition that lactation suppresses ovulation, it is possible that a young mother in good condition might achieve greater inclusive fitness if she kills a new-born daughter in the hope that her next offspring will be a son. Of course, factors such as the life history stage of the mother must be taken into account when calculating costs and benefits of infanticide.

Other proximate mechanisms of sex ratio manipulation suggested for primates include the timing or frequency of copulation (for humans, see James 1980; Lawrence 1941) and prezygotic mechanisms involving factors such as motility of sperm and its resistance to acidity (Burley 1982). The possibility that animals may influence the sex ratio of offspring produced by other group members is suggested by data on harassment of pregnant females and immature animals. In a rhesus laboratory colony, Simpson et al. (1981) find that pregnant females carrying daughters receive more aggression than those carrying sons. In a captive pigtail macaque group, females pregnant with daughters are more likely to need medical attention for wounds than those carrying sons; females requiring medical attention are at a higher risk of spontaneous abortion and stillbirth (Sackett 1980; Sackett et al. 1975). Silk (1983) reviews studies of captive bonnets and free-ranging toque macaques (Dittus 1979, 1980) showing that immature females are more likely than immature males to be harassed by adults. Dittus finds that immature females are also more likely than males to be excluded from feeding sites. This combination resulted in the class of immature females suffering the highest rate of mortality during a drought (Altmann 1980:41 questions some of Dittus' assumptions, however). Silk, Samuels, and Rodman (1981) report that while much of the mortality among juvenile female bonnets results from aggression by adult females, this is not so in the case of the deaths of juvenile males.

Studies Among Alloprimates
Four studies have utilized alloprimate data to test propositions derived from sex ratio theory (Altmann 1980; Silk, Clark-Wheatly, Rodman, and Samuels 1981; Simpson and Simpson 1982; and Wolfe 1983; see also Silk 1983). To these should be added Clark's (1978) paper on local resource competition in galagos. Further, many studies contain data on differential treatment of male

and female infants and juveniles, which may reveal tactics in the service of sex ratio manipulation (especially important are Berman 1980; Cheney 1978; Dittus 1977, 1979, 1980; Kurland 1977; Pusey 1983; and Simpson et al. 1981).

Altmann's (1980) field study of yellow baboons contains a test of the Trivers-Willard model. She finds that high-ranking females tend to produce daughters (nineteen of twenty-nine births over seven years), while lower-ranking mothers tend to produce sons (fifteen of twenty-two births). If we assume that high rank equates with "better condition," this result contradicts the model. Altmann argues, however, that high-ranking mothers can affect the reproductive fates of daughters, but not those of sons. Since there is a positive correlation between maternal rank and daughter's position in the dominance hierarchy, a high-ranking female who produces a daughter can be confident that she will achieve high rank. If high rank confers an advantage in reproductive competition (e.g., access to food during short-ages, freedom from harassment), the daughter will obtain fitness benefits from this position. In contrast, males disperse from their natal troops, and their positions in other troops are not related to maternal rank, meaning that a high-ranking female producing a son cannot be sure he will achieve reproductive success. The certain success of daughters will, on the average, result in higher inclusive fitness than the uncertain fate of sons. The logic for a low-ranking mother is reversed. Her daughter will be at a reproductive disadvantage due to low rank, while her son will have the same uncertain reproductive future as males produced by high-ranking females. Depending upon the probability of male reproductive success, a low-ranking female might achieve higher inclusive fitness if she gambles on sons.

Altmann's test raises issues that are also relevant to the other studies on this topic. For example, exact probabilities of reproductive success for each sex-dominance class need to be calculated. Are daughters of lower-ranking females at such a great disadvantage compared to those of higher-ranking females? Altmann predicts that infant mortality rate will vary inversely with rank, but finds instead a statistically nonsignificant tendency for greater infant mortality among high-ranking mothers. Low-ranking mothers may experience more harassment than high-ranking females experience from animals interested in their infants. However, they appear to cope by being restrictive mothers and by staying near specific adult males (Altmann 1980). Altmann et al. (1978) show that restrictive mothers may not be at a reproductive disadvantage under normal ecological conditions, suggesting a minimal difference in the reproductive potential of females of different ranks.

Another issue is whether the reproductive success of sons is totally uncorrelated with maternal rank—e.g., might high-ranking mothers produce stronger or more socially adept sons? If there is some correlation, high-ranking females might do better to produce equal numbers of males and females. Furthermore, if there is a correlation between male success and maternal rank, the gamble taken by a low-ranking mother who produces a son is even greater than previously thought, requiring that the disadvantages of producing a daughter be concomitantly higher.

Simpson and Simpson (1982) examine data for twenty-one years in a rhesus lab colony to show that high-ranking mothers tend to produce daughters (thirty-one of fifty-three births) and low-ranking ones, sons (fifty-four of eighty-six births). The authors agree with Altmann's interpretation of this situation. Simpson et al. (1981) report that mothers of males are more likely to conceive in the following breeding season than mothers of females. This suggests that the difference between probability of male and female reproductive success in different rank classes must be very large, for otherwise low-ranking females would produce as many, if not more, infants over a lifetime than high-ranking females. Anderson and Simpson's (1979) finding that female rank is not related to reproductive success in this colony is congruent with this interpretation.

Simpson and Simpson (1982) address the issue of proximate mechanisms by testing a maternal stress hypothesis, predicting that frequent harassment might result in a biased sex ratio. They find no bias in the sex ratio of offspring produced by ten females who were above the median on aggression received from other animals. They also note that a stress hypothesis does not explain the ability of high-ranking females to bias their sex ratio toward daughters.

Silk, Clark-Wheatly, Rodman, and Samuels (1981) and Silk (1983) review twelve years of data from a bonnet lab colony and find that low-ranking females tend to produce sons (75 of 120 births), while high-ranking females exhibit no bias (43 of 83 births were males). Silk (1983) combines the local resource competition model and the Trivers-Willard model to explain her results and those of Altmann and of Simpson and Simpson. Her model has three conditions: (1) size and growth of local troops are regulated by resource availability; (2) males disperse from their natal troops; and (3) females do not disperse. Silk argues that under these conditions females reduce the resource competition they and their daughters will face by acting to limit the number of unrelated or distantly related females in the group. This could be accomplished either by harassing pregnant females or by attacks on immatures (see also Silk and Boyd 1983).

Under Silk's model, low-ranking females who produce sons avoid harassment and ensure that their offspring will reach maturity. The model does not predict the sex ratio of high-ranking females, and unlike Altmann and Simpson and Simpson, Silk finds no sex ratio bias in their offspring. Whether this is a species difference, the result of captivity, or the outcome of different probabilities of reproductive success for offspring is not clear.

Wolfe (1983) examines data on three breeding seasons of the Arashiyama B troop of Japanese macaques and finds no association between female rank and sex ratio of offspring. She also notes that matriline rank does not correlate with sex ratio. The publication of these negative results is important, for, as noted by Clutton-Brock (1982), when a new topic sparks the interest of researchers there is a tendency to report only positive data sets.

All of the studies just reviewed exhibit weaknesses. For example, the Trivers-Willard model requires that the difference between male and female variance in lifetime reproductive success be at least moderate. However, as noted by Wasser (1983:380), statistics for variance in lifetime reproductive success are not available for any species of alloprimate. Also, none of the studies adequately controls the potentially confounding factors of female age and reproductive life history strategies. In spite of these shortcomings, three of the four studies do provide some support for the suggestion that a modified version of the Trivers-Willard model applies to some alloprimates (red deer are an example where the original model applies, see Clutton-Brock et al. 1984). However, it must be kept in mind that we have no idea how many negative results there may be that remain unpublished. More careful studies, conducted in wider range of species, are needed before a final statement can be made on whether, and if so, how, sex ratio theory relates to the alloprimates. Of special interest would be studies of species which do not meet the conditions of Silk's model. Thus, data on sex ratio in species where females disperse and males do not (Wrangham 1980) would be welcome.

Studies Among Humans
Five studies have utilized one or more of the three models discussed above to examine sex ratio variation among humans (Alexander et al. 1979; Chagnon et al. 1979; Dickemann 1975, 1979a,b, 1981; Essock-Vitale 1984; and Hughes 1981). Each deserves some review, although only the Chagnon et al. and the Essock-Vitale papers contain proposition tests.

Chagnon et al. (1979) note that variations away from the 105:100 sex ratio at birth (the secondary sex ratio) that is assumed to characterize humans usually favor males and are commonly explained as the outcome of preferential female infanticide. In turn, preferential female infanticide is explained in terms of its supposed role in adjusting group size to environmental resources. In this paper, the authors reject the assumption that all male-biased sex ratios in preindustrial societies result from preferential female infanticide (see also Dow 1983; Yengoyan 1981), and argue that observed sex ratios in different age classes among the Yanomamo can be explained by sex ratio theory without invoking infanticide.

The authors argue that Yanomamo parental investment extends far past weaning and that the resources expended on males old enough to engage in warfare must be included in the calculation of total parental effort. Given

Fisher's model, the fact that Yanomamo males exhibit a higher mortality than females during the period of parental investment should mean that more of them are produced at birth. The data on reported births that are analyzed by Chagnon et al. (1979) provide a rough estimate of a secondary sex ratio at 129:100, a statistically significant deviation from the assumed human standard of 105:100, and one that supports Fisher's model.

As noted earlier, such a strongly biased sex ratio would normally be explained in terms of preferential female infanticide. However, Chagnon et al. provide evidence that this is not the case for the Yanomamo. For example, they calculate the average interval between the birth of a male and the previously born child to be 3.43 years. If female infanticide were practiced, the interval between females and previously born children should be greater than the male figure. In fact, it is only 3.37 years, discrediting the infanticide hypothesis.

Chagnon et al. (1979) also conduct two tests of the Trivers-Willard model. First, they note that males of the largest lineage in a village have better chances of finding mates and thus a higher, and more predictable, level of reproductive success than males of smaller lineages. They therefore predict that larger lineages will specialize in producing sons and smaller ones in daughters. The data provide no support for this prediction. A second prediction, that headmen (equated with higher rank or better condition) bias the sex ratio of their offspring toward males, is also not supported.

Two explanations are offered for why the Yanomamo data fail to support the Trivers-Willard model. First, it may be that neither relative lineage size nor headmanship accurately predicts reproductive success of offspring. If so, a basic condition of the model, correlation between parental condition and reproductive success of offspring, is violated. Second, unlike societies where women can be exchanged for valuables, the Yanomamo marriage system ideally operates by sister exchange. Thus, families need daughters if sons are to have mates, and this may restrict any tendency to specialize in offspring of one sex.

These results suggest that the Trivers-Willard model may be more relevant to societies with heritable wealth differences, organized along class or caste lines, than to more "equalitarian" societies, like the Yanomamo. In fact, Trivers and Willard claim that data from class structured societies support their model:

> ... the model can be applied to humans differentiated on a socioeconomic scale, as long as the RS [reproductive success] of a male at the upper end of the scale exceeds his sister's, while that of a female at the lower end of the scale exceeds her brother's. A tendency for the female to marry a male whose socioeconomic status is higher than her will, other things being equal, tend to bring about such a correlation, and there is evidence of such a bias in female choice in the United States [Trivers and Willard 1973:91].

A partial test of the hypothesis that the secondary sex ratio is affected by socioeconomic status in a complex society is in Essock-Vitale's (1984) article on the reproductive history of individuals in the *Forbes'* sample of the 400 "richest people in America" for the year 1980. The Trivers-Willard model predicts that births in this group should exhibit a male-biased sex ratio; a prediction disconfirmed by the fact that the observed 109:100 ratio does not differ significantly from chance. Unlike the Yanomamo data, this result suggests that humans lack the physiological mechanisms that are needed to adjust secondary sex ratios to situations of changing resource availability or to track the reproductive potential of offspring.

Of course, cultural mechanisms may allow parents to manipulate the sex ratio of their offspring after birth. Alexander (1974:369) suggests that preferential female infanticide is more likely to be practiced by the upper strata in polygynous societies that exhibit wealth stratification. This behavior allows the elite to concentrate resources in sons who will become polygynous and achieve great reproductive success. Dickemann's reviews (1975, 1979a,b, 1981) of stratified preindustrial societies in northern India, Europe, China, and elsewhere support this suggestion. Although these reviews do not contain proposition tests, they are impressive in the number of cultural practices that are explained in part by reference to class or caste differences in the predictability and variability of reproductive success. For example, Dickemann relates preferential female infanticide, rules of celibacy, bars to widow remarriage, and suicide to the need to remove high-status women from the breeding pool.

In contrast to the Trivers-Willard model, there is little evidence of preferential male infanticide in the lower strata of the societies discussed by Dickemann. Since many males are removed from the breeding population by homicide, poverty, and celibacy, it would appear that lower strata parents could do better by specializing in the production of females. Irons (Chagnon and Irons 1979:255) speculates that while these males have a lower chance for reproductive success than their sisters, their labor power assists their parents in raising females who will be reproductively successful. This assistance will be especially important when doweries enable women to "marry up." The children of women in hypergynous marriages may be protected against the factors that produce high infant and juvenile mortality in their class of origin. Further, the sons of such women might have a higher probability of reproductive success than the same woman's brothers. In either event, the parents and brothers of these women might increase their inclusive fitness by working to help them amass a doweries.

Dickemann's reviews are wide ranging, and only specialists in the areas she covers can evaluate the validity of her data. However, given the limitations of the historical record, she makes a strong case for the relevance of the Trivers-Willard model to stratified polygynous societies. The recurrence of the same practices in widely different cultures is especially interesting. However, it should be noted that many of the behaviors analyzed by Dickemann can also be seen as the outcome of strategies designed to maximize the economic position and/or prestige of the elite. As noted previously, these explanations are not mutually exclusive, since both wealth and prestige may be proximate paths to inclusive fitness.

Alexander et al. (1979) use Fisher's model in their exploration of intersocietal variation in human sexual dimorphism of stature. They note that populations of African origin exhibit both low dimorphism and a secondary sex ratio near unity. In contrast, Amerindian, Asian, and European populations are characterized by greater dimorphism and a secondary sex ratio biased toward males. The authors argue that both traits are related to greater male mortality in warfare and in mate competition, in the manner described by Fisher. Unfortunately, the data they use to illustrate these points are very limited, rendering the discussion unconvincing.

Finally, Hughes (1981) analyzes societies that exhibit preferential female infanticide but do not exhibit high male mortality in warfare. He mathematically models Trivers and Willard's suggestion that if one sex dispenses altruism to the other, parents will bias the sex ratio toward the altruistic sex. His model shows that unless the additional gain in offspring created by altruism is great, female infanticide will not be favored. Hughes does not test his model against the ethnographic record.

Thus far there are too few empirical tests to judge the applicability of sex ratio theory to humans. The Chagnon et al. (1979) study is very interesting, but it needs to be replicated in other groups exhibiting high male mortality in warfare. Such replications are especially needed for groups outside of South America, since there is some evidence that the ABO locus may have an influence on secondary sex ratio (Berlin and Millard 1983; Millard and Berlin 1983), and the high frequency of the 0 allele among South American indians would also predict masculine-biased sex ratios. Unfortunately, except in the case of certain industrial societies, data on the secondary sex ratio are difficult to obtain. The sex ratio data that are reported by ethnographers often refer to children, and not to the sex ratio at birth. Furthermore, the data often come from societies that have experienced contact-induced diseases, which may have affected the observed sex ratio.

TESTS INVOLVING ALLOPARENTAL BEHAVIOR

Alloparenting describes a situation wherein an animal other than the mother carries or cares for an infant. A problem with the term is that sometimes the infant is subjected to awkward handling or abuse. Quiatt (1979) suggests the neutral term "infant handling," but alloparenting has been accepted by most writers. The distribution and evolution of alloparental care in mammals and birds is discussed by Riedman (1982). Hrdy (1976),

McKenna (1979, 1981), and Quiatt (1979) are the best reviews of the behavior among alloprimates.

There is great variation in the ease with which infants are taken from their mothers. In general, New World monkeys exhibit a great deal of alloparental behavior, but the close genetic relationships between group members means that this behavior is best seen as nepotism or paternal investment. Hanuman langur mothers willingly give up their infants soon after birth; Hrdy (1981b) notes that an infant may spend up to 50 percent of its first day of life in the possession of allomothers. Macaque and baboon mothers are more reluctant to release their infants, although there is great variation within the subfamily Cercopithecinae. McKenna (1979) argues that the difference between the Colobines and the Cercopithecines results from the evolution of specialized feeding adaptations, which allow Colobine females to exist in groups with little feeding competition. The lack of competition means that rank and dominance considerations do not play the role they do among baboons and macaques. McKenna suggests that relaxed allomothering in the Colobines may not serve the same functions as allomothering among the Cercopithecines. He also makes the important point that analyses of the current costs and benefits of allomothering may not reveal the origin or evolution of the behavior.

There is a lively debate among primatologists and sociobiologists over the evolution and functions of alloparental behavior. The key issue is benefit: Of the three actors (mother, infant, alloparent), who gains from the interaction? There is no consensus, and at least seven answers have been advanced to explain the evolution of allomothering (allopaternal behavior was discussed under male parental investment). The "mother relief" hypothesis sees the mother as the beneficiary, gaining time away from her infant to forage or to regain strength. The "learning to mother" hypothesis argues that allomothers gain valuable experience with infants before giving birth themselves. The "adoption" hypothesis suggests that the main benefit goes to the infant, who has an increased chance of being adopted if anything happens to its mother. A hypothesis of "group cohesion" views the social ties generated by allomothering as creating social stability. The "selfish allomother" hypothesis sees the allomother as attempting to reduce the competition for resources that she or her offspring face by lowering the inclusive fitness of the infant and its kin. The "status elevation" position suggests that allomothering creates bonds between females of different ranks, probably to the advantage of lower-ranking females. Finally, Quiatt (1979) argues that allomothering does not have a specific adaptive function separable from the functions of maternal behavior. He sees maternal skills as the behavioral complex selected, with allomothering merely being an expression of female interest in infants. Quiatt also suggests two fortuitous effects of allomothering: (1) an increase in the inclusive fitness of the allomother through kin selection, because infants of her matriline are more readily available; and (2) negative selection against the inadequate mothering of females who allow their infants to be taken by animals of other matrilines.

Few of these hypotheses have been empirically tested. Support for Quiatt's position is claimed by Scollay and DeBold (1980), who find that the majority of allomaternal interactions in their langur colony occur between young females and young infants. The authors argue that this result discredits all but the "learning to mother" hypothesis. However, this hypothesis is rendered questionable by the fact that as allomothers age there is a decline in infant handling skills. Scollay and DeBold accept Quiatt's argument and suggest that all females will allomother, but that rates will vary with idiosyncratic interest in infants.

Caine and Mitchell (1980) suggest that since rhesus are less tolerant of one another than bonnets, rhesus maternal behavior has been subject to greater selection pressure. They argue that if Quiatt is correct, bonnet females will be less interested in infants and will exhibit less allomothering than rhesus. This prediction is supported in two samples of immature animals, but the authors note the need for a test utilizing adults.

The "selfish allomother" hypothesis has been supported by a number of studies. Wasser and Barash (1981) suggest that the following predictions derived from this hypothesis have been supported by one or more tests: (1) younger, more vulnerable, infants will be targets of allomothering more often than older infants; (2) both nulliparous and multiparous females will allomother and often mistreat infants; (3) high-ranking females will allomother more often than low-ranking females, since they can take the infants of lower-ranking animals; (4) infants of low-ranking mothers will experience more allomothering than those of high-ranking mothers; (5) females who are pregnant or who are cycling and near ovulation will allomother more than females who are cycling but who did not conceive when they ovulated; (6) mothers will resist allomothers. Silk's (1980b) finding that bonnet mothers resisted "kidnap" attempts and that interlineage attempts outnumber intralineage attempts supports the "selfish allomother" position, as does Kurland's (1977) discovery that Japanese macaque females are interested in the infants of other matrilines and that there is an inverse correlation between infant-allomother relatedness and awkward allomothering. However, Kurland also finds that infants of low-ranking mothers do not experience more allomothering and that there is no rank-related difference in toleration of allomothering by mothers. These results do not support the "selfish allomother" hypothesis.

The strongest support for the "selfish allomother" hypothesis comes from a field study of female yellow baboons (Wasser 1983). Wasser suggests that in this species, allomothering is a tactic in a complex strategy of reproductive competition between females. He notes that the threat of dehydration and the fact that baboon milk is low in protein mean that infants need almost constant access to their mothers. An allomother who removes an infant from its mother may be endangering the life of the infant. Wasser tests six predictions derived from the selfish allomother hypothesis and finds them all supported by his data: (1) newborns (under three months) are more likely to be taken than older infants who are less vulnerable and who can more effectively resist; (2) both nulliparous and multiparous females handle infants and treat them roughly, in spite of the maternal experience of the latter; (3) high-ranking females handle infants more frequently than low-ranking females; (4) the offspring of low-ranking mothers are handled more frequently than those of high-ranking females; (5) females about to give birth handle infants more frequently than females in other reproductive states (perhaps as a means of lowering their offspring's competition); and (6) mothers resist infant handling, especially by females with the most to gain by harming the infant, i.e., females about to give birth.

Wasser reviews alternative theories of infant handling behavior and suggests that allomothering may have evolved for different reasons in different species. He argues that the selfish allomother hypothesis is most likely to be applicable when the females involved are not closely related or when the population frequently experiences periods of low resource availability. The relationship between resource availability and patterns of allomothering among howler monkeys is discussed by Jones (1981), who finds that in poor environments, the most frequently observed dyad is infants of low-ranking mothers with high-ranking females. In contrast, in good environments, the offspring of high-ranking mothers are often handled by low-ranking females. Jones notes that the "good" environment of a laboratory group may explain why Scollay and DeBold (1980) find no relationship between maternal rank and allomothering in their langur colony.

The "learning to mother" hypothesis has also received some empirical support. First, Kurland (1977) finds that awkward handling of infants by Japanese macaque females declines with allomaternal age. Second, studies with langurs (McKenna 1981; Scollay and DeBold 1980), Japanese macaques (Kurland 1977), vervets (Lancaster 1971), and other species, show that nulliparous females spend more time allomothering than multiparous or primiparous females. However, Silk (1980b) finds that nulliparous bonnet females do not account for the majority of "kidnap" attempts, contradicting the "learning to mother" position. Finally, Nishida (1983) finds that nulliparous females are the most frequent infant handlers in a troop of chimpanzees in the Mahale mountains. However, three of Nishida's findings support the selfish mother hypothesis: (1) grooming prior to infant transfer is shorter when the allomother is a sister of the mother; (2) a mother retrieves an infant less quickly when the allomother is the mother's sister; and (3) lactating females rarely interact with infants other than their own, but tend to be abusive when they do so.

Johnson et al. (1980) find support for the "mother relief" hypothesis in a study of captive vervets. Allomothering in this group is unrelated to maternal restrictiveness, but is correlated with genetic relatedness in a complex manner. When infants are most vulnerable (birth to one month) siblings are the most likely allomothers, and mothers usually permit infant handling. The authors speculate that the mother benefits by gaining time to build up her strength. After the second month, mothers tend to quickly retrieve infants from allomothers, sometimes using aggression to do so. This forces potential infant handlers to direct their attention to nonsibling infants, producing the distribution of allomothering seen in Japanese and bonnet macaques. In further support of the "mother relief" hypothesis, Hrdy (1981a:217) cites Whitten's finding that among free-ranging vervets, females whose infants are being allomothered consume more food than mothers who are carrying their infants.

Allomaternal behavior among free-ranging patas is explained by Zucker and Kaplan (1981) in terms of the benefits it provides to infants. The authors note that prior work on vervets suggests that allomothering may be a facultative trait, with different expressions in safe and dangerous environments. Lancaster (1971) found that juvenile females were the most frequent allomothers in a vervet troop that was observed in a fairly safe environment in Zambia; while multiparous females played this role in a troop studied in the threatening urban environment of Durban, South Africa (Krige and Lucas 1974). Zucker and Kaplan (1981) observe a patas troop sharing a habitat with two troops of socially more aggressive rhesus and find that multiparous females are the most frequent allomothers and that the majority of allomothering episodes are affiliative. They note that patas exhibit a dispersed foraging pattern and take rapid flight when confronted with danger. During such flights, a female may grab the nearest infant, a practice which may be facilitated by prior allomothering interactions.

Finally, the "adoption hypothesis" is supported by examples of adoptions in several species. These are reviewed in Hrdy (1976) and in McKenna (1981).

To summarize, the distribution of costs and benefits of allomothering has not yet been described for any species that exhibits the behavior. At present, the "selfish allomother" hypothesis appears to have the greatest support for Cercopithecine species, but may not be relevant to the Colobines. Allomothering may serve varied functions in different species and probably cannot be explained by a single factor. Perhaps more than any other topic in primate sociobiology, the discussion of allomothering brings to the forefront some of the problems of testing sociobiological hypotheses. Thus, we have Quiatt's warning that many behaviors that appear to be in need of an adaptive explanation may only be by-products of selection for totally different behaviors. Furthermore, the necessity of discovering the intraspecific variation in a behavior before creating adaptive stories on the basis of costs and benefits calculated in a single troop, or in a series of troops inhabiting similar environments, is illustrated by Zucker and Kaplan's work. Finally, McKenna's argument that the currently observed costs and benefits of a behavior may not be relevant to an explanation of its origin and evolution is an important warning in this debate, and applies as well to much of the literature in sociobiology.

CHAPTER 7

Sexual Selection Theory I: Inbreeding and Sexual Dimorphism

INTRODUCTION

The next three chapters review primate research that is relevant to sexual selection theory. In this chapter, some concepts of sexual selection theory are introduced, and empirical research on the topics of mate selection vis-à-vis inbreeding and sexual dimorphism is reviewed. Research on the relationship between rank and reproductive success among alloprimates is discussed in Chapter Eight. Finally, Chapter Nine examines propositions that are relevant to competition for reproductive success among humans.

The decision to treat the topics of inbreeding and sexual dimorphism in a separate chapter may need some justification. The subjects are alike in that both have been the center of controversy over whether natural selection, or sexual selection, or some combination of these forces is most important in the explanation of their origin and evolution. Although questions over the relative role of natural and sexual selection do arise in connection with some of the topics covered in Chapters Eight and Nine, they have not stimulated the debates that have characterized work on inbreeding and sexual dimorphism. Further, since both topics have generated a great deal of theoretical discussion and empirical research, the review of this material in a single chapter has allowed me to keep the following chapters down to a more manageable size.

SEXUAL SELECTION THEORY

The concept of sexual selection, and its relationship to natural selection, is one of the most frequently debated topics in evolutionary biology (Andersson 1982a,b; Arnold 1983; Bertin and Stephenson 1983; Borgia 1979; Dominey 1983; Fisher 1930; Searcy and Yasukawa 1983; Slatkin 1984; Wade 1979; Wade and Arnold 1980; West-Eberhard 1983; Zahavi 1975). As in most areas of sociobiology, the theoretical work on sexual selection is far more sophisticated than the empirical research that has been conducted among the primates. I will, therefore, merely introduce the basic concept of sexual selection in this section and will refer to the complexities of the theory only if they are relevant to those topics which have generated empirical research.

Darwin emphasized the role that the hostile forces of nature play in creating differential reproductive success among the members of a population. Natural selection theory involves demonstrating how the evolution of the traits that are useful in the "struggle for existence" can be explained in terms of this differential success. However, Darwin also observed that animals often possessed traits which seemed to be unrelated to the struggle for existence. Even more strangely, in some cases animals exhibited traits which actually appeared to lower their chances of withstanding the hostile forces of nature. Many of these "useless" traits were sexually dimorphic, being possessed, or possessed in elaborate form, by members of only one sex. Darwin often accounted for the evolution of such traits by the process of sexual selection—the differential mating success of individuals.

Sexual selection may operate through one or both of two pathways: selection by competition and selection by preference. Selection by competition, also called intrasexual competition, occurs when members of one sex compete for mating access to members of the other. The competition may be direct—as when males herd estrous females and prevent other males from copulating with them—or indirect, as when animals compete for territory or resources, and the opposite sex bases mating decisions on quality of territory or quantity of resources. Selection by competition can create intense selective pressure on the morphological structures and/or behavioral patterns that are involved in competition (West-Eberhard 1983) and is often utilized to explain the evolution of the animal "weapons" that are used only in intraspecific combats, the ornamentation that signals competitive ability, and other such phenomena.

Selection by preference, also labeled intersexual or epigamic selection, occurs when members of one sex prefer mating with the individuals that possess particular traits or exhibit specific forms of traits (e.g., brightest color, longest tail). Selection by preference has helped to explain the evolution of "useless" traits—those that cannot be explained through the operation of natural selection or selection by competition (e.g., the tails of peacocks). There is a major controversy over the importance, or even the existence, of selection by preference, especially when it involves female choice (see Fedigan 1982; Halliday 1983a; O'Donald 1983a,b; and Taylor and Williams 1982 for reviews). Some aspects of this controversy will be discussed in the next chapter.

TESTS OF SEXUAL SELECTION THEORY AMONG ALLOPRIMATES

Introduction
A complete study of sexual selection requires information on two inter-related topics. First, the causes of patterns of mate competition that are characteristic of different species or of different populations in the same species must be discovered. This problem was reviewed in Chapter Three, where the evolution of different mating systems (monogamy, polygyny, promiscuity, etc.) was related to the ecological factors of predation pressure and resource distribution. Once the causes of mating systems are identified, the analysis shifts to a description of how different systems of mate competition shape the morphological and behavioral characteristics of a species or a population. Aspects of this second topic are the concerns of this chapter. Of course, these processes "feedback" on one another through time, and any separation is only an analytic device that permits the discussion to be ordered.

As noted above, most of the empirical research applying sexual selection theory to the alloprimates centers on the question of rank and will be discussed in the next chapter. The main topics of this section are the relevance of mate selection to the problem of inbreeding and the influence of sexual selection on sexual dimorphism in morphology and behavior.

Mate Selection and Inbreeding
Sexual selection theory holds that animals have been selected to compete for matings as a way of maximizing inclusive fitness. If we assume that all members of the sex that is competed for are of equal quality (i.e., that there are no fitness-related differences between them), a simple measure of sexual selection is the variance in mating success of the competing sex. However, if members of the sex competed for do vary in quality, then variance in mating success may not be an adequate measure of sexual selection. For example, a male who mates with four females, each producing a single birth has greater mating success—but the same reproductive success—as a male who mates with two females, each of whom produces twins (assuming the offspring are equally fit).

One factor determining the quality of a potential mate is the coefficient of relatedness that he or she shares with the choosing individual. Numerous studies have shown that in many species, matings between close relatives lead to inbreeding depression: the offspring conceived by these matings have lower reproductive potential than the offspring of noninbred matings. This lower potential may result from numerous factors, including birth defects, smaller size, and so on. On the surface, it seems clear that animals should avoid mating when inbreeding depression is a probable outcome.

However, sociobiology's strategy metaphor suggests that inbreeding may not be inherently bad. The amount and type of inbreeding exhibited by a species, or a population, may depend upon the costs/benefits of inbreeding versus the costs/benefits of outbreeding. Bateson (1983) provides a summary of the hypothetical costs/benefits most frequently associated with inbreeding and outbreeding:

Costs of Inbreeding
1. Deleterious genes more likely to be fully expressed.
2. Beneficial interactions (heterozygous advantage or over-dominance) between different alleles at same genetic locus lost.
3. Offspring insufficiently variable for one or other to cope with a varying environment.
4. Offspring more like each other and so compete more intensely.

Costs of Outbreeding
1. Genes required for adaptation to particular environment lost or suppressed.
2. Co-adapted gene complexes broken up by recombination.
3. In polygynous species advantage of having extra-closely related offspring lost and parental genes less well represented in next generation.
4. Infection from pathogens carried by mate more likely.
5. Travelling into another population costly and dangerous.
6. Acquired skills useful in one environment not appropriate in another.
7. Mismatch of habits acquired by mates in different environments disrupts parenting [Bateson 1983:259; see also Partridge 1983].

Avoidance of the costs of outbreeding can be viewed as benefits of inbreeding and vice versa. Bateson notes that all of these costs/benefits will not necessarily operate for one particular species and that the balance between those which do will determine the optimal breeding strategy vis-à-vis inbreeding for each species.

Research on mate selection with reference to inbreeding among allo-primates has centered on three major questions. First, is there evidence for inbreeding depression among alloprimates? Second, is there evidence that mating strategies are influenced by the possibility of inbreeding depression? Third, if there is such evidence, what proximate mechanisms regulate inbreeding? I will examine each of these questions in turn.

There are data indicating that the necessity of avoiding inbreeding depression might have been a significant factor in the evolution of alloprimate reproductive strategies. A review of captive groups of various species by Ralls and Ballou (1982) reveals that in fiften of sixteen colonies, inbred animals exhibit a higher rate of infant mortality than outbred animals. This suggests that the close inbreeding that is characteristic of some colonies would be strongly selected against in natural populations.

Inbreeding depression in a colony of hamadryas baboons is indicated by the findings that the progeny of inbred matings are at a higher risk of lymphoma (Crawford and O'Rourke 1978) and exhibit lower mean values on anthropometric measurements (O'Rourke 1979) than the offspring on noninbred matings.

Finally, in a field study of olive baboons, Packer (1979a) reports the case of an adult male who transferred into a troop containing close female relatives. Fifty percent of the infants sired by this male died before the age of one month, compared to only sixteen percent of the infants sired by nonnatal males (see Moore and Ali 1984:97–98 for a discussion of Packer's results).

These three studies suggest that inbreeding depression can lower the reproductive success of closely related animals who mate. There is some evidence that the level of inbreeding required to create inbreeding depression may vary from species to species. For example, some troops of bonnet macaques appear to be highly inbred (Wade 1979) without exhibiting the expected inbreeding depression. Unfortunately, there are no empirical studies with alloprimates measuring either the potential benefits of inbreeding or the costs of outbreeding. This information is needed before it can be argued that the pattern of mate selection exhibited by an individual or a group is an adaptive response to the problem of inbreeding depression. At present, we know only that in some species, inbreeding depression may result when close relatives mate.

This leads to the second question: Do alloprimates avoid matings when inbreeding depression might result? There is evidence that at least some species exhibit incest avoidance with close relatives. Many primatologists have noted that in natural populations, mating between close relatives is precluded by dispersal patterns (see below). Several studies suggest that even when close relatives reside in the same troop, mating is avoided. Mother-son and brother-sister matings occur less frequently than might be expected in the few troops where this problem has been investigated. For example, Murray and Smith (1983) find that in captive groups of stumptail macaques, mounts between mother-son and maternal sibling dyads occur less frequently than would be expected if mating were random. Studies with rhesus macaques on Cayo Santiago demonstrate that mother-son matings are rare (Missakian 1973; Sade 1968). Further, when sexual activity between close relatives does occur, it often lacks attributes of mature sexuality (see Bischof 1975; Bixler 1981a,b; Demarest 1977 for reviews of inbreeding avoidance among alloprimates).

Most studies of inbreeding avoidance analyze only relationships through females. However, if inbreeding depression is a significant risk in a species, we would expect that paternal relatives would also avoid mating. In an important study Smith (1982) utilizes paternity exclusion techniques to test this possibility in a rhesus colony. Since the offspring of a single male may be raised in different matrilines, early social experience cannot serve as a proximate cue creating inbreeding avoidance, as has been suggested in the case of matrilineally related animals. Smith speculates that kin recognition, similar to that demonstrated by Wu et al. (1980) for pigtails, might be a proximate cue preventing inbreeding among paternally related animals. However, results indicate that no inbreeding avoidance exists between these relatives. In fact, two or three infants resulted from father-daughter matings. Smith notes that in free-ranging groups, father-daughter mating may be prevented if the average tenure of males in higher ranks does not exceed the time it takes their daughters to reach sexual maturity. Brief male tenure in higher ranks and migration of young males might keep the level of inbreeding between patrilineal relatives low in natural populations, but further research is needed to verify this hypothesis (especially given the difficulty of establishing a link between high male rank and mating success—see the next chapter).

To answer the second question, there is evidence for the existence of an inbreeding avoidance between maternal relatives in some species of alloprimates. This does not mean that inbreeding never occurs, only that it is less common than might be expected if mating were random. The question of whether such avoidance arose through natural or sexual selection has not been addressed with empirical tests. The possibility that the rarity of close inbreeding is merely the result of processes of competition for mates, which have nothing to do with inbreeding avoidance, has not been ruled out in any of these cases. Finally, there is no evidence for, and one empirical result against, the hypothesis that paternal kin avoid inbreeding.

Given the evidence for incest avoidance among at least matrilineal relatives in some species, the final question is: What proximate mechanisms are involved in lowering the level of inbreeding within a species? The mechanisms that have been suggested for alloprimates include: (1) familiarity reducing sexual excitement; (2) relative dominance positions preventing mother-son matings; (3) female preference for mating with unfamiliar males; and (4) dispersal patterns. Each of these four mechanisms has received mixed support from field studies.

The familiarity hypothesis postulates that animals are not sexually stimulated by the individuals with whom they interact during critical periods in their early lives. This situation is often identified as the Westermarck Effect, after the theorist who argued that one source of incest avoidance among humans is the fact that children are not sexually attracted to peers who were in close contact with them during early childhood (see below). The Westermarck Effect means that both males and females would seek sexual contact with unfamiliar partners. If familiarity is correlated with genetic relatedness, as it often is for matrilineal relatives, the possibility of inbreeding is reduced. It should be noted that some inbreeding may occur if unfamiliar partners are not available.

Support for the familiarity hypothesis is provided by Itiogawa et al.'s (1981) study of mother-son mating inhibition among Japanese macaques. The authors caged a mature male with his mother for three breeding seasons and found that the dyad avoided ejaculatory mounts, although both performed adequately with other animals. The authors note, too, that the male also failed to be sexually interested in a familiar female who was unrelated to him.

A second proximate mechanism that prevents inbreeding may involve dominance relationships between animals. Sade (1968) observed that a rhesus male on Cayo Santiago mated with his mother only after he began to dominate her physically. If most males do not dominate their mothers before emigrating from the natal troop, mother-son mating would rarely occur. However, the dominance interpretation is questioned by Johnson et al.'s (1982) finding that during the breeding season male Japanese macaques frequently mate with females who dominate them outside of the breeding season. Furthermore, Murray and Smith (1983) find that dominance relationships do not explain the inbreeding avoidance they observed in stumptail macaques.

The hypothesis that female preference for mating with unfamiliar males may be an adaptation to lower inbreeding is supported by data on mate choice among olive baboons (Packer 1979a). Packer argues that under certain cost/benefit ratios, sexually mature males residing in their natal troops should attempt to mate with close female relatives in spite of the risk of inbreeding depression. The factors that determine whether such attempts will profit a male include: (1) the risks of emigration; (2) the chances of reproductive success in other troops; (3) the resistance offered by the females; (4) the competition of other males in the natal troop; and (5) the lower inclusive fitness received if the female bears an offspring with lower than average reproductive potential (i.e., the risk of inbreeding depression). Packer suggests that both competition from older, nonnatal males and female choice are responsible for reducing the level of inbreeding. Females should be less willing than males to engage in incest, because, in terms of lifetime reproductive potential, inbreeding depression is more costly for them. The observation that three of five females consorting with natal males presented to other males during the consort, but that only two of thirty-nine females consorting with nonnatal males did so, supports Packer's argument. These results suggest that competition for females and female unwillingness to mate may be proximate mechanisms that create male emigration, which in turn lowers the probability of inbreeding.

Moore and Ali (1984) review some alternative explanations of female preference for "strange males," which do not hypothesize a functional relationship with inbreeding avoidance. One is that females choose to mate with transferred males because by the very act of successfully joining a troop against the resistance of resident males, these males have demonstrated that they carry "good genes" (see Chapter Eight). A second possibility is that females mate with as many males as possible in order to increase the genetic diversity of their offspring. Finally, females may mate with transferring males to confuse the issue of paternity, in order to forestall infanticide attempts or to gain paternal investment from a number of males. At present the field data that are needed to select among these alternatives are not available.

The fact that in many animal species members of one sex leave the natal troop before or near puberty is often explained as an evolved adaptation to reduce or eliminate inbreeding. Recent studies of alloprimates have seriously questioned this interpretation, often arguing that dispersal patterns are the outcome of intrasexual competition over food and mates (reviewed in Moore and Ali 1984). The only proposition test is by Dobson (1982), who suggests that if inbreeding avoidance is the major factor creating juvenile dispersal in mammals, then half of all species should exhibit female dispersal, since this would be just as effective as male dispersal in achieving the goal. In a sample of fifty-seven species (with twenty-one species of alloprimates) where one sex disperses, forty-six exhibit male dispersal. Dobson hypothesizes that competition for mates is the main factor determining dispersal and predicts that species with polygynous or promiscuous mating will exhibit male dispersal, while monogamous species will exhibit female dispersal by both sexes. His sample supports this prediction.

A study of dispersal by male vervets (Cheney and Seyfarth 1983) illustrates the necessity of calculating the cost/benefit ratio of inbreeding and outbreeding before predicting the behavior of a species. The authors find that young vervets do not disperse randomly from their natal troops, which would be an optimal strategy if avoidance of inbreeding were the major function of dispersal. Instead, they tend to transfer together with a brother or peer into groups that have received members of their natal troop in the past. This pattern can be explained in part by the finding that during intergroup meetings, troops that have exchanged males in the past tend to exhibit less aggression and more affiliative behavior than troops that have not done so. Cheney and Seyfarth suggest that, compared to males who enter troops with no prior exchanges, the males that transfer into troops with prior exchanges with their natal troop may experience less aggression from residents. While this strategy lowers the potential costs of transferring, it increases the risk of inbreeding depression. Cheney and Seyfarth suggest that for young vervets the costs of inbreeding depression do not exceed the costs of randomized transfer (predation risk, aggression from residents).

However, the balance may shift during the life of an animal. Cheney and Seyfarth postulate that older males might transfer a second or a third time, thereby lowering the probability that they might mate with their daughters or nieces. They suggest that these older males may be more likely to join distant groups, since the costs of transferring for an adult male may not be as great as those for a juvenile male. An empirical test of this two-stage transfer process and its implications for inbreeding avoidance would be very interesting.

To summarize, the role that inbreeding depression and the necessity to avoid it has played in the evolution of alloprimate behavior is still an open question. Given the evidence for interspecific variation in inbreeding, it is unlikely that a unitary explanation linking mate selection, inbreeding avoidance, specific proximate mechanisms, and inbreeding depression can be formulated. However, progress in testing theories of inbreeding avoidance is promised by the recent willingness of researchers to conceptualize inbreeding as part of a complex calculus of the costs and benefits that are associated with mate selection.

Sexual Dimorphism

Sexual dimorphism exists when the sexes of a species exhibit significant differences in body size, ornamentation (e.g., hair distribution, coloring), or behavior. A major theoretical problem in evolutionary biology has been the explanation of such dimorphism. In this section, I review several empirical studies relating sexual selection to sexual dimorphism—especially in body size—among the alloprimates. Before doing so, however, it is necessary to identify some of the problems of separating the effects of natural and sexual selection in the evolution of sexual dimorphism.

Since sexual dimorphism in body size is the trait most frequently discussed in this section, I will use it to illustrate the alternative perspectives of sexual and natural selection. In many alloprimate species, the average body length for males is significantly longer than that for females. While some of the size difference may be environmentally caused, there probably is a strong genetic component to the dimorphism. A natural selection explanation of this dimorphism is that different body lengths are adaptive responses to the different environments that are inhabited by the sexes. As Lande formulates the rule: "To assign natural selection as the primary cause requires ecological observations that males and females follow different ways of life and employ the dimorphic character(s) adaptively in their distinct modes of survival or reproduction" (1980:292). For example, if males forage over greater distances than females and encounter more predators, a larger body size might be selected for, as predators remove smaller males. Since females do not experience as much predation pressure, there is no selection for larger bodies, and sexual dimorphism evolves. Alternatively, sexual dimorphism may evolve if smaller females outreproduce larger females, and if males are not under selection for reduced body size. A mathematical treatment of various natural selection explanations of sexual dimorphism is found in Slatkin (1984).

A sexual selection explanation of body length dimorphism assumes that most of the size difference between the sexes cannot be explained by adaptation to different niches, but rather results from the variance in mating success experienced by one of the sexes. The most common explanation is that larger males have greater mating success than smaller males. This may be the result of selection by competition—as when larger males dominate smaller males and prevent them from mating with females, or when bigger individuals monopolize high-quality territories, capable of supporting more than one female, while smaller individuals obtain no territory or one capable of supporting only a single female. However, larger males might also be favored by selection by preference, if females prefer to mate with larger males, independent of the size of the males' territories or success in competing with other males (this is unlikely for a trait like body size, but may be important in explaining the evolution of sexually dimorphic coloring or ornamentation; see Chapter Eight). Lande summarizes:

> Sexual selection is implicated as the major cause of a sexual dimorphism when this reaches its fullest development at sexual maturity, perhaps only in the mating season, and if the dimorphic character functions mainly in one sex to confer a mating advantage on individuals with more extreme development of the character [Lande 1980:293].

Lande also notes (1980:293) that an observed correlation between a dimorphic character and either ecological adjustment or mating success does not automatically reveal the origin of the dimorphism. It is possible for a dimorphism originally generated by sexual selection to result in the sexes exploiting different environments and for the dimorphic character to function adaptively in these niches. The reverse process, ecologically generated dimorphisms leading to differential mating success, may also occur.

Price's (1984a; see also 1984b) review of explanations for the evolution of sexual dimorphism in body size provides a useful conceptualization of the difference between natural and sexual selection. He defines three types of selection which may operate on the body size (or any trait) of a sex. *Survival selection* arises from differential mortality and selects for the body size with greatest survival potential. *Fertility selection* arises from differences in fertility and selects for the body size with the greatest fertility potential. And, finally, *sexual selection* arises from variance in mating success and selects for the body size with the greatest mating potential. The optimal body size for a sex will be a compromise between these three forces, and if the sexes are exposed to different combinations of the forces, sexual dimorphism may result.

Price uses his model to describe three common hypotheses for the evolution of sexual dimorphism. The niche variation hypothesis states that survival selection in the environments inhabited by males and females creates different optima for body size. In one version, where the sexes inhabit different environments during the nonbreeding season, both sexes evolve toward their optimum size for survival, and sexual dimorphism results. In a second version, more dimorphic pairs are reproductively more successful than less dimorphic pairs during the breeding season, because they can exploit a wider range of resources. In this case, neither sex may achieve its survival optimum.

The fertility selection hypothesis assumes that both sexes inhabit the same environment and are therefore under the same survival selection for body size. For some reason, however, variance in female fertility is related to body size. A common assumption is that smaller females may invest more energy in reproduction than larger females. In this case, fertility selection causes females to be "drawn off" the survival optimum, while males stay on it, resulting in the evolution of sexual dimorphism. Since fertility selection does not arise from variance in mating success, it is best conceptualized as a form of natural selection.

Price notes that the sexual selection hypothesis is usually invoked when variance in male reproductive success is correlated with body size. Usually, larger or stronger males are assumed to be more attractive to females or more successful in mate competition. The selection for increased body size results in males evolving off the optimum for survival. If females are not concurrently experiencing selection for larger size, they stay on the optimum, and sexual dimorphism results. Of course this process can involve traits other than, or in addition to, body size. For example, Clutton-Brock, Albon, and Guiness (1982) note that the growth pattern of young red deer is sexually dimorphic. Reproductive success in adult males is positively correlated with body size and muscle strength, and young males divert most of the energy gained from food into development of these traits, instead of storing body fat. Evidence that the male growth pattern created by sexual selection has drawn males off the optimal body configuration for survival is provided by the fact that in severe winters males experience higher mortality than females, who devote much more energy to the production of body fat.

It should be noted that the image of a sex attaining a body configuration that is optimal for survival is only a way of conceptualizing the interaction between natural and sexual selection and is not expected to be observed in reality (even if such optima could be calculated). For example, Lande (1980) points out that even moderate genetic correlation between homologous characters of the sexes will make selection for sexual dimorphism a very slow process. However, if sexual (or fertility) selection is intense on one sex, such correlations might also pull the other sex off the survival optimum.

The problem of unraveling the effects of natural and sexual selection is evident in the studies that have been done of sexual dimorphism in body morphology among the alloprimates. The most commonly tested prediction is that as mating systems deviate from strict monogamy, creating greater variance in male reproductive success, the degree of sexual dimorphism that is characteristic of a species increases. Although selection by either competition or preference can theoretically explain increased sexual dimorphism, the former is usually implicated. Before reviewing the holospecies tests of this hypothesis, it should be noted that Darwin argued that sexual selection could operate in monogamous species if males compete for access to the earliest maturing or most fertile females. Thus, it is theoretically possible for a monogamous species to exhibit greater variance in male reproductive success than a polygynous or promiscuous species. Unfortunately, data on the variance in male and female lifetime reproductive success are not available for any aloprimate species, and we must make do with indirect measurements based on mating systems.

Alexander et al. (1979) examine breeding system and sexual dimorphism in body length for twenty-two species of alloprimates and find a direct correlation between dimorphism and two indirect measures of male-male competition for mates, mean and maximum harem size. The same relationship is observed in fifteen pinniped and seventeen ungulate species (I discuss the results obtained with human data below).

Alexander et al. address the problem of separating the effects of natural and sexual selection in their discussion of three alternative hypotheses for the evolution of sexual dimorphism: "... (1) division of labor in parental effort (Ralls 1976, Myers 1978); (2) differential use of resources by members of mated pairs (Selander 1966, 1972), or (3) intrasexual competition in three-dimensional environments" (1979:409). Predation pressure is suggested as another factor in the evolution of sexual dimorphism, but this may work through sexual selection. The authors note that these explanations might be relevant to their findings, but that:

> Effects like those above could either dilute or enhance differences in amounts of sexual dimorphism between monogamous and nonmonogamous species deriving from differences in sexual competition. They are, however, unlikely to explain widespread correlations between degrees of sexual dimorphism and degrees of polygyny in two-dimensional [e.g., terrestrial] environments. The significance of the comparisons in three different taxonomic groups ... strongly suggest that the relevant variable is the greater pressure of sexual competition among males, associated with their generally low parental effort and high mating effort [Alexander et al. 1979:410].

Studies of body length and weight dimorphism by Clutton-Brock and Harvey (1977), Clutton-Brock et al. (1977), Leutenegger (1978, 1982), and Gaulin and Sailer (1983b) have duplicated the relationship described by

Alexander et al. (1979), although the specifics vary. Sexual dimorphism in canine size has also been shown to be related to mating system in a similar manner (Leutenegger and Kelly 1977). A major element in each of these studies is the amount of interspecific variance in sexual dimorphism in body length, weight, or canine size that is left unexplained by the mating system variable. For example, the Pearson's correlation coefficient between mean harem size and sexual dimorphism in the Alexander et al. sample is 0.40, which explains only 16 percent of the variance in dimorphism. Similarly, only 9 percent of the variance is explained by the correlation between sexual dimorphism and maximum harem size ($r = 0.30$). The low explanatory value of the mating system variable may mean only that this indirect measure is a poor indicator of variance in male reproductive success. On the other hand, it might indicate that sexual selection is only one of numerous forces acting on the evolution of sexual dimorphism and that species must be examined individually to discover the combination of forces relevant to them. Leutenegger and Kelly (1977) provide an excellent illustration of this second alternative, identifying allometry, environment (aboreal, terrestrial, semiterrestrial), predation pressure, predictability and distribution of food, energy yields of food, and locomotion patterns, along with mate competition, as factors implicated in the evolution of sexual dimorphism of one or more alloprimate species.

The relative importance of sexual selection in the evolution of sexual dimorphism of body weight and canine size is explored in a multivariate holospecies study by Leutenegger and Cheverud (1982). Their results indicate that allometry explains most of the variance in these traits, although sexual selection may have a minor influence. The authors present a model demonstrating that selection for larger body size in both sexes will produce increased sexual dimorphism if phenotypic variation or variation in heritability of size is greater in one sex than in the other. They suggest that natural selection for larger body size in terrestrial alloprimates (permitting increased day range length and better protection against predators) explains most of the variation in sexual dimorphism observed among alloprimates.

Gaulin and Sailer (1983b) criticize the Leutenegger and Cheverud study on statistical grounds and demonstrate that when allometry is controlled, there is still a significant relationship between sexual dimorphism in body weight and mating system. This paper contains an interesting discussion of the relationship between body size and the expression of sexual dimorphism. The authors argue that for reasons of metabolism and energy, male competition is likely to result in sexual dimorphism in body size in large species, but sexual dimorphism in other traits (e.g., behavior, coloring) in smaller species.

In a second paper, Gaulin and Sailer (1983a) utilize data on diet to calculate a rough estimate of the ecologically optimal body weights for males and females in fifty-three alloprimate species. They predict that in species with promiscuous or polygynous mating systems, the observed body weight of males will deviate more often than the weight of females from the ecologically optimal weight, while in monogamous species the observed weight of both sexes will be fairly close to the optima. Both predictions are supported, but the crude measure for optimal body weight renders the findings only preliminary. As better data on the diet of various species become available, Gaulin and Sailer's conclusions should be subjected to more refined testing.

Popp's (1983) model of the relationship between ecology and male mating strategies, reviewed in Chapter Three, contains a discussion of the influence of natural and sexual selection on sexual dimorphism. He argues that in baboons the least dimorphism in body size occurs in arid environments, where smaller size is advantageous, due to lower caloric requirements, and where male-male avoidance is the most common mating strategy (gelada and hamadryas baboons). Popp notes that while both gelada and hamadryas baboons are often considered to exhibit extreme dimorphism, the sexes actually differ little in body mass. The impressive mantles of fur sported by males in these species might be the outcome of sexual selection acting in a situation where the evolution of larger size is opposed by natural selection.

Popp suggests that baboons that inhabit less arid environments exhibit increased size, but that the sexes respond in different manners to the more abundant energy in these environments. Although females of species in less arid environments have invested some energy in larger body size, most of the additional energy has been put into higher reproductive effort. In contrast, males invest the extra energy in larger body size and in mating strategies emphasizing male-male dominance and male-male exclusion. Since the increase in female body size from arid to less arid environments is more "conservative" than that of the male, sexual dimorphism increases with rainfall.

Popp's model indicates that consideration of both natural and sexual selection is necessary to explain the evolution of sexual dimorphism in baboons. His argument also points to the need for data on variance in lifetime reproductive success of both sexes. As noted in Chapter Three, unimale troops in arid environments have the same mating system as unimale troops in less arid environments, but since the former are based on male-male avoidance and the latter on male-male exclusion, both the variance in male lifetime reproductive success and the strength of the operation of sexual selection may differ greatly in the two settings. Tests of Popp's argument, using other groups of alloprimates inhabiting widely different environments, such as the macaques or the langurs, promise interesting results.

Two holospecies studies examine the possible influence of sexual selection upon the morphology of one of the sexes. Harvey et al. (1978) demonstrate that females in species with unimale troops have smaller canines relative to body size than females of species with monogamous or with multimale troops. They suggest that females in monogamous troops are often involved in territorial defense, while those in multimale troops may use their canines in agonistic encounters with both males and other females. In contrast, females in unimale troops are assumed to compete with one another only rarely, especially since they are often closely related (see also Robinson 1982).

Harcourt, Harvey, Larson, and Short (1981) explore the relationship between mating system and male genital size with a sample of thirty-three alloprimate species. They demonstrate that males of species in which females mate with different males in a relatively short time span have larger testes, relative to body size, than males of species with different mating patterns. This relationship is logical if larger testes allow males to produce greater amounts of sperm per ejaculation. Dziuk (1982) notes that timing of copulation relative to ovulation is probably more important than number of sperm per ejaculation in determining reproductive success, but Harcourt (1982) argues that if males cannot determine the time of ovulation, those inseminating females with the greatest number of sperm might have some competitive advantage over other males.

The testing of propositions relating sexual selection to the evolution of behavioral traits is not well advanced for the alloprimates. In many cases, sexually dimorphic traits can be explained with an adaptive scenario implicating either natural or sexual selection, or both. Thus, many of the studies of rank and reproductive success discussed in the next chapter can be examined as examples of the operation of sexual selection. Unfortunately, few empirical studies have attempted to contrast the two scenarios, either one against the other, or either against the null hypothesis that the traits under investigation are not the result of functional adaptations. Thus, only two studies, both concerning mate guarding, will be reviewed under this topic.

In a study of intertroop encounters among free-ranging baboons in South Africa, Cheney and Seyfarth (1977) find that females often present to males outside their troop. Such presentations may be a proximate factor in male transfers. The authors note that in ninety percent of the intertroop encounters, at least one male attempted to herd females in his troop away from the other troop. Herding behavior might be explained in terms of sexual selection theory. Males with the greatest access to females are more likely to herd than those with less access, with the alpha male responsible for 85 percent of the observed herding. Further, on occasions when the alpha male herded only a single female, he usually chose a sexually cycling rather than a lactating female.

Cubicciotti and Mason's (1978) study of different patterns of "jealousy" exhibited by caged squirrel and titi monkeys can be interpreted as an example of sexual selection producing dimorphic behavioral patterns. The authors predicted that among the monogamous titi monkeys, both sexes would move closer to their opposite sex cagemates when a stranger of the opposite sex was introduced. In contrast, squirrel monkeys were not expected to exhibit this pattern, since the species normally lives in multimale troops. The squirrel monkeys and the male titi monkeys exhibited the expected behaviors, but the female titi monkeys did not move closer to their mates when new females were introduced. Cubicciotti and Mason interpret their results from a parental investment framework, arguing that males in monogamous species are more concerned with paternal certainty than males in multimale troops, because in monogamous New World alloprimates males frequently provide high levels of infant care. They suggest that female titi monkeys should not be concerned if their mates copulate with other females as long as they show no sign of breaking the current bond. However, evidence of female defense of territory in many monogamous species suggests that in at least some alloprimate species, females do not tolerate the presence of other females. It is impossible at present to judge whether this intolerance serves to protect the pair bond, to prevent resource competition, or to do both.

Summary
Empirical work among alloprimates designed to test the role of sexual selection in explanations of inbreeding avoidance and sexual dimorphism in morphology and behavior is fairly well advanced. The major problem thus far is the difficulty of testing sexual selection explanations of these traits against alternative natural selection or nonfunctional explanations. In cases where natural selection and sexual selection are assumed to have interacted in the evolution of a trait, clearer statements of the interaction are usually required before testing can proceed.

In spite of these problems, it is clear that work on both inbreeding avoidance and sexual dimorphism of body morphology provides some of the strongest support for the applicability of the sociobiological paradigm to alloprimates. The strengths and weaknesses of the research on inbreeding avoidance were summarized earlier. In the case of sexual dimorphism of body morphology, it appears that most theorists would agree that while sexual selection is probably implicated in the evolution of body size dimorphism, it is not the only variable so implicated, and its strength relative to these other variables is still an open research question. Work conducted thus far suggests a number of future research directions. First, future research on sexual dimorphism should be multivariate rather than bivariate. Second, researchers must examine the interactions between various types of sexual dimorphisms. Oxnard (1983) and Ralls (1977) suggest the necessity for such investigations. Oxnard subjects body measurements of eighteen genera of alloprimates to multivariate analyses and finds that there are at least seven different types of body morphology dimorphisms in his sample. It is possible that each of these has been influenced by different combinations of natural and sexual selection. This possibility recalls Gaulin and Sailer's (1983b) point that the form of dimorphism may vary in species of different sizes. Ralls (1977:918) notes that dimorphisms of secondary sexual characteristics, such as their distribution, coloring, genital swelling, etc., must be integrated with size dimorphism in any complete model of the effects of sexual selection. Popp's (1983) hypothesis that ecological limitations on body size in hamadryas and gelada baboons affects the distribution of hair in these species indicates the value of such integration.

Finally, the role of sexual selection in the evolution of behavioral dimorphisms is at this time a subject of debate and the topic of little empirical research beyond that connected with rank. Tests of alternative hypotheses for such dimorphisms will no doubt be forthcoming in the near future. •

TESTS OF SEXUAL SELECTION THEORY AMONG HUMANS

Mate Selection and Inbreeding

The topics of inbreeding avoidance and the incest taboo have played central roles in human sociobiology. For example, in each of Wilson's books (1975a, 1979; Lumsden and Wilson 1981, 1983), the argument that incest taboos can be explained as the outcome of the avoidance of mating with close kin due to the deleterious effects of inbreeding has been advanced as an example of sociobiology's applicability to human beings (see Bixler 1981a,b and van den Berghe 1983 for reviews of this topic). As with the alloprimates, we can review this topic by seeking to answer three questions: Is there evidence that inbreeding depression affects humans? Is there evidence that human mating systems are influenced by the possibility of inbreeding depression? What proximate mechanisms regulate inbreeding?

The evidence that in at least some human groups individuals who mate with close relatives risk inbreeding depression is very strong (reviews in Adams and Neel 1967; Schull and Neel 1965; Stern 1973). Sociobiologists frequently cite Seemanova's (1971) study of Czechoslovakian women who produced infants with close relatives (fathers, brothers, sons) and with unrelated males on this point. The infants produced by matings with relatives ran far higher risks of serious birth defects and early infant mortality than those created by noninbred matings. Bittles (1979) points out that Seemanova did not control for some factors which could affect the health of the infants (maternal age, physical and psychological health of the parents), but it is unlikely that control of these would totally explain the greater risk experienced by children of inbred matings.

Livingstone (1980) criticizes explanations of human incest taboos that derive the taboos from the deleterious effects of inbreeding when he notes that the level of inbreeding producing inbreeding depression will vary with population structure. He cites Sanghvi's (1966) finding of a high incidence of uncle-niece marriage in South India and Spielman et al.'s (1977) estimate that the inbreeding coefficient in some Yanomamo villages is as high as 0.5 as illustrations of this point. In an earlier article (1969), he notes that the small group sizes assumed to be characteristic of early humans would have resulted in deleterious genes being rapidly selected out of a population. From this perspective, the threat of inbreeding depression would not have been a major factor in the evolution of human mating systems until population sizes increased with the adoption of full-time horticulture.

The question of whether the necessity of avoiding inbreeding influenced by the evolution of human mating systems has been answered positively by a number of sociobiologists. The two most commonly cited pieces of evidence are: (1) the fact that incest between primary relatives (parent-offspring and sibling-sibling) appears to occur less frequently than expected by chance in all human societies, and (2) the universal existence of the cultural rules of incest taboos and exogamy (marriage outside the family).

We have few data on the frequency of matings between primary relatives in any society. It has been suggested that the amount of primary relative incest has recently increased in the United States, but it is unclear whether this perception is an accurate reflection of reality or the outcome of the increased attention recently given to the subject of incest. Opponents of sociobiology sometimes argue as if any matings between primary relatives disconfirm the sociobiological hypothesis that inbreeding depression shaped human mating practices. However, this is a misreading of the hypothesis. Failure of proximate mechanisms serving to reduce incest and the lack of mating alternatives may explain observed cases of incest without casting doubt on the validity of a sociobiological interpretation.

Sociobiologists frequently argue that incest taboos, and the necessity for family exogamy created by their operation, can be explained by reference to the problem of inbreeding depression. At one level this argument fails, because it does not take into account the complex symbolic meanings of incest and marriage in human societies (see especially Needham 1971; Schneider 1976). Careful cultural analyses of incest rules indicate that they cannot be reduced to simple statements about who can and cannot mate. Cultural anthropology conclusively demonstrates that cultural concepts of incest cannot be explained only as responses to the necessity of avoiding inbreeding depression. However, sociobiologists argue that it is not their intent to explain the intersocietal variation in the concepts of incest, but only to suggest that the ultimate cause of incest taboos, however conceptualized, is the avoidance of inbreeding depression.

No studies have empirically tested sociobiological and nonsociobiological interpretations of the low incidence of primary relative incest and the existence of incest taboos/exogamy rules. At present, the arguments on both sides are plausibility arguments, and there is little evidence of a quick resolution. There is one aspect of this problem, however, which has generated several holocultural investigations by sociobiologists: the institution of first-cousin marriage. Many societies prescribe or prefer marriage with a first cousin, a situation which seems guaranteed to result in some degree of inbreeding depression (Schull and Neel 1965; Stern 1973). Several solutions to this apparent paradox have been advanced by sociobiologists.

A preliminary comment is in order before reviewing these studies. In many societies, the requirement to marry a first cousin really means that Ego must marry an individual of the terminological category that contains his genetic first cousin. Thus a society may have a rule of first-cousin marriage and still exhibit few matings between genetic first cousins. Only an analysis of actual marriages will reveal the risk of inbreeding depression experienced in such a society. Mathematical models and empirical observations of societies with prescribed first-cousin marriage have demonstrated that only a minority of marriages follow the ideal rule, suggesting that most unions exhibit a lower risk of inbreeding depression.

One of the more interesting approaches to first-cousin marriage rules is suggested by Bateson's (1980, 1982, 1983) experiments on optimal outbreeding among Japanese quail. As noted earlier, Bateson argues that mate choice should be influenced by the balance between the costs/benefits of inbreeding and outbreeding. Using choice tests, Bateson shows that Japanese quail prefer to mate with animals exhibiting slight phenotypic differences from the animals surrounding the chooser in early life. Since the latter are usually close relatives, too great a phenotypic resemblance might signify a high degree of relatedness, with an associated risk of inbreeding depression. Too little phenotypic resemblance might indicate that the costs associated with outbreeding would be too high. For Japanese quail, the mate choice that optimally balances the costs/benefits of inbreeding and outbreeding is the first cousin.

Bateson's work may have some relevance to human mate choice and first-cousin marriage, but at present there is no evidence on this point. Of course, in many human societies, marriages may be arranged with little reference to the sexual and/or social attraction between the participants, making it difficult to apply Bateson's paradigm. However, if mate choice has evolved in some manner to reflect the balance between inbreeding and outbreeding, the failure rates of arranged marriages might provide some clue as to the operation of personal preference. Of course, mating preferences will not explain the presence or absence of rules of first-cousin marriage, but they may have some effect on such rules.

Another explanation of first-cousin marriage is suggested by van den Berghe's (1980) holocultural study, which shows that rules permitting or prescribing cross-cousin marriage are usually found in horticultural societies with unilineal descent. In a second article (1983) he provides a conjectural history of human social evolution to explain this distribution. He argues that in small-scale band societies, nepotism organizes social life, but that with the advent of horticulture and warfare, societies attain population sizes greater than can be effectively organized by nepotism. A response to this problem is the creation of unilineal descent groups, but this results in few chances to provide nepotism to close relatives in other lineages. According to van den Berghe, when in these societies Ego marries a first cousin, he is not only getting a mate but also receiving "extra nepotism," due to the genetic relationship between himself and his spouse. A male marrying beyond the range of first cousin will receive less, or no, extra nepotism, and presumably will have a lower inclusive fitness relative to males who married first cousins. Beyond noting the association between horticulture, unilineal descent, and first-cousin marriage rules, van den Berghe does not test his hypothesis. It is difficult to see how he can demonstrate that horticultural societies with rules promoting first-cousin marriage are optimizing some value (social cohesion, population size, etc.?), while those forbidding such marriages are either: (1) also optimizing the same value by barring such marriages or (2) failing to optimize the same value.

Hughes (1980) argues that the risk of inbreeding depression should result in the banning of first-cousin marriages, but finds two conditions under which the benefits might outweigh the risks of such marriages. The first is when few unrelated partners are available, and the second is when individuals possess resources which cannot easily be divided among heirs. In the latter case, Hughes suggests, Ego gives the resources to few offspring and through first-cousin marriage assures that these offspring are closely related. Hughes finds that of the ninety-seven societies in the *Ethnographic Atlas* that prefer or prescribe first-cousin marriage, seventy are characterized by average community sizes of under two hundred, supporting his first condition. He utilizes indirect measures, such as bride-price and residence rule, as proxies for resource divisibility and finds support for his second condition. However, these indirect measures are not very convincing.

Hughes concludes his article with a short discussion of why state-level societies usually ban first-cousin marriages. He cites studies by Otterbein and Otterbein (1965) and by Kang (1976), which indicate that first-cousin marriage is associated with frequent feuding, and argues that this might be the result of "an unusual willingness on the part of individuals to sacrifice themselves on behalf of exceptionally high [sic] related kin" (Hughes 1980:317). The desire of states to limit such feuding is seen as a cause for the ban on first-cousin marriages in these societies. Unfortunately, this argument is not subjected to an empirical test.

Alexander (1979) and Greene (1978) explore intersocietal variation in rules concerning first-cousin marriage by relating marriage rules to paternal certainty and kinship terminology. Greene demonstrates that when paternal certainty falls below 1.0, cousin types will differ in relatedness to Ego. For example, when $p = 0.9$, cross-cousins will have an r of 0.1018, matrilateral parallel cousins an r of 0.1131, and patrilateral parallel cousins one of 0.0917. The average for parallel cousins is 0.1024 (note that these calculations do not take into account the degree of relatedness between husbands and the potential sexual partners of their spouses). Greene suggests that if marriage rules function to reduce inbreeding, there is less reason to bar marriage with cross-cousins than with parallel cousins. Of fifty societies in the SCCS that permit marriage with either cross-cousins or parallel cousins, but not with both, forty-eight bar marriage with parallel cousins. It is obvious that coefficients of relatedness are not the entire story, however, since Greene's reasoning indicates that marriage with patrilateral parallel cousins carries the least risk of inbreeding depression and therefore should be the most popular form of first-cousin marriage. Greene's sample demonstrates that this is not the case.

Alexander notes that the genetic asymmetries described by Greene can explain the common practice of terminologically distinguishing cross-cousins and parallel cousins. He argues that when parallel cousins have a higher r with Ego than cross-cousins, the former will be lumped with siblings in the category of nonmarriageable relatives. Alexander tests his argument by comparing the cousin terminologies of societies with sororal polygyny (where MZCs may be Ego's half siblings, and brothers sometimes have access to each other's wives) with those of monogamous societies. In societies with sororal polygyny, parallel cousins are assumed to be more closely related to Ego than cross-cousins. Alexander finds that societies with sororal polygyny tend to exhibit Iroquois cousin terminology (i.e., parallel cousins distinguished from cross-cousins and lumped with siblings) while monogamous societies have either Eskimo (cross-cousins and parallel cousins lumped together and distinguished from siblings) or Hawaiian (all cousins lumped with siblings) terminology.

Ruse (1979, 1982) has cited Alexander's study as one of the strongest pieces of evidence for the validity of applying sociobiological principles to the explanation of human cultural rules. Alternative explanations of why some societies terminologically distinguish parallel and cross-cousins might focus on the fact that in lineage systems, these two cousin types belong to different lineages, with parallel cousins being members of Ego's group. Gray (unpublished manuscript) utilizes a log-linear technique to examine the interplay between cousin terminology, polygyny, descent rule, and cousin marriage rule and finds that the distinction between sororal polygyny and monogamy does account for a statistically significant portion of the variance in cousin terminology, although not as much as the portion explained by descent rule or cousin marriage rule. This result provides additional support for Alexander's position, since it indicates that his explanation is not redundant with existing cultural explanations of this trait.

In a final study of first-cousin marriage, Ember (1975) reverses the usual question and asks why some societies do not extend marriage prohibitions to first cousins. He argues that societies desire to increase their size, and that traits such as the incest taboo function to prevent inbreeding depression. If first-cousin marriages have a negative affect on population growth, Ember's position suggests that they should be banned. His holocultural study shows that two types of societies are likely not to forbid first-cousin marriages: (1) those with large breeding pools, where marriages between genetic first cousins are probably rare; and (2) small societies which have been depopulated, where the risk of inbreeding depression is more acceptable than having a large portion of the population remain unmarried. It should be noted that Ember's interpretation does not explain why some societies not only neglect to ban first-cousin marriages but make them a preferred marriage form—a situation which would seem to increase the incidence of first-cousin marriage and, hence, of inbreeding depression.

Greene (1978) identifies another cultural rule which may be related to avoidance of inbreeding depression, when she tests the prediction that the level of female extramarital sexual activity in a society is inversely correlated with rules demanding community exogamy. She argues that high levels of extramarital sex reduce the degree of relatedness between individuals in a community, lowering the need for institutionalized mechanisms of in-breeding avoidance. In a sample from the SCCS this prediction is supported, although the distribution does not quite reach statistical significance.

The institution of royal incest has also been subjected to sociobiological analyses. Van den Berghe and Mescher (1980) argue that this institution usually occurs in association with hypergamy and royal polygyny. They suggest that royal males maximize their inclusive fitness by following two strategies. First, by mating with their sisters or daughters, they can produce children who are related to them with an r of 0.75, but only at some risk of inbreeding depression. This risk may be offset by the second strategy of mating with large numbers of unrelated females. Since royal women cannot marry lower-status males, their position depends upon the possibility of marriage into other royal households. If there is little likelihood of such marriages, these females should accept the one option open to them and mate with a close male relative, in spite of the risk of inbreeding depression. Van den Berghe and Mescher's explanation is plausible, but they provide no method of testing their argument. Unfortunately, such a test would require data on the risks of inbreeding depression, the likelihood of marriages for royal women, and the degree of polygyny for societies which no longer practice this type of marriage.

The studies just reviewed suggest that the avoidance of inbreeding depression has been a major factor shaping the evolution of human mating systems and cultural rules. The final topic examined in this section involves the search for proximate mechanisms of inbreeding avoidance. The most obvious of these is, of course, the influence of incest taboos. Most anthropologists assume that these rules have some influence on the actual behavior of individuals. However, there is evidence of great variation in the effectiveness of incest rules in actually preventing inbreeding (Fox 1980; Needham 1971; Schneider 1976).

Of greater sociobiological interest is the possible operation of the Westermarck Effect. Westermarck (1899, 1922) suggested that an aversion to sexual contact obtains between people raised in the same household before the age of six. The Westermarck Effect is an excellent example of an evolutionary rule of thumb, since for most of human history, people who were raised in the same household would have been close genetic relatives, and matings between them might have resulted in inbreeding depression. Three situations have provided strong support for the hypothesis that the Westermarck Effect operates among humans.

The first situation involves the finding that unrelated males and females raised communally in Israeli Kibbutzim very rarely marry, although they are not forbidden to do so (Spiro 1958; Talmon 1964; Shepher 1971, 1983). Shepher (1971) analyzes data on almost three thousand marriages within these communities and finds only thirteen couples where both partners were raised in the same peer group. In most of these thirteen marriages, the partners were not in the same unit before the age of six. This suggests that there might be a critical period for the development of sexual aversion. Shepher and others note that the pattern of sexual activity seems to be congruent with the marriage data, with little adolescent sexual activity occurring between members of the same peer group (however, see Kaffman 1977).

In an examination of *sim-pua* marriages in Taiwan, Wolf (1976; see also 1966, 1968, 1970; Wolf and Huang 1980) shows that these marriages, which are between unrelated individuals raised from early childhood in the same household, exhibit lower reproductive success and seem to be less sexually satisfying than alternative marriage forms wherein the partners do not grow up in the same household. Wolf and Huang's study (1980) is especially important, because a number of alternatives to the Westermarck hypothesis (nutrition, health, economic status, etc.) are tested and rejected.

The most recent addition to the empirical literature on the Westermarck Effect is McCabe's (1983) study of patrilateral parallel first-cousin (FBD-FBS) marriage in a southern Lebanese village. The children of brothers interact frequently during childhood, and the relationship between such opposite-sex dyads closely resembles that of brothers and sisters. McCabe demonstrates that FBD-FBS marriages exhibit higher divorce and lower fertility than other types of marriage, including those between first cross-cousins. She argues that divorce and fertility rates are both indirect measures of sexual satisfaction and that her work supports the Westermarck hypothesis. An interesting question raised by this research is: Why is a marriage form that results in lower reproductive success both normatively preferred and popular (about 20 percent of the marriages in this village)?

These three studies lend impressive support to the hypothesis that the Westermarck Effect acts as an evolutionary rule of thumb in reducing the amount of inbreeding in humans. As discussed earlier, there is some evidence that a similar phenomenon occurs among some alloprimates, although the problem of rank clouds the issue. It is important to note that the existence of the Westermarck Effect does not adequately explain either the origin or the present distribution of incest taboos. For example, the effect cannot explain the extension of incest taboos to nonrelatives who are not raised with Ego. Nor does it explain the taboo on father-daughter and mother-son matings. Finally, many cultural anthropologists argue that if sexual aversion arises between primary family members, it is difficult to understand why a taboo is necessary to forbid mating between these individuals. Many of the references cited above address this last point, but none in a totally convincing manner.

The hypothesis that the Westermarck Effect is relevant to the origin of rules that regulate first-cousin marriage is tested in a holocultural study by Ember (1975). He argues that in communities with local endogamy, there is a high probability that first cousins will grow up together and therefore develop sexual aversion. In contrast, communities with exogamous marriages are likely to have residence rules that place at least some first cousins in different villages during childhood. Ember predicts that societies characterized by local endogamy will not permit marriages with first cousins. This prediction is not supported in a sample of 717 societies, nor is a second prediction, that societies with smaller endogamous communities will be less likely to permit first-cousin marriage than societies with larger endogamous communities. The indirect nature of Ember's measure of the Westermarck Effect and the fact that cousin marriage rules provide little evidence relevant to the problem of sexual attraction render his tests rather weak (see McCabe 1983 for other criticisms).

To summarize, I believe that the following points are particularly relevant to the sociobiological argument that the evolution of human mating systems has been strongly influenced by the necessity to avoid inbreeding depression. First, the evidence for inbreeding depression in modern societies is strong, but the level of inbreeding that a society can sustain without serious effects on population size or individual reproductive success seems to be variable. Second, there is a serious lack of data on the variance in reproductive success or inclusive fitness experienced by children resulting from different levels of inbreeding. Third, the evidence for the existence of the Westermarck Effect is strong, but how this relates to either the origin or the evolution of incest taboos is not clear. While the risk of inbreeding depression and the Westermarck Effect combine to provide a plausible explanation for a human tendency to avoid inbreeding, the combination does not, at least by itself, explain why such avoidance is formalized in normative rules or why these rules are manipulated in ways that apparently violate sociobiological logic (i.e., placing taboos on distantly or unrelated individuals while permitting matings between closer relatives). This is not to say that the sociobiological explanation of inbreeding avoidance might not be the core of an accepted ultimate explanation of incest taboos, only that it is not currently so, and that it will never be the entire story.

Sexual Dimorphism
As in the case of the alloprimates, the relationship between mating systems (indirect measures of the intensity of sexual selection) and sexual dimorphism in morphology and behavior has been an important topic in human sociobiology. Alexander et al. (1979), Gray and Roberts (1984), Gray and Wolfe (1980, 1982c), Handwerker and Crosbie (1982), Munroe and Munroe (1976), Low (1979), and Wolfe and Gray (1982a,b) all explore various aspects of this relationship.

The key paper in this set is by Alexander and his colleagues. As noted earlier, the authors found that the alloprimate species that are characterized by polygynous or promiscuous mating systems exhibit greater sexual dimorphism in body length than species with monogamous mating systems. The authors also present data on mean male and female height for ninety-three human societies and demonstrate the following points: (1) sexual dimorphism of stature ranges from a low of 1.047 to a high of 1.116, with a mean of 1.076, a figure the authors use to classify humans as "mildly polygynous" (1979:416); (2) when the sample is divided into societies exhibiting monogamy and those exhibiting polygyny, there is no difference in the mean stature dimorphism of these two categories; and (3) when the sample is divided into societies exhibiting ecologically-imposed monogamy, socially-imposed monogamy, and polygyny, there is a statistically significant difference between the mean stature dimorphism of the ecologically-imposed monogamy category (1.068) and the means of the other two categories (both 1.078).

As noted in Chapter Three, Alexander et al. argue that in societies with socially-imposed monogamy, the level of male-male competition over mates equals or exceeds the level found in many polygynous societies. A male may be formally married to a single female but may have mistresses or concubines. The wealth necessary for such arrangements is not evenly distributed, making the variance in male reproductive success greater than would be expected from the description of these societies as monogamous. A second factor that increases such variance is high male mortality in the warfare that is characteristic of these societies (see below). Thus, human societies with socially-imposed monogamy and those with polygyny correspond to alloprimate species with polygynous or promiscuous breeding systems; while societies exhibiting ecologically-imposed monogamy correspond to species with monogamous breeding systems. Given these equations, the observed difference in sexual dimorphism of stature in the human sample supports the predictions of sexual selection theory.

The holocultural test of the relationship between mating system and sexual dimorphism is only one component in a very complex argument. The strength of the Alexander et al. analysis becomes clearer when these other components are examined. For example, the authors argue that their characterization of humans as a mildly polygynous species is supported by the fact that several features of human biology and behavior would be interpreted as evidence of a mating system characterized by intense male-male competition over mates if observed among nonhuman animals. Thus, compared to females, human males: (1) mature later; (2) exhibit a higher mortality rate before and after the onset of reproductive activity; (3) senesce more rapidly; (4) are conceived in greater numbers; (5) receive greater parental investment; and (6) are favored by individuals in upper economic strata.

Another component of the argument involves the relationship between male mortality in warfare and sex ratio theory. Alexander et al. (1979) note that in societies with high male mortality due to warfare or mate competition, many males will die before receiving the amount of parental investment devoted to the average female. Fisher's model of the population sex ratio (see Chapter Six) predicts that parents should balance investment in the sexes and compensate for the high rate of male "failures" by starting greater numbers of males. Alexander et al. predict that societies with polygyny or socially-imposed monogamy will exhibit a male-biased primary or secondary sex ratio. The practices of preferential female infanticide and neglect may permit more precise adjustments of the sex ratio.

As noted in Chapter Six, information on human primary or secondary sex ratio is limited, but Alexander et al. argue that what is available supports their model. Especially important is the rough correlation they find between sexual dimorphism and secondary sex ratio. They note that Eveleth's (1975) ranking of geographic races from the most to the least dimorphic (Amerindians, Asians, Europeans, Africans, and New Guinea natives) is positively correlated with male-biased secondary sex ratios.

Alexander et al. are unclear about what conclusions are to be drawn from the results of their holocultural test and other arguments. The central problem is whether intersocietal variation in secondary sex ratios and sexual dimorphism of stature is at least partially explained by genetic differences between societies. In one passage the authors seem to suggest that intersocietal genetic variation is irrelevant:

> There is probably no good reason yet for accepting that differences in degrees of sexual dimorphism between ecologically monogamous and other humans actually reflect genetic differences between populations with different marriage systems. Ecologically imposed monogamy seems to occur in what would usually be termed marginal habitats such as the Arctic or the edges of deserts. Nutrition is likely to be less than optimal, and improved nutrition may increase sexual dimorphism. To the extent that such effects are caused by males responding more dramatically to increased nutrition (Tobias 1962), a polygynous background is implied [Alexander et al. 1979:420–421].

If it is assumed that there are no genetic differences relevant to intersocietal variation in sexual dimorphism, it is difficult to see why Alexander et al. took the trouble to conduct a holocultural test; the results would not be analogous to the alloprimate findings demonstrating that species with different genotypes exhibit different degrees of sexual dimorphism in a manner predicted by sexual selection theory. Under the assumption of no intersocietal genetic variation relevant to sexual dimorphism, the only conclusion that could have emerged from the investigation is that the human genotype codes for a certain level of sexual dimorphism congruent with our "mildly polygynous" past, but that inadequate nutrition or other factors may prevent full expression of this genotypic potential. We are left with the assertion that the average sexual dimorphism of 1.076 exhibited by humans is a reflection of our polygynous past. However, this assertion may be questioned on at least two grounds. First, it is possible that the degree of genotypic potential for sexual dimorphism characteristic of humans arose from factors other than sexual selection. Nutrition, heat or cold stress, sexual differentiation of niche utilization, predator pressure, etc. could be the ultimate factors explaining the dimorphism observed by Alexander et al. This does not deny that sexual selection might have been involved in the evolution of human sexual dimorphism in some manner, only that it has not been shown to be the primary ultimate factor. Second, it is not clear that Alexander et al. are correct in asserting that human sexual dimorphism is of the same magnitude as that found in mildly polygynous alloprimate species. The mean dimorphism for the monogamous species in the Alexander et al. sample is 1.026, while the mean for the six most mildly polygynous species (measured by mean harem size) is 1.124. The human mean falls almost exactly in the middle of these figures. If there is an allometric relationship between body size and sexual dimorphism (Leutenegger and Cheverud 1982, but see Alexander et al. 1979:410), one would be justified in claiming either a monogamous or a polygynous past for humans on the basis of these figures.

In their summary section of their paper, Alexander et al. appear to argue that at least some of the intersocietal variation in sexual dimorphism is related to genotypic differences between populations with different mating systems:

> In regard to degrees of sexual dimorphism and amounts of male-bias in the neonate sex ratio, the human populations studied by Eveleth and Tanner (1976) rank alike. . . . This correspondence, in view of the selective effects of polygyny . . . raises the possibility that both sets of data may reflect genetic differences [Alexander et al. 1979:435].

In this passage, the authors seem to hypothesize that different intensities of male-male competition for mates produce different selective pressures on sexual dimorphism and secondary sex ratio, and that the history of these pressures is reflected in intersocietal variation in the genes that are relevant to at least these two traits. Under this interpretation, the results obtained with humans are analogous to those obtained with alloprimates.

In spite of this rather important ambiguity, it is clear that the Alexander et al. paper is one of the most important in human sociobiology. Although the dependent variable is morphological rather than behavioral, the possibility that differences in the degree of male-male competition over mates might have influenced sex ratios, infanticide, warfare, and other aspects of human evolution requires that cultural anthropologists rethink some of the issues raised by this paper.

Gray and Wolfe (1980) raise questions about the methodology of the holocultural test in Alexander et al. (1979), noting, for example, that the rating of societies on the mating system variable was not done by independent coders and that several cases of questionable data were included in the sample. Utilizing a sample of 140 societies, Gray and Wolfe retest the relationship between marriage system (measured by Murdock's 1967 "monogamy," "limited polygyny," and "general polygyny" codes) and sexual dimorphism and fail to replicate the results obtained by Alexander et al. However, this retest does not employ the distinction between eco-logically-imposed monogamy and socially-imposed monogamy. To correct for this, Wolfe and Gray (1982b) remove state-level societies from Mur-dock's monogamy category and place them in the general polygyny category. The twenty-two monogamous societies in this revised sample exhibit a mean dimorphism of 1.072, compared to 1.077 for the limited polygyny societies, and 1.074 for the general polygyny/state societies. None of the differences reach conventional levels of statistical significance, and the moderate level of dimorphism in the general polygyny/state category runs counter to the predictions of the Alexander et al. model.

Wolfe and Gray (1982a) argue that the results obtained by Alexander et al. can be explained in part by Bergmann's rule that stature varies inversely with latitude. They suggest that for reasons involved with heat conservation or dissipation, peoples in arctic and equatorial regions will exhibit shorter stature than peoples in the middle latitudes (although some peoples in dry equatorial regions will exhibit a tall, linear body form, see Hiernaux 1977; Hiernaux et al. 1975). Since sexual dimorphism is directly correlated with stature, they predict that the greatest dimorphism will be found among peoples in the middle latitudes. This prediction is supported in a sample of 237 societies. Furthermore, when the societies in the Alexander et al. sample are classified by latitude, they also support the Wolfe and Gray prediction. When latitude is controlled, the relationship between marriage system and sexual dimorphism of stature found by Alexander et al. disappears.

The studies by Gray and Wolfe cast doubt on the argument that intersocietal variation in human sexual dimorphism can be explained by variation in marriage systems. However, several weaknesses of these studies should be noted. First, Gray and Wolfe's use of the ratings on polygyny from the *Ethnographic Atlas* does not precisely correspond to the Alexander et al. division of societies into ecologically-imposed monogamy, socially-imposed monogamy, and polygyny. Once a formal statement on the distinction between the two types of monogamy is available, this problem should be corrected. Second, latitude is only an indirect measure of the climatological variables of interest to Gray and Wolfe. A more adequate study, using better measures of heat and cold stress, is necessary. Finally, Gray and Wolfe do not examine the total model advanced by Alexander et al. For example, they do not investigate intersocietal variation in the secondary sex ratio. Unfortunately, data on this variable are not available for most of the societies utilized to study sexual dimorphism of stature, and a systematic investigation is therefore not possible.

In a preliminary investigation, Gray and Roberts (1984) attempt to deal with the warfare component of the Alexander et al. model. In a sample of seventy-two societies, the authors demonstrate that while Murdock's scores on polygyny are not correlated with sexual dimorphism, frequency of warfare is, with societies scored as "infrequent warfare" exhibiting less sexual dimorphism than those scored as "frequent warfare." A multivariate analysis reveals no interaction effects between warfare and marriage system, but suggests that the association between warfare and sexual dimorphism may be an artifact of the correlation of these variables with latitude. More detailed analyses of these results are necessary, but at first glance they do support certain components of the Alexander et al. model. However, warfare may operate directly upon sexual dimorphism without involving sexual selection, or sexual selection may be a by-product of warfare conducted for ecological or sociological reasons having no bearing on mate competition. Only future research will clarify these relationships.

Before concluding this review of the Alexander et al. model, it is worthwhile to engage in some speculation. If, for the sake of argument, we accept that the ultimate cause of human sexual dimorphism is male-male competition for mates as manifested in polygyny and/or mortality in warfare, the question arises of why holocultural tests have provided only equivocal support for the hypothesis that intersocietal variation in sexual dimorphism is related to these variables. An obvious answer is that societies exhibiting low male-male competition for mates have arrived at this state only recently, and that sexual dimorphism has not yet had time to reflect relaxed selection pressure. As selection for male height continues to decline in these societies, we would expect to observe reduced dimorphism, reflecting underlying changes in the genotype. This position is not improbable, but it merely asserts the validity of the hypothesis that the holocultural research was designed to test.

A second, more speculative response, concerns the effect of culture on male-male competition for mates. Sexual dimorphism increases with polygyny in the alloprimates because larger males are assumed to achieve a higher proportion of successful (i.e., fertile) matings than smaller males. If there is no association between male size and successful matings, sexual dimorphism will not evolve, all else being equal. The major unanswered question for humans is whether there is an association between male height and relative mating success in societies with male-male competition for mates. That is, in polygynous societies, do taller males obtain more (or higher-quality) wives or achieve more premarital or extramarital copulations than shorter males? Of course the latter considerations also apply to males in monogamous societies. Also, in societies with warfare, do shorter males suffer higher mortality in battle? If the answers to both these questions are negative, we would not expect sexual dimorphism to be related consistently to either polygyny or warfare.

There are good reasons for suggesting that culture may act so as to negate any link between male stature and mating success. The fact that marriages in many societies are arranged independently of the wishes or physical characteristics of the partners and are often based on economic considerations is one of the reasons. The fact that warfare is often conducted with weapons and tactics which do not seem to provide taller males an advantage is another. The possibility of a relationship between male height and mating success and/or survival in warfare needs to be tested in small-scale societies. While the results of such tests could not automatically be projected into the evolutionary past, they might provide a basis for more informed speculation. Schumacher's (1982) finding that in Italy taller individuals outcompete shorter people for higher positions in white-collar, blue-collar, and pink-collar occupations (an advantage that remains when social background and formal training are controlled) is relevant to this problem if occupational success is positively correlated with reproductive success or inclusive fitness in this society (see Irons 1979b for a discussion of cultural goals and inclusive fitness).

Two other studies of sexual dimorphism of stature are available. Munroe and Munroe (1976) test Wilson's (1975a) hypothesis that increased sexual dimorphism occurs in species where animals exhibit marked sexual dimorphism in activities. They argue that among humans, a high level of male involvement in child care indicates low sexual dimorphism in activities and should be inversely related to sexual dimorphism of stature. This prediction is supported in a sample of twelve societies. Munroe and Munroe also test Wilson's hypothesis by using sex differentiation in subsistence tasks as the independent variable and find in a sample of seventeen societies that "task dimorphism" is directly correlated with sexual dimorphism of stature. Gray and Wolfe (1982b) conceptualize the relationship between father-child contact and sexual dimorphism of stature in terms of parental investment and sexual selection theory and also predict a negative association between level of father-child interaction and dimorphism. Forty-three societies classified as exhibiting little proximity between fathers and offspring (Barry and Paxson 1971) have a mean sexual dimorphism of 1.077, which compares to a mean of 1.074 for the nineteen societies with frequent proximity. This difference is in the predicted direction, but does not reach statistical significance. A second test of the parental investment argument involves the prediction that societies with inheritance rules favoring wife's offspring would exhibit less sexual dimorphism of stature than those with other inheritance rules. The results do not support the prediction. In the same article, the authors also fail to find an association between the sexual division of labor and sexual dimorphism of stature in a sample of 179 societies. This result contradicts the Munroe and Munroe finding noted earlier.

In an innovative holocultural study, Low (1979) explores human ornamentation in the light of sexual selection theory. She observes that all societies in her sample exhibit some sexual dimorphism in ornamentation and argues that the messages communicated by male ornamentation will differ from those carried by female ornamentation. Female ornaments communicate statements of sexual availability, maternal fitness, sexual receptivity, and the power and/or wealth of mates. In contrast, male ornaments communicate about sexual fitness (including proper group membership) and potential for parental investment (wealth and success tokens). Low predicts that societies with lower levels of male-male competition for mates will exhibit both less overall ornamentation and less sexually dimorphic ornamentation than societies with marriage systems indicative of higher levels of competition. This prediction is supported in her sample.

Low's results are interesting, but difficult to interpret. For example, her finding that societies with ecologically-imposed monogamy have low ornamentation scores might also be explained in terms of cultural complexity, since this marriage form seems to be associated with simpler societies. Low published her scores on both ornamentation and marriage system, so alternative explanations for her results can be tested easily.

The role of sexual selection in producing sexually dimorphic human behavioral traits has been discussed by many theorists, but empirical work on this topic is surprisingly limited. Sociobiological explanations of dimorphism in behaviors relevant to mating and reproduction have been discussed at monograph length by Daly and Wilson (1978), Hrdy (1981a), and Symons (1979), and in numerous articles. The empirical work in this area will be discussed in Chapter Nine. A more general behavioral dimorphism is examined by Handwerker and Crosbie (1982), who misinterpret sociobiological theory as predicting that human males will dominate females in all social interactions. They test this hypothesis by having college students who are strangers to one another play a game. They find that dominance in this situation is not explained by sex, but rather by social variables, such as expectations, participation, and resources. The authors note several shortcomings of their study and these, combined with their misinterpretation of sociobiological theory, render their research inadequate as a test opposing a sociobiological and a nonsociobiological perspective. The theory of mating strategies does not predict that males will dominate females in all social settings. In novel situations, a male's best strategy might be to defer to the females, or to interact with them as equals. Factors such as differences in resources and expectations are precisely the variables that evolutionary biologists would expect to influence male-female interactions.

Summary

The empirical work on the relationship between sexual selection and inbreeding is among the strongest in human sociobiology. Evidence for the existence of inbreeding depression and the operation of the Westermarck Effect seems fairly convincing. Still unclear are the following: (1) What is the relationship between natural and sexual selection in this case? (2) How does the genetically-based tendency to avoid inbreeding relate to cultural constructs such as incest taboos? (3) Are first cousins optimal mates as regards balancing inbreeding and outbreeding, and does this explain any of the intersocietal variation in rules concerning cousin marriage?

The Alexander et al. (1979) explanation of intersocietal variation in sexual dimorphism of stature currently raises more problems than it settles. The plausibility of their model depends upon the validity of their distinction between different types of monogamy and on the congruence of the stature data with the data on sex ratios. Unfortunately, the data on the secondary sex ratio, especially from small-scale societies, are limited. Further, the coding of societies are exhibiting socially-imposed monogamy or ecologically-imposed monogamy needs refinement. The model would be strengthened if a correlation between stature and inclusive fitness or reproductive success could be demonstrated in several small-scale societies exhibiting polygyny and/or warfare. The relationship between climate and sexual dimorphism proposed by Wolfe and Gray (1982a) is based on an indirect measure, and this work needs to be replicated utilizing measures such as temperature, altitude, and humidity.

Research on other morphological and behavioral dimorphisms has only just started among humans. Low's (1979) article on ornamentation is interesting, but alternative hypotheses for her results need to be tested.

CHAPTER 8

Sexual Selection Theory II: Rank Theory

INTRODUCTION

Use of the concepts of dominance and rank to describe the behavior and social structure of alloprimates is controversial. Theoretical and methodological critiques have been vigorous (see Bernstein 1970, 1981; Gartlan 1968; Hinde 1978; Rowell 1974), as have the responses to such criticisms (see the commentaries in Bernstein 1981). Although opponents of the concepts make some very telling points, both concepts continue to function as major organizing principles in primatology. This debate is of great interest for its own sake, but in this chapter I restrict my attention to those aspects of the argument that are relevant to the hypothesis that rank and dominance behavior either cause or are consequences of sexual selection. However, the reader should bear in mind that while the idea of rank is usually treated unproblematically in this chapter, an intense debate on the validity of the concept continues.

The relationship between rank, dominance behavior, and sexual selection is a major topic in primatology (see especially Berenstain and Wade 1983; Bernstein 1976; Deag 1977; Fedigan 1983; Lancaster 1978; Robinson 1982; and, for other animals, Dewsbury 1982). The basic question is whether rank is related to sexual selection of either type: selection by competition or selection by preference. This question is usually approached by testing the hypothesis that individuals of high rank achieve greater mating success than individuals of low rank. We will see, however, that this simple question conceals a host of complexities. The remainder of this chapter consists of four main sections: male rank and selection by competition, male rank and selection by preference, female rank and selection by competition, and female rank and selection by preference. In each section, four questions will be examined: (1) What basic predictions should be made? (2) What are the difficulties of testing these predictions? (3) What significant tests have been conducted? (4) What are the alternative explanations (those not utilizing sexual selection theory) for the results obtained? The answers to the second and last questions are often the same for each of the sections and are discussed in detail only in the section on male rank and selection by competition.

MALE RANK AND SELECTION BY COMPETITION

Basic Predictions

The studies concerning rank and sexual selection that are reviewed in this chapter usually conceptualize rank as an independent variable and mating success as a dependent variable. Before describing the basic predictions examined by these studies, it is important to recall that investigations using rank as the dependent variable are also possible. Some studies combine ecological factors and reproductive strategies into a model explaining variance in the importance of rank-related behavior across an order or other taxonomic group. Several investigations of this type were reviewed in the chapter on ecological sociobiology. Others examine the factors influencing the rank attained by individuals. At various points in this volume, maternal rank, parental investment, body size, nutrition, socialization experience, etc. have been identified as relevant to this question. When the questions of whether there is a heritable component to rank and, if so, how this component is related to either mating success or reproductive success, are examined, these factors can be conceptualized as proximate mechanisms creating sexual selection.

Although she is not concerned with separating selection by competition from selection by preference, Fedigan's (1983) formulation of what she labels the priority-of-access-to-estrous-females (PAEF) model captures the essence of the proposed relationship between male sexual selection by competition and rank:

> (1) in multimale primate societies, males compete for a position in a dominance hierarchy; (2) males then have access to estrous (i.e., fertile) females in direct relation to the rank they hold in the dominance hierarchy; (3) since access to fertile females is believed to lead to reproductive success, dominant males will sire the most offspring and contribute a disproportionately high number of genes to the next generation; (4) thus, the genetically

based aspects of high dominance rank are perpetuated; and (5) an obvious corollary is that dominant males are presumed to carry the fittest genes [Fedigan 1983:96].

Fedigan's formulation indicates some of the criteria that must be met before we can conclude that sexual selection by competition is the ultimate mechanism responsible for the evolution of rank-related behavior. Point (4) indicates that researchers must identify those behavioral traits vital to achievement of rank which are genetically based and heritable. It is assumed that these are the traits upon which selection is acting, and a strong test of the sexual selection hypothesis would demonstrate intrasexual variation in the genotypes that are relevant to the production of these traits. Point (3) serves to remind us that the model demands evidence that the lifetime reproductive success of high-ranking males is greater than that of lower-ranking males. Only those components of lifetime reproductive success that are produced by variance in success in male-male competition over mates can be utilized in such comparisons. This limitation eliminates variation due to female preference, natural selection, demographic "accidents," and so on. Finally, point (4) also suggests that the strongest support for the hypothesis would be from studies demonstrating that, on the average, the descendants of high-ranking males outreproduce those of low-ranking males for at least one more generation.

Unfortunately, primatologists working with single populations for brief periods cannot meet any of these criteria. Thus, as in the case of nepotism theory, we must resort to indirect tests of the sexual selection hypothesis. The basic prediction, that in a given troop, high-ranking males will achieve greater mating success than lower-ranking males, is the most frequently tested. However, as was true for the "interaction of relatives" tests of nepotism theory, even when a study provides results congruent with this prediction, the number of alternative explanations means that the test lends only the weakest support for the sexual selection hypothesis.

Problems in Testing the Basic Prediction
Five factors create difficulties for testing the basic prediction. The first is the identification of those aspects of rank that are relevant to sexual selection. The second and third factors involve the measures of dominance and mating success used in tests of the prediction. The fourth concerns incidental variables that act to create the impression of a correlation between mating success and male rank, when in fact the association is a by-product of the relationship of these variables with the incidental variables. Finally, the fifth factor involves variables that act to depress the observed correlation between male rank and mating success, resulting in an incorrect decision to accept the null hypothesis of no association between rank and mating success.

1. *The issue of rank.*   The first problem is a central issue in the debate over rank: What is the biological reality of rank, and which aspects of rank are heritable? Bernstein's (1981) distinction between dominance relationships and dominance ranks illustrates the problem:

> The confusion of dominance relationships (which involve two or more individuals) with dominance ranks (which are assigned to a single individual) has obscured the possible evolutionary basis of dominance relationships. If benefits accrue to dominant members of pairs, then those attributes which allow an animal to establish dominance can be selected. Dominance per se and dominance ranks, on the other hand, cannot be genetically transmitted since they constitute relationships with other individuals rather than absolute attributes. Dominance rankings in particular may be useful for describing behavioral patterns within a group, but they may reflect our own ability to count rather than any important variable in social organization [Bernstein 1981:419].

At first glance, Bernstein's point, although correct, seems to have little bearing on the testing of the basic prediction. Let us assume that the ranks achieved by animals mirror genetic differences that are relevant to behavioral traits involved with obtaining rank. For example, assume that the highest-ranking animal has genes coding for more "aggressiveness" than the second-ranking animal, and so on down the hierarchy. Or, if "social intelligence" correlates with rank, assume that high-ranking animals have genes coding for "better" social intelligence than low-ranking animals. If achieved rank is correlated with a single behavioral trait in this manner, it is probably legitimate to use the phrase "rank is selected" when describing selection for these behaviors. Thus, Berenstain and Wade (1983) and Deag (1977) argue that the tendency to dominate competitors is selected in some species. Animals manifest this tendency not only during competition for limited resources but when also dominant animals harass subordinates even though no resources are at stake. Berenstain and Wade note that while actual dominance relationships are affected by many factors, there will be a high correlation between achieved rank, difference in competitive ability, and tendency to dominate others. Because factors other than dominance may determine the outcome of competition over mates (see below), the observed correlation between rank and mating success is expected to be less than perfect, but still high enough to make talk of selection for high rank valid.

Whether or not the equation: "observed rank hierarchy accurately mirrors phenotypic variation in a single behavioral trait, which, in turn, accurately mirrors genotypic variation relevant to this trait" holds for a particular species is an empirical question. If it does not, it makes no sense to talk of selection for high rank in that species. Theorists have discussed at least two circumstances in which the equation might not hold. First, variation in a single behavioral trait might not adequately explain the rank hierarchy of a group. For example, while fighting ability or competitiveness may be one route to high rank in a population, weaker males might achieve high position by forming coalitions with other males, while still others might enlist the support of females to obtain high rank. Achieved rank can also be influenced by a host of "accidental" factors having nothing to do with genetic variation. Thus, a male's learning history might affect his ultimate rank, as might demographic "accidents," such as the presence or absence of siblings or unrelated peers, loss of mother in early life, etc. These accidents and alternative paths to high rank should not be seen merely as "noise," serving to reduce the expected correlation between rank and a single underlying behavioral trait. For example, Bernstein (1981) suggests that in some species, achievement of rank is context-dependent, such that behaviors serving to promote high rank in one generation or breeding season might not do so in the next. In this situation, the genes creating increased mating success via high rank in one period might not do so in the next period. Discussions phrased simply in terms of selection for high rank would be rather misleading in these circumstances.

A second circumstance, wherein the equation does not hold, occurs if there is no genetic variation relevant to the behavioral trait that is correlated with rank. Assume, for example, that competitiveness is the trait relevant to achievement of rank. A cohort of males could have the same genotype relevant to competitiveness, and yet a rank hierarchy will form based on nonheritable traits (e.g., the alpha male weighs more than his equally competitive peers, etc.). High rank might be associated with mating success in this situation, but the lack of genetic variation means that it would be improper to speak of selection for high rank.

These issues are far from settled, and it is likely that the validity of using phrases such as "rank is selected" will vary from species to species. For the present, the reader should be aware that such phrases are often shorthand statements, and should examine any study with an eye toward identifying which behavioral traits are assumed to be under selection.

2. *Measures of dominance.* A second difficulty in testing the basic prediction is the measurement of dominance. The methodological issues involved are well rehearsed in the alloprimate literature, and I will merely identify the major topics. Eaton (1974) criticizes early studies relating rank to mating success because the concepts of dominance and rank were often inconsistently defined and were based on subjective measures. He also notes that the effects of ties, rank reversals, and transitive relationships (X dominates Y, who dominates Z, who dominates X; see Bernstein 1981:423) were often not considered in the construction of rank hierarchies. When examining studies of rank, especially those conducted prior to the mid-1970s, the reader should always identify the researcher's definition of

dominance or rank and evaluate how hierarchies were constructed. Further, the skew of the hierarchy should be noted—does the alpha male always dominate subordinates, or does he merely win a certain percentage of encounters? Although skew is difficult to summarize in a single statistic, it is an important factor in determining the variance in male mating success in a population. Unfortunately, no alloprimate studies have related skew to variance in reproductive success.

Another problem is that researchers often use different forms of agonistic behavior to assign rankings. Some observe displacements when resources (food, mates, space) are at stake. Others examine patterns of threats and appeasement gestures. Still others work only with data from actual fights. Finally, some develop their rankings from a combination of all three types of data. One of these options is not inherently more correct, and the most appropriate option depends upon the behavioral traits the researcher assumes to be under selection. On the other hand, it is not clear that each will provide the same ranking in all species or even within the same study group. In any event, proper evaluation of a study requires examination of the behaviors that were used to assign rankings.

A special problem is created when rankings are determined by the outcomes of agonistic encounters over a limited resource (e.g., a peanut thrown between two animals, or an estrous female introduced into a cage with two males). Outcomes might indeed reflect dominance relationships, but they might also reflect asymmetries in resource holding potential (RHP) that are not related to dominance (e.g., fatigue, temporary social support, etc.) or asymmetries in the payoffs for obtaining the resource (e.g., an apple is more important to a hungry male than a sated one, and the former might be more willing to fight for it; see Chapais 1983; Parker 1974, 1982, 1983). One way of coping with this problem is to test or observe each pair in several different sets of circumstances and with different resources at stake. It should be noted that in dominance matrices derived from observed encounters, the fewer the encounters between two animals, the greater the chance that a non-rank-related asymmetry is concealing a dominance relationship. Unfortunately, the few encounters between them can also be evidence that one animal is so dominant that the subordinate avoids situations in which conflict is possible.

The influence of asymmetries in RHP or payoffs creates the further problem of when to measure a rank hierarchy. For example, in seasonal breeders, patterns of displacement during the breeding season may not be congruent with those observed during the nonbreeding season. While this might indicate that the null hypothesis of no relationship between rank and mating success should be accepted, it could also mean that different payoff asymmetries operate when access to estrous females, rather than access to food or space, is at stake.

The problems of measuring dominance should indicate the care that must be taken in evaluating the results of various empirical studies. Different measures of dominance and different methods of constructing rank hierarchies might make it difficult to compare the results of one investigation with those of another.

3. *Measures of mating success.* A third methodological problem involves the measurement of mating success. The ideal statistic would measure only the portion of each male's lifetime reproductive success that is created by the matings he wins through competition with other males (either directly, as when males fight over females, or indirectly, as when high-ranking males gain automatic access to estrous females). The statistic would ignore components of a male's lifetime reproductive success due to natural selection, demographic accidents, and female preference (see below). At present, we have no data on male lifetime reproductive success in any alloprimate species, and therefore no study has attempted to calculate such a statistic. The tests reviewed below all use the indirect measures of either mating activity or total reproductive success over a span of time.

The use of such indirect measures is unsatisfactory. Note that what needs to be measured is the portion of a male's reproductive success that is created by differential mating access. The number of infants sired by a male may not be an adequate indirect measure of this variable, since other factors may be responsible for differential male reproductive success. For example, infertile males may enjoy high rank and disproportionate access to estrous females without this being evidenced by paternity exclusion tests. Variations in female quality may affect the number of infants sired by different males, as may male qualities unrelated to rank. Thus, studies utilizing rank-related differences in the number of infants sired as evidence for sexual selection by competition usually accept the assumption that such differences are the direct result of differential mating success. Unfortunately, few of these studies provide evidence for making this assumption.

Numerous indirect measures of male mating success have been used in the studies reviewed below: number of days observed mating, number of mounts, number of mounts with ejaculation, number of females mated with, number of consortships, number of matings during conception cycle, number of matings during the period of highest probability of conception, frequency of mating, number of days consortship observed, overall sexual behavior, and so on. The major problem with these types of measures is that we are not sure that the different mating activities translate into the differential reproductive success necessary for sexual selection to operate. There is some evidence that they do not. Stern and Smith (1984), for example, investigate eight behavioral measures of mating success, involving both consort behavior and copulatory behavior, in three laboratory groups of rhesus macaques. Correlation of these behavioral measures with paternity, as established by paternity exclusion tests, indicates that none of the measures accurately predicts male reproductive success. A similar result is reported by Curie-Cohen et al. (1981) for a zoo troop of rhesus.

Fedigan (1983:106) argues that there is little evidence that the various behavioral measures of reproductive success are comparable across situations or species. She also notes that when researchers have data on several forms of sexual behavior in a single group, the usual situation is for only some of them to be correlated with male rank. At present we do not know which behaviors most accurately predict male reproductive success, and therefore we cannot say which are the most appropriate to use in tests of the basic prediction.

Dunbar (1982b, 1983) addresses another facet of the indirect measurement problem when he distinguishes between instantaneous and lifetime reproductive success. He notes that a male's reproductive success is determined by his mating success and by his tenure at different ranks and suggests that males may achieve equal reproductive success with different combinations of these factors. For example, a male who monopolizes all the females in a troop for a few breeding seasons and then ceases to mate (maximizing instantaneous success) may achieve no more reproductive success than one who copulates with only a few females each year but maintains this rate of mating over many breeding seasons (maximizing lifetime success). This means that a comparison of the mating success of males over one or two breeding seasons does not accurately measure the variance in male reproductive success; it gives too much weight to those males maximizing instantaneous reproductive success. Only long-term studies will indicate whether or not these two tactics result in differential reproductive success.

Other problems confront the use of indirect measures of male reproductive success, but these will be introduced during the reviews of studies where they are relevant.

4. *Confounding variables, I.* Another topic concerns factors that increase the probability that a researcher will incorrectly reject the null hypothesis of no association between male rank and reproductive success. These are confounding variables, which must be controlled in any study of rank and mating or reproductive success. A major factor is the association between observability and high rank. Drickamer (1974a) notes that in many multimale troops, because high-ranking males are more visible than subordinates their sexual activity is more likely to be observed by a researcher, creating an artificial association between mating success and rank. In a study of the La Parguera colony of rhesus macaques, Drickamer finds statistically significant, positive correlations between male rank and a series of sexual behaviors. However, the relationships do not reach statistical significance when rank-related observability is controlled.

In most early studies of rank and sexual behavior, fieldworkers merely recorded all observed sexual behavior. Jeanne Altmann (1974) argues that since all animals and all behaviors are not equally visible, data from such ad libitum sampling should not be used to calculate rates of behavior. Simple corrections for observability in data collected through ad libitum sampling do not solve this problem. Fedigan (1983:108) suggests that the importance of the problem depends both upon the species under study and the field conditions. She notes that observers working in open terrain, with small groups, or with groups exhibiting minimal dispersal, have a good chance of observing all copulations and therefore might be justified in using data gathered by ad libitum sampling to calculate behavioral rates. The same is true for observers of species where sexual activity is restricted to long-lasting consortships or where only one to two females are in estrus at any given time. However, there is no doubt that the strongest methodology involves focal animal sampling, where subordinates are observed as frequently as the dominant males. In any event, evaluation of a study requires knowledge of how the data on sexual behavior were gathered and which, if any, techniques were used to control for rank-related observability.

This material suggests that a common mating tactic of subordinate males is to "sneak" copulations while out of sight of dominant males. It should be noted that conditions of captivity may prevent lower-ranking males from adopting this tactic. If there are few places in which subordinates can escape the gaze of dominants, the correlation between rank and mating success is likely to be higher than it would be in a free-ranging troop. The same situation may obtain in provisioned troops if feeding occurs in a small, open area, and if observation is restricted to the feeding site. Studies on rank and mating in captive and provisioned troops should include an evaluation of the alternative mating strategies that are open to subordinates.

Several studies have suggested that both male age and tenure in a troop are related to rank in some species (references in Fedigan 1983:111–112). Although there are exceptions (see especially Strum 1982), the hypothesis that these variables, rather than rank per se, are responsible for variance in male mating success has rarely been examined. Unfortunately, if the correlation between rank and either of these variables is fairly high, there is little chance of examining the influence of rank while controlling for the effects of age or tenure. Alternative explanations relating tenure or age to male reproductive success are discussed below.

5. *Confounding variables, II.*   A final topic involves factors that increase the risk that the researcher will incorrectly accept the null hypothesis of no relationship between male rank and mating success. These are confounding variables lowering the correlation between mating success and rank. Here I will briefly note several of the most important and will deal with them more fully when they affect specific studies (see reviews in Berenstain and Wade 1983; Chapais 1983; Fedigan 1983).

The first factor involves the timing of estrus. In species where only a single female is in estrus at any given time, the alpha male is predicted to monopolize her. However, when several females are in estrus simultaneously, the cost of monopolizing them may be too great, giving lower-ranking males a chance to mate (a formal model is presented in S. Altmann 1962a,b). In these circumstances, the alpha male's choices may be explained by variation in female quality. For example, he may monopolize females only during the time when copulation is most likely to result in conception. If there are rank-related quality differences between females (e.g., fertility, health of infants produced), he may concentrate on mating with high-ranking females. If there are age-related differences in quality, he may monopolize females of the highest-quality age group. Presence or absence of a recent offspring may affect female quality. A prediction derived from these considerations is that the alpha males of seasonally breeding species will achieve a smaller percentage of total copulations than their counterparts in nonseasonal breeding species. However, the correlation between ordinal rank and rank in proportion of total copulations should not differ in the two types of species.

Female defensibility (Berenstain and Wade 1983) and differences in female quality may combine to produce situations where the alpha male does not achieve as much mating success as might be expected. If estrous females are easily defensible, the alpha male may be able to monopolize them. However, when estrous females are less defensible, males may have to restrict their attention to the highest quality females, lowering the total proportion of matings achieved by the alpha male. Factors making estrous females less defensible include synchronous estrus, large distances between animals, female unwillingness to mate, long consortships as a requirement for mating, and so forth.

Another factor depressing the correlation between rank and mating success involves the number of males present in a troop and the age differences between them. In small populations with few males, or where the alpha male is significantly older than his rivals, the association between rank and number of copulations may be quite strong. However, as more males enter the troop, or as rivals more closely resemble the alpha male in age and social experience, the proportion of copulations achieved by the alpha male may decline.

A fourth set of variables acting to lower the correlation between rank and mating success involves differences in resource holding potential (RHP) or asymmetries in payoffs (Chapais 1983) between pairs of males in specific situations. In any given situation, differences in RHP may create outcomes not predicted by the hypothesis that higher-ranking males will monopolize matings. For example, on one occasion the alpha male may be wounded, and a threat from a subordinate will suffice for the latter to obtain an estrous female. On another occasion, a subordinate might obtain a female by calling upon close kin for support against a dominant male. An example of a payoff asymmetry which might affect the outcome of an encounter between two males is female preference. If a female has a close relationship with a subordinate male, he may fight to deny the alpha male access to her with more tenacity than he would if another female were at stake. On the other hand, a dominant male might be less willing to fight for her, because the attachment to the subordinate might mean that monopolizing her would require extra effort (Bachmann and Kummer 1980 describe such a situation for hamadryas baboons).

Female preference may lower the correlation between rank and mating success independently of payoff asymmetries. Females may not allow themselves to be monopolized by a high-ranking male if any one of the following conditions obtains: (1) he is a natal male, and the females are attempting to avoid inbreeding; (2) they have mated with him in the past and prefer "stranger" males, with novel genotypes, in order to assure genetic variability in their offspring; (3) they prefer mating with a variety of males, to lower the risk of infanticide or to increase the number of males willing to provide paternal investment; (4) they prefer older males, who have demonstrated their genetic quality by survival; or (5) they prefer males with phenotypic traits other than those necessary to obtain high rank (e.g., less aggressive males).

The two final factors serving to lower variance in male mating success in multimale troops are rather speculative and have not yet been the subject of empirical research. One involves nepotism: Might an alpha male permit closely related subordinates access to estrous females when he can prevent it? The inclusive fitness rewards of such behavior would have to be high to offset the potential loss to the alpha male's personal reproductive success, but the theoretical possibility of such nepotism remains open. The other factor involves Vehrencamp's (1983a,b) concept of skew. In circumstances where a minimal number of adult males are required for group survival, might the alpha male permit some matings between subordinates and estrous females in order to keep males in the troop?

Relevant Studies
The relationship between male rank and mating success has been studied mainly in the genera *Papio* and *Macaca*. I will review the studies for each genus separately, and then discuss studies in other groups.

1. *Studies of baboons (Papio).* Studies by DeVore (1965, olive) Hall and DeVore (1965, olive and chacma), Hausfater (1975, yellow), Packer (1979b, olive), Saayman (1971, chacma), and Seyfarth (1978, chacma) provide partial or full support for the basic prediction that among baboons, high rank is positively correlated with male mating success. On the other hand, recent studies of olive baboons by Smuts (1982) and Strum (1982) find no support for this prediction, and even suggest that there is a negative correlation between rank and mating success in this species.

As is characteristic of all pioneering research, the early studies of DeVore (1965) and Hall and DeVore (1965) are marked by methodological weaknesses. Measures of dominance are not adequately described, data on sexual behavior were gathered ad libitum, and no statistics are reported. When the data are examined closely, they provide only moderate support for the basic prediction. DeVore's (1965:277) table of matings by males in the SR group of olive baboons shows that the most dominant male achieved the greatest number of completed copulations, but the Spearman correlation coefficient between rank and completed copulations (0.63) is not statistically significant. Hall and DeVore (1965:60) use two measures of dominance to rank the males of the SR group ("success-failure on experimental food-incentive tests" and "dominance-subordination in 'natural' situations") and find that these provide different orderings; and that both orderings differ from the one presented by DeVore (1965:277). These alternative orderings result in nonsignificant Spearman coefficients (both 0.34) for the relationship between rank and completed copulations. DeVore also suggests that while dominant animals mate only when females are maximally tumescent (and presumably most likely to conceive), subordinate males often mate during periods of partial tumescence. However, the results from the SR group demonstrate that four of six males mated only during full tumescence, while the two lowest-ranking males were less selective. The biological significance of this difference is unclear.

The other troop of olive baboons examined in DeVore (1965) provides no support for the basic prediction. The alpha male in the SV group was not observed to mate, and the Spearman coefficient between rank and completed copulations is a nonsignificant -0.02. Finally, in the S group of chacma baboons (Hall and DeVore 1965), the alpha male achieved more copulations than the two lower-ranking males, but the third-ranking male mated more often than the second-ranking.

Although the correlations between rank and mating success in the DeVore and the Hall and DeVore studies are not statistically significant, the authors conclude that rank and mating success are related. A reason for this position may be the way the proposed relationship is conceptualized. If we predict only that the alpha rank is associated with disproportionate mating success and make no prediction about the association between rank and mating success for animals below the alpha rank, a demonstration that the alpha male achieves more matings than expected by chance counts as support for the basic prediction. Under these conditions, the results in the SR and S groups support the basic prediction (chi-square test created by contrasting the alpha male against all others equaling 7.1 and 19.5 respectively, $p < 0.01$), but those of the SV group do not. In contrast, if we predict that mating success varies systematically with rank and that the second-ranked male will be more successful than the third-ranked male, and so on down the hierarchy, a rank order correlation coefficient is in order.

Under these conditions, none of the troops supports the basic prediction. Although primatologists usually assume that the second conceptualization applies to most alloprimates, the former would be as biologically significant. Studies of rank and mating success should be evaluated from both of these perspectives.

Using data on sexual behavior collected by ad libitum sampling, Saayman (1971) studied a troop of chacma baboons containing three adult males and thirty-one adult females. While the males did not differ on number or mean length of consorts, the alpha male followed more females, achieved more mounts, and had more total ejaculations than the other males. It is difficult to say whether these differences were relevant to reproductive success. Saayman notes that consorts were formed at the peak of female sexual swelling, suggesting that the number of consorts is the best indirect measure of reproductive success in this troop. Since there were no rank-related differences between males in the number of consorts, the different levels of sexual activity within consorts may not reflect differential reproductive success.

The high number of females per male (10.3) in Saayman's troop is of interest. It is at least 2.5 times greater than in any of the other baboon troops discussed here. DeVore (1965) notes that the low number of females per male in the SR troop (1.16) was associated with high intermale tension and frequent incomplete copulations, while both these elements were missing in the SV troop containing 2.4 females per male. The relatively equal distribution of mating success in Saayman's troop may reflect a similar dynamic.

Using systematically collected data on both dominance and sexual activity in a chacma baboon troop, Seyfarth (1978) presents a test of Altmann's (1962a,b) mathematical model of the relationship between male rank, mating success, and distribution of estrus. Altmann notes that in species where consortships are a component of mating, the alpha male may be able to consort with only one female at a time. When two females enter estrus simultaneously, the second-ranking male should monopolize the additional (perhaps lower-quality) female. As more females enter estrus simultaneously, still lower-ranking males should achieve mating success. Seyfarth demonstrates that on eight of the nine occasions when only one female was in estrus, the alpha male consorted with her. On the occasions when there were two females in estrus, both males formed consortships. These results match the predictions of Altmann's model. However, Seyfarth notes that while Altmann assumes that the distribution of matings will be the outcome of male-male competition, in this troop female preference for the alpha male appears to play the vital role in determining male mating success.

Altmann's model is subjected to a more sophisticated test in Hausfater's (1975) volume on dominance and reproductive success in a yellow baboon troop at Amboseli. Hausfater's work is one of the most methodologically sound studies of this topic, using focal animal sampling techniques to collect data on sexual activity and carefully describing the construction of rank hierarchies. Since males frequently changed ranks during the course of his fourteen-month study, Hausfater analyzes the reproductive success of different ranks, rather than that of individual males.

Altmann's model is tested with data on matings during the third day prior to deturgescence of the sexual skin (D-3), the time when matings are most likely to result in conception (Hendrickx and Kraemer 1969). A second data set of matings during the potential fertile period of D-7 to D-1 was also used. The greatest number of females in estrus on a single day was three, leading to the prediction that only the first three ranks would engage in copulation. However, nine of fourteen ranks mated on D-3 days, while thirteen of the fourteen ranks did so on days D-7 to D-1. Further, the three highest ranks did not conform to the predictions of the model, with the alpha rank mating less often than predicted, and the second and third ranks more often. Finally, two females gave birth to viable offspring during the study, and the alpha male was not observed to have mated with either during the conception cycle. These findings suggest that Altmann's priority-of-access model does not explain mating patterns in this troop.

Although Hausfater's data do not support the Altmann model, they do reveal a relationship between rank and mating success. The Spearman coefficient between rank and frequency of mating on D-3 days is 0.70, which rises to 0.75 when days D-7 to D-1 are considered. Hausfater notes that this correlation explains about 56 percent of the variance in mating success. Rank-related differences in reproductive strategies might explain why low ranks achieve more matings than expected. Hausfater notes that high ranks tend to be more selective in mating than low ranks, tending to mate only on a few cycle days, especially around day D-3, and with only a few favored females. In contrast, lower ranks tend to consort on more cycle days and with any available female, but they may mate at times that are less than optimal for conception. Hausfater suggests that the first rank might be achieving the greatest number of productive copulations without suffering the costs of consorting, while lower ranks achieve some reproductive success, but only by accepting the costs of consortships.

An important aspect of Hausfater's study is his discussion of how the rank history of males over a lifetime relates to differential reproductive success. After demonstrating that each rank exhibits a specific rate of mating success, he notes that frequent rank changes might result in little variance in the lifetime reproductive success of males:

> It may be . . . that every adult male baboon in his lifetime occupies each dominance rank for the same amount of time as does every other male. If so, then, in the long run, all males would be expected to have an equal total lifetime reproductive success. Even if, as is more likely, males differ in the

sequence of ranks that they occupy and in the duration of rank occupancy, the total reproductive success of all males may still be equal. For example, in this study second ranking males had a higher reproductive success than did fifth ranking males, but fifth ranking males had longer durations of rank occupancy, on the average, than did second ranking males. Thus, to achieve any given level of reproductive success, a male may either occupy second rank and reproduce at a high rate for a short period of time or occupy fifth rank and reproduce at a low rate for a longer period of time. The end results in terms of total reproductive success, however, could be equal [Hausfater 1975:140–141].

A male's tenure in a particular rank can be influenced by numerous factors, including the presence of opponents, female support, and rank-related mortality risks. Unfortunately, there is little information on these factors for any alloprimate group (however, see Hausfater et al.'s 1982 computer simulations of the influence of some life history factors on male reproductive success).

Hausfater's argument, that the evolutionary implications of rank-related variance in mating or reproductive success must be interpreted in light of the lifetime rank histories of males, identifies a major difficulty with short-term studies of this problem. A study attempting to show that rank is linked to mating success through the mechanism of sexual selection by competition must demonstrate not only that in a given population genetic variation between males is partially responsible for different patterns of lifetime rank occupancy, but also that different patterns of occupancy are correlated with varying amounts of mating and/or reproductive success. The first demonstration requires genetic data which will probably not be available in the near future. The second requires data on rank history and mating success over the lifetimes of males. Such data are not currently available for any alloprimate population. Thus, brief studies reporting a positive correlation between male rank and mating success must be interpreted with care, for in the absence of life history data they provide only the weakest support for the sexual selection hypothesis. On the other hand, short-term studies showing no correlation between rank and reproductive success cannot be taken as conclusive evidence that the hypothesis does not apply to a given population, since for brief periods the operation of different reproductive strategies might conceal lifetime associations between rank and reproductive success.

A final report of a positive relationship between male rank and mating success is Packer's (1979b) four-year study of three olive baboon troops at Gombe. For transferred males, the amount of consorting activity is significantly correlated with rank, as is the amount of consorting on day D-3 of conception cycles. Unlike Hausfater, Packer finds that the alpha male consorted on day D-3 of the conception cycle in fifteen of twenty-one pregnancies. The methodology of Packer's study (dominance defined by supplantations, focal animal sampling, etc.) and the number of males involved (twenty-seven in three groups) makes it one of the strongest reports supporting the basic prediction.

Two methodologically sophisticated studies of olive baboons at Gigil, Kenya (Smuts 1982, Strum 1982) do not support the basic prediction. Both find negative or nonsignificant correlations between male rank and measures of mating success; in Strum's case, the negative correlation reaches statistical significance when rank is correlated with consort rank on days D-3 to D-7 of conception cycles. The authors explain their surprising results by arguing that social relationships not involving dominance may be vital to male mating success. Smuts finds that older males, who generally have wider social networks, are more successful at mating during conception cycles than the younger males, who generally outrank them. Her results suggest that older males limit mating not only to certain females and to certain days during a cycle but also to certain cycles. If this is the case in other species, the positive association between high level of sexual activity and male rank that is evidenced in other studies may not reflect a true relationship between rank and reproductive success. High-ranking males in these studies may be mating more often, but in terms of conception, the matings may be "wasted" efforts. However, if males achieve mating success by creating positive social relationships with females, their efforts may not be wasted, for sexual interactions might be one route by which younger males develop relationships with females.

Strum explains the negative association between mating success and rank by noting that male rank is inversely correlated with tenure in the troop. Male newcomers to the troop rank above long-term residents, but the latter possess the social skills that allow them to monopolize females during conception cycles without engaging in aggression. Their ability to avoid fights may be a result in part of females preferring to associate with these familiar males. Strum suggests that newcomers use aggression to integrate themselves into the troop and to gain time to learn the social skills necessary for mating success. She also notes that adult males frequently transfer between troops, and that their lifetime reproductive success therefore depends upon such factors as the number of transfers they make, the time they remain in each troop, and the number of resident males and females in each troop.

The implications of Smuts' and Strum's results are not yet clear. It is possible that the negative correlations they observe are confined to their troops, or to a given time period, or to a single species; only further research will decide. On the other hand, if the findings are applicable to other situations, and if future investigations replicate them in other species, it would seem obvious that the basic prediction is not an adequate description of the relationship between male rank and reproductive success. However, even this conclusion would not totally invalidate the hypothesis that rank and reproductive success are linked through the mechanism of sexual selection by competition. If only the most domineering males (however measured) gain entry into a troop, and if the higher-ranking members of a cohort of young males forge the widest social networks, rank achieved as a newcomer might be an accurate indicator of reproductive success. Once again, only data on variance in lifetime reproductive success will resolve this issue.

2. *Studies of macaques, (Macaca).*   Berenstain and Wade (1983:218) note that female defensibility among the macaques is generally lower than among the baboons, and they predict that the relationship between male rank and mating success will be weaker in the former genus. Two reasons for lower defensibility are (1) that macaques tend to be seasonal breeders, and (2) that many species do not signal ovulation by morphological changes, such as sex swellings. Studies on rank and mating success among macaques appear to support Berenstain and Wade's argument. Many find a positive relationship between rank and mating success, but the correlations are generally lower than among baboons, and the evidence suggests that major differences in mating success exist between "classes" of males (e.g., "high, medium, low," or "central, peripheral, outside"), but often not between the males within a class.

The majority of studies have involved rhesus macaques. Early research on the provisioned groups on Cayo Santiago suggested a positive association between rank and various measures of mating success (Carpenter 1942; Conaway and Koford 1964; Kaufmann 1965; Sade 1968). Although suggestive, these studies are limited, because data on sexual behavior were collected by ad libitum sampling, and the measures of dominance and the techniques for constructing rankings are often not described. In a slightly later study, Loy (1971) correlates rank and number of observed matings in group F on Cayo Santiago and finds that while the Spearman coefficient (0.48) between these variables is not statistically significant, the four "high" and four "mid-ranking" males copulated more frequently than the four "low" males (68, 97, 22 copulations per class, respectively). Mid-ranking males outperformed high-ranking males, but this may be because the alpha male left the troop in the second month of the breeding season. Loy also finds that males concentrate their mating on the central portion of the estrous cycle and that the three classes did not differ in this respect. Kaufmann (1965) had reported that dominant males did not limit their mating to particular portions of the cycle, but Carpenter (1942) found that the most dominant male preferred to mate with females at mid-estrus.

Two recent studies with laboratory groups of rhesus provide no support for the basic prediction. There is no association between rank class (high vs. low) and number of mounts in a troop of rhesus at the Yerkes facilities (Wilson 1981), and Shively et al. (1982) find a nonsignificant Spearman coefficient (0.57) between rank and copulation frequency in a troop at Davis.

Both these studies are methodologically more sophisticated than the early work cited above. The negative results are especially important because, as noted earlier, captivity might reduce the mating options open to subordinate males, which should increase the correlation between rank and mating success.

Altmann's priority-of-access of model has been tested twice with rhesus data. Suarez and Ackerman (1971) use the Cayo Santiago data of Carpenter, Conaway and Koford, and Kaufmann to test the relationship between rank and three measures of mating success. Of ten tests, five show acceptable agreement between the predictions of the model and the field data. The authors point out (1971:220) that if the original researchers did not gather their data by random sampling, the estimates of mating probabilities would be biased, perhaps invalidating the tests. Unfortunately, the original papers contain little information on sampling, rendering the validity of Suarez and Ackerman's work questionable.

A more adequate test of Altmann's model utilizes data from group F on Cayo Santiago and finds that the model does not predict the observed distribution of matings during the time ovulation is most likely to occur (OV-1 period). Chapais (1983) finds that the alpha male mates less frequently than predicted by the model and that males below the third rank mate more frequently than expected. Thus, Altmann's model fares no better among rhesus macaques than it does among baboons.

Several studies test the association between rank and mating success while attempting to control the confounding variable of rank-related differences in observability. As noted earlier, when Drickamer (1974a) controls observability, the significant correlations between rank and measures of mating success in the La Parguera rhesus become nonsignificant. Curie-Cohen et al. (1983) and Stern and Smith (1984) were also cited earlier as suggesting that paternity and observed mating frequencies are not highly correlated. Chapais (1983) finds a Kendall correlation coefficient of 0.45 between rank and frequency of copulation during OV-1 periods in the first half of the breeding season of Cayo Santiago's group F, but when observability is controlled, the coefficient falls to a nonsignificant 0.07.

Paternity exclusion techniques have been utilized in several laboratory studies with rhesus. Duvall et al. (1976) examine the reproductive success of eight males over two breedings seasons and find no significant correlation between rank and reproductive success in the first year, but a strong association in the second year. Although doing better than expected under a hypothesis of no rank-related differences in paternity, the alpha male did not sire the most offspring in the group; this was accomplished by a male who ranked seventh in the first year and third in the second. Duvall et al.'s results have been cited as evidence both for and against the basic prediction. Smith (1981) notes that the study group had been newly formed and that rank relations were not stable over the two years. He points out that the four lowest-ranking males during the first breeding season sired over half the infants produced in the first birth season, and that by the second breeding season, they had displaced three out of four of the first breeding season's top-ranking males. The four upstarts then produced from 63 percent to 85 percent of the infants of the second birth season. These considerations lead Smith to suggest that changes in rank may follow from, rather than be the cause of, changes in reproductive success (see Smith 1980).

Curie-Cohen et al. (1983) examine the associations between rank, mating and paternity for eight years in a zoo troop of rhesus. In each year, male rank accurately predicts both frequency of copulation and average duration of copulation (dominant males copulate longer), with the alpha rank usually obtaining about 70 percent of the copulations in a year. In spite of this, the alpha rank sired only from 13 percent to 32 percent of the troop's infants, and was outreproduced by the beta rank, which was responsible for from 30 percent to 48 percent of the infants. The authors suggest that over a lifetime, alpha males still might outreproduce subordinates, however, because they sire infants earlier in life and continue to produce them throughout adulthood. These results do not discredit the idea that rank is related to reproductive success, but they do illustrate the necessity for life history data. Perhaps most importantly, they also indicate that measures of mating success may not be valid indicators of reproductive success.

Smith (1980, 1981) uses paternity exclusion to study reproductive success in small groups of rhesus housed in outdoor cages at Davis. He reports a statistically significant Spearman coefficient of 0.76 between rank and possible paternity in these groups (1981). For the three cages with four potential fathers, he calculates that the alpha and beta ranks would average from 2.7 to 4.5 infants per year, while the third and fourth ranks would average only from 0.8 to 2.7 (1980). In a more recent study, Stern and Smith (1984) examine paternity and mating success in three groups of rhesus at Davis. Their results agree with those of Curie-Cohen et al., in that mating success does not accurately indicate reproductive success and that the alpha male was not the most successful sire in two of the three groups. However, unlike Curie-Cohen et al., Stern and Smith find no correlations between male rank and various measures of sexual activity.

Stern and Smith's findings contradict Smith's earlier work showing a positive correlation between rank and paternity in the Davis rhesus. The authors note that the groups in the earlier study contained few potential sires (four maximum), the Stern and Smith study involved groups with from five to twelve adult and subadult males. They argue that a positive correlation between rank and reproductive success might obtain only when groups contain few breeding males, and/or exhibit a stable dominance hierarchy. This argument is combined with a discussion of the hypothesis that the mating system of rhesus and other alloprimates evolved to optimize female, and not male, mate choice. Stern and Smith suggest that the sexes may exhibit different mating strategies, with females attempting to choose their mates and males trying to maintain priority-of-access mating. The demography of a troop might determine which strategy is the more effective at any given time, with small population size or population decline favoring priority-of-access mating, and population growth favoring female choice. The authors note that most studies reporting a positive relationship between male rank and reproductive success have been conducted in groups containing few breeding males or in those where females have little chance to choose between males (e.g., no place to escape the dominant male). With regard to the hypothesis that male-male competition for rank is associated with sexual selection by competition, it should be noted that Stern and Smith's model permits sexual selection to play a major role in evolution, for the occurence of population "bottlenecks" would place a premium on high rank, even if rank were not associated with differential reproductive success during periods of population growth.

Studies of male rank and mating success among Japanese macaques, all using ad libitum sampling to collect sexual data and none controlling for observability, have achieved mixed results. For the Koshima troop, Tokuda (1961–62) finds a strong correlation between rank and number of copulations in four brief periods (nineteen days maximum) in four breeding seasons. Enomoto (1974) notes that the top five ranking males in the Jigokudani troop copulated more frequently than lower-ranking males, but that these five mated independently of rank. Stephenson (1975) discovers positive correlations between rank and several measures of mating success in the Arashiyama-B and Miyajima troops, but finds that mid-ranking, subleader males achieve more ratings than high-ranking, leader males in the Koshima troop. When Takahata (1982) examines mating for two breeding seasons in the Arashiyama-B troop, he finds that among sexually mature males (over 4.5 years of age), his strongest indirect measure of reproductive success, number of females mounted with ejaculation, is significantly associated with rank in both seasons. However, when only adult males (over ten years of age) are considered, there was a significant association only in the last half of the second breeding season. Takahata also notes that the three highest-ranking adult males accounted for only 15 percent of the copulations in conception cycles, compared to 24 percent for mid-ranking adult males, 28 percent for low-ranking adult males, and 31 percent for subadult males (the remainder were with solitary males). He concludes that among adult males, rank is not related to reproductive success.

Two studies of the Oregon Japanese macaque troop (Eaton 1974; Hanby et al. 1971) provide ambiguous results. Hanby et al.'s five-month study shows high-ranking males scoring higher than middle-ranking or low-ranking males on five measures of sexual behavior, but the differences reach statistical significance only on the number of ejaculatory mounts. Nevertheless, the alpha male achieved 23 percent of the observed ejaculations, against an expected 4 percent under the hypothesis that rank is unrelated to mating success. Eaton's study over one breeding season produces no significant correlations between rank and a series of activities related to mount initiation and termination. For example, the Spearman coefficient between rank and mounts terminating in ejaculation is 0.097. Eaton concludes that rank is not related to mating success in this troop. However, the alpha male did achieve more mounts terminating in ejaculation than would be expected if the alpha position were not rewarded by higher mating success (12 percent of total, versus 5 percent expected).

Other species of macaques have not been as well studied as the rhesus and Japanese macaques, and I will discuss them only briefly. Studies of bonnets have generally shown no association between rank and mating success (Simonds 1974; Sugiyama 1971; but see Glick 1980). Shively et al. (1982) find an inverse correlation between rank and copulatory frequency in a captive troop of bonnets. An inverse correlation between age and rank in this group suggests that the youngest, lowest-ranking males are the most sexually active.

Shively et al. (1982) find a strong positive correlation between rank and copulatory frequency in a captive group of crab-eating macaques, echoing Angst's (1975) report from a zoo group that the alpha male engages in more mounts than other males. Wheatley (1982) observed a free-ranging troop and also finds that the alpha male achieves the greatest number of copulations.

Mating success in a free-ranging troop of Barbary macaques was studied by Taub (1980). The mating pattern of this species involves consociations, defined by Taub (1980:292) as ". . . transitory but exclusive sexual association. . . ." During each day of estrus, a female may establish several such consociations with different males. Taub finds that male rank is significantly related both to the number of consociations achieved and to the number of females consociated with during the study. The alpha male engaged in a mating strategy different from that of the other males. The majority of consociations of nonalpha males were originated by females, while the alpha male originated the majority of his consociations. Witt et al. (1981) utilize paternity exclusion techniques in a study of rank and reproductive success in a small zoo group of Barbary macaques and find that the alpha rank outreproduced two other ranks. Unfortunately, the small number of males in the troop and the conditions of captivity make it impossible to generalize this result to free-ranging troops.

3. *Studies in other genera.* The relationship between rank and mating success has rarely been investigated in species other than the macaques and baboons. However, interesting work has been done in a chimpanzee community at Gombe (McGinnis 1979; Tutin 1979; reviewed in Tutin and McGinnis 1981). The authors observe three different mating patterns.

During opportunistic mating, a single female may be mounted by all the males in the vicinity, and the males do not appear to compete for access. Seventy-three percent of the copulations observed by Tutin followed this pattern. In possessive matings, comprising 25 percent of the copulations, dominant males may temporarily prevent lower-ranking males from copulating with an estrous female. Possessiveness was most common on the day of, and two days prior to, presumed ovulation and was a tactic frequently exhibited by the alpha male. Finally, in consortships, a male and an estrous female leave the community and avoid other animals. Only two percent of the copulations in the group occurred in consortships, yet at least half of the conceptions resulted from them. Tutin and McGinnis note that consortships are dangerous, due to possible encounters with noncommunity chimpanzees and to the aggressive reunions that may occur when the partners return to their community.

Both McGinnis and Tutin find that frequency of male participation in restrictive mating patterns (possessiveness and consortship) is not related to age, male aggression toward females, or dominance rank. However, high male participation in restrictive mating is directly correlated with three measures of affiliative behavior with females: time spent with estrous females, time spent grooming estrous females, and frequency of sharing food with females. Both authors suggest that female choice plays an important role in the formation of consortships. However, the data do indicate that the alpha male's strategy of possessiveness may result in his achieving slightly higher reproductive success than other males.

A study of a chimpanzee group in the Mahale mountains made by Nishida (1979) provides evidence that high-ranking males achieve more copulations than lower-ranking males. However, Nishida collected his mating data by ad libitum sampling, and it is difficult to compare his work with the more methodologically sophisticated studies of McGinnis and Tutin.

In two studies, Struhsaker (1967, 1975) reports direct correlations between male rank and mating success. The first involves two groups of free-ranging vervet monkeys, and the second a group of red colobus in Kibale Forest, Uganda. Dixson et al. (1975) report that in a laboratory setting, high rank in male talapoins is associated with mounting greater numbers of females. Finally, Jones (1981) finds that in a free-ranging group of howlers, the alpha male achieved 47 percent of the copulations, the beta male 32 percent, and the gamma male 21 percent.

4. *Summary.* Given the widespread acceptance of the idea that one reward of high rank for male alloprimates is increased mating success, it is surprising to see how little empirical work demonstrates a positive correlation between these variables. At the same time, the basic prediction is given some support by the fact that the alpha male usually achieves a

disproportionate degree of reproductive and/or mating success in most of the studies reviewed. Probably the most important conclusion of the review is that the hypothesis relating male rank to sexual selection cannot be adequately tested with the data at hand. The necessity for information on the lifetime reproductive histories of males, including the possible costs of achieving and maintaining high rank, was illustrated repeatedly. Until such data are available, the question of how male rank is associated with mating and reproductive success remains open.

Alternative Explanations

Several explanations of why males strive to achieve high rank that do not implicate sexual selection are briefly discussed in this subsection. Deag's (1977) list of the advantages gained by winners of agonistic interactions serves as a starting point for a review of rewards of high rank which may not be related to differential mating success, but still might result in a male's achieving higher inclusive fitness. Since many of these rewards also influence the inclusive fitness of females, I will also note their possible effects upon this sex.

1. *Access to food and water.* The importance of this factor for an animal's inclusive fitness varies with the ecological circumstances. In periods of resource abundance, there may be little rank-related variation in the nutritional status of animals. However, even during extremely good periods the access of high-ranking animals to higher-quality foods, or to foods in short supply, might result in differential inclusive fitness. Further, if lower-ranking males achieve nutritional parity with dominant males only by feeding longer on poorer-quality resources or by foraging away from the main body of the troop, they may not be able to invest as much time as dominant animals do in social interactions with females. As suggested above, such interactions may form the basis of mating relationships.

When resources are scarce, differential access may result in rank-related variability in nutrition or mortality. The former may affect the ability of females to conceive, bear, and rear infants or of males to compete for matings. Wrangham (1980) finds that during a period of severe water shortage, lower-ranking male and female vervets had higher mortality rates than high-ranking animals. Studies of toque macaques by Dittus (1979) and of Japanese macaques by Mori (1979) demonstrate correlations between low rank and increased mortality in groups experiencing population decline. However, Gouzoules et al. (1982) note several studies suggesting that the reproductive success of females of different ranks might not vary even in extremely adverse conditions.

2. *Increased feeding efficiency.* In searching for food, high-ranking animals might not need to avoid other animals and might experience fewer disruptions while feeding than subordinate animals. Increased feeding

efficiency could lead to increased inclusive fitness through several mechanisms. For example, the extra time a subordinate animal puts into feeding might be converted into mating effort by a high-ranking animal.

3. *Ability to aid kin.* Dominant animals can often interfere in agonistic interactions between subordinates with little danger of retaliation. High-ranking animals successfully interceding on behalf of kin (see Chapter Four) might increase their own inclusive fitness. Cheney (1977) describes this process in chacma baboons, noting that maternal aiding of offspring is a major factor in determining the rank of juvenile and subadult animals. Offspring of dominant females are more likely than the offspring of lower-ranking mothers to be aided by their mothers when threatened or attacked. High-ranking defenders are less likely to be threatened or attacked, and their interventions are more likely to be successful than those of subordinate females (see Berman 1980 for rhesus data).

Bernstein (1976; see also Duvall et al. 1976) proposes a model relating male rank to lifetime reproductive success in the absence of rank-related variance in mating success. He argues that high-ranking males are control animals, protecting the troop from external dangers. Bernstein sees protection as paternal investment and argues that protective males ensure the survival of their offspring. As a male ages, the proportion of younger troop members closely related to him increases, even if he has not fathered a disproportionate number of offspring. Bernstein also argues that a male's willingness to protect the troop and his skill at forming alliances with other males make him attractive to females. The end result is that females preferentially mate with higher-ranking males, selecting for social skills and willingness to defend the troop, not for competitiveness per se. A critique of Bernstein's model by Berenstain and Wade (1983:221–222) argues that because noninvesting males have their offspring protected by investing males, but suffer none of the risks assumed by investors, Bernstein's system could evolve only under the unlikely condition of trait-group selection.

4. *Participation in social interaction.* This benefit might assume various forms, each related to inclusive fitness in a different manner. For example, a major factor in the social life of many alloprimates is grooming, and rank may be related to the probability that a given animal will groom, or will be groomed by, others. Seyfarth (1976, 1980) notes that among both chacma baboons and vervets, high-ranking females are attractive to potential groomers. Using grooming to create alliances with high-ranking females may permit a subordinate to avoid some of the disadvantages of her position, perhaps increasing her reproductive success. However, Seyfarth notes that this strategy's utility may be limited by competition for access to dominant females, which might result in females being able to groom only those adjacent to them in the rank hierarchy. The dynamics identified by Seyfarth may not apply to all alloprimates. Silk (1982) notes that bonnet

macaque females do not concentrate grooming on rank-adjacent females, nor do they intervene in agonistic situations on behalf of females who groom them frequently.

An area where male rank might be related to ability to participate in social life is illustrated by the work of Smuts (1982) and Strum (1982) which shows that agonistic behavior and high rank are means by which young olive baboons enter a troop.

5. *Summary.* This brief discussion of alternative explanations of male dominance behavior indicates the lack of data on this topic. The rarity of alternative arguments and the shortage of empirical work relevant to them does not mean that the sexual selection hypothesis is validated, but only that primatologists have only recently begun to look at rank from new perspectives. Formulation and testing of alternative explanations will undoubtedly increase in the near future.

MALE RANK AND SELECTION BY PREFERENCE

Basic Prediction

The hypothesis that sexual selection by preference is responsible for the evolution of male rank systems has not been examined in detail by alloprimate sociobiologists. However, the issue of female mate choice is frequently raised by theorists who object to an exclusive focus on the role of male rank in alloprimate mating systems. Emphasis on female choice is usually found together with demonstrations that dominant males achieve lower mating or reproductive success than expected under the hypothesis that male rank is the only factor that determines the distribution of mating. However, female preference for mating with high-ranking males can also be viewed as the reason that dominant males achieve disproportionate mating success. At present, few alloprimate studies have explicitly adopted the view that females prefer to mate with high-ranking males, or have attempted to test it in opposition to the view that male-male competition is the main variable responsible for observed mating patterns.

A case can be made for the hypothesis that the system of male rank and dominance behavior that is characteristic of a species evolved through a process of sexual selection by preference if the following points are demonstrated: (1) that the species exhibits no rank-related differences in the ability of males to withstand the hostile forces of nature (i.e., rank systems are not the outcome of natural selection); and (2) that rank-related variance in male mating activity is not the outcome of male-male competition for access to mates, but rather that it arises from the desire of females to mate with the most dominant males (i.e., rank systems are not the outcome of sexual selection by competition). The major problem in establishing these points is that the hypotheses of sexual selection by competition and sexual selection by preference both predict the same distribution of mating activities, with dominant males mating more often than subordinate males.

The limited amount of work that has been done on female mate choice among the alloprimates means that the problem of sexual selection by preference cannot be addressed in detail (for general reviews see Andersson 1982b; Arnold 1983; Borgia 1979; Bradbury and Gibson 1983; Fisher 1930; Halliday 1983a,b; O'Donald 1983a,b; Taylor and Williams 1982; Zahavi 1975). At present, we have only a few empirical studies on female choice. Several studies that are relevant to the basic prediction that females prefer to mate with dominant males will be reviewed, after some theoretical complications have been discussed.

Problems Testing the Basic Prediction
Halliday (1983a) argues that the hypothesis that female mate choice is an evolved adaptive trait, implying that sexual selection by preference may have been involved in its evolution, is supported if a researcher demonstrates three points: (1) that female mating is not random, meaning that all males do not have equal chances of mating success; (2) that the variance in male mating success results from female behavior and is not the outcome of male actions; and (3) that females mating with preferred males have higher fitness than those mating with less preferred males. Evidence on the first point is conclusive for the alloprimates. The material reviewed in the next subsection relates to the second point. There are no existing alloprimate data on the third point, nor can any be collected until the phenomenon female choice has been demonstrated.

Demonstrations that mating patterns are strongly influenced by female choice confront most of the difficulties discussed in the section on testing the basic prediction relating male rank to mating success. Furthermore, the nature of the data that are needed to distinguish female choice from male choice is not clear. Most convincing would be experiments allowing females to choose mates free of male coercion. Several experiments of this type are described in the next subsection, but it is difficult to say how the results relate to free-ranging animals. A high correlation between the ranks of sexual partners may indicate female-female competition over access to high-ranking males, but it can also indicate synchronous estrus and dominant males restricting their attention to the highest-quality females (assuming that high rank is equivalent with high female quality).

Before reviewing studies on female choice, it is necessary to raise briefly the "lek paradox" and the "good genes" problems. I do so not because there are adequate primate data on these subjects, but because these ideas are so seductive that newcomers to sociobiology may not be aware of the complexities of demonstrating the operating of sexual selection by prefer-ence. The problems arise when we ask which features of a male might make him the preferred mate of all the females in a group. In many mating systems, the answer involves the benefits provided by the male—benefits allowing females to achieve greater reproductive success. For example, if dominant males hold the most productive territories, then females should prefer to mate with them, all else being equal. If dominant males protect their mates and offspring from harassment by other animals, they should be the preferred mates. A male's willingness to provide paternal investment may be another feature that females use to select mates.

However, in mating systems such as leks, males provide nothing to females except sperm. Yet females often act as if they were choosing between males, even if it is only by refusing to mate until the most dominant male is revealed. Several population geneticists (reviewed in Arnold 1983; Taylor and Williams 1982) have argued that in systems where males contribute nothing but sperm, selection on the phenotypic traits that females use to distinguish between males will be intense, and any genetic variance responsible for the phenotypic variation in these traits will be rapidly eliminated. Thus, a species will quickly reach the point where phenotypic variation between males on the traits in question is due totally to environmental factors. This means that a female selecting a bird with a long tail, for example, is no more certain that her offspring will exhibit a long tail than a female who mates with a short-tailed male. Taylor and Williams (1982) review several models purporting to solve the problem of how female choice is maintained in the face of rapid loss of genetic variance in fitness and conclude that none solves it. On the other hand, some theorists (see Arnold 1983; O'Donald 1983a) see the paradox as not being applicable to the real world, since the condition of zero variance in the genes that are relevant to fitness is not likely to be stable. The intricacies of this debate need not be addressed here. However, arguments that alloprimate females select mates on the basis of criteria other than such benefits as protection or paternal investment must address the lek paradox and show how it would not apply to the species in question.

The "good genes" argument holds that females choose mates on the basis of traits indicating that the male carries genes that are optimal for survival or for success in male-male competition for mates. However, models of sexual selection often suggest that female preference for specific characteristics may lead in some cases to selection for genotypes which are less than optimal for survival or male-male competition (see Fisher 1930; Arnold 1983). Again, I will not rehearse all the pros and cons of this argument, but only suggest that explanations applying the concept of selection for "good genes" must always be paired with a consideration of the possible effects of natural selection and sexual selection by competition.

Relevant Studies
Several studies investigate the hypothesis that animals of similar ranks tend to mate with one another. If female choice is the cause of this pattern, it may

indicate that all females prefer to mate with high-ranking males and that competition results in a "like rank phenomenon." On the other hand, if male choice is the operative factor, the like rank phenomenon should be less clear, since dominant males are expected to mate with females of all ranks, unless prevented by conditions of low female defensibility. Low defensibility would create the like rank phenomenon if high-ranking males concentrate their attention on the highest-ranking females, but the outcome would probably still not be as marked as under conditions of female-female competition.

Three studies of Japanese macaque sexual activity find the like rank phenomenon in this species (Stephenson 1975; Takahata 1982; Wolfe 1979). Witt et al. (1981) report that in their zoo troop of Barbary macaques, the two males of lower rank produced infants with lower-ranking females but the alpha male produced offspring with females of all ranks. This result suggests the operation of male choice. Finally, two studies of rhesus macaques find no evidence of a like rank phenomenon. Loy's (1971) article describes a study of mating relationships in a group on Cayo Santiago; while Small and Smith's (1982) paternity exclusion tests demonstrate that the ranks of an infant's mother and father are independent. Their results cannot be explained simply as the outcome of male choice, however, since mid-ranking and low-ranking males produced infants with both high-ranking and low-ranking females. It is clear that the empirical tests do not yet allow a decision on the existence of the like rank phenomenon.

Experiments with nonprimates have supported the hypothesis that females prefer to mate with dominant males or with males exhibiting certain features. I mention a few significant studies to indicate the type of data that is needed to investigate the topic of female choice among alloprimates. Huck and Banks (1982a,b; see Carr et al. 1982 for rats) use tether tests to show that female brown lemmings voluntarily spend more time near, and are more willing to copulate with, the victors of male-male agonistic interactions. They also show that in a triad composed of a dominant male, a subordinate male and a female, both male-male agonism and female choice are responsible for the greater mating success of the dominant male. Andersson (1982a) experimentally demonstrates female preference for a character not related to dominance by elongating the tails of some male widowbirds and shortening those of others. Males with elongated tails achieved greater mating success than those with normal sized or shortened tails. She also shows that males with shortened tails held their territories as long as those with normal sized tails. This lack of association between ability to hold territory and tail size suggests that females preferring males with long tails are not using the tail as a signal of males' ability to provide resources.

The relationship between female choice and fitness of offspring is the subject of an interesting experiment by Partridge (1980). She finds that the offspring of female *Drosophilia* allowed to select their mates exhibited higher larval competitive ability than the progeny of females assigned mates at random. This may indicate some variance in male genotypic fitness which was detected by the females, but Arnold (1983:90) notes that the experiment does not demonstrate genetic variation in the mate choice of females and that the results can be interpreted as showing that there is genetic variance in larval competitive ability which is correlated with some sexually selected trait.

Finally, Marjarus et al. (1982) use two-spot ladybirds to demonstrate that female preference may be subject to selection. Through artificial selection, they managed to more than double the preference level for a certain type of male in just four generations. In control groups, the preference level did not change during the experiment.

There are few experimental studies of female choice among alloprimates (see Hrdy 1981a; Fedigan 1982:282–285). Eaton (1973) finds that female pigtail macaques who are allowed to manipulate cage doors tend to associate with males who do not attempt to injure them. Female choice for less aggressive, more sociable males among rhesus is documented in cage release studies by Herbert (1968) and by Michael et al. (1978). Michael and Saayman (1967) report that both male and female rhesus exhibit mate preferences, and that decisions about association may be more strongly influenced by such preferences than by the reproductive state of alternative partners. Bachmann and Kummer (1980) demonstrate both male and female partner preferences among hamadryas baboons and show that the strength of a female's preference may determine whether other males attempt to interfere in her consortships. Interestingly, the two most dominant males did not take female preference into account when interfering with consorts, which suggests that female choice may be overridden by the wishes of dominant males.

Hausfater (1975, yellow baboons) and Seyfarth (1978, chacma baboons) both conclude that females in their free-ranging troops exhibit a positive preference for dominant males. Seyfarth, for example, notes that most of the females in his troop presented only to the alpha male and that on the two occasions when two females were in estrus at the same time, both presented exclusively to the alpha male and turned their attention to the subordinate only after the dominant male had selected his consort.

Marsh (1979) addresses the problem of female choice in the context of troop transfer decisions made by red colobus females. In this species, harem takeovers sometimes lead to infanticide, and Marsh suggests that females evaluate the new harem holder's chances of attaining a tenure long enough for his infants to be past the point of vulnerability when a new male invades. If this probability is too low, females choose to transfer to another troop. Although we do not know which features females use to evaluate males, it seems safe to assume that they would prefer more dominant males.

Finally, Dunbar and Sharman (1983) examine a number of studies of baboons and find negative correlations between female-biased adult sex ratios and birth rate and between female-biased adult sex ratios and rainfall, but a positive correlation between rainfall and birth rate. They suggest that as the sex ratio in troops becomes biased against males, female competition for access to males—either for mating or for protection—increases social stress. The increased stress may cause more females to experience anovulatory cycles, lowering the birth rate. Rainfall is implicated in the model by its effects on female health and hence, reproduction, and by its influence on the adult sex ratio. Although Dunbar and Sharman do not demonstrate that competition for access to dominant males is particularly intense, this hypothesis could be tested in the field.

In contrast to the positive results of these studies, work by Jay (1965, langurs), Saayman (1971, chacma baboons), Smuts (1982, olive baboons), and Strum (1982, olive baboons), showing low-ranking males achieving high mating success, includes cases where high-ranking males may not be preferred by females. Tutin (1979) suggests that chimpanzee females do not exhibit a preference for the alpha male. As noted earlier, females choice determines whether or not a male achieves a consortship. If a female protests or refuses to stray from the community, a male has little chance of consorting with her. The features that chimpanzee females might be using to select males as consorts are suggested by the positive correlation between the frequency of a male's consorts and three behavioral patterns: time spent associating with estrous females, time spent grooming estrous females, and frequency of food sharing with females. Tutin and McGinnis (1981) suggest that females may be selecting for affiliative behavior on the part of males. However, they note that selection for this trait may be counterbalanced by the negative effect it might have on male survival. Finally, they observe that once the alpha male directs mating overtures toward an estrous female, she may have little chance to reject him, regardless of his willingness to engage in affiliative behavior.

The limited evidence that we have does not provide strong support for the position that females exhibit a preference for mating with high-ranking males. We are left with the problem of identifying which features might make males attractive to females and permit sexual selection by preference to operate. There are few studies on this problem. As noted above, nonaggressiveness has been implicated in female mate choice. Fedigan (1982) notes that friendship bonds have been related to consortships in some species of baboons, but that they do not appear to influence the choice of female Japanese macaques. A preference for older males has been suggested for rhesus (Kaufmann 1965) and for Japanese macaque females (Hanby et al. 1971). Packer (1979b, olive baboons) finds that older males consort more frequently than might be expected by their dominance ranks, but suggests that this may result from their experience in forming coalitions rather than from female preference for older males. As discussed in Chapter One, display behavior was related to mating success in one troop of

Japanese macaques (Modahl and Eaton 1977), but not in the troops studied by Wolfe (1981a). A situation perhaps limiting the possibility of sexual selection by preference would be a female preference for mates with novel genotypes, or "stranger males" (reviewed in Moore and Ali 1984; Berenstain and Wade 1983:225).

The need for more empirical research on alloprimate female mate choice is obvious. There are numerous questions which such research must address, but in the present context, we are interested mainly in the basic prediction that females prefer to mate with dominant males. Existing evidence appears not to support this prediction, but it is too early to reject the hypothesis. If alloprimate females base mate choices on traits other than dominance, these traits must be identified and their influence tested in situations where females have freedom to exhibit their preferences. Finally, data are required on the effect of mating choices on female fitness. These data would allow us to discover, for example, whether females mating with dominant males produce offspring with higher fitness than those mating with subordinate males. Until such evidence is available, the hypothesis that male ranking and dominance behavior evolved through sexual selection by preference remains untested.

Alternative Explanations
Since there is little evidence that female alloprimates exhibit a preference for mating with dominant males, alternative explanations are not required at present. Should such a preference be demonstrated in a species, the most likely alternative explanation would involve the possible rewards a female might gain from association with dominant males. Suggested rewards, including lower harassment (see Galdikas 1981; see also Wrangham 1980), better access to resources, paternal investment, etc., have been discussed previously.

FEMALE RANK AND SELECTION BY COMPETITION

Basic Prediction
A hypothesis explaining the evolution of female dominance hierarchies by sexual selection by competition would suggest that females compete for mating access to males, and that differential access is responsible for rank-related variation in female reproductive success. The simplest prediction that can be derived from this hypothesis is that female rank is positively correlated with mating success (e.g., number of copulations, number of partners). The research reviewed below clearly indicates that there is little evidence to support this prediction. Further, sociobiologists note that there is no theoretical reason to suggest that female rank behavior evolved through sexual selection by competition. As Trivers (1972) points out, the

sex that provides the greater parental investment is usually a limited re-source over which members of the opposite sex compete. Among allopri-mates, females normally fulfill this role. While the mating success of one male results in a reduction of the reproductive success of other males, this is not usually true for females. Thus, there is no good reason for arguing that dominant females will prevent subordinates from mating (monogamous alloprimates may be an exception, but here the issue seems to be access to paternal investment, not to mating per se). The fact that a female will probably mate during estrus, regardless of her rank, means that variance in female mating success is usually much lower than that of males. This, in turn, suggests that any variance in female reproductive success probably does not result from differential mating activity produced by female-female competi-tion over males.

On the other hand, in many alloprimate species, females invest energy in obtaining and maintaining rank. Sociobiological theory suggests that they are unlikely to do so unless they obtain benefits which translate into increased reproductive success or inclusive fitness. It is assumed that these benefits offset the costs of striving for, or holding, rank. As will be discussed in the subsection on alternative hypotheses, the most commonly postulated benefits of female rank include access to food and water and freedom to harass other animals while themselves escaping harassment. Our basic prediction thus becomes that high-ranking females achieve greater repro-ductive success or inclusive fitness than low-ranking females, although this may not result from rank-related differences in mating activity. Note that results congruent with this prediction can be interpreted from a number of alternative perspectives, including both sexual selection and natural selec-tion theory.

Problems in Testing the Basic Prediction

Many of the problems involved in the testing of predictions that relate male rank to sexual selection are relevant to tests of explanations of the evolution of female rank. Definition of rank and measurement of dominance, although less often addressed in discussions of female rank, remain problematic. The relationship between female age and rank is a possible confounding variable in any investigation. For example, if younger females rank lower than older females, and if age is inversely correlated with infant survival, a test of the prediction that the rank-related variance in infant survival is evolutionarily significant must demonstrate such variance within age classes. If either frequency of copulation or number of partners is utilized as a measure of mating success, the observability of females, as well as males, must be controlled. Other confounding variables are discussed during reviews of the studies where they apply.

Calculation of female reproductive success appears comparatively simple, requiring only a count of the offspring produced during a female's lifetime.

Unfortunately, no study of an alloprimate group has spanned the lifetimes of a large number of females. Researchers have had to rely on several indirect measures of reproductive success, including rate of infant production over short time spans, infant survival rates, age when first offspring is produced, and so forth. The validity of these indirect measures has not been established. For example, females who give birth a year earlier than their cohorts may, on the average, produce one more offspring over a lifetime than their competitors. However, Wilson et al. (1983) show that in rhesus, such "early" mothers fail to conceive in the year following their first births more often than "normal" mothers. Over a lifetime, early and normal mothers appear to produce about the same number of infants. Several long-term studies currently underway will eventually permit calculation of lifetime female reproductive success, but until they do so, indirect measures must suffice.

The Relevant Studies

1. *Rank and mating success.* Studies relevant to the prediction that female rank is correlated with differential mating success require few comments. Work with Japanese macaques demonstrates that female rank does not predict number of ejaculations received (Hanby et al. 1971), number of mounts and/or copulations (Hanby et al. 1971; Enomoto 1974), or number of sexual partners (Hanby et al. 1971; Stephenson 1975). Takahata (1982) finds a positive correlation between rank and number of observed mounts for two breeding seasons in the Arashiyama-B troop, but notes that the greater mating success of higher-ranking females does not translate into higher conception rates (Takahata 1980).

Results with rhesus are less clear, with some studies finding female rank uncorrelated with number of ejaculations received (Wilson 1981), number or rate of mounts and/or copulations (Wilson 1981; Wilson et al. 1982), or number of partners (Wilson 1981). However, Wilson et al. (1982) discover an interesting rank-related difference in mating strategies. They note that most females mate with a number of males in a single day and that consortships (in the sense of the female limiting copulation to one male) usually occur only when both partners are of high rank. The implications of this difference are not yet clear. Finally, Chapais' (1983:220) Cayo Santiago data demonstrate significant correlations between female rank and both number of observed copulations (Spearman's $r = 0.30$) and number of partners (Spearman's $r = 0.40$).

There are few studies of female rank and mating success in other species. Taub's (1980) tables of Barbary macaque consociations indicate that female rank is not correlated with the number of such associations, or with the number of male consociates, or with how the associations are initiated or terminated. Loy (1981) finds no correlation between rank and number of copulations in a patas troop at La Parguera. Dunbar and Dunbar (1977) discover no rank-related differences in the number of mounts with ejaculation among gelada baboons. Finally, Dixson et al. (1975) note that female rank is not related to number of copulations in laboratory groups of talapoins.

Although there are some exceptions, the impression given by these studies is that female-female competition is not reflected in correlations between rank and measures of mating success. As expected, since females are the limited resource, they have no trouble obtaining mates.

2. *Rank and number of offspring.* No study of an alloprimate group compares the lifetime reproductive success of females of different ranks. However, several studies have examined rank-related differences in number of infants produced over a short time span. These studies usually have the disadvantage that if age is correlated with rank, differences in the number of infants produced may reflect age-specific fertility, rather than rank. Most of the studies reviewed do not control for this possibility.

Two studies of Japanese macaques (Gouzoules et al. 1982; Wolfe 1983) find no evidence of a relationship between rank and number of offspring (fecundity). Gouzoules et al. (1982) examine eight years of data on the provisioned Arashiyama-West corral troop and conclude that individual rank is not correlated with fecundity. As is true for many macaque troops, Arashiyama-West is split into matrilines of different ranks. Gouzoules et al. demonstrate that the matrilines do not differ in fecundity. Since matriline rankings do not always accurately predict the dominance relationships between individuals, the individual dominance hierarchy was calculated and divided evenly into high-ranking, mid-ranking, and low-ranking females. These three classes do not exhibit different levels of fecundity. The authors also use a measure of individual dominance, consisting of the proportion of adult females each female dominated at the time she gave birth. A Spearman correlation between this measure and fecundity is significant ($r = 0.49$), but does not explain a great deal of the variance in fecundity. The relationship is offset by the fact that this measure of dominance has an even stronger inverse correlation with infant mortality rates. In other words, dominating a larger proportion of adult females is associated with greater infant production, but also with a greater risk of infant death during the first year of life. Finally, Gouzoules et al. take a subsample of females who were mature when the study started and who survived the entire eight years and calculate a mean rank over this period for each of them. This mean rank score shows no correlation with fecundity.

An important issue addressed in the Gouzoules et al. study is the generational stability of rank. They examine the rankings of the six matrilines from 1957 to 1979 and find little stability over time. For example, the highest-ranking matriline in 1957 ranked number four in 1964, number two in 1972, and number three in 1979. An even more significant result is their comparison of the relative ranks (proportion of adult females dominated) of eight matriarchs with those of their first daughter, first granddaughter, and first great-granddaughter. None of the intergenerational correlations were significant. For example, Nose dominated 93 percent of the adult females in 1957, her first daughter dominated 67 percent when she matured, her first granddaughter 53 percent, and her first great-granddaughter only 35 percent. If relative rank is not maintained over generations, multigenerational studies are required to assess the evolutionary significance of female rank, for it would be incorrect to assume that daughters of high-ranking females inherit the advantages of their mothers (for an opposite conclusion on rank stability in baboons, see Hausfater et al. 1982).

Gouzoules et al.'s (1982) results are echoed by the finding that over a period of three birth seasons (1976 to 1978), fecundity was unrelated to either individual rank or matriline rank in Japan's provisioned Arashiyama-B troop (Wolfe 1983).

Results of studies with rhesus are more ambiguous. Anderson and Simpson's (1979) eighteen years of data from a laboratory group indicate that female rank is unrelated to fecundity. In a study arriving at a different conclusion, Sade et al. (1976) use data on mortality and natality collected during a two-year period among five social groups on Cayo Santiago to construct a life table for females and to calculate the Intrinsic Rate of Natural Increase (r, not to be confused with Hamilton's r) for both social groups and for matrilines within social groups. They combine the top-ranking matriline of each social group and calculate the r of this category as 0.094. This compares to an r of −0.039 for the category composed of the lowest-ranking matriline from each group, and an r of 0.021 for the category composed of all the matrilines that were neither highest nor lowest ranking. Thus, high-ranking matrilines achieve greater growth than middle-ranking or low-ranking matrilines. The data presented by Sade et al. do not indicate whether this difference is the result of differential natality or mortality, but the authors speculate that females of high-ranking matrilines reproduce earlier in life than those of low-ranking matrilines (see below). An unfortunate aspect of the Sade et al. study is that social group J, which had only two matrilines, had to be omitted from the analysis of the relationship between r and matriline rank. Group J's rate of increase was over three times greater than that of the other social groups. Interestingly, group J appears to be the lowest-ranking group in the study (perhaps excepting group L), outranked even by the smaller group M, with an r of −0.236. A closer examination of group J would undoubtedly prove to be interesting.

Another study suggesting that female rank may be related to fecundity is Dittus' (1979) study of nine groups of toque macaques at Polonnaruwa, Sri Lanka. He shows that high-ranking females have more daughters and more total offspring surviving to the age of reproduction than either middle-ranking or low-ranking females, who do not differ on these measures.

Dittus' study occurred during a drought, and his troops exhibited zero population growth. He presents data indicating that the greater reproductive success of high-ranking females results from the fact that their daughters obtain more food than those of lower-ranking females. This suggests that rank-related differences in fecundity might not be implicated in Dittus' results.

There are few studies of fecundity and female rank other than those of macaques. The best case for a positive association between these variables is Dunbar and Dunbar's (1977; see also Dunbar 1980) work among gelada baboons. The authors find a strong correlation between rank and number of offspring under 4.25 years of age. Their explanation of this finding will be discussed below. Two other studies fail to find correlations between rank and fecundity. Loy (1981) notes that fecundity over the three years of his patas study is not affected by female rank, and Dolhinow et al. (1979) report that in a laboratory group of langurs, number of offspring produced is independent of rank.

3. *Rank and conception rate.*   Another indirect measure in studies of rank and reproductive success is the probability that a female of a given rank will conceive during the breeding season. The predictions usually tested are that high-ranking females have a greater probability of conceiving, or a lower probability of experiencing a sterile year, than lower-ranking females.

Two studies of rhesus find positive correlations between female rank and probability of conception. With six years of data from the La Parguera colony, Drickamer (1974b) demonstrates that high-ranking females have a greater probability of giving birth in a year than middle-ranking or low-ranking females. Unfortunately, no statistical tests are presented, and it is difficult to tell whether the differences between high-ranking and middle-ranking Indian-born females, and between middle-ranking and low-ranking La Parguera-born females, are significant. The simplest summary of Drickamer's work is that high-ranking females have about a ten percent greater probability of giving birth in a given year than low-ranking females. Six years of birth data for rhesus housed in various groupings at the Yerkes Field Facility show that high-ranking females have fewer sterile years (7.8 percent) than middle-ranking (18.9 percent) and low-ranking (21.3 percent) females (Wilson et al. 1978). Gouzoules et al. (1982:1146) criticize the statistical methodology of this study and demonstrate that the three rank classes do not differ from the expected values from the mean number of sterile years.

Three studies fail to find a correlation between rank and probability of conception. As noted above, Takahata (1980) reports no significant association between these variables in two birth seasons of the Arashiyama-B troop of Japanese macaques. In fact, low-ranking females over six years of age have a statistically nonsignificant higher probability of conception (76.1 percent) than middle-ranking (61.1 percent) or high-ranking (60.7 percent) females of similar age. Paul and Thommen (1984) examine five years of births in a Barbary macaque group housed in an outdoor enclosure and find no relationship between rank and number of sterile years. Finally, data on probability of conception in three troops of free-ranging vervets during three breeding seasons indicate no relationship between rank and conception probability (Cheney et al. 1981).

The few existing studies thus provide little support for the hypothesis that higher-ranking females enjoy greater reproductive success because they exhibit fewer sterile years than lower-ranking females. However, it should be noted that none of these studies examines the complete reproductive histories of a cohort of females.

4. *Rank and birth date.*   If there is an optimal period in the birth season for delivery, it might be predicted that high-ranking females would give birth closer to it than lower-ranking females. However, it is difficult to specify such a period. It might be that infants born earlier in the breeding season achieve developmental landmarks sooner than later-born infants, giving them sociological advantages which may translate into greater reproductive success. Another argument for viewing an early birth date as optimal is that the mothers of later-born infants might be more likely to experience sterile years than mothers of earlier-born infants. This might result from the sociological problem of having to care for a very young infant during the breeding season or from lack of time to recover from the physiological stress of gestation and birth (of course, mothers of earlier-born infants will be nursing more voracious infants during the breeding season, which is also a physiological stress).

Paul and Thommen's (1984) study of Barbary macaques provides ambiguous support for a relationship between female rank and timing of birth. Among females ten years or older, higher-ranking mothers tend to give birth earlier than lower-ranking mothers. However, high rank is associated with later birth dates for females under ten years of age. Unfortunately, the authors do not control for the presence or absence of an infant in the previous year and do not statistically evaluate the differences in the percentages they report. Wilson et al. (1978) find no individual rank-related differences in timing of birth in their rhesus groups; nor do matrilines differ on this variable. Finally, Wolfe's (1983) Japanese macaques exhibit no relationship between rank and timing of birth over a three-year period. When the author controls for presence of an infant in the previous birth season, by calculating the correlation between rank and timing only for females who did not have infants in the previous season, she finds that higher-ranking females gave birth significantly earlier in one season, but not in the other two. Wolfe also tests and rejects the hypothesis that high-ranking females are more likely to give birth in the middle of the birth season.

In summary, there is little evidence that timing of birth is related to female rank. Existing studies indicate that maternal age and reproductive history (nulliparous or multiparous, presence or absence of infant, etc.) are more important than rank in predicting the timing of birth.

5. *Rank and age at first birth.* If daughters of high-ranking females give birth earlier in life than those of lower-ranking females, high-ranking mothers may have greater numbers of grandoffspring than lower-ranking mothers. Further, the advantage of high-ranking mothers might increase over the generations if their daughters also exhibit early parturition. Several studies examining the hypothesis of rank-related differences in age at first birth are reviewed in this subsection.

Drickamer (1974b) shows that although daughters of high-ranking and middle-ranking rhesus do not differ in mean age at first birth (3.9 vs. 3.8 years), they do exhibit statistically significant earlier parturition than daughters of low-ranking females (4.4 years). However, Gouzoules et al. (1982) note that the 6.6-month birth season of this population means that this six-month difference may have few demographic implications, since many of the first births of higher-ranking females will occur in the same birth season as the first births of low-ranking females. Since Drickamer's data show that the time of birth within a birth season is not correlated with infant survival, Gouzoules et al. conclude that Drickamer's results do not clearly indicate a reproductive advantage for high-ranking and middle-ranking females.

Data from seventy-eight rhesus born in the Yerkes Field Facility colony indicate a relationship between age at first birth and maternal rank (Wilson et al. 1983). Of the females who gave birth at thirty-six months (twelve months earlier than the average female) 75.0 percent were from high-ranking, 18.7 percent from middle-ranking, and 6.3 percent from low-ranking matrilines, a statistically significant difference. However, the authors note that only 44.4 percent of the daughters of high-ranking matrilines exhibited early first parturition. Further, of the nine infants produced by early parturition females who had reached the age of three, only two (22.2 percent) exhibited early parturition. Since the population average of early maturers is 20.5 percent, this is not significantly different from expectations.

Wilson et al.(1983) compare the subsequent reproductive histories of early and normal maturers and find that early parturition may not lead to increased lifetime reproductive success. Compared to normal maturers, an early maturer is more likely to have a sterile year following her first birth, perhaps due to a greater failure to conceive. The authors suggest that this negates the reproductive advantage of early maturation, with early and normal maturers achieving equal lifetime reproductive success. However, they also note that the first offspring of an early maturing female enters the breeding pool a year earlier than those of normal maturing females, which might allow the former to obtain greater numbers of grandoffspring. Unfortunately, there are no data available on this last point.

In Paul and Thommen's (1984) Barbary macaque group, mean age at first birth is 4.77 years. The authors find that only two of seventeen low-ranking, but four of seven high-ranking four-year-old females gave birth earlier, recalling Wilson et al.'s (1983) finding that while early maturers are more likely to come from high-ranking matrilines, high rank is not a guarantee of early parturition.

Studies of the two Arashiyama troops of Japanese macaques find no support for the prediction of rank-related differences in age at first birth. Wolfe's (1983) analysis of Arashiyama-B shows no individual rank differences between females who first gave birth at five years and those exhibiting first parturition at six years. Wolfe unexpectedly finds a statistically significant relationship between matriline rank and age at first birth, with females of lower-ranking matrilines more likely to give birth at five years than those of higher-ranking matrilines, a finding opposite to that expected from the hypothesis. Gouzoules et al. (1982) find no relationship between either matriline rank or individual rank and mean age at first birth or number of females giving birth at five years of age in the Arashiyama-West troop.

A final article, a ten-year study of bonnet macaques housed at Davis finds that although there is great variance in the age of first parturition, it is unrelated to female rank (Silk, Clark-Wheatley, Rodman, and Samuels 1981).

On balance, the evidence does not strongly support the hypothesis that high-ranking females exhibit an earlier age of first parturition than their lower-ranking cohorts. Two of the three supporting studies were conducted with rhesus macaques, while two of the nonsupporting studies were done with Japanese macaques, so there may be a species difference to account for the results, but there are no theoretical reasons to predict such a difference.

6. *Rank and infant mortality.* A final means through which high-ranking females might achieve disproportionate reproductive success would exist if it is shown that their infants have a greater chance of reaching reproductive maturity. Several studies examine the hypothesis that infants of high-ranking mothers have a greater chance of survival over a given period (usually the first year of life) than those of low-ranking females.

Drickamer (1974b) reports that among Indian-born females in the La Parguera rhesus colony the infants of low-rank mothers had a 24.3 percent chance of dying before six months, compared to 10.9 percent for those of middle-rank mothers and 10.3 percent for those of high-rank mothers. There were no rank-related differences in survival to six months in the infants produced by colony-born females. Drickamer suggests that the latter is the case because colony-born females are younger, and the offspring of younger mothers suffer higher mortality rates. Gouzoules et al. (1982:1145) reanalyze Drickamer's data and discover that mothers of different ranks did not produce infants that varied significantly from the mean mortality rate of the population. It is not clear, however, whether Gouzoules et al.'s failure to find a significant difference in mortality rates is due to their lumping both Indian- and colony-born females in the same test.

The Yerkes rhesus studied by Wilson et al. (1978) show a rank-related difference in infant loss (stillbirth plus mortality before six months), with low-ranking females exhibiting statistically significant greater loss (32.2 percent) than either middle-ranking (21.1 percent) or high-ranking (15.5 percent) mothers. Gouzoules et al. (1982:1146) note that the major cause of the difference is infant mortality within one month of birth and demonstrate that the rank classes do not significantly differ from one another when compared with the mean rate of infant mortality within one month.

Silk, Clark-Wheatley, Rodman, and Samuels (1981) find a relationship between maternal rank and infant survival to six months in the bonnet macaques at Davis, with infants of high-ranking females showing higher survival than those of low-ranking females of similar age. Finally, Paul and Thommen (1984) note a high survival rate to one year (92.1 percent) in their Barbary macaque troop, but find that high-ranking females have a lower percentage of infants who die before one year (0.0 percent) than either middle-ranking (14.3 percent) or low-ranking (8.8 percent) females. Unfortunately, the authors' presentation of their data makes statistical tests of their results impossible.

Studies failing to find a correlation between rank and infant survival include Gouzoules et al. (1982) and Wolfe (1983) for provisioned Japanese macaques, Anderson and Simpson (1979) for laboratory rhesus macaques (survival at least one week), Altmann (1980) for free-ranging yellow baboons, Cheney et al. (1981) for free-ranging vervets, and Dolhinow et al. (1979) for laboratory langurs. Glander (1980) notes a curvilinear relationship in a group of free-ranging howler monkeys, with infants of middle-ranking mothers exhibiting the lowest mortality rate.

The relationship between rank and infant survival is still not clear. Studies with a wider range of species and with species under several different resource regimes are needed before the association between these variables can be established. As indicated below, several alternative explanations that have nothing to do with sexual selection by competition may explain rank-related differences in infant mortality.

7. *Summary.* Studies relevant to several possible mechanisms whereby female rank may be correlated with reproductive success were reviewed in this subsection. The conclusion of the review must be that none of the mechanisms has been strongly supported by the empirical research. While several studies of rhesus macaques suggest that high rank is associated with greater reproductive success in this species, the methodological shortcomings of these studies make such a conclusion premature. In general, studies with other macaques and with other genera have not revealed a relationship between female rank and various mechanisms of reproductive success.

Obviously more work on this topic is needed. It may be that rank is related to variance in reproductive success in only certain types of rank systems. Hrdy and Hrdy's (1976) distinction between rank systems based on age, genealogy, and reproductive value bears examination in this light. Other alternative explanations are discussed in the following subsection.

Alternative Explanations

As noted earlier, the hypothesis that female rank behavior evolved through, and is maintained by, sexual selection by competition has no empirical support. Results of studies on rank and differential reproductive success have been mixed. Researchers finding correlations between these variables have advanced a number of explanations which do not implicate sexual selection for their results. A few of these alternative explanations are briefly discussed in this subsection.

An important correlate of high rank among females might be priority access to food and water. In fact, measures of dominance are frequently calculated from differential access to such resources. A simple prediction derived from this point is that high-ranking females are better nourished than low-ranking females and, consequently, achieve greater reproductive success. Nutrition may affect a female's ability to conceive, to carry a fetus to term, or to feed a neonate. It may also affect the general health of an infant. Other researchers suggest that the length of interbirth intervals, too, may be affected by nutrition.

Although assuming a relationship between rank, access to food, and reproductive success appears to be a matter of common sense, there is actually little relevant empirical evidence for such a connection (see Dittus 1979). Small (1981) finds that high-ranking females in a laboratory group of rhesus have higher fat index scores during the winter than middle-ranking or low-ranking females. This is surprising, because laboratory conditions usually mean that lower-ranking females can obtain as much food as the high-ranking ones. Small speculates that rank-related variance in fat index is probably greater in free-ranging troops of rhesus. The relationship between rank and fat may be evolutionarily significant, if fatter females have higher chances of survival during severe food shortages than their thinner cohorts. Further, it has been argued (Frisch 1984; Frisch and McArthur 1974) that ovulation occurs only when females attain a certain threshold level of body fat. Lower-ranking females may fall below this threshold more frequently than higher-ranking females. Small finds no association between fat index and probability of giving birth in her group, but notes that in captive groups low-ranking females, although thinner than dominant females, may still not fall below the fat level that is critical for ovulation.

Important discussions of access to food and water are found in Gouzoules et al. (1982) and Fedigan (1983). Gouzoules et al. note that the omnivory of many macaque and baboon species might lower variance in female nutritional status. While high-ranking females have easy access to the most valuable foods, subordinates may achieve adequate nutrition without a great deal of additional effort by concentrating on less valued resources. If subordinates do not experience too many additional risks (e.g., predation) or energetic costs (e.g., increased search or feeding time), this may mean that females of different ranks produce about the same number of offspring over a lifetime.

Gouzoules et al. (1982) and Wolfe (1983), among others, suggest that high-ranking females may have the potential to outreproduce subordinates, but that this potential is not realized until a troop experiences nutritional deprivation. This view predicts that when resources are abundant and a group's population is expanding, there will be no rank-related differences in female reproductive success. Data from the Arashiyama troops are congruent with this argument. Gouzoules et al. note that the fact that several of the studies finding positive correlations between rank and reproductive success are from provisioned or laboratory groups appears to contradict this analysis. However, as noted in the review of relevant studies, reanalysis of some of these investigations places their conclusions in doubt.

The evolutionary importance of female rank and access to resources may thus depend upon how frequently a group experiences poor ecological circumstances. Results of studies by Wrangham (1981, vervets), Mori (1979, Japanese macaques), and Dittus (1979, toque macaques) indicate that when such environments are encountered, low-ranking females suffer higher mortality than high-ranking females. However, studies of vervets (Cheney et al. 1981) and yellow baboons (Altmann 1980) that experienced resource restriction do not demonstrate correlations between female rank and reproductive success, suggesting that resource scarcity might have to be quite severe before the reproductive benefits of high rank are realized.

The argument that rank-related differences in female reproductive success become significant only when resource restriction make it physio-logically impossible for low-ranking females to match their superordinates in infant production and/or care is questioned by Sugiyama and Ohsawa's (1982) analysis of the demographic effects of provisioning in the Ryozen A troop of free-ranging Japanese macaques. Births in the troop during artificial feeding are compared to those that occurred after provisioning had been discontinued. The authors find that under provisioning, the central (high-ranking) females exhibit an earlier age at first parturition, a greater age-specific natality rate, and a lower infant mortality rate than peripheral (low-ranking) females. In the nonprovisioned condition, central and peripheral females exhibit similar ages at first parturition and age-specific natality rates, and the difference in infant mortality rates decreases slightly. Since the Gouzoules et al. (1982) and Wolfe (1983) arguments suggest that resource abundance lowers rank-related variance in female reproductive success, the results in the Ryozen A troop clearly do not support their positions. Perhaps other long-term studies of troops observed during both resource abundance and restriction will resolve this apparent contradiction.

An issue that has been absent from the discussion up to this point is that of the possible costs of rank. Cheney et al. (1981) raise this point when they note that most studies finding positive correlations between rank and reproductive success have been conducted with troops which either are provisioned and/or are located in environments where predation is not a major problem. The authors argue that such conditions may increase the benefits of high rank, while decreasing the costs of holding such a position. As noted previously, their study of free-ranging vervets demonstrates no relationship between rank and reproductive success. This is in part because high-ranking adult females experience a higher mortality rate than their low-ranking cohorts. Moreover, the causes of mortality differ between rank classes, with subordinates being more likely to die from illness and dominants being at greater risk from predation. Cheney et al. suggest that the deaths of low-ranking females may result from lack of access to food and water during the dry seasons. The reasons why high-ranking females are more vulnerable to predation are not clear, but the authors note that they give alarm calls more frequently and are more aggressive during intertroop encounters than subordinates. Fluctuation of resources over time may be the major factor determining whether the costs of holding high rank are offset by the benefits accruing to the holder. If a troop has frequently encountered periods of resource restriction in the past, and if adult or infant mortality are negatively correlated with rank, a strategy of competing for high rank might be the outcome of natural selection.

An interesting aspect of the Cheney et al. (1981) study is the problem of rank-related differences in reproductive success in good environments. If the risk of death from predation remains the same when a troop experiences a period of resource abundance, we might predict that in such conditions better-nourished, lower-ranking females, suffering fewer deaths from illness, might actually outreproduce high-ranking females. Only future research will indicate the validity of this prediction.

Another study identifying the costs of high rank is Glander's (1980) investigation of howler monkeys. He finds that alpha females experience the greatest rate of infant mortality (100 percent), but that females in the ranks just below the alpha position produce more offspring surviving to one year than females of lower ranks. Glander suggests that these middle-rank positions are the prizes that females compete for, and he argues that the only way for females to obtain them is to first achieve the alpha position. Perhaps future research will indicate whether females who retain low-ranking positions all their lives achieve greater lifetime reproductive success than females who become alpha females, experience a period of low reproductive success, and then attain a middle rank, with its high reproductive success.

A final explanation of the rank-related variance in reproductive success that is observed in some species involves the physiological effects created when female-female competition is manifested through physical harassment. Several studies demonstrate that social stress may interfere with a female's reproductive cycle (Alverez 1973; Bowman et al. 1978; Hearn 1978; Hendrickx and Nelson 1971; Rowell 1970; Sassenrath 1970; Sassenrath et al. 1969). If low-ranking females undergo more social stress than high-ranking females, they may experience more anovulatory cycles and more postconception failures than their more dominant cohorts. The Dunbar (1980) and Dunbar and Dunbar (1977) discovery of a positive correlation between female rank and reproductive success in gelada baboons is explained in this manner. Dunbar and Dunbar (1977) observe no rank differences in amount of sexual activity, and they report that females do not interfere with one another's consortships. However, physical attacks by dominant females on subordinates increase by almost 50 percent when the latter enter estrus. This statistic may well underestimate the stress that subordinate estrous females experience, since the constant reception of threats may also affect their physiology. The effects of this stress may be indicated by the fact that subordinates take longer to conceive than dominants. Wasser (1983) also argues that female-female competition occurs by means of reproductive suppression in certain species (see also Silk and Boyd 1983). He predicts that low-ranking females will receive more attacks during certain critical periods (early preovulatory stage and first trimester of pregnancy) than high-ranking females. This prediction is confirmed in a free-ranging troop of yellow baboons. Several studies reviewed in the section on sex ratio theory also noted that female-female competition may be responsible for the varying sex ratios that are produced by females of different ranks (Chapter Six).

A major problem in this model of rank and reproductive success is determining how much stress low-ranking females experience in free-ranging groups. In captivity, subordinates often cannot avoid females who dominate them, and therefore they may be subject to prolonged periods of high social stress. In contrast, in wild groups they may move to the periphery of the troop to avoid harassment. After reviewing the literature on the subject, Deag (1977) concludes that subordinate animals in the wild may not experience enough social stress to produce physiological changes of a magnitude that would affect their reproduction. Dunbar and Dunbar's (1977) analysis may apply only to species exhibiting unimale troop organizations, where females who desire to mate must maintain contact with the male. In contrast, Deag's observation may be particularly relevant to species with multimale groups, where subordinates of both sexes may avoid superiors and still mate.

Summary

The material just reviewed indicates that the relationship between female rank and reproductive success, if any, is still not clearly defined for the alloprimates. There is almost no evidence that female rank hierarchies have evolved through sexual selection by competition. The fact that most studies find no relationship between rank and amount or type of mating activity indicates that any rank-related variance in reproductive success results from evolutionary processes other than sexual selection. However, there is still much research to be done on the issue of female mate choice. The available evidence suggests that females frequently prefer males other than the most dominant, and it would be interesting to know if such preferences are the outcomes of positive choices on the part of the females, or if they are by-products of female-female competition for access to better-quality mates.

While there are several good empirical studies of the relationship between female rank and reproductive success, the need for more careful investigations is obvious. Some of the issues to be addressed by these future studies were identified in the earlier discussion. In any study, the nature of the rank system of the species must be examined, the mechanisms through which differential reproductive success is achieved (e.g., harassment, infant mortality, birth date) identified, and the resource situation of the group delineated. Studies must also confront the problem of the costs of rank and how these affect female lifetime reproductive success. Finally, if researchers argue that natural and/or sexual selection is responsible for the evolution of female dominance behavior, there is a need for data on the heritability of relative rank or dominance behavior and for evidence that the offspring of high-ranking females maintain a reproductive advantage in relation to their lower-ranking competitors.

FEMALE RANK AND SELECTION BY PREFERENCE

Since among alloprimates, it is the females who are being competed for, there is no theoretical reason for predicting that they will exhibit traits evolved through sexual selection by preference. The females who possess such traits (or exaggerated versions of them) would enjoy higher mating success than those without them, because they would be more attractive to males. Studies reviewed earlier fail to establish differential mating success among alloprimate females. Several investigations have revealed male preference for certain age classes of females (which class depends on the species), but there is no reason to argue that the female age is somehow involved in the operation of sexual selection by preference. As noted earlier, a like-rank mating phenomenon might indicate some sexual selection by preference, but evidence for such a phenomenon is very weak. Finally, the most obvious candidate for the role of a trait evolved through sexual selection by preference, the sexual swellings associated with estrus, varies widely between species and has been shown not to correlate with male preference for specific females, but rather with the timing of copulations.

SUMMARY

That increased fitness is one of the rewards of high rank appears to be one of the common sense assumptions of many social scientists. The preceding discussion indicates, however, how complex primatologists have found the situation to be. In general, the evidence for the basic prediction that high rank is directly correlated with increased mating and reproductive success in males and/or females is very weak. Perhaps the most important lesson of the review is that there are a large number of factors that affect the correlation between rank and reproductive success in any group. Until empirical studies manage to control these factors, the relevance of any specific study to the basic prediction will remain ambiguous.

It should be noted that while existing studies do not clearly demonstrate that rank is related to reproductive success, they also do not allow us to reject this hypothesis. Proponents of the hypothesis can point to theoretical and methodological difficulties in all of the studies that fail to find a correlation between rank and reproductive success. It is obvious that the relationship between rank and inclusive fitness will be a controversial topic in alloprimate sociobiology for some time to come.

CHAPTER 9

Some Human Reproductive Strategies

INTRODUCTION

This chapter reviews a miscellaneous collection of studies relating to the manners in which humans achieve reproductive success. Much of the research can be subsumed under sexual selection theory, but because the theory is rarely systematically developed, I will not organize the chapter around the issues of selection by competition and selection by preference. All the investigations assert that humans act so as to maximize their reproductive success; this being, in most circumstances, the most effective means of maximizing inclusive fitness. Although the view is sometimes implicit, the authors of these studies see their work as contrasting the sociobiological hypothesis of maximization of reproductive success against various theories emphasizing human freedom from such "biological" considerations. However, the exact relationship between the sociobiological hypothesis and alternative perspectives varies from author to author.

The studies discussed in this chapter touch on so many topics and relate to one another in so many ways that any organization is bound to be somewhat artificial. I will, however, divide the chapter into four subdivisions: (1) studies on the relationship between cultural goals and reproductive success, including a discussion of the demographic transition; (2) studies relating social power and marriage forms (cross-cousin marriage, polyandry, etc.) to reproductive success; (3) studies of the reproductive strategies of individuals; and (4) studies relating reproductive strategies to the evolution of human longevity and menopause. It should be noted, however, that the studies in the first three subdivisions often deal with similar problems and should be considered together.

CULTURAL GOALS AND REPRODUCTIVE SUCCESS

The major paper in this subsection is Irons' (1979b) examination of wealth and reproductive success among the Yomut Turkman. Irons notes that human behavior is goal directed, and that societies differ in the goals they define as worth achieving. For example, pastoralists may be socialized to strive to control a large herd, while Yanomamo males are taught to strive for recognition as fierce men. Irons defines cultural success as achievement of those goals which a society sees as indicating that a person is an admired member of the group. An opponent of sociobiology might suggest that the large intersocietal variation in definitions of cultural success is an example of a human trait which cannot be explained by the discipline's focus on maximization of reproductive success. However, Irons argues that there is a close relationship between cultural and biological success and that changes in one may track changes in the other:

> I suggest as a hypothesis that in most human societies cultural success consists in accomplishing those things which make biological success (that is, a high inclusive fitness) probable. While cultural success is by definition something people are conscious of, they may often be unaware of the biological consequences of their behavior. . . . As a result of environmental change, what has been defined in the past in a particular society as worth achieving may cease to make a high inclusive fitness probable. When this happens, I hypothesize, members of the society gradually redefine their goals to make them correspond with those things which will increase the probability of a high inclusive fitness. This hypothesis is derived from the following more general theoretical principle: Human beings track their environments and behave in ways in which, given the specific environment in which they find themselves, maximize inclusive fitness; what is observed as culture and social structure is the outcome of this process [Irons 1979b:258].

It is important to note what Irons does not say here. He is not arguing that genetic differences between societies are responsible for varying definitions of cultural success. In fact, there are no genes for specific definitions of cultural success. Rather, all human beings have been selected to maximize inclusive fitness, and definitions of cultural success are the outcomes of the interaction of this universal tendency with ecological, social, and cultural factors.

Irons illustrates his hypothesis with data on wealth and reproductive success among the Yomut. He first argues that the accumulation of wealth is a Yomut cultural goal. A maximization of wealth goal is opposed to a sufficing strategy, under which individuals and households stop working once they have enough wealth to meet their basic needs. Sahlins (1972) suggests that the worker-to-consumer ratio is an important factor in the production of wealth, and argues that if households with a better ratio for wealth production actually do accumulate wealth over time, while those with a worse ratio do not, we can conclude that the former are acting to accumulate capital. In a paper discussed below, Irons (1980) utilizes Sahlins' argument and demonstrates that Yomut households act as if they were attempting to accumulate capital. In the paper under review, he merely notes that households attempt to accumulate wealth beyond the consumption needs of members and that there are clear differences in the wealth of households.

Having demonstrated that the Yomut seek to accumulate wealth, Irons shows that wealth is positively correlated with fitness. Data on fertility and mortality indicate that the wealthier half of the population achieves greater Darwinian fitness (i.e., reproductive success and survivorship) than the poorer half. The two categories differ significantly on age-specific male fertility and on age-specific male and female mortality rates for the first twenty years of life. The difference in age-specific female fertility rates is in the predicted direction, but is not statistically significant. Thus, the results support Irons' hypothesis that individuals do increase their fitness through the proximate mechanism of wealth accumulation.

Irons also examines variation in male and female reproductive success, showing that the variance for males is much greater than that for females. To illustrate the difference, he uses data on fertility and mortality rates to calculate the expected number of offspring of individuals with different amounts of wealth. In the wealthier half of the population, 100 males will produce 442 sons and 371 daughters, while 100 males in the poorer half will produce only 239 sons and 225 daughters. One hundred wealthy females will produce 305 sons and 256 daughters, while 100 poor females will produce only 257 sons and 242 daughters. Of course, if wealth tends to be stable, the gap in inclusive fitness between rich and poor will widen with each passing generation.

Finally, Irons investigates the question of whether wealthy individuals achieve greater Darwinian fitness at the expense of close relatives. If this were the case, it could be argued that such individuals were reducing their inclusive fitness, and Irons would have to demonstrate that their increased Darwinian fitness outweighed the costs they imposed upon their relatives (devalued by the coefficient of relatedness). The data indicate that brothers of wealthy males also tend to be wealthy, suggesting that wealthy males do not cheat their brothers out of chances for reproductive success.

Irons indicates that the greater Darwinian success of the wealthy stems from several factors. They have better diets, receive better medical care, and work less at strenuous or dangerous tasks. Males from wealthy families marry earlier than those from poor families, because they more quickly accumulate the bridewealth necessary to contract marriages. Wealthy males also remarry more quickly than poor males after the death of a wife, and they are also more likely to be polygynous. Irons demonstrates that polygyny is the main reason for the widening of the gap between fertility rates of wealthy and poor males as they grow older.

Irons' results provide strong preliminary support for his hypothesis that cultural success is positively related to Darwinian fitness. However, one's position on the redundancy problem is likely to affect how this study is interpreted. A sociocultural anthropologist who is unwilling to accept the sociobiological perspective can point out that the associations between wealth, natality, and mortality rates are so logical and so obvious that recourse to an evolutionary explanation is not required. A much stronger test case for Irons' argument would be that of a society where the achievement of cultural goals does not lead to an accumulation of wealth or other resources that have a straightforward relationship to Darwinian fitness. A society that stresses the pursuit of religious goals demanding celibacy, or at least a delay in reproductive activity, would be an interesting test case. Irons himself identifies another important test case when he notes that wealthy individuals in societies which have undergone the demographic transition often limit the size of their families (see below).

Unfortunately, Irons' (1979b) failure to discuss the methodological problems of identifying images of cultural success weakens his presentation. At some points in his discussion, he appears to hold that such goals must be present in the consciousness of actors, and that individuals must know they are striving to achieve these goals. This view would suggest that the proper methodology for this type of research involves having informants articulate their goals. However, Irons does not employ this methodology in his Yomut study. Instead, he postulates the existence of a goal of accumulation of wealth from his background knowledge of the culture and from his data on the economic activities of households. Does this indicate that images of cultural success may remain outside the consciousness of actors? Might individuals articulate one image of cultural success having nothing to do with fitness, while in reality striving to achieve a "hidden" goal related to increased fitness (e.g., a scholar who consciously strives only to resolve theoretical problems, but "actually" is working to enhance his or her personal reputation)? A further problem with defining the relationship between images of cultural success and fitness occurs when a society offers many such images. In the small-scale societies discussed by Irons (Yanomamo, Nuer, Yomut), it may be permissible to argue that the members of the society agree upon a single image of cultural success (or, at most, one for each sex), but this is certainly not true in more complex social systems. There is probably no simple relationship between images of cultural success and Darwinian fitness in these more complex societies, but only additional research, conducted with adequate concern for the methodological problems of identifying models of cultural success, will resolve this question.

At the end of his discussion, Irons notes that in societies which have experienced the demographic transition, wealthier individuals tend to utilize contraception to limit family size. Since wealth is often an image of cultural success in such societies, this situation would appear to invalidate Irons' general argument. In fact, the lower fertility rate of the upper and middle classes in industrial societies is often cited as conclusive evidence that sociobiological theories postulating selection for behaviors that maximize inclusive fitness do not apply to humans (see Lande 1978). Since this point is such an important one in the debate between human sociobiologists and their opponents, I will take this opportunity to examine some of the positions on it.

Irons suggests two possible explanations for why wealthy individuals might limit family size. First, he notes that in industrial societies, fertility limitation is often a component of a strategy of status elevation or status maintenance. Higher socioeconomic status is accompanied by lower mortality rates. Thus, it is possible that while wealthy individuals have fewer offspring, these offspring have a higher survivorship than the children of lower classes, resulting in the wealthy achieving greater inclusive fitness. The second alternative suggested by Irons is that ". . . the novelty of modern social environments is such that the proximate behavioral mechanisms which were adaptive in pre-industrial societies are no longer adaptive" (1979b:272). In other words, striving for cultural success was associated with Darwinian fitness until the demographic transition, but for various reasons this is no longer true. This alternative should perhaps be accepted only as a last resort, for it has the taste of special pleading, introduced only to save the sociobiological perspective when predictions derived form it are not verified. Acceptance of this position would indicate that the tracking of environments hypothesized by Irons is a rather slow process, since the demographic transition has been underway for over a hundred years. At the same time, there can be no doubt that environmental change can result in a mismatch between behavior and environment, and therefore this argument can never be dismissed out of hand.

Other explanations of the fertility behavior of wealthy individuals in societies which have achieved the demographic transition are reviewed by Barkow and Burley (1980). They reject Alexander's (1974) argument that in the past humans often responded to an increase in resources by reducing the quantity of offspring, in order to invest more in each child (a movement from a r-strategy to a K-strategy). They argue that only so many resources can be invested in a child to increase its probability of reproductive success.

After a given point, additional investment will be wasted and could be better invested in producing additional offspring. Barkow and Burley suggest that the wealthy reach this point fairly frequently and therefore should be expected to produce offspring at a higher rate than they do. They note that it is possible to argue that the behavior of the wealthy would make sense in the environment of evolutionary adaptation of our species, since the point where the K-strategy would not pay off would rarely be reached in a hunting-gathering economy. However, as noted above, such "novelty of modern environments" arguments should be accepted only as a last resort.

Barkow and Burley's explanation of the lower fertility of the wealthy argues that such behavior is in fact nonadaptive. In other words, wealthy people who limit fertility are behaving in a manner that does not maximize inclusive fitness. Barkow and Burley see this maladaptive situation as an accidental by-product of selection for human intelligence. In an earlier article, on the concealment of ovulation, Burley (1979) hypothesizes that early human females attempted to escape the pain and danger associated with giving birth to large-brained infants by avoiding copulation during ovulation. Concealment of the time of ovulation from the female is a result of this situation. However, Burley emphasizes that intelligence and behavioral flexibility have also been selected for in the course of human evolution. Barkow and Burley argue that these traits allow females to avoid the pain and danger of childbirth, as well as pursue goals requiring a reduction in family size. In other words, the intelligence of human females leads them to desire a smaller family size, and in certain societies the availability of contraception allows them to achieve this goal. The authors note that both the attractiveness of children and cultural ideologies favoring natality may counterbalance female desire to pursue nonreproductive goals. The authors also suggest that the amount of control that females have over their fertility will be a more accurate predictor of reduced population growth than economic growth, with greater female autonomy associated with smaller family size. They note that the current literature neither refutes or supports this hypothesis.

An empirical study bearing on these issues is Essock-Vitale's (1984) analysis of the reproductive histories of individuals on *Forbes'* list of the 400 wealthiest Americans. She finds that the wealthy women on the list or the wives of men on the list average 3.1 children ever-born, while the average for the general population is 2.7 children. A subsample of women with completed reproductive histories shows that the wealthy women average 3.4 ever-born children, as contrasted with an average of 2.9 for white women of similar ages. Essock-Vitale also notes that the survivorship of the children of the wealthy is higher than that of the average population. She illustrates the reproductive advantages of the wealthy by comparing the number of offspring surviving to age twenty that would be produced by a theoretical cohort of 100 wealthy women, 100 white women in the general population, and 100 nonwhite women. These numbers are 307, 223, and 255 offspring, respectively.

Essock-Vitale's results indicate that in the United States, as among the Yomut, wealth is associated with higher Darwinian fitness. Her work suggests a need to re-examine the commonly-held impression that the wealthy are at a reproductive disadvantage in industrial societies. For example, while the poor may exhibit larger families than the rich, a higher proportion of the poor may fail to produce a family. Essock-Vitale cites U.S. census data indicating that the proportion of married women remaining childless decreases with wealth. It is obvious that clarification of the relationship between wealth and reproductive success in industrial societies remains one of the major tasks of future research in human sociobiology.

Another piece of innovative research relating cultural success to reproductive success is Barkow's (1977) examination of conformity to ethos in two Nigerian communities. This work differs from Irons' approach, in that Barkow considers how genetic variation between populations might be relevant to different cultural goals.

Barkow notes that the literature on the interaction between culture and biology usually asks one of two of questions. The first is whether individuals who follow culturally prescribed behavior patterns increase their inclusive fitness. This is the question posed by Irons in his research on wealth and reproductive success among the Yomut. The second question asks whether, and to what extent, biological evolution tracks cultural evolution. Barkow notes that this tracking might involve the genetic assimilation of cultural characteristics. As an example of such a process, he cites Brues' (1959) argument that different technologies select for different body forms. Brues argues, for example that the spear would favor tall, lean individuals, while the bow-and-arrow would favor males with thick, muscular arms. The introduction of the bow-and-arrow into a group with bodies appropriate to spear use might eventually result in changing the distribution of alleles for body form, in which case biological evolution would have tracked cultural change.

According to Barkow, at least four points must be demonstrated before a genetic assimilation argument relevant to a behavioral trait can be accepted:

> (1) that those individuals who were most readily socialized into the trait in question enjoyed an increase in biological fitness; (2) that the ease with which one is socialized into the trait is at least partly under genetic control; (3) that the population is at least a relative genetic isolate; and (4) that the process had been continuing for a sufficient number of generations to affect allele frequencies meaningfully [Barkow 1977:412].

He notes that his research is designed to test only the first point in this process and suggests that he has no evidence on points (2) and (4), and that point (3) is, in fact, not true of his population.

Barkow's fieldwork took place in two Nigerian communities. The Muslim Hausa place a high value on a trait Barkow labels as "inhibitedness," while the non-Muslim Maguzawa Hausa do not. Inhibitedness is defined as ". . . maintaining a constant demeanor of friendly cheerfulness regardless of actual inner state" (Barkow 1977:415). The trait is operationalized by mention of three emotional topics ("shame," "adultery," and "sexual activity") in Thematic Apperception Test (TAT) stories, with the males who mention such topics less frequently being scored as more inhibited. Barkow demonstrates that in the Muslim group, inhibited males had more living children than less inhibited males. Among the Maguzawa, where inhibitedness is not admired, there is no correlation between this trait and the number of living children. Barkow also examines the relationship between wealth and reproductive success and finds that in both villages, wealthier men have more living children than poorer men, although the t-test statistics for the difference are not statistically significant in either village.

Barkow's results are interesting, but conceptual and methodological problems mar his study. For example, he does not demonstrate that men who scored highest on the inhibitedness trait were those most easily socialized into it. Perhaps many strongly resisted socialization but finally discovered that (outward) conformity was necessary for social or economic success. Unless independent evidence for ease of socialization is provided, the relevance of Barkow's results to the first point of the genetic assimilation argument remains questionable.

Second, Barkow's use of a projective test to measure inhibitedness is problematic. He scored men as inhibited if they did not mention sex acts, shame acts, or adultery in the TAT stories they produced. Actually, the trait most related to number of children was the mention of adultery, with males who mentioned it frequently scored as less inhibited and characterized by fewer children. It is possible, however, that objectively, males with more children have less reason to be concerned about adultery than other men, and that their failure to mention this theme is merely a reflection of the fact that their wives are less likely to engage in such behavior. A second possible argument is that males who mentioned sexual themes more often were actually not less inhibited, but rather more concerned about sexual activity. Barkow does not provide an age breakdown of responses for his sample; nor does he compare the responses of men in childless marriages with those in marriages that had produced children. Finally, projective test theory suggests an alternative scoring of the TAT stories. Barkow scores males as inhibited if they did not mention emotional topics in their stories. However, projective tests are predicated on the assumption that the test's ambiguous stimuli, and the fact that the test setting is outside normal social experience, both force and permit individuals to express components of their personalities which are ordinarily repressed. From this perspective, it could be argued that males who mentioned emotional topics most frequently are those who are the most inhibited in ordinary social settings.

Finally, Barkow's statistics are not convincing. For example, for each topic there is a possible score of 13.0 mentions by an individual. Barkow's Table One shows that although the Muslims and Maguzawa do differ, the frequency of mention is not high for either group. The comparison producing the greatest t-statistic has the Muslims mentioning sex acts with a mean frequency of 0.05 and the Magazawa with a mean frequency of 0.22. While statistically significant, it is difficult to believe that a difference of such small magnitude plays a major role in social life. Unfortunately, Barkow's table of correlations coefficients between mentions of each topic and number of children does not permit adequate analysis of his results. Finally, in his test of the association between wealth and number of children, Barkow does not control for age, making his results difficult to interpret or to compare with those obtained by Irons or Essock-Vitale.

In summary, the studies reviewed in this section can be seen as attempts to define the mutual influences between cultural norms and reproductive strategies. Irons' position, that humans have evolved so that cultural definitions of success will closely track strategies most likely to optimize inclusive fitness, receives some support from the data on wealth and reproductive success, but must be replicated in societies characterized by images of cultural success which do not lead to rewards instrumentally related to higher Darwinian fitness. Of course, if no such societies can be located, Irons' position would be strongly supported. It is clear that the problem of the demographic transition requires much more research and will remain an obstacle to the wide acceptance of human sociobiology until it is satisfactorily resolved. Finally, Barkow's suggestion that cultural traits might be subject to genetic assimilation is theoretically interesting, but his empirical work is not adequate to provide even a preliminary test of his argument.

REPRODUCTIVE SUCCESS AND MARRIAGE PATTERNS

Studies reviewed in this section seek relationships between reproductive success and marriage patterns. In so doing, they often implicitly relate cultural success to biological success by suggesting that individuals who achieve certain types of culturally preferred marriages may achieve higher Darwinian fitness than those who are forced to settle for less preferred unions. I do not discuss in this section the studies reviewed in Chapter Three concerning the fertility of polygynous marriages, but their relevance to the topics addressed in this chapter is clear.

Chagnon and his colleagues have twice utilized demographic data from the Yanomamo to investigate relationships between form of marriage and reproductive success. Chagnon et al. (1979) examine whether headmen achieve greater reproductive success than other males. Since headmen are usually respected by the Yanomamo, we can view this study as another test of Irons' (1979b) argument that in human societies cultural success leads to biological success. When males over the age of thirty-five are compared, headmen average 8.6 children, while non-headmen average only 4.16, a statistically significant difference. Further analysis indicates that this difference results from the fact that headmen obtain more wives than nonheadmen (an average of 3.6 versus 2.4). There is no significant difference in the fertility of the wives of headmen and nonheadmen. Thus, the reproductive advantage of headmen appears to stem solely from their ability to accumulate more wives than other males. Chagnon (1979b) argues that the reward of extra wives, and the resultant enhancement of reproductive success, are major reasons why individuals accept the burdens of headmanship in societies without wealth differentials.

The politics and demography of Yanomamo cross-cousin marriage are examined in Chagnon (1980). In an analysis too detailed to review here, he demonstrates that such marriages solve a number of the problems that stem from mate competition in this society. Of interest to the present discussion in Chagnon's test of the hypothesis that marriages between genetically-related partners will be reproductively more successful than those between unrelated individuals. In a sample of 259 marriages, he finds that the per-marriage fertility rate for unions between unrelated individuals is 1.92, which compares with a rate of 2.26 for marriages between related partners. Unfortunately, Chagnon does not evaluate the statistical significance of this difference. He also demonstrates that marriages between actual first cross-cousins are reproductively more successful than marriages between other consanguineal kin.

While Chagnon notes the superior reproductive performance of certain marriage types, he does not explain this phenomenon beyond noting that some marriage types might mitigate the problems of mate competition. However, he does suggest that first cross-cousin marriage may not be the optimum reproductive strategy for every member of the society:

> My suspicion . . . is that cross-cousin marriages represent an adaptive strategy for only a fraction of the Yanomamo population, i.e., for those individuals who were fortunate enough to have a highly successful grandfather—someone who, through polygyny, produced large numbers of sons and daughters and whose sons and daughters built on their "kinship fortunes" through reciprocal marriage alliance by giving their children in marriage to each other as implied in the "ideal model" [Chagnon 1980:560].

Chagnon's argument is important for research on marriage institutions, because it suggests that the ideal model or the formal rules governing marriage may benefit only a minority of a society's population. This might mean that individuals with the wrong characteristics who follow the formal rules may exhibit lower reproductive success than a researcher would predict, given their adherence to the rules. An adequate examination of the relationship between marriage rules and reproductive success must identify the options available to individuals in different circumstances. These options, Chagnon suggests, will be determined in part by the inclusive fitness maximization strategies adopted by their ancestors and by demographic "luck" (e.g., the sex of siblings, mortality patterns, the demographic situation of other individuals, etc.). Chagnon's work illustrates the complexity of sorting this out in a small-scale society like the Yanomamo; the difficulties facing researchers in more socially complex societies will be many times greater.

Another proposition concerning Yanomamo reproductive strategies is tested in Chagnon (1982). He notes that male-male competition for mates increases with greater numbers of lineages in a village. Given Yanomamo marriage rules, the ideal situation for a male is to be a member of a village composed of two lineages that trade women with one another (e.g., cross-cousin marriage). Older men seeking to increase their inclusive fitness by providing mates for their younger brothers and/or sons may attempt to bring village composition closer to this ideal. Chagnon argues that village fissions may result from the social machinations of such men and predicts that when villages fission, the daughter villages will exhibit a more dualistic structure than the mother village. To test this prediction, he examines four fissions, producing eight new villages, and calculates the percentage of males belonging to the two largest lineages in each village. Compared to the mother villages, this percentage increased (indicating a more dualistic structure) in five of the daughter villages, decreased in two, and remained the same in one. Chagnon concludes that these results support his hypothesis. He also provides data indicating that an important part of the reproductive strategy of a Yanomamo male is to surround himself with siblings and cross-cousins (potential sources of women), while separating himself (and his offspring) from parallel cousins and distant male relatives who would compete with him or his offspring and brothers for wives.

A holocultural study that is indirectly related to Chagnon's demonstration that Yanomamo headmen achieve greater reproductive success than their fellows is Betzig's (1982) study of despotism and reproductive success in twenty-four nonstate and early state societies. Her research can be viewed as another demonstration that cultural success is correlated with biological success if we assume that individuals in hierarchical societies strive to obtain power. Betzig argues that as societies become larger and increase in hierarchical complexity, individuals with the authority or ability to resolve conflicts of interest do so in manners beneficial to their own inclusive fitness. Her sample indicates that as groups become more complex, power holders tend to dictate the settlement of conflicts rather than to negotiate compromises between contending parties. Often disputes are settled in ways that increase the power of the authorities. Further, as social complexity increases, power holders charge or extort increasingly higher prices (fines, fees, bribes, etc.) to intervene in disputes. These rewards are often diverted to uses that increase the inclusive fitness of the authorities. Finally, Betzig demonstrates that social complexity is directly correlated with the number of wives and concubines that the leaders are permitted.

Betzig notes that the despotism of power holders and their accumulation of wealth and women declines in more modern states. To explain this, she refers to Alexander's (1975; Alexander et al. 1979) discussions of social monogamy in state societies. Recall that Alexander argues that in an environment of intense interstate competition, the survival of the modern state may demand high levels of social cooperation, and that such cooperation cannot be maintained when resource skew is too great. Betzig adds to this picture the argument that increased specialization of labor in modern states may mean that groups are better able to resist the efforts of power holders to settle conflicts despotically or to extract disproportionate amounts of resources from them.

Historical research by Faux and Miller (1984) on Mormon polygyny is interesting in light of Betzig's and Irons' arguments. The authors discover that the members of the hierarchy of the early Mormon Church who were related to Joseph Smith (the founder of the Church) averaged more wives and more offspring than members who were unrelated to Smith. Among members of the hierarchy appointed by Smith, his relatives averaged 24.2 offspring, as compared to 11.4 for unrelated members.

Further analysis by Faux and Miller illustrates Betzig's and Alexander's position that the necessities of social cooperation may force power holders to forego extraction of resources from those with less power. Polygyny, originally a secret practice restricted to the governing hierarchy of the Church, was eventually extended to the general membership, although the right to a polygynous marriage was subject to the approval of the hierarchy. The authors note that the men who were granted permission for polygynous marriages differed from monogamists in being either religiously or economically prominent, and they suggest that the central hierarchy used polygyny as a means of creating alliances with such individuals. Faux and Miller also show that while the central hierarchy might have given up some potential for increased fitness by extending polygyny to the general membership, they still averaged more wives and more offspring than the average polygynist who did not belong to the hierarchy. The latter, in turn, were reproductively more successful than the average monogamist.

The studies just reviewed are all concerned in one way or another with the topics of social power, marriage system, and reproductive success (see also Dickemann 1979a,b, 1981). They generally support the argument that individuals who achieve social power (political or economic) utilize such power to increase their inclusive fitness or reproductive success. Of course, alternative, nonsociobiological explanations could be offered for the results obtained by these authors. However, it is clear that sociobiology offers a simple perspective which ties these studies of widely disparate topics together perhaps more neatly than nonsociobiological explanations are able to do.

An empirical study suggesting that cultural success may not be related to biological success is Beall's and Goldstein's (1981) investigation of polyandry in a Tibetan population residing in Nepal. The authors note that polyandry is a common form of marriage in this population and that wealthy males marry polyandrously more frequently than poorer males, even though the former could afford to support individual wives. Since the culturally successful engage in polyandry, Beall and Goldstein argue that if sociobiological theory is correct, polyandrous marriages will exhibit greater Darwinian fitness than monogamous marriages—perhaps due to higher infant survival, as a result of the greater paternal investment that is characteristic of polyandrous families. The hypothesis is not supported by their data, however, since monogamous marriages exhibit higher mean rates of infant survival than polyandrous marriages. The authors calculate that the inclusive fitness of a male with three brothers is five times greater if all the brothers marry monogamously than if they marry a single woman. Beall and Goldstein suggest that polyandry is a strategy that is employed to maintain or increase the wealth of households, even at the cost of sacrificing inclusive fitness. Of course, if wealth is converted over the long run (several generations?) into inclusive fitness, as Irons (1979b) suggests is the case for the Yomut, then the Tibetan data do not disprove the sociobiological hypothesis that, under the ecological circumstances of this population, polyandry maximizes inclusive fitness. Unfortunately, Beall and Goldstein do not have the long-term data needed to resolve this question.

Weigel and Taylor (1982) criticize the Beall and Goldstein article by invoking some of the arguments suggested by Chagnon (1980). They note that the authors err in using population means to calculate fitness estimates. This method assumes that all males in the population have the same expected reproductive success for a given marriage type, a situation that, as Chagnon demonstrates, is not true of the Yanamomao and is probably not true of the Tibetan population. Weigel and Taylor argue that the expected reproductive success of different marriage types will depend on numerous variables, including wealth, occupation, number of kin, etc. Males differing on these variables can be expected to make different marriage choices. The authors conclude that Beall and Goldstein do not have the data necessary to disprove the sociobiological hypothesis that polyandry is positively correlated with inclusive fitness in this population. However, they also note that the amount of data required to reject any sociobiological hypothesis is so great that the usefulness of the theory may be nil: "Perhaps sociobiology will prove to be a relatively unusable theory for human behavior because it is difficult to test, and is therefore nonfalsifiable" (Beall and Goldstein 1982:408; see Hughes 1982 for another perspective on polyandry).

The final set of studies reviewed in this section involve Irons' ingenious attempts at using empirical data to test predictions derived from an individual selection perspective against those derived from the group selection perspective of Wynne-Edwards (1962). Irons (1980) argues that Wynne-Edwards sees certain species as regulating population so as to remain below their environment's carrying capacity. This is sometimes done by having individuals compete for the tokens that are required for breeding (i.e., dominance position, territory, etc.). When population density is low, the tokens are available to most animals, but once density exceeds a certain threshold, a lower proportion of individuals achieve tokens and population is automatically regulated. If environmental conditions are related to the availability of tokens, this process will regulate population around an equilibrium point. Along with most sociobiologists, Irons argues that the Wynne-Edwards hypothesis is difficult to accept, because it places selection at the level of the group: groups which fail to regulate their population eventually become extinct. He notes that once a gene encouraging "cheating" (i.e., using resources conserved by nonbreeders to reproduce without obtaining a token) enters a population of noncheaters, its bearers will outreproduce individuals bearing the genes for population regulation.

Irons considers the role of bridewealth among the Yomut as an appropriate test case of these perspectives. He suggests that the group selection perspective would see bridewealth as a conventionalized token, which acts to limit fertility as increases in population density make bridewealth more difficult to obtain. The amount of bridewealth demanded by the Yomut is large, averaging two to four years of income for a family of median wealth in the community where Irons worked. Further, it is fixed by tradition and is not subject to negotiation. Irons notes that in the last thirty years the Yomut have become richer, due to the introduction of mechanized agriculture. The value of patrimonies received during the last twenty years is almost twice that of those received more than twenty years ago. He postulates that the Wynne-Edwards position would predict that the Yomut should have responded to the more abundant resources with an increase in fertility. The greater availability of wealth, when combined with the fixed bridewealth, means that males should have been able to marry earlier in life, producing a concomitant decrease in age of marriage for females and a resultant increase in fertility. The data indicate no support for this prediction. The age at first marriage for Yomut females has not significantly changed during the past thirty-nine years. Data on trends in female fertility are more difficult to interpret. Irons compares the completed fertility of women at age thirty for three age groups (thirty to thirty-nine; forty to forty-nine; fifty to fifty-nine) and shows that younger women exhibit slightly higher fertility, even though they are not marrying earlier than women in the past. Finally, the data on mortality demonstrate that age-specific mortality rates for both males and females have declined over the last thirty years.

Irons concludes that there is no support for the idea that the Yomut regulate their population in response to resource availability. Increased wealth has brought higher population growth, but the mechanisms involved seem to be lower mortality rates and a slight increase in female fertility, perhaps due to better diet or less dangerous work. Irons interprets both these mechanisms as a relaxing of Darwin's "hostile forces of nature" and thus as not relevant to the group selection argument. He sees the key point against the Wynne-Edwards position as the fact that the greater availability of a token, bridewealth, did not result in a lower age of marriage for females.

The individual selection hypothesis argues that an increase in resources will result in individuals increasing their reproduction, independently of access to any token. Irons argues that the mechanisms through which additional resources are used to achieve greater fitness, either increasing fertility or lowering mortality, or both, are not predicted by the individual selection perspective. He reveiws his data on wealth, fertility, and mortality, showing that wealth is positively correlated with fertility and inversely correlated with mortality rates. Finally, as discussed above, he demonstrates that the Yomut do strive to attain wealth, perhaps as the proximate step in achieving greater Darwinian fitness.

Irons' test of the Wynne-Edwards hypothesis is one of the few pieces of sociobiological research to test empirically a group selection and an individual selection explanation of the same phenomenon. Unfortunately, it fails to resolve some very important questions. For example, the thrust of the Wynne-Edwards position is that as a population approaches carrying capacity, increasingly limited access to tokens results in lower population growth. However, Irons does not demonstrate that the Yomut population of thirty years ago was near the carrying capacity of its environment and therefore was engaging in fertility limitation. Perhaps the age of first marriage for females thirty years ago reflected attempts to maximize fertility in a population not in danger of exceeding its resources. If so, even greater resource abundance would not be expected to result in a lowering of this age. A better test for the Wynne-Edwards hypothesis would be a case where resources were observed to be shrinking, not growing.

Irons also does not show that lowering the age at first marriage for women would result in greater fertility. Data on age of menarche and length of adolescent sterility are needed to decide this question. Irons (1982) notes that the Yomut delay coresidence of spouses for three or more years after marriage. During this period, sexual activity is not permitted. Since average age at first marriage is about fifteen years, copulation for females usually begins around age eighteen, with a first birth at nineteen. Irons (1982) also notes that data on age of first menses suggest that Yomut women do not become fecund until about age eighteen. These facts suggest that decreasing the age at first marriage for females below the age of fifteen would not result in a significantly higher rate of fertility. A lower age would allow earlier coresidence, but if eighteen remained the average age of fecundity, this earlier coresidence would not result in increased fertility. This line of thought suggests that the reason why increased availability of the bridewealth token is not correlated with lower age of first marriage for females is that a reduction in this age would not create increased reproductive success.

Irons (1980) does not explore trends for the age at first marriage of males in his paper. Have increased resources resulted in earlier marriages for males, and, if so, does this have an influence on fertility rates? Although female age at marriage is more important than male age for overall fertility rates, the latter could be important if, by marrying earlier, males are marrying young females who in the past would have become wives of older men. If younger men copulate more frequently than older males, a reduction of the age gap between spouses might increase fertility in a manner postulated by Wynne-Edwards. Furthermore, studies reviewed in Chapter Three indicate that the fertility of wives in polygynous marriages is lower than that of women in monogamous unions. If increased resources and lower age of marriage for males have reduced the percentage of women in polygynous marriages, the fertility rates might also increase in a manner congruent with the Wynne-Edwards position.

The failure of the Yomut to lower the average age at first marriage for females also raises some questions for the individual selection perspective. It is clear that Irons holds that such a reduction is one path to increased fitness and that he sees the failure of the Yomut to take it as discrediting the group selection argument. However, the individual selection argument also predicts that individuals will choose actions increasing their reproductive success. If earlier age of marriage is one such action, why have not more individual Yomut selected it, thereby creating a significant reduction in the age at first marriage? In other words, the behavior of the Yomut does not appear to support either prediction.

Another paper by Irons (1982) also makes use of data on Yomut population trends to test hypotheses drawn from the individual and group selection perspectives. He once again examines the data on age at first marriage of females and finds that it does not support the Wynne-Edwards position. However, there is a significant difference between this paper and the one just reviewed (1980) in how the data are applied to the Wynne-Edwards position. In the earlier paper, Irons tests the prediction that:

> If the Yomut homeostatically regulate their population density in the manner suggested by Wynne-Edwards, they should respond to an increase in resources by lessening social limitation of fertility. This should be reflected in earlier and earlier marriage as resources per person increase [Irons 1980:426].

In contrast, in the 1982 paper, Irons uses his data to test the hypothesis that:

> [For] The Yomut . . . . resources/person have increased dramatically in a short time. This also means that if we move back in time we are looking at a

time of lowered resources. Thus, moving back in time we should see the population regulating mechanisms having a progressively stronger effect in restraining reproduction. That is to say, the group-level adaptation hypothesis predicts that, as we look at how demographic parameters change as we move back in time, we will see ... an increasing exclusion of women from marriage.... [Irons 1982:7].

This second perspective solves one of the difficulties of the 1980 paper, but only at the cost of destroying its value. In the 1982 paper, Irons cites data on age at marriage, first menses, and coresidence to demonstrate that in the past the delay in coresidence did not mean that Yomut women suffered a loss of fertility. In other words, the Yomut living in the period prior to the increase in the value of patrimonies were already maximizing fertility. To Irons, this fact indicates that the group selection argument is incorrect, for under conditions of lower resources per person, the Yomut did not limit their fertility. However, such an interpretation invalidates the discussion in Irons' 1980 paper, for, as noted earlier, if the age at first marriage for women in the past was already maximizing fertility, then reducing this age would not increase reproductive success, and the failure of increased resources to result in a lower age at first marriage is expected.

Irons' 1982 argument is validated only if he demonstrates that in the past the Yomut were near the carrying capacity of their land and that this was correlated with greater difficulty in obtaining bridewealth. Is it possible that, although the cost of bridewealth was high in the past, the Yomut were wealthy enough so that most males could accumulate it fairly early in life? Again, data on trends in the age at first marriage for males are vital to the interpretation of Irons' results. Until these data are presented, Irons' argument remains untested.

Irons (1982) also tests the prediction that under conditions of resource limitation, fertility was reduced by having widows remain unmarried. He finds that the recent increase in resources available to the Yomut is correlated with an increase in the probability of widow remarriage. This finding supports the group selection position, but Irons argues that such support is rather weak, because in the past only a few potentially fertile years were lost by widows who did not remarry. He also suggests that the behavior of widows in the earlier time period can be explained in terms of the individual selection perspective. Widows might have chosen to remain unmarried and invest resources in their offspring in an attempt to increase inclusive fitness. Male relatives of a widow or of her deceased husband might have supported or encouraged the widow not to remarry, since they often gained thereby the labor of the woman and her children or because they were concerned with the well being of their relatives.

Irons' paper (1982) also contains a test of a prediction derived from the Divale and Harris (1976) explanation of the male supremacist complex. Divale and Harris argue that in many preindustrial societies, endemic warfare is a mechanism that adjusts population to resources. Population size is affected by warfare, not only because of combat deaths but also because groups desiring to produce the maximum number of male warriors often resort to preferential female infanticide, in order to raise more males to adulthood. Divale and Harris test their theory by examining the sex ratio of children (under age fourteen) and adults in 561 populations. In societies exhibiting warfare at the time of the census, the sex ratio for children was 128 males to 100 females, and the ratio for adults was 101 males to 100 females. In contrast, societies where warfare had ceased over twenty-six years before the census had a childhood sex ratio of 106 males to 100 females, close to the secondary sex ratio assumed to be typical of humans (however, see Chagnon et al. 1979). Interestingly, the adult sex ratio in these societies was low, with 92 males for 100 females.

Warfare among the Yomut ceased in 1925, but flared up again between 1941 and 1949. Irons' data show the Yomut sex ratio in 1894 to be about 112:100. In the decade between 1944 and 1954, the sex ratio fell to about 107:100. By 1974, it had risen again and was even higher than in 1894, about 114:100. Unfortunately, Irons' results are difficult to interpret, because he does not identify the age groups from which his sex ratio statistics are derived. Divale and Harris' argument applies to the juvenile sex ratio most directly affected by female infanticide and least affected by male mortality in warfare. However, it is clear that the sequence of changes in Yomut sex ratio does not match the predictions of the Divale and Harris model, especially since the ratio with the greatest masculine bias occurs during a pacified period. Unfortunately, while Irons notes that his results do not support the Divale and Harris model, he does not discuss how an individual selection perspective would explain the observed changes in sex ratio.

The final test in Irons' paper (1982) involves an individual selection argument and examines whether Lack's rule applies to the Yomut. Lack (1954, 1968) studied the relationship between clutch size and number of fledglings in birds and found that the modal clutch size produced the largest number of fledglings. Irons predicts that the Yomut women with the most common level of fertility would have the highest number of surviving adult progeny. When data on the reproductive histories of women over forty are examined, they do not support the prediction. The modal number of births is eight, but women giving birth to from nine to sixteen children have greater numbers of surviving children than women producing only eight children. A subsample of women older than sixty years exhibits a slightly better fit with Lack's rule, but still does not support the prediction. Irons concludes that in this case, the individual selection hypothesis is not supported by the empirical data. However, he also notes that the test might be unfair, because the environments faced by different women may not be the same (due to differences in wealth), and because the Yomut environment fluctuates over time, while Lack's rule applies to single breeding seasons and to situations where all females confront the same environment.

Irons' work provides some support for the hypothesis that the individual selection perspective can explain much Yomut behavior. His attempts to derive testable predictions from the group selection perspective are ingenious, but not always totally convincing. Although his Yomut research relating changes in resources to manipulation of fertility is marred by the apparent contradiction between the 1980 and 1982 papers, it does point to the type of data that are required to conduct convincing tests of either group or individual selection arguments.

Because the studies reviewed here touch on so many different topics, it is not easy to summarize this subsection. It is clear that the work relating social power, marriage forms, and reproductive success is some of the strongest research in human sociobiology. Although redundant nonsociobiological hypotheses can be advanced to account for each individual finding, sociobiology's ability to subsume the results under a few basic principles is impressive. On the other hand, the work by Beall and Goldstein and by Irons serves to remind us how difficult it is to move from merely interpreting events as conforming to the sociobiological perspective to attempting to falsify specific predictions derived from that perspective.

SOME MISCELLANEOUS REPRODUCTIVE STRATEGIES

The studies reviewed in this subsection all deal with strategies that individuals adopt to increase their reproductive success. Whereas the studies in the preceding subsection were mainly concerned with the analysis of the causes and consequences of marriage systems, those in this subsection inquire as to how individuals manipulate their social environments to achieve reproductive success. I will divide the subsection into those strategies which are applicable to both males and females (couples), those adopted only by males, and those adopted only by females.

1. *Strategies of couples.* In the chapter on rank theory, I noted that the problem of male and female quality is an issue in sexual selection theory. Theorists in human sociobiology rarely address this problem directly, but there are several studies of human mate selection and assortative mating that do provide a base for future research into this topic. For example, Thiessen and Gregg (1980) discuss the possibility that kin selection may have played a role in the evolution of positive assortative mating (see also van den Berghe 1983):

> Positive assortment increases the genetic potential for altruism (reduces its cost) and increases the number of each parent's genes among the offspring without an additional reproductive effort. Cast within this framework it is understandable why natural selection would favor positive assortment, at least up to the point where inbreeding results in deleterious consequences. The other side of the coin is that disassortative mating which diminishes

gene similarity among family members and restricts kin selection must be offset by substantial reproductive advantages in order for the strategy to succeed. Thus, disassortative mating is less likely to evolve [Thiessen and Gregg 1980:116].

An implication of Thiessen and Gregg's argument for individual reproductive strategies is that couples composed of people who resemble one another on many behavioral and/or morphological traits, or on certain key traits, may be reproductively more successful than couples composed of individuals who are not congruent on these traits. Thiessen and Gregg demonstrate that among dating couples in college, those who show positive assortment tend to remain together longer than those who do not. The same effect is found for both friends and married couples. The authors also use data from Clark and Spuhler (1959) to support their position. These data indicate that the greater the positive assortment exhibited by a couple, the more children the couple produced. The magnitude of the correlation between positive assortment on any single trait and reproductive success is not strong (0.09 is the highest), but for nineteen traits, the correlation was positive for seventeen, a very consistent pattern.

If positive assortative mating is based on selection for gene homology, as suggested by Thiessen and Gregg, the manner in which the gene affects the phenotype may not matter. This leads Thiessen and Gregg to predict that individuals should positively assort on abnormal as well as on normal traits. They review literature indicating that positive assortment occurs for a wide range of physical and psychological abnormalities. However, the authors note that there are many alternative hypotheses that might account for this situation (differential association, etc.).

Burley (1983) identifies a major weakness in Thiessen and Gregg's argument when she notes that the fact that the partners tend to resemble one another on various traits does not prove that "like attracts like," as suggested by the positive assortment argument. She argues that the same outcome could occur if the following conditions were met: (1) both sexes provide parental care; (2) there is phenotypic variation in traits indicating ability to provide such care (i.e., mates vary in quality); and (3) all individuals seek to mate with the highest-quality individuals. In such circumstances, high-quality individuals will mate with one another, leaving lower-quality individuals to mate among themselves. This makes it appear as if "like prefers like," but, in fact, all individuals have the same mate preferences (for mates with traits indicating high quality). Burley's argument stands as a potential alternative to Thiessen and Gregg's analysis, and future research will have to decide which explanation applies to humans. For certain traits, laboratory tests may provide a partial answer to this question. For example, an individual who is permitted to select between pictures of members of the opposite sex might reveal a preference for traits similar to his or her own

(Thiessen and Gregg's position) or might exhibit a preference for traits which all members of his or her sex consider attractive (Burley's position). Allowing individuals to choose partners for experimental tasks might permit analysis of preference for behavioral traits.

Studies by Paterson and Pettijohn (1982) and by Lockard and Adams (1981) examine the relationship between age and mate selection in the United States. Paterson and Pettijohn argue that since females mature earlier than males, they should prefer older males who are equally mature. At the same time, older males should prefer younger females, who have greater reproductive value, all else being equal. Examination of 275 marriages occurring in an Ohio county during a fifty-year period reveals that grooms are older than their brides in over 75 percent of the couples. Paterson and Pettijohn's interpretation is plausible, but suffers from the problem that we cannot tell whether the observed situation is the result of female choice, male choice, or both. It is possible, for example, that females do not prefer older males, but for economic and/or social reasons are forced to accept them as husbands.

Lockard and Adams (1981) postulate an ideal life history strategy within the American mating system:

> . . . a mating strategy . . . males might adopt with greater likelihood than females, would be to mate as early as socially feasible with a female of approximately the same age. Upon her approaching menopause, he might then abandon her to mate again with a younger female still in her reproductive years . . . . a female strategy might be to mate for life with a male possessing, or potentially capable of possessing . . . resources to help rear young . . . and [after menopause] . . . to aid offspring in their reproductive behavior. . . . [Lockard and Adams 1981:177–178].

The authors test their theory by examining the relative ages of partners in opposite-sex dyads in a Seattle shopping center. They find that younger males tend to be with females around their own age, while older males are frequently with younger females. However, older females are rarely observed with younger males. Examination of divorce and remarriage records in King County, Washington, also support their argument, with divorced males tending to remarry younger women. Finally, Lockard and Adams utilize birth records to demonstrate that dyads matching their ideal model have more births than other types of dyads.

One of the more controversial papers investigating reproductive strategies is Weinrich's (1977) discussion of the different sexual practices of the working and middle classes of industrialized nations. In this paper, he argues that class-related differences in sexual behavior illustrate variant reproductive strategies and result from the differences in resource predictability that are experienced by these two classes. He also notes that racial variation in sexual behavior in the United States can be explained from the same perspective. Although much of Weinrich's discussion centers on male reactions to income predictability, I examine his study in this section because female responses to the same factors are obviously implicated in his argument.

Weinrich relates predictability of resources over time to the willingness of males to invest in stable pair bonds. He argues that males encounter a cost in maintaining such bonds, but that the reproductive returns from them are low. Males facing unpredictable resource futures should not invest in developing and maintaining a pair bond which might produce future offspring who cannot be provided for and might not survive. When resources are unpredictable, males should adopt an opportunistic mating pattern, emphasizing rapid reproduction during the periods when resources are abundant. Under such conditions, a male might desire females who demand a minimum of investment before becoming pregnant. The life history strategies of males in unpredictable resource environments may take a number of shapes. Some males may mate with a large number of females and provide no paternal investment for the resultant offspring. Others may create bonds with single mates and provide paternal investment when resources are abundant, but leave once they become scarce. Either way, males should not invest too much in the maintenance of the pair bond itself. In contrast, males facing predictable resource futures should be willing to invest in order to maintain pair bonds. The reproductive strategy of such males foregoes the quantity of offspring produced by males facing unpredictable resource futures and, instead, concentrates on the higher quality of children that can be produced through the long-term cooperation of a male and female. Unfortunately, Weinrich does not answer the important question of whether or not the children of stable pair bonds exhibit higher survival or have greater chances of reproductive success than those produced outside of such bonds.

Data from various sources indicate that in the United States, working-class men face more unpredictability in resource futures than middle-class men. They are more likely to be injured or killed on the job and to experience more frequent and longer periods of unemployment. Further, the lower pay of most working-class jobs means that individuals holding them are less likely to be able to create a cushion against periods of economic misfortune.

Weinrich first tests his hypothesis by examining data on the "Conjugal Role Relationship" (or CRR—see Bott 1957; Rainwater 1960, 1965). A joint CRR exists when the spouses do not have a strict division of labor and often share tasks. In contrast, in segregated CRRs, each spouse performs gender-specific tasks and usually does not undertake a task in the domain of the other member. Weinrich relates CRR to reproductive strategies by arguing that a pair may select from several child-rearing strategies. He defines two opposite poles on a continuum of such strategies. In one case, the individual learns the tasks appropriate to his or her role and does them regardless of personal inclination or ability. He or she does not undertake tasks assigned to the other gender. Weinrich argues that an individual adopting this strategy is capable of frequent partner changes. The strategy at the opposite end of the continuum is one in which the individual performs the tasks he or she is most competent at, regardless of whether or not these tasks are gender appropriate. Such an individual seeks to find a spouse who complements his or her weaknesses. Weinrich argues that the latter strategy is very effective in raising offspring, since children are not harmed by the union of individuals who are not really good at performing their standard roles (as sometimes happens in the first strategy). However, reproductive speed is lost, because it takes time to find a mate with complementary skills. The first strategy leads to a segregated CRR, and Weinrich predicts that it will be associated with working-class families. In contrast, the second strategy leads to a joint CRR and is predicted to characterize families in the middle class. Rainwater's (1965) study of 168 American families supports Weinrich's assertion, 88 percent of the upper-middle-class families exhibit a joint CRR and the remainder an intermediate form; while seventy-two percent of lower-class families exhibit a segregated CRR. Only four percent of white families and no black families in the lower class are characterized by a joint CRR.

Weinrich also tests the influence of resource predictability on sexual activity by reviewing studies that compare the sexual behavior of different classes. He shows that higher resource predictability (measured by occupation, education, or income level) is associated with the following traits: (1) higher probability and greater frequency of engaging in sexual activity unlikely to result in conception; (2) less extramarital sex in the early years of marriage, but more in later years; (3) less extramarital sex over the course of a marriage; (4) later age of first coitus; (5) more petting prior to marriage; and (6) less use of prostitutes. Weinrich views each of these results as indicating that individuals with predictable resource futures tend to invest resources (including sexual activity) in creating and maintaining their pair bonds, rather than in achieving the maximum rate of reproduction.

A possible objection to Weinrich's argument is the hypothesis that it is the level of income, rather than its predictability, that is responsible for the observed class-related differences in sexual behavior. Weinrich attempts to eliminate this hypothesis by noting that members of the West German working class experience incomes as low as the American working class, but that their jobs are more stable, indicating higher resource predictability. A study by Sigusch and Schmidt (1971) finds that class-related differences in sexual behavior in Germany are not as great as in the United States. This finding indicates that income predictability is probably more important than level of income in producing reproductive strategies in industrial societies.

Weinrich devotes a major portion of his paper to an examination of nonsociobiological explanations of his results. His entire discussion will not be detailed here, but several points bear review. First, he notes that certain nonsociobiological ("environmentalistic") theories adequately explain some of the results he presents, but that no environmentalistic theory explains them all. For example, environmentalistic theories emphasizing socialization might explain why middle-class individuals achieve first coitus late in life, but they do not explain why, once these individuals are married, they are more likely to engage in sexual activity that is unlikely to result in conception. Weinrich suggests that his evolutionary explanation is superior to environmentalistic explanations, because it encompasses more of the data. Second, Weinrich notes that environmentalistic explanations based on early childhood socialization confront the problem that individuals who change classes frequently exhibit the pattern of sexual behavior that is characteristic of their acquired class, and not that of their class of origin. He argues that this indicates that an individual's current economic circumstances are probably more important than socialization in determining sexual behavior. Weinrich identifies an interesting phenomenon requiring further research when he notes that individuals who change classes frequently exhibit the sexual patterns of the acquired class long before they actually enter it. This might be explained from the sociobiological perspective by arguing that individuals anticipate their adult resource future and adjust their sexual behavior accordingly. On the other hand, an environmentalistic interpretation might suggest that it is the adoption of a class-specific sexual pattern that creates class mobility in the first place. Weinrich does not totally reject this alternative, but notes that it cannot explain all of his results.

Before leaving Weinrich's presentation, it bears emphasizing that he explicitly rejects the idea that there are genetic differences between classes relevant to sexual behavior or tendencies to invest resources in pair bonds. His argument is that differences in resource predictability have existed long enough for humans to have been selected to track fluctuations in such predictability with behavioral flexibility.

Weinrich's paper is one of the most interesting in human sociobiology, indicating as it does how the theory can be tested in industrial societies. What is more, the paper carries important social policy implications. For example, if reproductive strategies are generated in response to income predictability and not to early sexual socialization, then sex education aimed at lowering the number of "undesired" pregnancies in lower-income groups may not be successful without concomitant changes in the economic circumstances of these groups. Weinrich (1977:113) cites studies from Sweden and the United States indicating that this may be the case in these countries.

The major response to Weinrich's paper has been Lande's (1978) criticism that Weinrich has the theory wrong. Lande argues that three features are necessary to characterize the role of resource availability in the production of reproductive strategies: predictability, variability, and the average amount of resources. Lande argues that concentrating only on predictability leads to incorrect predictions, and that the average level of resources is more relevant in the determination of reproductive strategies:

> When resources are superabundant (a high average level) with a large minimum availability, and survivorship is high, the reproductive schedule which maximizes the number of future descendants is one of early reproductive and high fecundity, regardless of the predictability or variability of the resources. When resources are scarce (a low average level) limited reproduction often yields the best chance of producing progeny which will survive to reproductive age [Lande 1978:95].

Thus, consideration of the average level of resources leads to predictions precisely opposite to those made by Weinrich. The working class, with its lower average level of resources, should concentrate those resources on maintaining the pair bond, producing a few children, and making sure that those children survive to reproduce. In contrast, individuals in the middle class have higher resource averages and should take risks to produce a larger number of children. Lande concludes that since humans are not acting as predicted, many have adopted a "maladaptive strategy" of limiting reproduction in the midst of abundant resources and thus are not attempting to maximize their reproductive success.

In his response to Lande, Weinrich (1978) argues that his definition of predictability takes into account Lande's idea of average level of resources. However, he is not clear as to how it does so. He further notes that his article was not concerned with the level of fertility, but rather with the strength of the pair bond. Finally, he notes that Lande's argument that upper-class and middle-class individuals who limit family size are acting maladaptively confuses the number of children born with the number who are raised to age of reproduction. However, Weinrich does not show that upper-class or middle-class families are actually raising more children to puberty than working-class families. As noted earlier in this chapter, more research is needed to resolve this last point.

In a wide-ranging speculative paper, Draper and Harpending (1982; see also Harpending 1980) explore the possible effects of male reproductive strategies on children by examining the psychological and anthropological literature on the topic of father-absence. Father-absent households occur into two distinct environments. The first, also discussed by Weinrich, is the environment among the poor in stratified societies. In this case, father-present households are the ideal norm of the society, and the poor are stigmatized for failing to conform. The second environment occurs in many horticultural societies, where marriages are stable, but where all males reside away from wives and children, usually in men's houses (Whiting 1964; Whiting et al. 1958; Whiting and Whiting 1975).

Along with Weinrich, Draper and Harpending argue that human behavioral flexibility means that reproductive strategies are responses to the environmental conditions faced by individuals. However, they are more interested in how the family circumstances experienced by children might influence the reproductive strategies they adopt as adults and suggest that there may be a sensitive-period for learning reproductive strategies during childhood. I will first review their argument as it relates to father-absence in stratified societies and then turn to their discussion of horticultural societies.

The literature on boys raised in father-absent households in the United States reveals two facts that Draper and Harpending find interesting. First, compared to boys from father-present households, these boys exhibit increased verbal, but decreased spatial and quantitative scores on tests of cognitive performance. The high verbal and low spatial-quantitative abilities of these boys form a pattern that is usually characteristic of females, and some theorists have suggested that such boys have been "feminized" or have adopted a feminine identity. Second, studies frequently find that father-absent boys are likely to engage in various forms of "hypermasculine" behavior, which many theorists see as a form of "protest masculinity." Draper and Harpending reject both the feminization and the protest masculinity positions and argue that the data are better explained if we assume that boys in father-absent households learn that the best route to reproductive success is not through high paternal investment, but rather through an opportunistic mating strategy based on seduction, manipulation of others, and preventing other males from gaining access to females. Under this assumption, the development of verbal skills is a necessary component of seduction and manipulation, while hypermasculine behavior serves both to warn away other males and to impress females.

Draper and Harpending see the increased spatial and quantitative skills of boys raised in father-present households as preparing them to engage in a reproductive strategy focused on paternal investment. As they phrase it, these boys are more interested in "things" than in "people." Because females will be attracted to them by their occupational skills, they do not need to develop the verbal skills necessary for seduction and manipulation.

Female reproductive strategies are also shaped by the presence or absence of the father. The authors suggest that girls growing up in father-present households will perceive that male parental investment is important for reproductive success and therefore will attempt to form stable pair bonds upon reaching adulthood. This strategy requires the testing of males' willingness to invest in offspring, which results in these women exhibiting the pattern of sexual behavior that Weinrich identifies as middle class. In contrast, women raised in father-absent households perceive stable pair bonds as less important for reproductive success (or as less possible to achieve) and exhibit Weinrich's working-class pattern of sexual behavior. In support of this analysis, the authors cite a study showing that when interviewed by males, adolescent females from divorced households were judged as more flirtatious and more interested in the interviewer than girls from father-present or widowed households. The subjects did not differ in their responses to female interviewers. The difference between girls from divorced households, who were most flirtatious, and those from widowed households, who are least, indicates that the mothers' attitudes toward males may play a role in determining the reproductive strategies of daughters. Widows idealized their deceased spouses, while divorcees tended to denigrate their ex-husbands.

Draper and Harpending have fewer data to support the extension of their theory to entire societies. However, they do note a cluster of traits generally found in societies with the father-absent household complex:

> (1) segregation of adult males from women and children in many daily activities, such as eating, sleeping, working, and resting; (2) high levels of aggression and competitive display among males, usually including much bombast and rhetoric and occasionally outright physical violence; (3) sex-role asymmetry, in which male dominance and female subordination are pervasively established in secular and sacred spheres of social organization; and (4) sex-role antagonism, by which we mean that men and women hold sterotypically negative and hostile attitudes towards the opposite sex [Draper and Harpending 1982:262–263].

Another trait commonly found in this cluster is a male fear of female pollution. Draper and Harpending speculate that this belief might be a result of males attempting to keep more fearful males away from women. Berndt's (1962) description of the sexual behavior of Kamano males indicates that such speculation is plausible.

Draper and Harpending briefly discuss the environmental and sociological factors that might determine whether a society exhibits reproductive strategies based on paternal investment or on manipulation and seduction, but they note that the connections are not yet well understood. Whiting (1964) and Whiting and Whiting (1975) explore this problem in greater detail, noting that societies with the father-absent household complex tend to be small-scale, horticultural groups without standing armies which are located in the tropics. The division between adult males and women and children is explained as a necessary preliminary to the development of fierce male warriors.

The Draper and Harpending research is subject to a number of criticisms. It is obvious, for example, that numerous nonsociobiological hypotheses might account for their results. Furthermore, not all studies on the effects of father-absence arrive at the same results as those discussed in their paper. Finally, their picture of sex antagonism in societies with father-absence seems to be drawn from data on certain highland New Guinea societies and ignores variations in other culture areas. However, the work is exciting, especially when combined with Weinrich's analysis of reproductive strategies. Consideration of Weinrich's conclusions in light of Draper and Harpending's work suggests several questions for further research. For example, Draper and Harpending emphasize the role of early childhood experience in determining reproductive strategies, while Weinrich stresses the resource circumstances an adult experiences and expects to confront in the future. Is it possible that these two factors might produce conflicting tendencies with regard to reproductive strategies? Thus, might an individual raised in a father-present household be less than effective when forced to adopt the reproductive strategy of seduction required by an unpredictable resource environment? Or, could some individuals be incapable of taking advantage of predictable resources because, having been raised in father-absent households, they cannot maintain a pair bond?

A stress on human behavioral flexibility in reproductive strategies is also implicit in Hartung's (1982b) discussion of self-deception. The theoretical groundwork for this discussion is suggested by Trivers (1971) and Alexander (1975) (see also Lockard 1980). In his analysis of reciprocal altruism, Trivers notes that this behavioral system is likely to be characterized by frequent attempts at cheating. Cheating should lead to the evolution of mechanisms to detect the propensity to cheat in others. In turn, as detection mechanisms become more accurate, there is selection for even more sophisticated cheating. Both Trivers and Alexander argue that cheaters who deceive themselves into thinking that they are not cheating give fewer cues that permit others to detect their propensity to cheat. In other words, self-deception and a resultant unawareness of our true motives have been selected for during human evolution.

Hartung suggests that males and females in stratified societies have different experiences with self-deception. He notes that people often use self-deception to adjust their self-esteem when they find themselves in situations where their full talents cannot be utilized. An example would be a man who is more talented than his boss and knows it; if his attitude demonstrates such an evaluation to his boss, he might lose his job. On the other hand, if he can deceive himself into thinking that he is actually less talented than his boss, his position will not be threatened. A second type of self-deception occurs when a man is faced with a job for which he knows he is not qualified. Communication of an attitude of self-doubt could result in the loss of the position. If a man deceives himself into thinking he is qualified for the job, then others may accept his right to the position. Further, Malinowski's theory of magic predicts that such a deception might actually result in an objectively better job performance.

The core of Hartung's article is that males in industrial societies get frequent practice at both self-deceiving up and self-deceiving down. In contrast, he argues that, until recently, most females often self-deceived down within the context of marriage, but had few chances to self-deceive up. Hartung suggests that when self-deceptions get too far out of line with reality, mental illness results. He predicts that, due to their differential practice with self-deception, males and females will differ in the types of mental illness relevant to self-esteem that they exhibit. Females are expected to be more at risk from "straight depression," while males are expected to exhibit illnesses combining depression with euphoria. Clinical statistics support his position, with the diagnosis of major depression exhibiting a sex ratio strongly biased toward females, and that of bipolar depression awarded to equal numbers of males and females. Hartung notes that if females are more likely than males to be seen by mental health practitioners, even when their illnesses are equally severe, the latter finding probably underestimates the prevalence of bipolar depression in males.

Hartung's article is significant as another example of a sociobiological explanation which may have important social policy implications. For example, his argument implies that different social arrangements will provide different chances for self-deceiving up and down and that this might be responsible for varying patterns of depressive illnesses. Thus, Egeland and Hostetter (1983) report that in an Amish sample there is no sex difference in unipolar major depression. Might this result from different opportunities for self-deception in the Amish community? An interesting prediction suggested by Hartung's work is that as women continue to enter the labor market and undertake positions requiring both self-deception up and self-deception down, the sex ratio of bipolar depression will change.

2. *Strategies of males.* Several studies have explored the reproductive strategies of males and have concluded that these are congruent with the predictions of sociobiological theory. For example, Mackey (1980) uses census data to examine the marital histories of American males and concludes that they "... are following an adequate, if complex, strategy more consonant than dissonant with sociobiological theory" (1980:419). By this he means that the majority of males marry once and remain with their wives and children throughout their lifetimes. Of the males who do divorce, most do not have offspring who would be raised without their influence. When they do remarry, it is usually with younger women who then produce children. Finally, men who divorce a second time usually divorce older women, who are unlikely to have any more children.

Mackey's study shows that the marital history of American males is not inconsistent with sociobiological theory, but his research cannot be said to support any particular aspect of the theory. He does not, for example, demonstrate that men who divorce their wives achieve reproductive success or inclusive fitness equal to, or greater than, males who remain married throughout life. As noted several times previously, population statistics cannot be used to demonstrate this point. Until the reproductive rates of different marital histories can be calculated and compared to the options open to males in different circumstances, it is difficult to determine what Mackey's results really mean.

A paper by Hawkes et al. (1981) on hunting practices among the Ache Indians of Paraguay attempts to compare predictions from an individual selection perspective with those derived from a limited needs model of labor. The authors argue that hunting to obtain game beyond the basic subsistence needs of a household may be a means by which males increase their inclusive fitness. The extra food may be given to less fortunate relatives or may be traded to women for sex. This view argues that individuals will hunt long after the amount of food required by their households is obtained. In contrast, the limited needs perspective suggests that males will obtain the amount of food necessary for the survival of their households and then stop work. Hawkes et al. use data on Ache hunting productivity to test three contrasting predictions derived from these perspectives.

The limited needs model suggests that on days when hunting is productive, males should stop hunting earlier than on days when it is unproductive. In contrast, the fitness maximization model suggests that males would hunt longer on these days. The data reveal no correlation between the quality of the hunting day and the time spent hunting, supporting neither prediction.

Hawkes et al. argue that the fitness maximization model predicts that better hunters will spend more time hunting than poorer hunters, while the limited needs model predicts the opposite. The data from the Ache support the former model. The authors review data on Dobe Bushman and Bisa hunters that are congruent with the Ache data. However, they note data on the Yanomamo that indicate that better hunters spend less time hunting than poorer hunters, a result congruent with the limited needs model. Hawkes et al. suggest that the Yanomamo may be a special case, because a male's absence while hunting may increase the chances that he will be cuckolded. They predict that Yanomamo males without wives and children would hunt more than males with families. Perhaps within the unmarried group, poorer hunters would hunt less than better hunters, as predicted by the fitness maximization model. So far these predictions have not been tested.

Finally, Hawkes et al. argue that the fitness maximization model predicts that hunters will spend more time hunting with the most efficient technology, while the limited needs model predicts the reverse. For the Ache, the shotgun is more efficient than the bow and arrow, but there is no differential use of these technologies, a situation supporting neither perspective. The authors do suggest that married Yanomamo males with guns will spend less time hunting than either unmarried or married males without guns. Again, these predictions have not been tested.

The results obtained by Hawkes et al. do not strongly support either of the models they attempt to test. The limited needs model receives no support and probably does not apply to the Ache. However, the fitness maximization model also receives little support. There are probably many different reasons individuals hunt, and to make a convincing case for the fitness maximization model, Hawkes et al. must demonstrate that better hunters achieve greater inclusive fitness due to their hunting skills. Up to the present time, they have not been able to do this.

Daly et al. (1982) review the literature on male sexual jealousy to defend the following thesis:

> ... there have evolved in *Homo sapiens* certain psychological propensities that function to defend paternity confidence. Manifestations include the emotion of sexual jealousy, the dogged inclination of men to possess and control women, and the use or threat of violence to achieve sexual exclusivity and control [Daly and Wilson 1982:11].

The bulk of the article consists of an examination of the ethnographies of several societies for which it has been claimed that women have great sexual freedom and males exhibit no signs of jealousy. Close reading of the ethnographies reveals numerous indications that at least some males do behave in manners indicative of jealousy. Daly et al.'s article is certain to be controversial, because it rejects anthropology's usual insistence on the extreme malleability of sexual drives (see also Hrdy 1981a; Symons 1979). Also, it denies the validity of various theories asserting that male sexual jealousy is the outcome of socialization within specific social and/or economic arrangements and that it will disappear if those arrangements are altered. It should be noted that Daly et al.'s position does not deny the possibility that societies may differ with regard to the display rules concerning jealousy, for this is well documented in the ethnographic record. However, the existence in a society of display rules limiting the overt expression of jealousy cannot be taken as evidence that males in that society do not experience this emotion. Unfortunately, testing such an argument is impossible if we are limited to the ethnographic record.

Daly et al. also briefly discuss the difference between male and female jealousy. Because of paternal uncertainty, male jealousy is expected to center upon the sexual act. In contrast, females are assumed to be more worried about potential loss of paternal investment and, whereas female jealousy is also universal, it is expected not to focus on the sexual act. This analysis suggests a biological basis for the double standard, with females more willing to accept the extramarital sexual activity of males so long as such behavior does not threaten the continued existence of the household. Unfortunately, the ethnographic record contains very few data on female jealousy, and it is currently impossible to test this argument.

Sure to produce even more controversy than Daly et al.'s argument on the biological origins of jealousy and other male reproductive strategies are the attempts to provide a sociobiological explanation of rape made by Shields and Shields (1983) and by Thornhill and Thornhill (1983). These articles make different assumptions concerning the genetic components of rape behavior, but both oppose environmentalistic theories, which suggest that rape is an act of male hostility toward females and has nothing to do with reproductive strategies.

The core of Shields and Shields' position is contained in the following passage:

> We suspect that during human evolutionary history, males that possessed a mating strategy that included rape as a facultative response were favored by natural selection over those that did not. Owing to rape's potential costs, men are not expected to rape indiscriminately. Rather, selection would be expected to favor a proximate control mechanism, that (1) maximized the probability that in any instance the benefits would, on average, exceed the costs, and (2) did not interfere unduly with alternative mating tactics with potentially higher payoffs (e.g., honest courtship). The probability of rape generated by such a program is expected to vary among individuals given identical proximate conditions (motivation and stimulus strength) owing to individual differences in rape thresholds, and to vary temporally and spatially for each male as a function of variation in the immediate proximate conditions [Shields and Shields 1983:123].

Shields and Shields argue that there are two polygenic substrates relevant to rape. The first is universal in males and consists of a "closed" behavioral program, with hostility to women and perception of female vulnerability linked to a tendency to engage in forced copulation. The second is an "open" program, which varies among individuals and consists of conscious and/or unconscious routines for evaluating the potential benefits and risks of rape. The authors suggest that the joint operation of these two programs means that all males have the potential to rape, but that variation in the level of female vulnerability and hostility toward females will determine how frequently rape occurs.

A crucial assumption of Shields and Shields' theory is that rape has some potential for increasing the number of offspring a man produces in his lifetime (or did so in the species' evolutionary past). Data to test this assumption and to demonstrate that males adopting a strategy of rape could not have achieved greater reproductive success by using other strategies are not available. However, the authors argue that their position predicts that the women most likely to be raped are those with the greatest reproductive value (i.e., where copulation is most likely to result in conception). A review of four studies of rape in the United States supports the prediction that the highest risk of rape is for teenagers and women in their early twenties. Shields and Shields point out that hypotheses arguing that rape is a behavior designed to subjugate women, one having nothing to do with sex, do not predict this age distribution, but rather would predict that rape will be randomly distributed or directed toward older, or more powerful, women.

As further support for their argument, Shields and Shields review the relevance of different combinations of hostility and female vulnerability to the frequency of rape. They note, for example, that in warfare, hostility toward females and female vulnerability are both high and that rape is common. The conditions least likely to promote rape are low hostility toward females and low female vulnerability. Shields and Shields argue that this last fact has social policy implications. They suggest that the most effective way of lowering the level of rape is to minimize the benefits and maximize the costs of engaging in such behavior. In other words, the frequency of rape will decline when potential rapists realize that there is a high probability that they will be apprehended and subjected to severe punishment. This does not mean that rape will disappear, for the potential benefits can never be reduced to zero, and males with no alternative mating options might be willing to risk severe punishment to pursue this strategy.

Thornhill and Thornhill's (1983) argument differs slightly from that of Shields and Shields by concentrating on the idea of conditional reproductive strategies. They suggest that all humans carry genes permitting the adoption of various reproductive strategies and that the strategies selected by individuals depend upon the conditions they encounter at a given time. Thornhill and Thornhill see the potential to engage in forced copulation as a human universal, but argue that once a male adopts a particular reproductive strategy, the alternatives may be rendered unsuitable. They suggest that socially-successful males will very rarely experience conditions where the benefits of rape outweigh the potential costs. This leads them to predict that rape is a strategy adopted by socially-unsuccessful males.

Thornhill and Thornhill derive eighteen predictions concerning rape from their argument and test some of these with data from the United States. They replicate Shields and Shields' finding that females near peak fertility are most likely to be victims of rape. They also show that men who rape are most likely to be around the age when competition for females is most intense, just prior to the usual age of first marriage. Using measures of social success, such as socioeconomic class, education, ethnicity, and occupation, they demonstrate that in the United States, less socially-successful males are most likely to rape. Finally, in a sample of twenty-nine preindustrial societies, they show that as the degree of polygyny increases, the punishment for rape also increases, perhaps because the more intense competition for females results in more males who are willing to attempt rape.

Some of the predictions discussed by Thornhill and Thornhill involve the reactions of victims and their spouses or relatives to rape. They argue that prereproductive and postreproductive females will have less trouble than fertile women in adjusting after being raped. They also suggest that females with husbands are less likely than unmarried females to report being raped, because the rape might result in the loss of economic support or paternal investment due to male paternal uncertainty. Unfortunately, the data necessary to test these predictions are not available.

As noted earlier, the papers on rape as a male reproductive strategy are destined to generate a great deal of debate. Dusek (1984) reviews sociobiological literature describing "rape" among nonhuman animals (Abele and Gilchrist 1977; Barash 1977; Lloyd 1980; Thornhill 1980) and concludes that the use of this term is inappropriate in these situations. The Shields and Shields and Thornhill and Thornhill papers are likely to be attacked on the grounds that they provide a biological rationale for male rape, and because they suggest that rape is not only an act of aggression against females. On the other hand, both papers argue that rape is best controlled by manipulating the costs and benefits of the behavior and by altering the social arrangements that serve to create high hostility toward females or high female vulnerability. Neither paper asserts that society is defenseless against rape, nor do they deny that male hostility toward females may be part of the proximate mechanism of rape. It is unlikely that this debate will be settled by empirical evidence, but it should be noted that the sociobiological perspective does offer a number of testable predictions and that the few that have been tested so far have been supported by the data.

3. *Strategies of females.* One of the weakest areas of research in human sociobiology is the investigation of female reproductive strategies. Of course, the strategies of both sexes are shaped in part by the tactics of the opposite sex, and several of the studies reviewed above consider female strategies as responses to male behaviors. However, the fact that females are the limited resource in the production of reproductive success suggests the necessity of reversing this emphasis. We need much more theoretical and empirical work on the causes and consequences of female strategies and on how female strategies shape male behaviors. Although some theorists have made significant contributions to this work (Daly and Wilson 1978; Hrdy 1981a; Irons 1983) many of the ideas on female strategies remain implicit, and there is little empirical work as of yet.

Irons' (1983) theoretical review of human female reproductive strategies, with an examination of three cases from the ethnographic record (Palteau Tonga, Tiwi, and Yomut), is the most sophisticated paper on this topic. He points out that females may use a number of strategies to achieve reproductive success, and identifies four: use of reciprocity to obtain parental care; family planning; the selection of high-quality mates; and the countering of male coercion. The ability of a female to employ these strategies depends upon a number of factors. Those discussed by Irons include her ability to obtain subsistence and/or to control resources independently of nonrelated males (especially mates) and the probability that she can rely on kin for access to resources necessary for her children. This last set of factors is, in turn, determined to a large extent by the economic and social systems of different societies. Thus, the ability of males to control female behavior may differ in hunting-gathering societies, as compared with horticultural or industrial societies. Irons' paper contains many suggestions on possible relationships between female strategies and the distribution of kin and resources, and these indicate several lines of empirical research which will no doubt be developed in the near future.

Symons (1979) argues that the responses of the sexes to erotic stimuli differ because they have different reproductive strategies. He reviews literature suggesting that males respond to a wider range of stimuli than females. This is predictable from the fact that females are the sex competed for and therefore may choose among numerous suitors. Further, matings that are "mistakes" (e.g., those with low-quality mates, or with mates refusing to provide parental investment) have a greater negative impact on the lifetime reproductive success of females than on that of males. Presumably, females can better avoid such mistakes if they are not easily aroused by erotic stimuli. Bixler (1983) makes a similar argument, suggesting that it is supported by the fact that males are more likely than females to exhibit various paraphilias. Bixler also reviews work by Kinsey et al. (1953), who found that females were three-to-five times more likely than males to be placed in the "X" category of individuals who did not respond erotically to either heterosexual or homosexual stimuli. Bixler's argument needs to be tested in a more recent sample, utilizing instruments that measure physiological indicators of arousal. A replication in a society with attitudes more accepting of female sexual behavior would also be of great interest.

An article on female mate selection by Mazur (1983) is a fitting end to this subsection. In a passage which is relevant to almost every study reviewed in this chapter, and to many in the rest of this volume, he reveals a frustration that many are likely to experience after examining the literature in human sociobiology:

> When observations are consistent with a straightforward interpretation of the theory, the theory is counted a success, though the hypothesis being tested is as obvious as that we are more likely to help kin than nonkin. When observations are inconsistent, the observations are discounted or the theory is reinterpreted until it is brought into line. Even behaviors so ostensibly inimical to fitness as homosexuality and suicide have been shown consistent with fitness enhancement, if one accepts certain felicitous subsidiary assumptions. To some extent these strategies are followed in all areas of science, but they appear to have reached, in sociobiology, the extremes that we have come to recognize in psychoanalysis [Mazur 1983:226, references omitted].

Perhaps in desperation, Mazur attempts to test what he considers to be a fairly straightforward prediction derived from sociobiological theory. He starts with the simple statement that nepotism theory predicts that individuals will frequently aid close relatives. He then notes that a female faced with a choice between two potential spouses of equal quality, one having siblings, and the other not, should prefer to marry the male with no siblings:

> Her reasoning is this: If my husband had a sib, they would share half their genes, the same protion [sic] that my husband shares with our child. Thus

my husband's inclusive fitness would be equally served if he took a risk for, or shared nonrenewable resources with, his sibling as our child. The sib would reciprocally aid my husband but be less likely to aid my child since they share only one-quarter of their genes. Thus my child loses more to the sib than he gains, and so my fitness will be maximized by choosing the sibless mate [Mazur 1983:226].

From this logic Mazur derives the prediction that in the United States there will be an inverse correlation between number of sibs and the probability of being married. He notes that this may not apply to females, since they are a limited resource. Using a survey sample of over 12,000 Americans, Mazur shows that there is no correlation between number of sibs and probability of never being married for either sex. When race, income, and education are controlled, the results do not change. In other words, the data indicate that females are not selecting mates in a manner maximizing their inclusive fitness or reproductive success.

Mazur notes that several reviewers of his paper did manage to make his results consistent with sociobiological theory. One suggested that the number of children a male's parents had might be a good indicator of his ability to produce and provide for offspring, making males from large families more attractive mates. However, this advantage is offset by the resource drain of a man's siblings, creating the zero correlation between marriage and number of sibs observed by Mazur. Another suggested that children of males with siblings may be protected from bad economic times, making such males attractive mates. Finally, Mazur suggests that sociobiologists can always argue that the observed pattern is the result of behaviors which were adaptive in the past but which are maladaptive in the current environment. Mazur does not resort to these alternatives and appears to accept his negative result at face value. However, he does not indicate whether he believes his result should be interpreted to mean that inclusive fitness theory does not apply to human behavior.

Before leaving Mazur's paper, it is perhaps worthwhile to recall the importance of the search for proximate mechanisms in human sociobiology. Mazur is correct that, given enough ingenuity, a theorist can probably fit any behavior into a sociobiological explanation. Since we do not have long-term records on human reproductive success, these explanations can probably never be falsified. However, the proximate mechanisms hypothesized by such explanations are probably more amenable to testing and falsification. For example, one of the alternative explanations for Mazur's results suggests that males from large families are attractive mates, but that there is no correlation between number of sibs and probability of being married, because this attractiveness is balanced by the demands of sibs for resources. We can postulate a number of proximate mechanisms which might be involved in such a system. Do females exhibit different genetically-based reproductive strategies, such that some are attracted to signals of high potential fertility while others find a lack of alternative investment possibilities more attractive? Or do these two factors never enter into genetically-based reproductive strategies? Either way, a search for proximate mechanisms of attraction might be a way to falsify this explanation.

REPRODUCTIVE STRATEGIES, LONGEVITY, AND MENOPAUSE

Mayer's (1980a,b; 1982) research on longevity and inclusive fitness is especially interesting because of his innovative use of the genealogies of four New England families to measure inclusive fitness. His results suggest that longevity is positively related to both reproductive success and inclusive fitness. One problem with his analysis of inclusive fitness is that he utilizes the "simple weighted sum" measure discredited by Grafen (1982; see also Hames 1984). However, since he demonstrates that longevity is related to number of offspring produced, his overall conclusions are probably not affected by this problem.

Mayer argues that longevity and care of the old may have been selected for among humans because of the increasing importance of accumulated experience in society. Further, their knowledge of rare events might have made older people valuable to their offspring. In his paper on the evolution of menopause (1982; see also 1984), Mayer suggests that the association between fertility and longevity might be related to an underlying heritable factor, which theorists have labeled "constitutional fitness" or "vigor." He speculates further that this factor may be related somehow to DNA repair.

Mayer (1982) tests the proposition that women who experience menopause achieve higher reproductive success and inclusive fitness than those who die before menopause. He speculates that menopause may have evolved in conditions where females might have achieved greater inclusive fitness by caring for relatives (especially grandchildren) than by reproducing too close to the age of death (see also Gaulin 1980). In a critique of this paper, Hames (1984) points to methodological problems with Mayer's test, suggesting that what was actually tested is the common sense prediction that the longer you live, the more kin will be born while you are alive. He suggests that Mayer should compare the reproductive success of women who died at the same age, but experienced menopause at different ages. Mayer's (1984) response to Hames clarifies some points in this debate, but leaves a number of problems unresolved. At present, Mayer's results are in need of further analysis and replication in another sample.

CONCLUSIONS

Perhaps the conflicting attitudes exhibited in Mazur's (1983) discussion of the difficulties encountered in testing sociobiological theory is the most accurate summary of this chapter on human reproductive strategies. Most of the studies reviewed make plausible cases that human reproductive behavior can be interpreted from a sociobiological perspective. However, most of the results can be interpreted from other theoretical perspectives, which often makes the sociobiological explanation redundant. With the exception of Irons' work, there are far too few attempts to falsify sociobiological predictions and to seriously test alternative explanations. On the other hand, we should recall the frequently stated argument that sociobiological theory provides an explanation for a greater range of phenomenon than any alternative perspective. Although it is too early to rule on the validity of this claim in the case of human reproductive strategies, the number of topics investigated in this chapter does lend surface support to this position.

APPENDIX

Some Recent Studies in Sociobiology

In this appendix, I briefly mention several important empirical studies in primate sociobiology that were published after the previous chapters were completed. The citations for these studies have been incorporated in the bibliography.

General

Lewontin et al.'s (1984) volume, *Not in Our Genes*, is an excellent critique of biological determinism and reductionism. The authors examine topics such as IQ, reductionist models of mental illness, and research on the biological basis of gender differences, as well as sociobiology. Although the arguments in the chapter on sociobiology repeat the common criticisms of the discipline, their location within the context of a wider discussion of biological determinism gives them added force. The authors devote a chapter to an interesting discussion of a "new biology," which will escape from the traps of determinism and reductionism, but it is not clear that such an approach totally rules out a sociobiology based on learning rules and conditional strategies.

Ecological Sociobiology

Silverberg (1984) notes a tendency of some sociobiologists to assume that the social system exhibited by one population is a species-specific trait. One cure for this is of course to conduct research on groups in various ecological settings. Another approach, illustrated in Lott's (1984) major review of intraspecific variation in the social systems of vertebrates, seeks to demonstrate how such variation may be the result of the interactions among conditional strategies, demographic factors, and ecological circumstances.

Nepotism Theory

A major study reviewed in Chapter Three was Wu et al.'s (1980) research indicating that young pigtail macaques can recognize half-siblings with whom they had not previously interacted. An attempt to replicate this result with a larger sample of pigtails fails to demonstrate this kin recognition effect (Fredrickson and Sackett 1984). Fredrickson and Sackett suggest that given their results, and the fact that the sample size of the original study was so small, there is no good evidence that alloprimates recognize kin through a mechanism of phenotype matching. The monkeys in the larger sample do demonstrate a social preference based on familiarity, which indicates that Bateson's (1983) interpretation of Wu et al.'s results from a framework of optimal outbreeding theory may not be correct or, at least, that it may not be relevant to the animals in Fredrickson and Sackett's sample.

Silk (1984b) uses genealogical data on a number of macaque populations to measure the average intensity of selection within families and between families. She notes that selection intensity within families estimates the strength of individual selection, while that between families estimates the strength of kin selection. Silk suggests that the relative strengths of selection intensities within and between families provides a means of examining the ongoing interaction between individual and kin selection in particular populations.

Finally, Dow (1984) re-examines Hawkes' (1983) analysis of kinship categories, genetic relatedness, and garden aid among the Binumarien. He introduces the concept of coancestral cooperation and suggests that unrelated individuals may often cooperate because they share a descendant in common. Hawkes' failure to take coancestral cooperation into account is one reason why garden aid and genetic kinship were not highly correlated in her sample. When Dow calculates the index of coancestry for Hawkes' sample, he finds that this statistic is superior to the coefficient of relatedness in predicting both gardening aid and social kinship distance.

Parental Investment Theory

Hinde (1983) has edited a volume on primate social behavior which contains a number of articles concerning alloprimate parental behavior. Although the papers rarely invoke ultimate causation, many of them contain research that is relevant to the proximate mechanisms hypothesized by sociobiologists.

Alloprimate paternal investment is examined in papers contained in a volume edited by Taub (1984). Dunbar (1984) investigates infant handling during agonistic encounters by male gelada baboons and shows that both the agonistic buffering and the progeny protection hypothesis appear to be valid for males in different circumstances. He also advances and provides support for a third hypothesis, that gelada males handle infants as a means of soliciting the social support of the infants' mothers.

Papers on the evolution of infanticide are found in a new volume edited by Hausfater and Hrdy (1984). Busse (1984) shows that chacma baboon females with infants behave differently than females without infants toward males who have recently entered the troop. Further, females with infants exhibit differential responses toward males who have been in the troop long enough to have sired their infants and those who entered too recently to be potential sires. Busse suggests that these behavioral differences are strategies against the males' potential for infanticide.

An interesting development of the Lumsden and Wilson (1981) model of gene-culture coevolution involves parent-offspring conflict theory. After suggesting that Trivers' (1974) model implies that children may demand more enculturation than is optimal for their parents' inclusive fitness, Lumsden (1984) argues that epigenetic rules probably reduce the potential for parent-offspring conflict over the transmission of culture. Unfortunately, his review of the anthropological literature on culture transmission does not really provide support for his argument.

Van Schaik and van Noordwijk (1983) examine data on neonate and infant sex ratios in a number of alloprimate groups and argue that social stresses involved with food availability and crowding explain most of the variability in these ratios. They find sex ratios biased toward males in captive groups that are assumed to be under high stress due to crowding and also in wild groups assumed to suffer from limited food resources. In contrast, female-biased ratios are observed in provisioned natural groups. The authors suggest a hypothesis of "density-dependent enforced sex ratio change" to explain their results. They argue that as stress increases, adult females direct aggression toward young animals, especially females. Low-ranking females, who are unable to protect their daughters against the attacks of superordinate females, are assumed to be especially sensitive to increased levels of social stress and are quick to terminate investment in daughters when stress becomes too great. The rapid elimination of the daughters of low-ranking females results in infant and juvenile sex ratio biased toward males. Van Schaik and van Noordwijk argue that mortality patterns in alloprimate groups indicate that, contrary to some theorists, females do not have the ability to manipulate the sex ratio of their offspring, and that only external factors are responsible for biased sex ratios. However, they noted that the only way to test these alternative hypotheses is to examine the sex ratio at conception.

Silk (1984a) provides an intrademic group selection model, which demonstrates that male-biased sex ratios can evolve in a manner suggested by Clark (1978), even when local group sizes are large.

Voland (1984) examines the relationship between economic resources and sex ratio manipulation in a German parish between 1720 and 1869. He finds that the first-born daughters of landholding families had lower rates of survival than their later-born siblings or the first-born daughters of farm laborers or tradesmen. This results, he suggests, from the fact that these families favored males in inheritance and that the marriage prospects for the daughters of such families were poor, compared to those of sons. Since families of smallholders, farmer laborers, or tradesmen had little to be inherited, and because their daughters frequently married hypergamously, the sex ratio of these families often exhibited a female bias. Voland finds no evidence that there were class-related differences in the primary or secondary sex ratio and argues that the patterns he observes are the result of different strategies of parental investment, which produce varying rates of infant survival. His results are congruent with Dickemann's (1979a) review of the literature on infanticide in state societies.

Human Reproductive Strategies

The question of cultural and biological success is examined in a literature review by Hill (1984). His original hypothesis is that the attainment of prestige is related to increased reproductive success in all human societies. However, a review of the literature on Tlingit potlatching and an analysis of the trends in British family size lead him to reject this hypothesis. For example, his earliest data (the cohort of parents born between 1800 and 1824) indicate that the British peerage has produced smaller families than the general population, a practice which continues to the present. Hill suggests that the correlation between prestige and reproductive success will be high in societies at or near the subsistence level of existence, but that when societies exceed this level the correlation will disappear. The destruction of a link between prestige and reproductive success comes about, Hill argues, because in societies with surplus income, individuals find themselves facing the law of diminishing returns as regards parental investment. The point is reached where extra investment in existing children will result in no additional increase in the reproductive success of the parents. When this occurs, individuals invest resources in gaining and maintaining prestige (potlatching, conspicuous consumption, etc.), even though increased prestige brings no additional reproductive success. Hill suggests that a striving for prestige is an outcome of our primate heritage of rank and attention structures. In any event, his main argument is that the lack of a relationship between prestige and reproductive success in societies with surplus income is an example of cultural goals becoming uncoupled from biological success.

Richardson and Boyd's (1984) explication of their dual inheritance model of genes and culture also addresses the problem of limitation of family size in societies achieving the demographic transition. They conclude that selection on nonparentally transmitted cultural variations can sometimes result in the spread of behaviors reducing genetic fitness, and argue that norms for smaller families may be an illustration of this situation. In other words, they agree with Barkow and Burley (1980) that limitation of family size is a maladaptive behavior, spreading only because among humans, cultural evolution is a stronger force than genetic evolution.

References

Abele, H., and S. Gilchrist
  1977   Homosexual Rape and Sexual Selection in Acanthocephalan Worms. Science 197:81–83.

Adams, M. S., and J. V. Neel
  1967   Children of Incest. Pediatrics 40:55–62.

Alcorta, Candace S.
  1982   Paternal Behavior and Group Competition. Behavior Science Research 17:3–23.

Alexander, Richard D.
  1971   The Search for an Evolutionary Philosophy of Man. Proceedings of the Royal Society of Victoria, Melbourne 84:99–120.

  1974   The Evolution of Social Behavior. Annual Review of Ecology and Systematics 5:325–383.

  1975   The Search for a General Theory of Behavior. Behavioral Science 20:77–100.

  1977   Review of Sahlins' The Use and Abuse of Biology. American Anthropologist 79:917–920.

  1979   Darwinism and Human Affairs. Seattle: University of Washington Press.

  1981a   Evolution, Culture, and Human Behavior: Some General Considerations. *In* Natural Selection and Social Behavior: Recent Research and New Theory. R. Alexander and D. Tinkle, eds. pp. 509–520. New York: Chiron Press.

1981b   Evolution, Social Behavior, and Ethics. *In* The Roots of Ethics. D. Callahan and H. Tristam, eds. pp. 307–338. New York: Plenum Press.

1981c   Natural Selection and Societal Laws. *In* The Roots of Ethics. D. Callahan and H. Tristam, eds. pp. 265–306. New York: Plenum Press.

Alexander, Richard D., John L. Hoogland, Richard D. Howard, Katharine M. Noonan, and Paul W. Sherman
1979   Sexual Dimorphisms and Breeding Systems in Pinnipeds, Ungulates, Primates, and Humans. *In* Evolutionary Biology and Human Social Behavior: An Anthropological Perspective. N. Chagnon and W. Irons, eds. pp. 402–435. North Scituate, Mass.: Duxbury Press.

Allen, L. L., P. S. Bridges, D. L. Evon, K. R. Rosenberg, M. D. Russell, L. A. Schepartz, V. J. Vitzthum, and M. H. Wolpoff
1982   Demography and Human Origins. American Anthropologist 84:888–896.

Altmann, Jeanne
1974   Observational Study of Behavior: Sampling Methods. Behaviour 48:1–41.

1978   Infant Independence in Yellow Baboons. *In* The Development of Behaviour: Comparative and Evolutionary Aspects. G. Burghardt and M. Bekoff, eds. pp. 253–277. New York: Garland.

1979   Age Cohorts as Paternal Sibships. Behavioral Ecology and Sociobiology 6:161–164.

1980   Baboon Mothers and Infants. Cambridge, Mass.: Harvard University Press.

Altmann, Jeanne, Stuart A. Altmann, and Glenn Hausfater
1978   Primate Infant's Effects on Mother's Future Reproduction. Science 201: 1028–1030.

Altmann, Stuart A.
1962a   A Field Study of the Sociobiology of the Rhesus Monkey, *Macaca mulatta*. Annuals of the New York Academy of Sciences 102:338–435.

1962b   Social Behavior of Anthropoid Primates: Analysis of Recent Concepts. *In* Roots of Behavior. E. Bliss, ed. pp. 277–294. New York: Harper.

1979   Altruistic Behavior: The Fallacy of Kin Deployment. Animal Behaviour 27:958–959.

Altmann, Stuart A., Stephen S. Wagner, and Sarah Lenington
1977   Two Models for the Evolution of Pologyny. Behavioral Ecology and Sociobiology 2:397–410.

Altmann, Stuart A., and Jeffrey Walters
1978   Review of Kurland's Kin Selection in the Japanese Monkey. Man 13:324–325.

n.d.   Critique of Kurland's "Kin Selection in the Japanese Monkey." Unpublished manuscript.

Alverez, F.
    1973 Periodic Changes in the Bare Skin of *Theropithecus gelada*. Primates 14:195–199.

Anderson, Donna M., and M. J. A. Simpson
    1979 Breeding Performance of a Captive Colony of Rhesus Macaques (*Macaca mulatta*). Laboratory Animals 13:275–281.

Andersson, Malte
    1982a Female Choice Selects for Extreme Tail Length in a Widowbird. Nature 299:818–820.

    1982b Sexual Selection, Natural Selection and Quality Advertisement, Biological Journal of the Linnean Society 17:375–393.

Angst, W.
    1975 Basic Data and Concepts on the Social Organization of *Macaca fascicularis*. *In* Primate Behavior: Developments in Field and Laboratory Research, vol. 4. L. Rosenblum, ed. pp. 325–388. New York: Academic Press.

Angst, W., and D. Thommen
    1977 New Data and A Discussion of Infant Killing in Old World Monkeys and Apes. Folia Primatologica 27:198–229.

Arnold, Stevan J.
    1983 Sexual Selection: The Interface of Theory and Empiricism. *In* Mate Selection. P. Bateson, ed. pp. 67–107. Cambridge: Cambridge University Press.

Axelrod, R., and W. D. Hamilton
    1981 The Evolution of Cooperation. Science 211:1390–1396.

Bachmann, C., and H. Kummer
    1980 Male Assessment of Female Choice in Hamadryas Baboons. Behavioral Ecology and Sociobiology 6:315–321.

Baer, Darius, and Donald L. McEachron
    1982 A Review of Selected Sociobiological Principles: Applications to Hominid Evolution. I. The Development of Group Social Structure. Journal of Social and Biological Structures 5:69–90.

Bailey, F. G.
    1969 Stratagems and Spoils. New York: Schocken.

Bales, Kelvin
    1980 Cumulative Scaling of Paternalistic Behavior in Primates. American Naturalist 116:454–461.

Barash, David P.
    1977 Sociobiology of Rape in Mallards (*Anas platyrhynchos*): Responses of the Mated Male. Science 197:788–789.

1982   Sociobiology and Behavior. 2d ed. New York: Elsevier.

Barash, David P., W. Holmes, and Penelope Greene
1978   Exact versus Probabilistic Coefficients of Relationship: Some Implications for Sociobiology. American Naturalist 112:355–363.

Barkow, Jerome H.
1977   Conformity to Ethos and Reproductive Success in Two Hausa Communities: An Empirical Evaluation. Ethos 5:409–425.

1982   Return to Nepotism: The Collapse of a Nigerian Gerontocracy. International Political Science Review 3:33–49.

Barkow, Jerome H., and Nancy Burley
1980   Human Fertility, Evolutionary Biology, and the Demographic Transition. Ethology and Sociobiology 1:163–180.

Barlow, George W.
1980   The Development of Sociobiology: A Biologist's Perspective. In Sociobiology: Beyond Nature/Nurture? G. Barlow and J. Silverberg, eds. pp. 3–24. Boulder: Westview Press.

Barnes, J. A.
1962   African Models in the New Guinea Highlands. Man 62:5–9.

Barry, Herbert, III, and Leonora M. Paxson
1971   Infancy and Early Childhood: Cross-Cultural Codes 2. Ethnology 10:461–508.

Barth, Fredrik
1966   Models of Social Organization. Royal Anthropological Institute Occasional Paper No. 23.

1967   On the Study of Social Change. American Anthropologist 69:661–669.

Bateson, Patrick P. G.
1978   Sexual Imprinting and Optimal Outbreeding. Nature 273:659–660.

1980   Optimal Outbreeding and the Development of Sexual Preferences in Japanese Quail. Zeitschrift für Tierpsychologie 53:231–244.

1982   Preferences for Cousins in Japanese Quail. Nature 295:236–237.

1983   Optimal Outbreeding. In Mate Choice. P. Bateson, ed. pp. 257–277. Cambridge: Cambridge University Press.

Beall, Cynthia M., and Melvyn C. Goldstein
1981   Tibetan Fraternal Polyandry: A Test of Sociobiological Theory. American Anthropologist 83:5–12.

Bekoff, M.
1983   The Development of Behavior from Evolutionary and Ecological Perspectives: Towards a Generic Sociobiology. In, The Evolution of Adaptive Skills:

Comparative and Ontogenetic Approaches. E. S. Gollen, ed. New York: Academic Press, in press.

Berenstain, Leo, Peter S. Rodman, and David Glenn Smith
1981   Social Relations between Fathers and Offspring in a Captive Group of Rhesus Monkeys. Animal Behaviour 29:1057–1063.

Berenstain, Leo, and Ted D. Wade
1983   Intrasexual Selection and Male Mating Strategies in Baboons and Macaques. International Journal of Primatology 4:201–235.

Berger, Joel
1983   Induced Abortion and Social Factors in Wild Horses. Nature 303:59–61.

Berlin, E. A., and A. V. Millard
1983   ABO Blood Groups and Sex Ratios in South America. Evolutionary Theory 6:257–273.

Berman, C. M.
1980   Early Agonistic Experience and Rank Acquisition among Free-Ranging Infant Rhesus Monkeys. International Journal of Primatology 1:153–170.

Berndt, Ronald M.
1962   Excess and Restraint. Chicago: University of Chicago Press.

Bernstein, Irwin S.
1970   Primate Status Hierarchies. In Primate Behavior. L. A. Rosenblum, ed. pp. 71–109. New York: Academic Press.

1976   Dominance, Aggression and Reproduction in Primate Societies. Journal of Theoretical Biology 60:459–472.

1981   Dominance: The Baby and the Bathwater. Behavioral and Brain Sciences 4:419–457.

Bertin, R. I., and A. G. Stephenson
1983   Towards a Definition of Sexual Selection. Evolutionary Theory 6:293–295.

Bertram, B. C. R.
1982   Problems with Altruism. In Current Problems in Sociobiology. King's College Sociobiology Group. pp. 251–267. Cambridge: Cambridge University Press.

Betzig, L. L.
1982   Despotism and Differential Reproduction: A Cross-Cultural Correlation of Conflict Asymmetry, Hierarchy, and Degree of Polygyny. Ethology and Sociobiology 3:209–221.

Bischof, N.
1975   Comparative Ethology of Incest Avoidance. In Biosocial Anthropology. R. Fox, ed. pp. 37–67. London: Malaby.

Bittles, A. H.
1979   Incest Re-assessed. Nature 280:107.

Bixler, Ray H.
1981a   Incest Avoidance as a Function of Environment and Heredity. Current Anthropology 22:639–654.

1981b   The Incest Controversy. Psychological Reports 49:267–283.

1983   "X" and the Single Girl: Of Parental Investment, Reproductive Strategies, and the Overly Cautious Female. Psychological Reports 53:279–282.

Blaustein, Andrew R.
1983   Kin Recognition Mechanisms: Phenotypic Matching or Recognition Alleles? American Naturalist 121:749–754.

Blaustein, Andrew R., and Richard K. O'Hara
1981   Genetic Control for Sibling Recognition? Nature 290:246–248.

1982   Kin Recognition in Rana cascadae Tadpoles: Maternal and Paternal Effects. Animal Behaviour 30:1151–1157.

Blick, J.
1977   Selection for Traits Which Lower Individual Reproduction. Journal of Theoretical Biology 67:597–601.

Bloch, Maurice
1977   The Past and the Present in the Present. Man 12:278–292.

Blurton Jones, N. G.
1984   A Selfish Origin for Human Food Sharing: Tolerated Theft. Ethology and Sociobiology 5:1–3.

Boggess, Jane
1979   Troop Male Membership Changes and Infant Killing in Langurs (Presbytis entellus). Folia Primatologica 32:65–107.

1980   Intermale Relations and Troop Male Membership Changes in Langurs (Presbytis entellus). International Journal of Primatology 1:233–274.

Boorman, S. A., and P. R. Levitt
1973   Group Selection on the Boundary of a Stable Population. Theoretical Population Biology 4:85–128.

1980   The Genetics of Altruism. New York: Academic Press.

Borgia, Gerald
1979   Sexual Selection and the Evolution of Mating Systems. In Sexual Selection and Reproductive Competition in Insects. M. Blum and N. Blum, eds. pp. 19–80. New York: Academic Press.

Bott, Elizabeth
1957   Family and Social Network: Roles, Norms, and External Relations in Ordinary Urban Families. London: Tavistock.

Bowman, L. A., S. R. Dilley, and E. B. Kaverne
1978   Suppression of Oestrogen-Induced LH Surges by Social Subordination in Talapoin Monkeys. Nature 275:56–58.

Bradbury, Jack W., and Robert M. Gibson
1983   Leks and Mate Choice. In Mate Choice. P. Bateson, ed. pp. 109–138. Cambridge: Cambridge University Press.

Broude, Gwen J., and Sarah J. Greene
1976   Cross-Cultural Codes on Twenty Sexual Attitudes and Practices. Ethnology 15:409–429.

Brues, Alice
1959   The Spearman and the Archer—An Essay on Selection in Body Build. American Anthropologist 61:457–469.

Burley, Nancy
1979   The Evolution of Concealed Ovulation. American Naturalist 114:835–838.

1982   Facultative Sex-Ratio Manipulation. American Naturalist 120:81–107.

1983   The Meaning of Assortative Mating. Ethology and Sociobiology 4:191–203.

Busse, Curt D.
1984   Tail Raising by Baboon Mothers toward Immigrant Males. American Journal of Physical Anthropology 64:255–262.

Butynski, Thomas M.
1982   Harem-Male Replacement and Infanticide in the Blue Monkey (Cercopithecus mitus stuhlmanni) in the Kibale Forest, Uganda. American Journal of Primatology 3:1–22.

Caine, Nancy C., and G. Mitchell
1980   Species Differences in the Interest Shown in Infants by Juvenile Female Macaques (Macaca radiata and M. mulatta). International Journal of Primatology 1:323–332.

Carpenter, C. R.
1942   Sexual Behavior of Free-Ranging Rhesus Monkeys (Macaca mulatta). Journal of Comparative Psychology 33:113–162.

Carr, W. J., Kenneth R. Kimmel, Steven L. Anthony, David E. Schlocker
1982   Female Rats Prefer to Mate with Dominant Rather than Subordinate Males. Bulletin of the Psychonomic Society 20:89–91.

Chagnon, Napoleon A.
1968   Yanomamo: The Fierce People. New York: Holt, Rinehart and Winston.

1974   Studying the Yanomamo. New York: Holt, Rinehart and Winston.

1975   Genealogy, Solidarity, and Relatedness: Limits to Local Group Size and Patterns of Fissioning in an Expanding Population. Yearbook of Physical Anthropology 19:95–110.

1979a   Mate Competition, Favoring Close Kin, and Village Fissioning among the Yanomamo Indians. *In* Evolutionary Biology and Human Social Behavior: An Anthropological Perspective. N. Chagnon and W. Irons, eds. pp. 86–132. North Scituate, Mass.: Duxbury Press.

1979b   Is Reproductive Success Equal in Egalitarian Societies? *In* Evolutionary Biology and Human Social Behavior: An Anthropological Perspective. N. Chagnon and W. Irons, eds. pp. 374–401. North Scituate, Mass.: Duxbury Press.

1980   Kin-Selection Theory, Kinship, Marriage and Fitness among the Yanomamo Indians. *In* Sociobiology: Beyond Nature/Nurture. G. Barlow and J. Silverberg, eds. pp. 545–571. Boulder: Westview Press.

1981   Terminological Kinship, Genealogical Relatedness and Village Fissioning among the Yanomamo Indians. *In* Natural Selection and Social Behavior: Recent Research and New Theory. R. Alexander and D. Tinkle, eds. pp. 490–508. New York: Chiron Press.

1982   Sociodemographic Attributes of Nepotism in Tribal Populations: Man the Rule-Breaker. *In* Current Problems in Sociobiology. King's College Sociobiology Group. pp. 291–318. Cambridge: Cambridge University Press.

Chagnon, Napoleon A., and Paul E. Bugos, Jr.
1979   Kin Selection and Conflict: An Analysis of a Yanomamo Ax Fight. *In* Evolutionary Biology and Human Social Behavior: An Anthropological Perspective. N. Chagnon and W. Irons, eds. pp. 213–238. North Scituate, Mass.: Duxbury Press.

Chagnon, Napoleon A., Mark V. Flinn, and Thomas F. Melancon
1979   Sex-Ratio Variation among the Yanomamo Indians. *In* Evolutionary Biology and Human Social Behavior: An Anthropological Perspective. N. Chagnon and W. Irons, eds. pp. 290–320. North Scituate, Mass.: Duxbury Press.

Chagnon, Napoleon A., and William Irons, eds.
1979   Evolutionary Biology and Human Social Behavior: An Anthropological Perspective. North Scituate, Mass.: Duxbury Press.

Chapais, Bernard
1983   Reproductive Activity in Relation to Male Dominance and the Likelihood of Ovulation in Rhesus Monkeys. Behavioral Ecology and Sociobiology 12:215–228.

Chapman, Michael, and Glenn Hausfater
1979   The Reproductive Consequences of Infanticide in Langurs: A Mathematical Model. Behavioral Ecology and Sociobiology 5:227–240.

Charlesworth, B., and E. R. Chanov
1980   Kin Selection in Age Structured Populations. Journal of Theoretical Biology 88:103–119.

Charnov, Eric L.
1983   The Theory of Sex Allocation. Princeton: Princeton University Press.

Cheney, Dorothy L.
   1977   The Acquisition of Rank and the Development of Reciprocal Alliances
          among Free-Ranging Immature Baboons. Behavioral Ecology and Sociobiology
          2:303–318.
   1978   Interaction of Immature Male and Female Baboons with Adult Females.
          Animal Behaviour 26:389–408.

Cheney, Dorothy L., and Robert M. Seyfarth
   1977   Behavior of Adult and Immature Male Baboons during Inter-Group
          Encounters. Nature 269:404–406.
   1980   Vocal Recognition in Free-Ranging Vervet Monkeys. Animal Behaviour
          28:362–367.
   1981   Selective Forces Affecting the Predator Alarm Calls of Vervet Monkeys.
          Behaviour 76:25–61.
   1983   Nonrandom Dispersal in Free-Ranging Vervet Monkeys: Social and
          Genetic Consequences. American Naturalist 122:392–412.

Cheney, Dorothy L., P. C. Lee, and Robert M. Seyfarth
   1981   Behavioral Correlates of Non-Random Mortality among Free-Ranging
          Female Vervet Monkeys. Behavioral Ecology and Sociobiology 9:153–161.

Chepko-Sade, B. Diane, and Thomas J. Olivier
   1979   Coefficient of Genetic Relationship and the Probability of Intragenealogical
          Fission in Macaca mulatta. Behavioral Ecology and Sociobiology 5:263–278.

Chepko-Sade, B. Diane, and Donald S. Sade
   1979   Patterns of Group Splitting within Matrilineal Kinship Groups: A Study of
          Social Group Structure in Macaca mulatta (Cercopithecidae: Primates). Be-
          havioral Ecology and Sociobiology 5:67–86.

Clark, Anne B.
   1978   Sex Ratio and Local Resource Competition in a Prosimian Primate. Science
          201:163–165.

Clark, P. J., and J. N. Spuhler
   1959   Differential Fertility in Relation to Body Dimensions. Human Biology
          31:121–137.

Clignet, Remi, and Joyce Sween
   1974   Urbanization, Plural Marriage, and Family Size in Two African Cities.
          American Ethnologist 1:221–242.

Clutton-Brock, T. H.
   1982   Sons and Daughters. Nature 298:11–12.
   1984   Reproductive Effort and Terminal Investment in Iteroparous Animals.
          American Naturalist 123:212–229.

Clutton-Brock, T. H., and S. D. Albon
  1982   Parental Investment in Male and Female Offspring in Mammals. *In* Current
         Problems in Sociobiology, King's College Sociobiology Group. pp. 223–247.
         Cambridge: Cambridge University Press.

Clutton-Brock, T. H., S. D. Albon, and F. E. Guinness
  1982   Competition between Female Relatives in a Matrilocal Mammal. Nature
         300:178–180.

  1984   Maternal Dominance, Breeding Success and Birth Sex Ratio in Red Deer.
         Nature 308:358–360.

Clutton-Brock, T. H., F. E. Guinness, and S. D. Albon
  1983   The Costs of Reproduction to Red Deer Hinds. Journal of Animal Ecology
         52:367–383.

Clutton-Brock, T. H., and Paul H. Harvey
  1977   Primate Ecology and Social Organization. Journal of Zoology 183:1–39.

Clutton-Brock, T. H., Paul H. Harvey, and B. Rudder
  1977   Sexual Dimorphism, Socionomic Sex Ratio and Body Weight in Primates.
         Nature 269:797–800.

Cohen, Yehudi A.
  1969   Ends and Means in Political Control: State Organization and the Punish-
         ment of Adultery, Incest, and the Violation of Celibacy. American Anthro-
         pologist 71:658–687.

Conaway, Clinton H., and Carl B. Koford
  1964   Estrous Cycles and Mating Behavior in a Free-Ranging Band of Rhesus
         Monkeys. Journal of Mammalogy 45:577–588.

Cox, Cathleen R., and Burney J. LeBoeuf
  1977   Female Incitation of Male Competition: A Mechanism in Sexual Selection.
         American Naturalist 111:317–335.

Crawford, M. H., and D. H. O'Rourke
  1978   Inbreeding, Lymphoma, Genetics and Morphology of the *Papio hamadryas*
         Colony of Sukhumi. Journal of Medical Primatology 7:355–360.

Crook, J. H.
  1970   The Socio-Ecology of Primates. *In* Social Behaviour in Birds and Mammals:
         Essays on the Social Ethology of Animals and Man. J. Crook, ed. pp. 103–166.
         New York: Academic Press.

  1971   Sources of Cooperation in Animals and Man. *In* Man and Beast:
         Comparative Social Behavior. J. Eisenberg and W. Dillion, eds. pp. 237–272.
         Washington, D.C.: Smithsonian Institution Press.

  1972   Sexual Selection, Dimorphism, and Social Organization in the Primates. *In*
         Sexual Selection and the Descent of Man, 1871–1971. B. Campbell, ed. pp. 231–
         281. Chicago: Aldine.

Crook, J. H., and, J. Gartlan
1966 Evolution of Primate Societies. Nature 210:1200–1203.

Cubicciotti, D. D. III, and W. A. Mason
1978 Comparative Studies of Social Behavior in *Callicebus* and *Saimiri:* Heterosexual Jealousy Behavior. Behavioral Ecology and Sociobiology 3:311–322.

Curie-Cohen, M., D. Yoshihara, C. Blystad, L. Luttrell, K. Benforado, and W. H. Stone
1981 Paternity and Mating Behavior in a Captive Troop of Rhesus Monkeys. American Journal of Primatology 1:335.

Curie-Cohen, Martin, Deborah Yoshihara, Lesleigh Luttrell, Kathy Benorado, Jean W. MacCluer, and William H. Stone
1983 The Effects of Dominance on Mating Behavior and Paternity in a Captive Troop of Rhesus Monkeys (*Macaca mulatta*). American Journal of Primatology 5:127–138.

Curtain, Richard
1977 Langur Social Behavior and Infant Mortality. Kroeber Anthropological Society Papers 50:27–36.

Curtain, Richard, and Phyllis Dolhinow
1978 Primate Social Behavior in a Changing World. American Scientist 66:468–475.
1979 Infanticide among Langurs—a Solution to Overcrowding? Science Today 13(7):35–41.

Daly, Martin
1978 Comment on Barkow. Current Anthropology 19:103–104.

Daly, Martin, and Margo I. Wilson
1978 Sex, Evolution and Behavior. North Scituate, Mass.: Duxbury Press.
1981 Abuse and Neglect of Children in Evolutionary Perspective. *In* Natural Selection and Social Behavior: Recent Research and New Theory. R. Alexander and D. Tinkle, eds. pp. 405–416. New York: Chiron Press.
1982a Homicide and Kinship. American Anthropologist 84:372–378.
1982b Whom Are Newborn Babies Said to Resemble? Ethology and Sociobiology 3:69–78.

Daly, Martin, Margo Wilson, and Suzanne J. Weghorst
1982 Male Sexual Jealousy. Ethology and Sociobiology 3:11–27.

Dawkins, Richard
1976 The Selfish Gene. Oxford: Oxford University Press.
1979 Twelve Misunderstandings of Kin Selection. Zeitschrift für Tierpsychologie 47:61–76.
1982 The Extended Phenotype: The Gene as the Unit of Selection. San Francisco: W. H. Freeman.

Dawkins, Richard, and H. Jane Brockmann
  1980   Do Digger Wasps Commit the Concorde Fallacy? Animal Behaviour
          28:892–896.

Dawkins, Richard, and T. R. Carlisle
  1976   Parental Investment, Mate Desertion and a Fallacy. Nature 131–132.

Deag, John M.
  1977   Aggression and Submission in Monkey Societies. Animal Behaviour
          25:465–474.

  1980   Interactions between Males and Unweaned Barbary Macaques: Testing the
          Agonistic Buffering Hypothesis. Behaviour 75:54–81.

Deag, John M., and John H. Crook
  1971   Social Behavior and "Agonistic Buffering" in the Wild Barbary Macaque
          Macaca sylvanus. Folia Primatologica 15:183–200.

Demarest, W.
  1977   Incest Avoidance among Human and Nonhuman Primates. *In* Primate Bio-
          Social Development: Biological, Social and Ecological Determinants. A.
          Chevalier-Skolnikoff and F. Poirier, eds. pp. 323–342. New York: Garland.

DeVore, Irven
  1965   Male Dominance and Mating Behavior in Baboons. *In* Sex and Behavior. F.
          Beach, ed. pp. 266–289. New York: John Wiley & Sons.

Dewsbury, Donald A.
  1982   Dominance Rank, Copulatory Behavior, and Differential Reproduction.
          Quarterly Review of Biology 57:135–159.

Dickemann, Mildred
  1975   Demographic Consequences of Infanticide in Man. Annual Review of
          Ecology and Systematics 6:107–137.

  1979a Female Infanticide, Reproductive Strategies, and Social Stratification: A
          Preliminary Model. *In* Evolutionary Biology and Human Social Behavior: An
          Anthropological Perspective. N. Chagnon and W. Irons, eds. pp. 321–367.
          North Scituate, Mass.: Duxbury Press.

  1979b The Ecology of Mating Systems in Hypergynous Dowry Societies. Social
          Science Information 18:163–195.

  1981   Paternal Confidence and Dowry Competition: A Biocultural Analysis of
          Purdah. *In* Natural Selection and Social Behavior: Recent Research and New
          Theory: R. Alexander and D. Tinkle, eds. pp. 417–438. New York: Chiron Press.

Dittus, Wolfgang
  1977   The Social Regulations of Population Density and Age-Sex Distribution in
          the Toque Monkey. Behaviour 63:281–321.

  1979   The Evolution of Behaviours Regulating Density and Age-Specific Sex
          Ratios in a Primate Population. Behaviour 69:265–301.

1980   The Social Regulation of Primate Populations: A Synthesis. *In* The Macaques: Studies in Ecology, Behavior and Evolution. D. Lindberg, ed. pp. 263–286. New York: Von Nostrand Reinhold.

Divale, William T., and Marvin Harris
1976   Population, Warfare, and the Male Supremacist Complex. American Anthropologist 78:521–538.

Dixson, A. F., Diane M. Scruton, and J. Herbert
1975   Behaviour of the Talapoin Monkey (*Miopithecus talapoin*) Studied in Groups, in the Laboratory. Journal of Zoology 176:177–210.

Dobson, F. Stephen
1982   Competition for Mates and Predominant Juvenile Male Dispersal in Mammals. Animal Behaviour 30:1183–1192.

Dolhinow, Phyllis
1977   Normal Monkeys? American Scientist 6:266.

Dolhinow, P., J. J. McKenna, and J. Vonder Har Laws
1979   Rank and Reproduction among Female Langur Monkeys: Aging and Improvement (They're Not Just Getting Older, They're Getting Better). Aggressive Behavior 5:19–30.

Dominey, W. J.
1983   Sexual Selection, Additive Genetic Variance and the "Phenotypic Handicap." Journal of Theoretical Biology 101:495–502.

Dorjahn, Vernon R.
1958   Fertility, Polygyny and Their Interrelations in Temne Society. American Anthropologist 60:838–860.

Dow, James
1983   Woman Capture as a Motivation for Warfare: A Comparative Analysis of Intra-Cultural Variation and a Critique of the "Male Supremacist Complex". *In* Rethinking Human Adaptation: Biological and Cultural Models. R. Dyson-Hudson and M. Little, eds. pp. 97–115. Boulder: Westview Press.

1984   The Genetic Basis for Affinal Cooperation. American Ethnologist 11:380–383.

Draper, Patricia, and Henry Harpending
1982   Father Absence and Reproductive Strategy: An Evolutionary Perspective. Journal of Anthropological Research 38:255–273.

Drickamer, Lee C.
1974a   Social Rank, Observability, and Sexual Behaviour of Rhesus Monkeys (*Macaca mulatta*). Journal of Reproduction and Fertility 37:117–120.

1974b   A Ten Year Summary of Reproductive Data for Free-Ranging *Macaca mulatta*. Folia Primatologica 21:61–80.

Dunbar, R. I. M.

1979a Population Demography, Social Organization, and Mating Strategies. *In* Primate Ecology and Human Origins. I. Bernstein and E. Smith, eds. pp. 65–88. New York: Garland.

1979b Structure of Gelada Baboon Reproductive Units. I. Stability of Social Relationships. Behaviour 69:72–87.

1980 Determinants and Evolutionary Consequences of Dominance among Female Gelada Baboons. Behavioral Ecology and Sociobiology 7:253–265.

1982a Adaptation, Fitness and the Evolutionary Tautology. *In* Current Problems in Sociobiology. King's College Sociobiology Group. pp. 9–28. Cambridge: Cambridge University Press.

1982b Intraspecific Variations in Mating Strategy. *In* Perspectives in Ethology, vol. 5. P. Bateson and P. Klopter, eds. New York: Plenum Press.

1983 Life History Tactics and Alternative Strategies of Reproduction. *In* Mate Choice. P. Bateson, ed. pp. 423–433. Cambridge: Cambridge University Press.

1984 Infant-Use by Male Gelada in Agonistic Contexts: Agonistic Buffering, Progeny Protection, or Soliciting Support? Primates 25:28–35.

Dunbar, R. I. M., and E. P. Dunbar

1977 Dominance and Reproductive Success among Female Gelada Baboons. Nature 266:351–352.

Dunbar, R. I. M., and M. Sharman

1983 Female Competition for Access to Males Affects Birth Rate in Baboons. Behavioral Ecology and Sociobiology 13:157–159.

Dusek, Val

1984 Sociobiology and Rape. Science for the People 16(1):10–16.

Duvall, Susan W., I. S. Bernstein, and T. P. Gordon

1976 Paternity and Status in a Rhesus Monkey Group. Journal of Reproduction and Fertility 441:25–31.

Dziuk, Philip

1982 Behaviour, Paternity and Testes Size. Nature 296:587.

Eaton, G. Gray

1973 Social and Endocrine Determinants of Sexual Behavior in Simian and Prosimian Females. *In* Primate Reproductive Behavior, vol. 2. C. Phoenix, ed. pp. 20–35. Basel: S. Karger.

1974 Male Dominance and Aggression in Japanese Macaque Reproduction. *In* Reproductive Behavior. W. Montagna and W. Sadler, eds. pp. 287–297. New York: Plenum Press.

Egeland, Janice A., and Abram M. Hostetter

1983 Amish Study, I: Affective Disorders among the Amish, 1976–1980. American Journal of Psychiatry 140:56–61.

Eisenberg, J. F., N. A. Mackenhirn, and R. Rudran
1972   The Relation between Ecology and Social Structure in Primates. Science 176:863–874.

Ember, Melvin
1974   Warfare, Sex Ratio, and Polygyny. Ethnology 13:197–206.

1975   On the Origin and Extension of the Incest Taboo. Behavior Science Research 10:249–281.

1983   Alternative Predictors of Polygyny. Paper presented at the Society for Cross-Cultural Research meetings.

Ember, Melvin, and Carol R. Ember
1979   Male-Female Bonding: A Cross-Cultural Study of Mammals and Birds. Behavior Science Research 14:37–56.

1983   The Evolution of Human Female Sexuality: A Cross-Species Perspective. To appear in Journal of Anthropological Research. (appeared in 1984, 40:202–210).

Emlen, Stephen T.
1980   Ecological Determinism and Sociobiology. In Sociobiology: Beyond Nature/Nurture? G. Barlow and J. Silverberg, eds. pp. 125–150. Boulder: Westview Press.

Emlen, Stephen, and L. Oring
1977   Ecology, Sexual Selection and the Evolution of Mating Systems. Science 197:215–223.

Enomoto, Tomoo
1974   The Sexual Behavior of Japanese Monkeys. Journal of Human Evolution 3:351–372.

Epple, G.
1977   Notes on the Establishment and Maintenance of the Pair Bond in Saquinus fuscicollis. In The Biology and Conservation of the Callitrichidae. D. Kleiman, ed. pp. 231–237. Washington, D.C.: Smithsonian Institution Press.

Essock-Vitale, Susan M.
1984   The Reproductive Success of Wealthy Americans. Ethology and Sociobiology 5:45–49.

Essock-Vitale, Susan M., and Michael T. McGuire
1980   Prediction from the Theories of Kin Selection and Reciprocation Assessed by Anthropological Data. Ethology and Sociobiology 1:233–243.

Etter, Martin A.
1978   Sahlins and Sociobiology. American Ethnologist 5:160–169.

Eveleth, Phyllis B.
1975   Differences between Ethnic Groups in Sex Dimorphism of Adult Height. Annals of Human Biology 2:35–39.

Eveleth, Phyllis B, and J. M. Tanner
  1976   World-Wide Variation in Human Growth. Cambridge: Cambridge University Press.

Fagen, R. M.
  1976   Three-Generation Family Conflict. Animal Behaviour 24:874–879.

Faux, Stephen F., and Miller, Harold L. Jr.
  1984   Evolutionary Speculations on the Oligarchic Development of Mormon Polygyny. Ethology and Sociobiology 5:15–31.

Fedigan, Linda M.
  1982   Primate Patterns: Sex Roles and Social Bonds. Montreal: Eden Press.

  1983   Dominance and Reproductive Success. Yearbook of Physical Anthropology 26:91–129.

Firth, Raymond
  1964   Essays on Social Organization and Values. London School of Economics Monographs on Social Anthropology 28:30–87.

Fisher, R. A.
  1930   The Genetical Theory of Natural Selection. New York: Dover Press.

Flinn, Mark
  1981a   Uterine vs. Agnatic Kinship Variability and Associated Cousin Marriage Preferences: An Evolutionary Biological Analysis. In Natural Selection and Social Behavior: Recent Research and New Theory. R. Alexander and D. Tinkle, eds. pp. 439–475. New York: Chiron Press.

  1981b   Behavioral Interactions in a Trinidadian Village: Testing Predictions from Kin Selection Theory. To appear in Ethology and Sociobiology.

Flinn, Mark V., and Richard D. Alexander
  1982   Culture Theory: The Developing Synthesis from Biology. Human Ecology 10:383–400.

Fox, Robin
  1980   The Red Lamp of Incest. New York: E. P. Dutton.

Fredlund, Eric V.
  1981   The Use and Abuse of Kinship When Classifying Marriages: A Shitari Yanomamo Case Study. To appear in Ethology and Sociobiology.

Fredrickson, W. Timm, and Gene P. Sackett
  1984   Kin Preferences in Primates (Macaca nemestrina): Relatedness or Familiarity? Journal of Comparative Psychology 98:29–34.

Freedman, Daniel
  1974   Human Infancy: An Evolutionary Perspective. Hillsdale, N.J.: Lawrence Erlbaum Associates.

  1979   Human Sociobiology. New York: Free Press.

Frisch, R. E.
1984   Body Fat, Puberty, and Fertility. Biological Reviews of the Cambridge Philosophical Society 59:161–188.

Frisch, R. E., and J. W. McArthur
1974   Menstrual Cycles: Fatness as a Determinant of Minimum Weight and Height Necessary for Their Maintenance or Onset. Science 185:949–951.

Furuichi, Takeshi
1983   Interindividual Distance and Influence of Dominance on Feeding in a Natural Japanese Macaque Troop. Primates 24:445–455.

Gadgil, Madhav
1982   Changes with Age in the Strategy of Social Behavior. Perspectives in Ethology 5:489–501.

Galdikas, Birute M. F.
1981   Orangutan Reproduction in the Wild. In Reproductive Biology of the Great Apes. C. Graham, ed. pp. 281–300. New York: Academic Press.

Gartlan, J. S.
1968   Structure and Function in Primate Society. Folia Primatologica 8:89–120.

Gaulin, Steven J. C.
1980   Sexual Dimorphism in the Human Post-Reproductive Life-Span: Possible Causes. Journal of Human Evolution 9:227–232.

Gaulin, Steven J. C., and Lee D. Sailer
1983a   Nutritional Constraints and Sexual Selection in the Evolution of Body Weight: Are Females the Ecological Sex? Unpublished manuscript.

1983b   Sexual Dimorphism in Weight among the Primates: The Relative Impact of Allometry and Sexual Selection. Unpublished Manuscript.

Gaulin, Steven J. C., and Alice Schlegel
1980   Paternal Confidence and Paternal Investment: A Cross-Cultural Test of a Sociobiological Hypothesis. Ethology and Sociobiology 1:301–309.

Gautier-Hion, A., and J.-P. Gautier
1978   Le Singe de Brazza: Une Strategie Originale. Zeitschrift für Tierpsychologie 46:84–104.

Getz, Wayne M., and Katherine B. Smith
1983   Genetic Kin Recognition: Honey Bees Discriminate between Full and Half Siblings. Nature 302:147–148.

Ghiglieri, Michael P.
1984   The Chimpanzees of Kibale Forest: A Field Study of Ecology and Social Structure. New York: Columbia University Press.

Ginsburg, Harvey J., and Shirley Miller
    1981   Altrusim [sic] in Children: A Naturalistic Study of Reciprocation and an
    Examination of the Relationship between Social Dominance and Aid-Giving
    Behavior. Ethology and Sociobiology 2:75–83.

Glander, Kenneth E.
    1980   Reproduction and Population Growth in Free-Ranging Mantled Howling
    Monkeys. American Journal of Physical Anthropology 53:25–36.

Glick, Barbara B.
    1980   Ontogenetic and Psychological Aspects of the Mating Activities of Male
    Macaca radiata. In The Macaques: Studies in Ecology, Behavior, and Evolution.
    D. Lindberg, ed. pp. 345–369. New York: Van Nostrand Reinhold.

Goldschmidt, William R.
    1966   Comparative Functionalism: An Essay in Anthropological Theory.
    Berkeley: University of California Press.

Goodall, Jane
    1977   Infant Killing and Cannibalism in Free-Living Chimpanzees. Folia Prima-
    tologica 28:259–282.

Gould, Stephen J., and Richard L. Lewontin
    1979   The Spandrels of San Marco and the Panglossian Paradigm. Proceedings
    of the Royal Society of London. B. Biological Sciences 205:581–598.

Gouzoules, Harold, Sarah Gouzoules, and Linda Fedigan
    1982   Behavioural Dominance and Reproductive Success in Female Japanese
    Monkeys (*Macaca fuscata*). Animal Behaviour 30:1138–1150.

Grafen, Alan
    1982   How Not to Measure Inclusive Fitness. Nature 298:425–426.

Grass, Harold J.
    1982   Kin Recognition in White-Footed Deermice (*Peromscus leucopus*. Animal
    Behaviour 30:497–505.

Gray, J. Patrick
    1984   A Guide to Primate Sociobiological Theory and Research. New Haven:
    Human Relations Area Files.

Gray, J. Patrick, and Joseph P. Roberts
    1984   Warfare, Polygyny, and Human Sexual Dimorphism. Paper presented
    before the Society for Cross-Cultural Research.

Gray, J. Patrick, and Linda D. Wolfe
    1980   Height and Sexual Dimorphism of Stature among Human Societies.
    American Journal of Physical Anthropology 53:441–456.

    1981   Parental Certainty, Subsistence, and Inheritance Revisited. Journal of
    Human Evolution 10:277–278.

1982a A Note on Brother Inheritance. Ethology and Sociobiology 3:103–105.

1982b Correlates of Monogamy in Human Groups: Tests of Some Sociobiological Hypotheses. To appear in Behavior Science Research.

1983 Human Female Sexual Cycles and the Concealment of Ovulation Problem. Journal of Social and Biological Structures 6:345–352.

Greene, Penelope J.
1978 Promiscuity, Paternity and Culture. American Ethnologist 5:151–159.

Hall, K. R. L., and Irven DeVore
1965 Baboon Social Behavior. In Primate Behavior. I. DeVore, ed. pp. 53–110. New York: Holt, Rinehart and Winston.

Halliday, Tim
1983a Do Frogs and Toads Choose their Mates? Nature 306:226–227.

1983b The Study of Mate Choice. In Mate Choice. P. Bateson, ed. pp. 3–32. Cambridge: Cambridge University Press.

Hames, Raymond B.
1979 Relatedness and Interaction among the Ye'kwana: A Preliminary Analysis. In Evolutionary Biology and Human Social Behavior: An Anthropological Perspective. N. Chagnon and W. Irons, eds. pp. 239–249. North Scituate, Mass: Duxbury Press.

1981 Untitled Paper. To appear in Ethology and Sociobiology.

1984 On the Definition and Measure of Inclusive Fitness and the Evolution of Menopause. Human Ecology 12:87–91.

Hamilton, William D.
1963 The Evolution of Altruistic Behavior. American Naturalist 97:354–356.

1964 The Genetical Evolution of Social Behaviour. Journal of Theoretical Biology 7:1–52.

Hanby, Jeannette P., L. T. Robertson, and C. H. Phoenix
1971 The Sexual Behavior of a Confined Troop of Japanese Macaques. Folia Primatologica 16:123–143.

Handwerker, W. Penn, and Paul V. Crosbie
1982 Sex and Dominance, American Anthropologist 84:97–104.

Harcourt, Alexander H.
1982 Reply to Dziuk. Nature 296:587–588.

Harcourt, Alexander H., Dian Fossey, and J. Sabater-Pi
1981 Demography of Gorilla gorilla. Journal of Zoology 195:215–233.

Harcourt, Alexander H., Paul H. Harvey, S. G. Larson, and R. V. Short
1981 Testis Weight, Body Weight and Breeding Systems in Primates. Nature 293:55–57.

Harpending, Henry
   1979   The Population Genetics of Interaction. American Naturalist 113:622–630.
   1980   Perspectives on the Theory of Social Evolution. Current Developments in Anthropological Genetics 1:45–64.

Harris, Marvin
   1979   Cultural Materialism: The Struggle for a Science of Culture. New York: Random House.

Harris, Marvin, and Edward O. Wilson
   1978   The Twig and the Envelope. The Sciences 18(8):10–15, 27.

Hartung, John
   1976   On Natural Selection and the Inheritance of Wealth. Current Anthropology 17:607–622.
   1977   An Implication about Human Mating Systems. Journal of Theoretical Biology 66:737–745.
   1980   Parent-Offspring Conflict—A Retraction. Journal of Theoretical Biology 87:815–817.
   1981   Paternity and Inheritance of Wealth. Nature 291:652–654.
   1982a   Polygyny and Inheritance of Wealth. Current Anthropology 23:1–12.
   1982b   Deceiving Down: Conjectures on the Management of Subordinate Status. Unpublished manuscript.
   1983   Matrilineal Inheritance: New Theory and Analysis. Paper read at the meetings of the American Anthropological Association.

Harvey, Paul H., Michael Kavanagh, and T. H. Clutton-Brock
   1978   Canine Tooth Size in Female Primates. Nature 276:817–818.

Hausfater, Glenn
   1975   Dominance and Reproduction in Baboons (Papio cynocephalus): A Quantitative Analysis. New York: S. Karger.

Hausfater, Glenn, Jeanne Altmann, and Stuart Altmann
   1982   Long-Term Consistency of Dominance Relations among Female Baboons (Papio cynocephalus). Science 217:752–754.

Hausfater, Glenn, and Sarah B. Hrdy, eds.
   1984   Infanticide: Comparative and Evolutionary Perspectives. New York: Aldine.

Hawkes, Kristen
   1983   Kin Selection and Culture. American Ethnologist 10:345–363.

Hawkes, Kristen, James O'Connell, Kim Hill, and Eric Charnov
   1981   How Much is Enough? Hunters and "Limited Needs." To appear in Ethology and Sociobiology.

Hearn, J. P.
1978 The Endocrinology of Reproduction in the Common Marmoset (*Callithrix jacchus*). *In* The Biology and Conservation of the Callitrichidae. D. Kleiman, ed. pp. 163–171. Washington, D.C.: Smithsonian Institution Press.

Heisler, I. L.
1981 Offspring Quality and the Polygyny Threshold: A New Model for the "Sexy Son" Hypothesis. American Naturalist 117:316–328.

Hendrickx, A. G., and D. C. Kraemer
1969 Observations on the Menstrual Cycle, Optimal Mating Time and Pre-implantation Embryos of the Baboon, *Papio anubis* and *Papio cynocephalus*. Journal of Reproduction and Fertility, Supplement 6:119–128.

Hendrickx, A. G., and V. G. Nelson
1971 Reproductive Failure. *In* Comparative Reproduction of Nonhuman Primates. E. Hafez, ed. pp. 403–425. Springfield, Ill.: Thomas.

Herbert, J.
1968 Sexual Preference in the Rhesus Monkey (*Macaca mulatta*) in the Laboratory. Animal Behaviour 16:120–128.

Hiernaux, Jean
1977 Long-Term Biological Effects of Human Migration from the African Savanna to the Equatorial Forest: A Case Study of Human Adaptation to a Hot and Wet Climate. *In* Population Structure and Human Variation. G. Harrison, ed. pp. 187–217. Cambridge: Cambridge University Press.

Hiernaux, Jean, P. Rudan, and A. Brambati
1975 Climate and the Weight/Height Relationship in Sub-Saharan Africa. Annals of Human Biology 2:3–12.

Hill, J.
1984 Prestige and Reproductive Success in Man. Ethology and Sociobiology 5:77–95.

Hill, Kim
1982 Hunting and Human Evolution. Journal of Human Evolution 11:521–544.

Hinde, R. A.
1978 Dominance and Role—Two Concepts with Dual Meaning. Journal of Social and Biological Structures 1:27–38.

Hinde, R. A., ed.
1983 Primate Social Relationships: An Integrated Approach. Sunderland: Sinauer Associates.

Hinde, R. A., and L. M. Davies
1972a Changes in Mother Infant Relationships after Separation in Rhesus Monkeys. Nature 239:41–42.

1972b   Removing Infant Rhesus from Mother for 13 Days Compared with Removing Mother from Infant. Journal of Child Psychology and Psychiatry 13:227–237.

Hinde, R. A., and Y. Spencer-Booth
1971   Effects of Brief Separation from Mother on Rhesus Monkeys. Science 173:111–118.

Holmes, Warren G., and Paul W. Sherman
1982   The Ontogeny of Kin Recognition in Two Species of Ground Squirrels. American Zoologist 22:491–517.

1983   Kin Recognition in Animals. American Scientist 71:46–55.

Hoogland, John L.
1981   Sex Ratio and Local Resource Competition. American Naturalist 117:796–797.

1983   Nepotism and Alarm Calling in the Black-Tailed Prairie Dog (Cynomys ludovicianus). Animal Behaviour 31:472–479.

Horrocks, Julia, and Wayne Hunte
1983   Rank Relations in Vervet Sisters: A Critique of the Role of Reproductive Value. American Naturalist 122:417–421.

Hrdy, Sarah Blaffer
1974   Male-Male Competition and Infanticide among the Langurs (Presbytis entellus) of Abu, Rajasthan. Folia Primatologica 22:19–58.

1976   Care and Exploitation of Nonhuman Primate Infants by Conspecifics Other than the Mother. Advances in the Study of Behavior 6:101–158.

1977   Infanticide as a Primate Reproductive Strategy. American Scientist 65:40–49.

1979   Infanticide among Animals: A Review, Classification, and Examination of the Implications for the Reproductive Strategies of Females. Ethology and Sociobiology 1:13–40.

1981a   The Woman that Never Evolved. Cambridge, Mass: Harvard University Press.

1981b   "Nepotists" and "Altruists": The Behavior of Old Females among Macaques and Langur Monkeys. In Other Ways of Growing Old. P. Amoss and S. Harrell, eds. pp. 59–76. Stanford: Stanford University Press.

1982   Positivist Thinking Encounters Field Primatology, Resulting in Agonistic Behavior. Social Science Information 21:245–250.

Hrdy, Sarah B., and Daniel B. Hrdy
1976   Hierarchical Relations among Female Hanuman Langurs (Primates: Colobinae, Presbytis entellus). Science 193:913–915.

Huck, U. William, and Edwin M. Banks
1982a   Differential Attraction of Females to Dominant Males: Olfactory Dis-

crimination and Mating Preference in the Brown Lemming (*Lemmus trimucronatus*). Behavioral Ecology and Sociobiology 11:217–222.

1982b   Male Dominance Status, Female Choice and Mating Success in the Brown Lemming, *Lemmus trimucronatus*. Animal Behaviour 30:665–675.

Huck, U. William, Robin L. Soltis, and Carol B. Cooper-Smith
1982   Infanticide in Male Laboratory Mice: Effects of Social Status, Prior Sexual Experience and Basis for Discrimination between Related and Unrelated Young. Animal Behaviour 30:1158–1165.

Hughes, Austin L.
1980   Preferential First-Cousin Marriage and Inclusive Fitness. Ethology and Sociobiology 1:311–317.

1981   Female Infanticide: Sex Ratio Manipulation in Humans. Ethology and Sociobiology 2:109–111.

1982   Confidence of Paternity and Wife-Sharing in Polygynous and Polyandrous Systems. Ethology and Sociobiology 3:125–129.

Hurd, James P.
1981   Sex Differences in Mate Choice among the Nebraska Amish of Central Pennsylvania. To appear in Ethology and Sociobiology. (A revised version appeared in Social Biology, 1983, 30:59–66.)

Irons, William
1979a   Natural Selection, Adaptation, and Human Social Behavior. *In* Evolutionary Biology and Human Social Behavior: An Anthropological Perspective. N. Chagnon and W. Irons, eds. pp. 4–39. North Scituate, Mass.: Duxbury Press.

1979b   Cultural and Biological Success. *In* Evolutionary Biology and Human Social Behavior: An Anthropological Perspective. N. Chagnon and W. Irons, eds. pp. 257–272. North Scituate, Mass.: Duxbury Press.

1979c   Investment and Primary Social Dyads. *In* Evolutionary Biology and Human Social Behavior: An Anthropological Perspective. N. Chagnon and W. Irons, eds. pp. 181–213. North Scituate, Mass.: Duxbury Press.

1980   Is Yomut Social Behavior Adaptive? *In* Sociobiology: Beyond Nature/ Nurture? G. Barlow and J. Silverberg, eds. pp. 417–463. Boulder: Westview Press.

1981   Why Lineage Exogamy? *In* Natural Selection and Social Behavior: Recent Research and New Theory. R. Alexander and D. Tinkle, eds. pp. 476–489. New York: Chiron Press.

1982   Some Tests of the Wynne-Edwards/Carr-Saunders Hypothesis. Paper read before the American Anthropological Association.

1983   Human Female Reproductive Strategies. *In* Social Behavior of Female Vertebrates. S. Wasser, ed. pp. 169–213. New York: Academic Press.

Isaac, Barry L., and William E. Feinberg
1982   Marital Form and Infant Survival among the Mende of Rural Upper Bambara Chiefdom, Sierra Leone. Human Biology 54:627–634.

Itani, Junichiro
1959 Paternal Care in the Wild Japanese Monkey, *Macaca fuscata fuscata.* Primates 2:61–93.

1982 Intraspecific Killing among Non-Human Primates. Journal of Social and Biological Structures 5:361–368.

Itiogawa, N., K. Negayama, and K. Kondo
1981 Experimental Study on Sexual Behavior between Mother and Son in Japanese Monkeys (*Macaca fuscata*). Primates 22:494–502.

Itzkowitz, Murray, and John Nyby
1981 A Parental Sex Difference in Child Custody Suits. Ethology and Sociobiology 2:147–149.

Jakubowski, Moshe, and Joseph Terkel
1982 Infanticide and Caretaking in Non-Lactating *Mus musculus:* Influence of Genotype, Family Group and Sex. Animal Behaviour 30:1029–1034.

James, William H.
1980 Time of Fertilisation and Sex of Infants. Lancet 8178:1124–1126.

Jay, Phyllis
1965 The Common Langur of North India. *In* Primate Behavior: Field Studies of Monkeys and Apes. I. DeVore, ed. pp. 197–249. New York: Holt, Rinehart and Winston.

Jenni, D.
1974 Evolution of Polyandry in Birds. American Zoologist 14:129–144.

Johnson, Candace, Cathy Koerner, Marty Estrin, and Deanna Duoos
1980 Alloparental Care and Kinship in Captive Social Groups of Vervet Monkeys (*Cercopithecus aethiops* sabaeus). Primates 21:406–415.

Johnson, Deanne F., Kurt B. Modahl, and G. Gray Eaton
1982 Dominance Status of Adult Male Japanese Macaques: Relationship to Female Dominance Status, Male Mating Behaviour, Season Changes, and Developmental Changes. Animal Behaviour 30:383–392.

Jones, Clara B.
1981 The Evolution and Socioecology of Dominance in Primate Groups: A Theoretical Formulation, Classification and Assessment. Primates 22:70–83.

Judge, Debra S., and Peter S. Rodman
1976 *Macaca radiata:* Intragroup Relations and Reproductive Status of Females. Primates 17:535–539.

Kaffman, M.
1977 Sexual Standards and Behavior of the Kibbutz Adolescent. American Journal of Orthopsychiatry 47:207–217.

Kang, Gay E.
  1976   Conflicting Loyalties Theories: A Cross-Cultural Test. Ethnology 15:201–
  210.

Kaplan, Jay R.
  1978   Fight Interference and Altruism in Rhesus Monkeys. American Journal of
  Physical Anthropology 49:241–250.

Kareem, A. M., and C. J. Bernard
  1982   The Importance of Kinship and Familiarity in Social Interactions between
  Mice. Animal Behaviour 30:594–601.

Kaufmann, John H.
  1965   A Three-Year Study of Mating Behavior in a Free-Ranging Band of Rhesus
  Monkeys. Ecology 46:500–512.

King's College Sociobiology Group
  1982   Current Problems in Sociobiology. Cambridge: Cambridge University
  Press.

Kinsey, A. C., W. B. Pomeroy, C. E. Martin, and P. H. Gebhard
  1953   Sexual Behavior in the Human Female. Philadelphia: Saunders.

Klahn, Jeff E., and George J. Gamboa
  1983   Social Wasps: Discrimination between Kin and Nonkin Brood. Science
  221:482–484.

Kleiman, D. G.
  1977   Monogamy in Mammals. Quarterly Review of Biology 52:39–69.

  1981   Correlations among Life History Characteristics of Mammalian Species
  Exhibiting Two Extreme Forms of Monogamy. In Natural Selection and Social
  Behavior: Recent Research and New Theory. R. Alexander and D. Tinkle, eds.
  pp. 332–344. New York: Chiron Press.

Kleiman, D. G., and J. R. Malcolm
  1981   The Evolution of Male Parental Investment in Mammals. In Parental Care
  in Mammals. D. Gubernick and P. Klopfer, eds. pp. 347–387. New York:
  Plenum Press.

Krige, P. D., and J. W. Lucas
  1974   Aunting Behaviour in an Urban Troop of Cercopithecus aethiops. Journal of
  Behavioural Science 2:55–61.

Kurland, Jeffrey A.
  1977   Kin Selection in the Japanese Monkey. New York: S. Karger.

  1979   Paternity, Mother's Brother, and Human Sociality. In Evolutionary Biology
  and Human Social Behavior: An Anthropological Perspective. N. Chagnon and
  W. Irons, eds. pp. 145–180. North Scituate, Mass.: Duxbury Press.

1980   Kin Selection Theory: a Review and Selective Bibliography. Ethology and Sociobiology 1:255–274.

Kurland, Jeffrey A., and Steven Gaulin
1979   Testing Kin Selection: Problems with r. Behavioral Ecology and Sociobiology 6:81–83.

Lack, David
1954   The Natural Regulation of Animal Numbers. Oxford: Oxford University Press.
1968   Ecological Adaptations for Breeding in Birds. London: Methuen.

Lacy, Robert C., and Paul W. Sherman
1983   Kin Recognition by Phenotype Matching. American Naturalist 121:489–512.

Lamb, Michael E.
1983   Early Mother-Neonate Contact and the Mother-Child Relationship. Journal of Child Psychology and Psychiatry 24:487–494.

Lancaster, Jane
1971   Play-Mothering: the Relations between Juvenile Females and Young Infants among Free-Ranging Vervet Monkeys (Cercopithecus aethiops). Folia Primatologica 15:161–182.
1978   Sex and Gender in Evolutionary Perspective. In Human Sexuality: A Comparative and Developmental Perspective. H. Katchadourian, ed. pp. 51–80. Berkeley: University of California Press.

Lande, Russell
1978   Are Humans Maximizing Reproductive Success? Behavioral Ecology and Sociobiology 3:95–96.
1980   Sexual Dimorphism, Sexual Selection, and Adaptation in Polygenic Characters. Evolution 34:292–307.

Latane, B., and J. Darley
1970   The Unresponsive Bystander: Why Doesn't He Help? New York: Meredith.

Lawick-Goodall, Jane V.
1967   Mother-Offspring Relationships in Free-Ranging Chimpanzees. In Primate Ethology. D. Morris, ed. pp. 287–346. Chicago: Aldine.

Lawrence, P. S.
1941   The Sex Ratio, Fertility, and Ancestral Longevity. Quarterly Review of Biology 16:35–79.

Laws, John W., and Julia Vonder Haar Laws
1984   Social Interactions among the Adult Male Langurs (Presbytis entellus) at Rajaji Wildlife Sanctuary. International Journal of Primatology 5:31–50.

Leacock, Eleanor
  1980 Social Behavior, Biology and the Double Standard. *In* Sociobiology:
        Beyond Nature/Nurture? G. Barlow and J. Silverberg, eds. pp. 465–488.
        Boulder: Westview Press.

Lenington, Sarah
  1981 Child Abuse: The Limits of Sociobiology. Ethology and Sociobiology 2:17–
        29.

Leutenegger, Walter
  1978 Scaling of Sexual Dimorphism in Body Size and Breeding Systems in
        Primates. Nature 272:610–611.

  1982 Scaling of Sexual Dimorphism in Body Weight and Canine Size in
        Primates. Folia Primatologica 37:163–176.

Leutenegger, Walter, and James Cheverud
  1982 Correlates of Sexual Dimorphism in Primates: Ecological and Size
        Variables. International Journal of Primatology 3:387–402.

Leutenegger, Walter, and James T. Kelly
  1977 Relationship of Sexual Dimorphism in Canine Size and Body Size to
        Social, Behavioral, and Ecological Correlates in Anthropoid Primates. Primates
        18:117–136.

Levinson, David, and Martin J. Malone
  1980 Toward Explaining Human Culture: A Critical Review of the Findings of
        Worldwide Cross-Cultural Research. New Haven: HRAF Press.

Lewontin, R. C., Steven Rose, and Leon J. Kamin
  1984 Not in Our Genes. New York: Pantheon.

Lightcap, Joy L., Jeffrey A. Kurland, and Robert L. Burgess
  1982 Child Abuse: A Test of Some Predictions from Evolutionary Theory.
        Ethology and Sociobiology 3:61–67.

Livingstone, Frank B.
  1969 Genetics, Ecology, and the Origins of Incest and Exogamy. Current
        Anthropology 10:45–62.

  1980 Cultural Causes of Genetic Change. *In* Sociobiology: Beyond Nature/
        Nurture? G. Barlow and J. Silverberg, eds. pp. 307–329. Boulder: Westview
        Press.

Lloyd, J.
  1980 Male *Photuris* Fireflies Mimic Sexual Signals of Their Females' Prey.
        Science 210:669–671.

Lockard, Joan S.
  1980 Speculations of the Adaptive Significance of Self-Deception. *In* The
        Evolution of Social Behavior. J. Lockard, ed. pp. 257–275. New York: Elsevier.

Lockard, Joan S., and Robert M. Adams
1981 Human Serial Polygyny: Demographic, Reproductive, Marital, and Divorce Data. Ethology and Sociobiology 2:177–186.

Loekle, Diane M., Dale M. Madison, and John J. Christian
1982 Time Dependency and Kin Recognition of Cannibalistic Behavior among Poeciliid Fishes. Behavioral and Neural Biology 35:315–318.

Lott, Dale F.
1984 Intraspecific Variation in the Social Systems of Wild Vertebrates. Behaviour 88:266–325.

Lovejoy, C. Owen
1981 The Origin of Man. Science 211: 341–350.

Low, Bobbi S.
1979 Sexual Selection and Human Ornamentation. *In* Evolutionary Biology and Human Social Behavior: An Anthropological Perspective. N. Chagnon and W. Irons, eds. pp. 462–487. North Scituate, Mass.: Duxbury Press.

Low, Bobbi S., and Katharine M. Noonan
1983 Resource Distribution and Reproductive Strategies. Paper read before the American Anthropological Association.

Loy, James
1971 Estrous Behavior of Free-Ranging Rhesus Monkeys (*Macaca mulatta*). Primates 12:1–31.

1981 The Reproductive and Heterosexual Behaviour of Adult Patas Monkeys in Captivity. Animal Behaviour 29:714–726.

Lumsden, Charles J.
1984 Parent-Offspring Conflict over the Transmission of Culture. Ethology and Sociobiology 5:111–129.

Lumsden, Charles J., and Edward O. Wilson
1981 Genes, Mind, and Culture: The Coevolutionary Process. Cambridge, Mass.: Harvard University Press.

1983 Promethean Fire: Reflections on the Origin of Mind. Cambridge, Mass.: Harvard University Press.

Mackey, Wade C.
1980 A Sociobiological Perspective on Divorce Patterns of Men in the United States. Journal of Anthropological Research 36:419–430.

Majerus, M. E. N., P. O. O'Donald, and J. Weir
1982 Female Mating Preference Is Genetic. Nature 300:521–523.

Marsh, C. W.
1979 Female Transfer and Mate Choice among Tana River Red Colobus. Nature 281:568–569.

Massey, Adrianne
   1977   Agonistic Aids and Kinship in a Group of Pigtail Macaques. Behavioral Biology and Sociobiology 2:31–40.

Mayer, Peter J.
   1980a   On the Evolution of Human Longevity: Evidence from New England Families 1600–1960. Paper read before the American Association of Physical Anthropologists.
   1980b   The Biocultural View of the Evolution of Human Longevity. Paper read before the Gerontological Society.
   1982   Evolutionary Advantage of the Menopause. Human Ecology 10:477–494.
   1984   Reply to Hames. Human Ecology 12:93–99.

Maynard Smith, J.
   1964   Group Selection and Kin Selection. Nature 201:1145–1147.

Mazur, Allan
   1983   Problems of Testing Inclusive Fitness Claims among Humans, with an Example on Sibship. Ethology and Sociobiology 4:225–229.

McCabe, Justine
   1983   FBD Marriage: Further Support for the Westermarck Hypothesis of the Incest Taboo? American Anthropologist 85:50–69.

McEachron, Donald L., and Darius Baer
   1982   A Review of Selected Sociobiological Principles: Applications to Hominid Evolution. II. The Effects of Intergroup Conflict. Journal of Social and Biological Structures 5:121–139.

McGinnis, Patrick R.
   1979   Sexual Behavior in Free-Living Chimpanzees: Consort Relationships. In The Great Apes. D. Hamburg and E. McCown, eds. pp. 429–439. Menlo Park: Benjamin Cummings.

McKenna, James J.
   1979   The Evolution of Allomothering Behavior among Colobine Monkeys: Function and Opportunism in Evolution. American Anthropologist 81:818–840.
   1981   Primate Infant Caregiving Behavior: Origins, Consequences, and Variability with Emphasis on the Common Indian Langur Monkey. In Parental Care in Mammals. D. Gubernick and P. Klopfer, eds. pp. 389–416. New York: Plenum Press.

Meikle, D. B., and S. H. Vessey
   1981   Nepotism among Rhesus Monkey Brothers. Nature 294:160–161.

Michael, Richard P., Robert W. Bonsall, and Doris Zumpe
   1978   Consort Bonding and Operant Behavior by Female Rhesus Monkeys. Journal of Comparative and Physiological Psychology 92:837–845.

Michael, Richard P., and G. S. Saayman
  1967   Individual Differences in Sexual Behavior of Male Rhesus Monkeys
         (*Macaca mulatta*) under Laboratory Conditions. Animal Behaviour 15:460–466.

Michod, Richard E.
  1979   Genetical Aspects of Kin Selection: Effects of Inbreeding. Journal of
         Theoretical Biology 81:223–234.
  1982   The Theory of Kin Selection. Annual Review of Ecology and Systematics
         13:23–55.

Michod, Richard E., and W. D. Hamilton
  1980   Coefficients of Relatedness in Sociobiology. Nature 288:694–697.

Milinski, Manfred
  1978   Kin Selection and Reproductive Value. Zeitschrift für Tierpsychologie
         47:528–529.

Millard, A. V., and E. A. Berlin
  1983   Sex Ratio and Natural Selection at the Human ABO Locus. Human
         Heredity 33:130–136.

Missakian, E. A.
  1973   Genealogical Mating Activity in Free-Ranging Groups of Rhesus Monkeys
         (*Macaca mulatta*) on Cayo Santiago. Behaviour 45:224–241.

Mitchell, G.
  1969   Paternalistic Behavior in Primates. Psychological Bulletin 71:399–417.

Mitchell, G., and E. M. Brandt
  1972   Paternal Behavior in Primates. *In* Primate Socialization. F. Poirier, ed. pp.
         173–206. New York: Random House.

Mitchell, G., G. Ruppenthal, E. Raymond, and H. Harlow
  1966   Long-Term Effects of Multiparous and Primiparous Monkey Mothering.
         Child Development 37:781–791.

Modahl, K. B., and G. C. Eaton
  1977   Display Behaviour in a Confined Troop of Japanese Macaques (*Macaca
         fuscata*). Animal Behaviour 25:525–535.

Moore, Jim
  1984   The Evolution of Reciprocal Sharing. Ethology and Sociobiology 5:5–14.

Moore, Jim, and Rauf Ali
  1984   Are Dispersal and Inbreeding Avoidance Related? Animal Behaviour
         32:94–112.

Morgan, Charles J.
  1979   Eskimo Hunting Groups, Social Kinship, and the Possibility of Kin
         Selection in Humans. Ethology and Sociobiology 1:83–86.

Mori, A.
1979 Analysis of Population Changes by Measurements of Body Weight in the Koshima Troop of Japanese Monkeys. Primates 20:371–397.

Muhsam, H. V.
1956 Fertility of Polygynous Marriages. Population Studies 10:3–16.

Mulder, Monique B., and T. M. Caro
1983 Polygyny: Definition and Application to Human Data. Animal Behaviour 31:609–610.

Munroe, Robert L., and Ruth H. Munroe
1976 Sociobiology: Another View. Reviews in Anthropology 3:556–558.

Murdock, George P.
1957 World Ethnographic Sample. American Anthropologist 59:664–687.

1967 Ethnographic Atlas. Pittsburgh: University of Pittsburgh Press.

1972 Anthropology's Mythology: Proceedings of the Royal Anthropological Institute of Great Britain and Ireland for 1971, 17–24.

Murdock, George P., and Suzanne F. Wilson
1972 Settlement Patterns and Community Organization: Cross-Cultural Codes 2. Ethnology 11:254–295.

Murray, R. Damel, and Euclid O. Smith
1983 The Role of Dominance and Intrafamilial Bonding in the Avoidance of Close Inbreeding. Journal of Human Evolution 12:481–486.

Myers, P.
1978 Sexual Dimorphism in Size of Vespertilionid Bats. American Naturalist 112:701–711.

Nash, L.
1978 The Development of the Mother-Infant Relationship in Wild Baboons. Animal Behaviour 26:746–759.

Needham, Rodney
1971 Remarks on the Analysis of Kinship and Marriage. In Rethinking Kinship and Marriage. R. Needham, ed. pp. 1–34. London: Tavistock.

Nishida, Toshisada
1979 The Social Structure of Chimpanzees of the Mahale Mountains. In The Great Apes. D. Hamburg and E. McCown, eds. pp. 73–121. Menlo Park: Benjamin Cummings.

1983 Alloparental Behavior in Wild Chimpanzees of the Mahale Mountains, Tanzania. Folia Primatologica 41:1–33.

Nishida, Toshisada, Shigeo Uehara, and Ramadhani Nyundo
1979 Predatory Behavior among Wild Chimpanzees of the Mahale Mountains. Primates 20:1–20.

O'Donald, Peter
1983a   Sexual Selection by Female Choice. *In* Mate Choice. P. Bateson, ed. pp. 53–66. Cambridge: Cambridge University Press.

1983b   Do Female Fruit Flies Choose Their Mates? A Comment. American Naturalist 122:413–416.

Orians, G. H.
1969   On the Evolution of Mating Systems in Birds and Mammals. American Naturalist 103:589–603.

O'Rourke, D. H.
1979   Components of Genetic and Environmental Variation in Hamadryas Baboon Morphometrics. American Journal of Physical Anthropology 50:469.

Otterbein, Keith F., and Charlotte S. Otterbein
1965   An Eye for an Eye, A Tooth for a Tooth: A Cross-Cultural Study of Feuding. American Anthropologist 67:1470–1482.

Oxnard, Charles E.
1983   Sexual Dimorphism in the Overall Proportions of Primates. American Journal of Primatology 4:1–22.

Packer, Craig
1977   Reciprocal Altruism in *Papio anubis.* Nature 265:441–443.

1979a   Inter-Troop Transfer and Inbreeding Avoidance in *Papio anubis.* Animal Behaviour 27:1–36.

1979b   Male Dominance and Reproductive Activity in *Papio anubis.* Animal Behaviour 27:37–45.

1980   Male Care and Exploitation of Infants in *Papio anubis.* Animal Behaviour 28:512–520.

Packer, Craig, and Anne E. Pusey
1983a   Adaptations of Female Lions to Infanticide by Incoming Males. American Naturalist 121:716–728.

1983b   Male Takeovers and Female Reproductive Parameters: A Simulation of Oestrous Synchrony in Lions (*Panthera leo*). Animal Behaviour 31:334–340.

Parke, R. D., and S. J. Suomi
1981   Adult Male-infant Relationships: Human and Nonhuman Primate Evidence. *In* Behavioral Development: The Bielefeld Conference. K. Immelmann et al., eds. pp. 700–725. Cambridge: Cambridge University Press.

Parker, G. A.
1974   Assessment Strategy and Evolution of Animal Conflicts. Journal of Theoretical Biology 47:223–243.

1982   Phenotype-Limited Evolutionarily Stable Strategies. *In* Current Problems in Sociobiology. King's College Sociobiology Group. pp. 173–201. Cambridge: Cambridge University Press.

1983   Mate Quality and Mating Decisions. *In* Mate Choice. P. Bateson, ed. pp. 141–166. Cambridge: Cambridge University Press.

Parker, G. A., and M. R. MacNair
1978   Models of Parent-Offspring Conflict. I. Monogamy. Animal Behaviour 26:97–110.

Partridge, Linda
1980   Mate Choice Increases a Component of Offspring Fitness in Fruit Flies. Nature 283:290–291.

1983   Non-random Mating and Offspring Fitness. *In* Mate Choice. P. Bateson, ed. pp. 227–255. Cambridge: Cambridge University Press.

Partridge, Linda, and L. Nunney
1977   Three-Generation Family Conflict. Animal Behaviour 25:785–786.

Paterson, Chris E., and Terry F. Pettijohn
1982   Age and Human Mate Selection. Psychological Reports 51:70.

Paul, Andreas, and Dieter Thommen
1984   Timing of Birth, Female Reproductive Success and Infant Sex Ratio in Semifree-Ranging Barbary Macaques. Folia Primatologica 42:2–16.

Pereira, Michael E.
1983   Abortion Following the Immigration of an Adult Male Baboon (*Papio cynocephalus*). American Journal of Primatology 4:93–98.

Popp, Joseph
1983   Ecological Determinism in the Life Histories of Baboons. Primates 24:198–210.

Price, Trevor D.
1984a   The Evolution of Sexual Size Dimorphism in Darwin's Finches. American Naturalist 123:500–518.

1984b   Sexual Selection on Body Size, Territory and Plumage Variables in a Population of Darwin's Finches. Evolution 38:327–341.

Pugesek, Bruce H.
1983   The Relationship Between Parental Age and Reproductive Effort in the California Gull (*Larus californicus*). Behavioral Ecology and Sociobiology 13:161–171.

Pusey, Anne
1983   Mother-Offspring Relationships in Chimpanzees after Weaning. Behaviour 31:363–377.

Quiatt, Duane
1979   Aunts and Mothers: Implications of Allomaternal Behavior of Nonhuman Primates. American Anthropologist 81:310–319.

Rainwater, L.
1960   And the Poor Get Children: Sex, Contraception, and Family Planning in the Working Class. Chicago: Quadrangle.

1965   Family Design: Marital Sexuality, Family Size, and Contraception. Chicago: Aldine.

Ralls, Katherine
1976   Mammals in Which Females are Larger than Males. Quarterly Review of Biology 51:245–276.

1977   Sexual Dimorphism in Mammals: Avian Models and Unanswered Questions. American Naturalist 111:917–938.

Ralls, Katherine, and Jonathan Ballou
1982   Effects of Inbreeding on Infant Mortality in Captive Primates. International Journal of Primatology 3:491–505.

Redican, William K.
1976   Adult Male-Infant Interactions in Nonhuman Primates. In The Role of the Father in Child Development. M. Lamb, ed. pp. 345–385. New York: John Wiley & Sons.

1978   Adult Male-Infant Relations in Captive Rhesus Monkeys. In Recent Advances in Primatology, vol. 1. D. Chivers and J. Herbert, eds. pp. 79–92. New York: Academic Press.

Richard, A. F., and S. R. Schulman
1982   Sociobiology: Primate Field Studies. Annual Review of Anthropology 11:231–255.

Richardson, P., and R. Boyd
1984   Natural Selection and Culture. BioScience 34:430–434.

Riedman, Marianne L.
1982   The Evolution of Alloparental Care and Adoption in Mammals and Birds. Quarterly Review of Biology 57:405–435.

Rijksen, Herman D.
1981   Infant Killing: A Possible Consequence of a Disputed Leader Role. Behaviour 78:138–168.

Riopelle, A., P. Hale, and E. Watts
1976   Protein Deprivation in Primates. VII. Determinants of Size and Skeletal Maturity at Birth in Rhesus Monkeys. Human Biology 48:203–222.

Robinson, James V.
1980   A Necessary Modification of Trivers' Parent-Offspring Conflict Model. Journal of Theoretical Biology 83:533–535.

Robinson, John G.
1982   Intrasexual Competition and Mate Choice in Primates. American Journal of Primatology, Supplement 1:131–144.

Rothstein, Stephen I.
1980   Reciprocal Altruism and Kin Selection Are Not Clearly Separable Phenomena. Journal of Theoretical Biology 87:255–261.

Rowell, Thelma E.
1970   Baboon Menstrual Cycles Affected by Social Environment. Journal of Reproduction and Fertility 21:133–141.

1974   The Concept of Social Dominance. Behavioral Biology 11:131–154.

1979   How Would We Know If Social Organization Were *Not* Adaptive? *In* Primate Ecology and Human Origins. I. Bernstein and E. Smith, eds. pp. 1–22. New York: Garland.

Rubenstein, D. I.
1982   Risk, Uncertainty and Evolutionary Strategies. *In* Current Problems in Sociobiology. King's College Sociobiology Group. pp. 91–112. Cambridge: Cambridge University Press.

Rubin, Paul H., James B. Kau, and Edward P. Meeker
1979   Forms of Wealth and Parent-Offspring Conflict. Journal of Social and Biological Structures 2:53–64.

Ruse, Michael
1979   Sociobiology: Sense or Nonsence. Dordrecht:Reidel.

1982   Darwinism Defended: A Guide to the Evolution Controversies. Reading, Mass.: Addison-Wesley.

Rutberg, Allen T.
1983   The Evolution of Monogamy in Primates. Journal of Theoretical Biology 104:93–112.

Saayman, G. S.
1971   Behavior of the Adult Males in a Troop of Free-Ranging Chacma Baboons (*Papio ursinus*). Folia Primatologica 15:36–57.

Sackett, Gene P.
1980   Receiving Severe Aggression Correlates with Fetal Gender in Pregnant Pigtail Monkeys. Developmental Psychobiology 14:267–272.

Sackett, Gene P., R. A. Holm, A. E. Davis, and C. E. Farenbuch
1975   Prematurity and Low Birth Weight in Pigtail Macaques: Incidence, Prediction, and Effects on Infant Development. *In* Proceedings of Symposia of the Fifth Congress of the International Primatological Society. S. Kondo et al. eds. pp. 189–205. Tokyo: Japan Science Press.

Sade, Donald S.
1968   Inhibition of Son-Mother Mating among Free-Ranging Rhesus Monkeys. *In* Science and Psychoanalysis, vol. 12: Animal and Human. J. Masserman, ed. pp. 18–38. New York: Grune and Stratton.

Sade, Donald S., Katherine Cushing, Peter Cushing, Janet Dunaif, Angel Figueroa, Jay R. Kaplan, Carol Lauer, Douglas Rhodes, and Jonathan Schneider
   1976   Population Dynamics in Relation to Social Structure on Cayo Santiago. Yearbook of Physical Anthropology 20:253–262.

Sahlins, Marshall
   1972   Stone Age Economics. Chicago: Aldine.
   1976   The Use and Abuse of Biology. Ann Arbor: University of Michigan Press.

Sanghvi, L. D.
   1966   Inbreeding in India. Eugenics Quarterly 13:291–301.

Sassenrath, E. N.
   1970   Increased Advanced Responsiveness Related to Social Stress in Rhesus Monkeys. Hormones and Behavior 1:283–298.

Sassenrath, E. N., L. J. Hein, and A. A. Kaita
   1969   Social Behavior and Corticoid Correlates in Macaca mulatta. In Proceedings of the Second International Congress of Primatology. C. Carpenter, ed. pp. 220–231.

Schaik, C. P. van
   1983   Why are Diurnal Primates Living in Groups? Behaviour 87:120–143.

Schaik, C. P. van, and J. A. R. A. M. van Hooff
   1983   On the Ultimate Causes of Primate Social Systems. Behaviour 85:91–117.

Schaik, C. P. van, and Maria A. van Noordwijk
   1983   Social Stress and the Sex Ratio of Neonates and Infants among Non-human Primates. Netherlands Journal of Zoology 33:249–265.

Schaik, C. P. van, Maria A. van Noordwijk, Rob J. de Boer, and Isolde den Tonkelaar
   1983   The Effect of Group Size on Time Budgets and Social Behavior in Wild Long-Tailed Macaques (Macaca fascicularis). Behavioral Ecology and Socio-biology 13:173–181.

Schaik, C. P. van, Maria A. van Noordwijk, Bambang Warsono, and Edy Suyriono
   1983   Party Size and Early Detection of Predators in Sumatran Forest Primates. Primates 24:211–221.

Schneider, David M.
   1976   The Meaning of Incest. Journal of the Polynesian Society 85:149–169.

Schubert, Glendon
   1982   Infanticide by Usurper Hanuman Langur Males: A Sociobiological Myth. Social Sciences Information 21:199–244.

Schull, W. J., and J. V. Neel
   1965   The Effects of Inbreeding on Japanese Children. New York: Harper and Row.

Schulman, Steven R., and Bernard Chapais
1980   Reproductive Value and Rank Relations among Macaque Sisters. American Naturalist 115:580–593.

Schulman, Steven R., and Daniel I. Rubenstein
1983   Kinship, Need, and the Distribution of Altruism. American Naturalist 121:776–788.

Schumacher, A.
1982   On the Significance of Stature in Human Society. Journal of Human Evolution 11:697–701.

Scollay, Patricia A., and Patricia DeBold
1980   Allomothering in a Captive Colony of Hanuman Langurs (*Presbytis entelleus*). Ethology and Sociobiology 1:291–299.

Searcy, William A., and Ken Yasukawa
1983   Sexual Selection and Red-Winged Blackbirds. American Scientist 71:166–174.

Seay, B.
1966   Maternal Behavior in Primiparous and Multiparous Rhesus Monkeys. Folia Primatologica 4:146–168.

Seemanova, Eva
1971   A Study of Children of Incestuous Matings. Human Heredity 21:108–128.

Selander, R. K.
1966   Sexual Dimorphism and Differential Niche Utilization in Birds. Condor 68:113–151.

1972   Sexual Selection and Dimorphism in Birds. *In* Sexual Selection and the Descent of Man, 1971–1971. B. Campbell, ed. pp. 180–230. Chicago: Aldine.

Seyfarth, Robert M.
1976   Social Relationships among Adult Female Baboons. Animal Behaviour 24:917–938.

1977   A Model of Social Grooming among Adult Female Monkeys. Journal of Theoretical Biology 65:671–698.

1978   Social Relationships among Adult Male and Female Baboons. I. Behaviour during Sexual Consortship. Behaviour 64:204–226. II. Behaviour throughout the Female Reproductive Cycle. Behaviour 64:227–247.

1980   The Distribution of Grooming and Related Behaviours among Adult Female Vervet Monkeys. Animal Behaviour 28:798–813.

Seyfarth, Robert M. and Dorothy L. Cheney
1984   Grooming, Alliances, and Reciprocal Altruism in Vervet Monkeys. Nature 308:541–542.

Shepher, Joseph
  1971   Mate Selection among Second Generation Kibbutz Adolescents and Adults: Incest Avoidance and Negative Imprinting. Archives of Sexual Behavior 1:293–307.

  1983   Incest: A Biosocial View. New York: Academic Press.

Sherman, Paul W.
  1980   The Limits of Ground Squirrel Nepotism. In Sociobiology: Beyond Nature/Nurture? G. Barlow and J. Silverberg, eds. pp. 505–544. Boulder: Westview Press.

Shields, William M. and Lea M. Shields
  1983   Forcible Rape: An Evolutionary Perspective. Ethology and Sociobiology 4:115–136.

Shively, C., S. Clarke, N. King, S. Schapiro, and G. Mitchell
  1982   Patterns of Sexual Behavior in Male Macaques. American Journal of Primatology 2:373–384.

Sigusch, V., and G. Schmidt
  1971   Lower-Class Sexuality: Some Emotional and Social Aspects in West German Males and Females. Archives of Sexual Behavior 1:29–44.

Silk, Joan B.
  1979   Feeding, Foraging and Food Sharing Behavior of Immature Chimpanzees. Folia Primatologica 31:123–142.

  1980a Adoption and Kinship in Oceania. American Anthropologist 82:799–820.

  1980b Kidnapping and Female Competition among Captive Bonnet Macaques. Primates 21:100–110.

  1982   Altruism among Female Macaca radiata: Explanations and Analysis of Patterns of Grooming and Coalition Formation. Behaviour 79:162–188.

  1983   Local Resource Competition and Facultative Adjustment of Sex Ratios in Relation to Competitive Abilities. American Naturalist 121:56:–66.

  1984a Local Resource Competition and the Evolution of Male-Biased Sex Ratios. Journal of Theoretical Biology 108:203–213.

  1984b Measurement of the Relative Importance of Individual Selection and Kin Selection among Females of the Genus Macaca. Evolution 38:553–559.

Silk, Joan B., and Robert Boyd
  1983   Cooperation, Competition, and Mate Choice in Matrilineal Macaque Groups. In Social Behavior of Female Vertebrates. S. Wasser, ed. pp. 315–347. New York: Academic Press.

Silk, Joan B., Cathleen B. Clark-Wheatley, Peter S. Rodman, and Amy Samuels
  1981   Differential Reproductive Success and Facultative Adjustment of Sex Ratios among Captive Female Bonnet Macaques (Macaca radiata). Animal Behaviour 29:1106–1120.

Silk, Joan B., Amy Samuels, and Peter S. Rodman
1981 The Influence of Kinship, Rank, and Sex on Affiliation and Aggression between Adult Female and Immature Bonnet Macaques (*Macaca radiata*). Behaviour 78:111–137.

Silverberg, James
1980 Sociobiology, the New Synthesis? An Anthropologist's Perspective. *In* Sociobiology: Beyond Nature/Nurture? G. Barlow and J. Silverberg, eds. pp. 25–74. Boulder: Westview Press.

1984 "Foreword" to A Guide to Primate Sociobiological Theory and Research, by J. Patrick Gray. pp. v–viii. New Haven: Human Relations Area Files.

Simonds, Paul E.
1974 Sex Differences in Bonnet Macaque Networks and Social Structure. Archives of Sexual Behavior 3:151–166.

Simpson, M. J. A., and A. E. Simpson
1982 Birth Sex Ratio and Social Rank in Rhesus Monkey Mothers. Nature 300:440–441.

Simpson, M. J. A., A. E. Simpson, J. Hooley, and M. Zunz
1981 Infant-Related Influences on Birth Intervals in Rhesus Monkeys. Nature 290:49–51.

Slatkin, Montgomery
1984 Ecological Causes of Sexual Dimorphism. Evolution 38:622–630.

Small, Meredith F.
1981 Body Fat, Rank, and Nutritional Status in a Captive Group of Rhesus Macaques. International Journal of Primatology 2:91–95.

1983 Females without Infants: Mating Strategies in Two Species of Captive Macaques. Folia Primatologica 40:125–133.

Small, Meredith F., and David Glenn Smith
1981 Interactions with Infants by Full Siblings, Paternal Half-Siblings, and Nonrelatives in a Captive Group of Rhesus Macaques (*Macaca mulatta*). American Journal of Primatology 1:91–94.

1982 The Relationship between Maternal and Paternal Rank in Rhesus Macaques (*Macaca mulatta*). Animal Behaviour 30:626–627.

Smith, David Glenn
1980 Paternity Exclusion in Six Captive Groups of Rhesus Monkeys (*Macaca mulatta*). American Journal of Physical Anthropology 53:243–249.

1981 The Association between Rank and Reproductive Success of Male Rhesus Monkeys. American Journal of Primatology 1:83–90.

1982 Inbreeding in Three Captive Groups of Rhesus Monkeys. American Journal of Physical Anthropology 58:447–451.

Smith, Eric A.
  1983   Evolutionary Ecology and the Analysis of Human Social Behavior. *In*
         Human Adaptation: Biological and Cultural Models. R. Dyson-Hudson and M.
         Little, eds. pp. 23–40. Boulder: Westview Press.

Smuts, Barbara
  1982   Special Relationships between Adult Male and Female Olive Baboons
         (*Papio anubis*). Ph.D. dissertation, Stanford University.

Snowdon, C. T., and S. J. Suomi
  1982   Paternal Behavior in Primates. *In* Nurturance, vol. 3: Studies of Develop-
         ment in Nonhuman Primates. H. Fitzgerald, J. Mullins, and P. Child, eds. pp.
         63–108. New York: Plenum Press.

Spielman, R. S., J. V. Neel, F. H. Li
  1977   Inbreeding Estimation from Population Data: Models, Procedures and
         Implications. Genetics 85:355–371.

Spiro, M. E.
  1958   Children of the Kibbutz. Cambridge, Mass.: Harvard University Press.

Stamps, Judy A., and Robert A. Metcalf
  1980   Parent-Offspring Conflict. *In* Sociobiology: Beyond Nature/Nurture? G.
         Barlow and J. Silverberg, eds. pp. 589–618. Boulder: Westview Press.

Stamps, Judy A., Robert A. Metcalf, and V. V. Krishnan
  1978   A Genetic Analysis of Parent-Offspring Conflict. Journal of Behavioral
         Ecology and Sociobiology 3:369–392.

Stein, David M., and Peter B. Stacey
  1981   A Comparison of Infant-Adult Male Relations in a One-Male Group with
         Those in a Multi-Male Group of Yellow Baboons (*Papio cynocephalus*). Folia
         Primatalogica 36:264–276.

Stephenson, Gordon R.
  1975   Social Structure of Mating Activity in Japanese Macaques. *In* Proceedings
         from the Symposia of the Fifth Congress of the International Primatological
         Society. S. Kondo et al., eds. pp. 63–115. Tokyo: Japan Science Press.

Stern, Bonnie R., and David Glenn Smith
  1984   Sexual Behavior and Paternity in Three Captive Groups of Rhesus
         Monkeys (*Macaca mulatta*). Animal Behaviour 32:23–32.

Stern, C.
  1973   Principles of Human Genetics. San Francisco: W. H. Freeman.

Struhsaker, Thomas T.
  1967   Social Behavior among Vervet Monkeys (*Cercopithecus aethiops*). Behaviour
         29:6–121.

1975   The Red Colobus Monkey. Chicago: University of Chicago Press.

Strum, S. C.
1982   Agonistic Dominance in Male Baboons: An Alternative View. International Journal of Primatology 3:175–202.

Suarez, Brian, and D. R. Ackerman
1971   Social Dominance and Reproductive Behavior in Male Rhesus Monkeys. American Journal of Physical Anthropology 35:219–222.

Sugiyama, Yukimaru
1971   Characteristics of the Social Life of Bonnet Macaques (*Macaca radiata*). Primates 12:247–266.

Sugiyama, Yukimaru, and Hideyuki Ohsawa
1982   Population Dynamics of Japanese Monkeys with Special Reference to the Effect of Artificial Feeding. Folia Primatologica 39:238–263.

Symons, Donald
1979   The Evolution of Human Sexuality. Oxford: Oxford University Press.

Takahata, Yukio
1980   The Reproductive Biology of a Free-Ranging Troop of Japanese Monkeys. Primates 21:303–329.

1982   The Socio-Sexual Behavior of Japanese Monkeys. Zeitschrift für Tierpsychologie 59:89–108.

Talmon, Y.
1964   Mate Selection in Collective Settlements. American Sociological Review 29:491–508.

Taub, David M.
1980   Female Choice and Mating Strategies among Wild Barbary Macaques (*Macaca sylvanus* L.). In The Macaques: Studies in Ecology, Behavior, and Evolution. D. Lindberg, ed. pp. 287–344. New York: Van Nostrand Reinhold.

Taub, David M., ed.
1984   Primate Paternalism: An Evolutionary and Comparative View of Male Investment. New York: Van Nostrand Reinhold.

Taylor, Peter D., and George C. Williams
1982   The Lek Paradox Is Not Resolved. Theoretical Population Biology 22:392–409.

Textor, Robert B.
1967   A Cross-Cultural Summary. New Haven: HRAF Press.

Thiessen, Del, and Barbara Gregg
1980   Human Assortative Mating and Genetic Equilibrium: An Evolutionary Perspective. Ethology and Sociobiology 1:111–140.

Thompson, Philip Richard
  1980   "And Who Is My Neighbor?" An Answer from Evolutionary Genetics.
         Social Science Information 19:341–384.

Thornhill, Randy
  1980   Rape in *Panorpa* Scorpionflies and a General Rape Hypothesis. Animal
         Behaviour 28:52–59.

Thornhill, Randy and Nancy W. Thornhill
  1983   Human Rape: An Evolutionary Analysis. Ethology and Sociobiology
         4:137–173.

Timmermans, P. J. A., W. G. P. Schouten, and J. C. M. Krijnen
  1981   Reproduction of Cynomolgus Monkeys (*Macaca facsicularis*) in Harems.
         Laboratory Animals 15:119–123.

Tobias, P. V.
  1962   On the Increasing Stature of the Bushman. Anthropos 57:801–810.

Tokuda, Kisaburo
  1961–62   A Study on the Sexual Behavior in the Japanese Monkey Troop.
            Primates 3(2):1–40.

Trivers, Robert L.
  1971   The Evolution of Reciprocal Altruism. Quarterly Review of Biology 46:35–
         57.

  1972   Parental Investment and Sexual Selection. *In* Sexual Selection and the
         Descent of Man, 1871–1971. B. Campbell, ed. pp. 136–179. Chicago: Aldine.

  1974   Parent-Offspring Conflict. American Zoologist 14:249–264.

Trivers, Robert L., and D. E. Willard
  1973   Natural Selection of Parental Ability to Vary the Sex Ratio of Offspring.
         Science 179:90–92.

Tutin, Caroline E. G.
  1979   Mating Patterns and Reproductive Strategies in a Community of Wild
         Chimpanzees (*Pan troglodytes* schweinfurthii). Behavioral Ecology and Socio-
         biology 6:29–38.

Tutin, Caroline E. G., and Patrick R. McGinnis
  1981   Chimpanzee Reproduction in the Wild. *In* Reproductive Biology of the
         Great Apes. C. Grahman, ed. pp. 239–264. New York: Academic Press.

van den Berghe, Pierre L.
  1979   Human Family Systems: An Evolutionary View. New York: Elsevier.

  1980   Incest and Exogamy: A Sociobiological Reconsideration. Ethology and
         Sociobiology 1:151–162.

  1983   Human Inbreeding Avoidance: Culture in Nature. The Behavioral and
         Brain Sciences 6:91–123.

van den Berghe, Pierre L., and G. M. Mescher
1980   Royal Incest and Inclusive Fitness. American Ethnologist 7:300–317.

van Wagenen, G., and H. R. Catchpole
1956   Physical Growth of the Rhesus Monkey. American Journal of Physical Anthropology 14:245–256.

Vehrencamp, Sandra L.
1983a   Optimal Degree of Skew in Cooperative Societies. American Zoologist 23:327–335.

1983b   A Model for the Evolution of Despotic versus Egalitarian Societies. Animal Behaviour 31:667–682.

Verner, J.
1964   Evolution of Polygyny in the Long-Billed Marsh Wren. Evolution 18:252–261.

Verner, J., and M. F. Willson
1966   The Influence of Habitats on Mating Systems of North American Passerine Birds. Ecology 47:143–147.

Voland, Eckart
1984   Human Sex-Ratio Manipulation: Historical Data from a German Parish. Journal of Human Evolution 13:99–107.

Wade, Michael
1977   An Experimental Study of Group Selection. Evolution 31:134–153.

1978   A Critical Review of the Models of Group Selection. Quarterly Review of Biology 53:101–114.

1979   The Evolution of Social Interactions by Family Selection. American Naturalist 113:399–417.

Wade, Michael L., and Stevan J. Arnold
1980   The Intensity of Sexual Selection in Relation to Male Sexual Behaviour, Female Choice, and Sperm Precedence. Animal Behaviour 28:446–461.

Wade, Ted D.
1979   Inbreeding, Kin Selection, and Primate Social Evolution. Primates 20:355–370.

Wasser, Samuel K.
1983   Reproductive Competition and Cooperation among Female Yellow Baboons. In Social Behavior of Female Vertebrates. S. Wasser, ed. pp. 349–390. New York: Academic Press.

Wasser, Samuel K. and David P. Barash
1981   The Selfish "Allomother": A Comment on Scollay and DeBold (1980). Ethology and Sociobiology 2:91–93.

Weatherhead, Patrick J., and Raleigh J. Robertson
  1979   Offspring Quality and the Polygny Threshold: "The Sexy Son Hypothesis."
  American Naturalist 113:201–208.

Weigel, Ronald
  1981   The Distribution of Altruism among Kin: A Mathematical Model. American
  Naturalist 118:191–201.

Weigel, Ronald M., and M. Margaret Taylor
  1982   Testing Sociological Theory with Respect to Human Polyandry: A Reply to
  Beall and Goldstein. American Anthropologist 84:406–408.

Weinrich, James D.
  1977   Human Sociobiology: Pair-Bonding and Resource Predictability (Effects of
  Social Class and Race). Behavioral Ecology and Sociobiology 2:91–118.

  1978   Reply to Lande. Behavioral Ecology and Sociobiology 3:96–98.

Werner, Dennis
  1979   A Cross-Cultural Perspective on Theory and Research on Male Homosexuality. Journal of Homosexuality 4:345–362.

Werren, J. H., M. R. Gross, and R. Shine
  1980   Paternity and the Evolution of Male Paternal Care. Journal of Theoretical
  Biology 82:619–631.

West, Mary M. and Melvin J. Konner
  1976   The Role of the Father: An Anthropological Perspective. In The Role of the
  Father in Child Development. M. Lamb, ed. pp. 185–217. New York: John Wiley
  & Sons.

West-Eberhard, M. J.
  1975   The Evolution of Social Behavior by Kin Selection. Quarterly Review of
  Biology 50:1–33.

  1983   Sexual Selection, Social Competition, and Speciation. Quarterly Review of
  Biology 58:155–183.

Westermarck, Edward
  1899   The History of Human Marriage. London: MacMillian.

  1922   The History of Human Marriage, vol. 2. New York: Allerton.

Western, Jonah D., and Shirley C. Strum
  1983   Sex, Kinship, and the Evolution of Social Manipulation. Ethology and
  Sociobiology 4:19–28.

Wheatley, Bruce P.
  1982   Adult Male Replacement in Macaca fascicularis of East Kalimantan, Indonesia. International Journal of Primatology 3:203–219.

Whiting, John W. M.
  1964   Effects of Climate on Certain Cultural Practices. In Explorations in Cultural
  Anthropology. W. Goodenough, ed. pp. 511–544. New York: McGraw-Hill.

Whiting, John W. M., Richard Kluckhohn, and Albert Anthony
  1958   The Function of Male Initiation Ceremonies at Puberty. *In* Readings in Social Psychology, 3d ed. E, Maccoby et al., eds. pp. 359–370. New York: Holt, Rinehart and Winston.

Whiting, John W. M. and Beatrice B. Whiting
  1975   Aloofness and Intimacy of Husbands and Wives: A Cross-Cultural Study. Ethos 3:183–207.

Williams, B. J.
  1980   Kin Selection and Cultural Evolution. *In* Sociobiology: Beyond Nature/Nurture? G. Barlow and J. Silverberg, eds. pp. 573–587. Boulder: Westview Press.

Williams, George C.
  1957   Pleiotrophy, Natural Selection, and the Evolution of Senescence. Evolution 11:398–411.

  1966   Adaptation and Natural Selection. Princeton: Princeton University Press.

  1971   Group Selection. Chicago: Aldine.

  1979   The Question of Adaptive Sex Ratio in Outcrossed Vertebrates. Proceedings of the Royal Society of London, B. Biological Sciences 205:567–580.

Wilson, David S.
  1975   A Theory of Group Selection. Proceedings of the National Academy of Sciences 72:143–146.

  1983   The Group Selection Controversy: History and Current Status. Annual Review of Ecology and Systematics 14:159–187.

Wilson, Edward O.
  1975a   Sociobiology: The New Synthesis. Cambridge, Mass.: Harvard University Press.

  1975b   Some Central Problems of Sociobiology. Social Sciences Information 14(6):5–18.

  1977   Biology and the Social Sciences. Daedalus 106:127–140.

  1978   The Nature of Human Nature. New Scientist 80(1125):20–22.

  1979   On Human Nature. Cambridge, Mass.: Harvard University Press.

  1980   A Consideration of the Genetic Foundation of Human Social Behavior. *In* Sociobiology: Beyond Nature/Nurture? G. Barlow and J. Silverberg, eds. pp. 295–306. Boulder: Westview Press.

Wilson, Mark E.
  1981   Social Dominance and Female Reproductive Behaviour in Rhesus Monkeys (*Macaca mulatta*). Animal Behaviour 29:472–482.

Wilson, Mark E., Thomas P. Gordon, and Irwin S. Bernstein
  1978   Timing of Births and Reproductive Success in Rhesus Monkey Social Groups. Journal of Medical Primatology 7:202–212.

Wilson, Mark E., Thomas P. Gordon, and Dennis Chikazawa
   1982   Female Mating Relationships in Rhesus Monkeys. American Journal of
   Primatology 2:21–27.

Wilson, Mark E., Margaret L. Walker, and Thomas P. Gordon
   1983   Consequences of First Pregnancy in Rhesus Monkeys. American Journal of
   Physical Anthropology 61:103–110.

Witkowski, Stanley R.
   1975   Polygyny, Age of Marriage, and Female Status. Paper read before the
   American Anthropological Association.

Witt, R., C. Schmidt, and J. Schmitt
   1981   Social Rank and Darwinian Fitness in a Multimale Group of Barbary
   Macaques (*Macaca sylvana* Linnaeus, 1758): Dominance Reversals and Male
   Reproductive Success. Folia Primatologica 36:201–211.

Wittenberger, James F.
   1980   Group Size and Polygamy in Social Mammals. American Naturalist
   115:197–222.

   1981a   Male Quality and Polygyny: The "Sexy Son" Hypothesis Revisited.
   American Naturalist 117:329–342.

   1981b   Animal Social Behavior. Boston: Duxbury Press.

Wolf, Arthur P.
   1966   Childhood Association, Sexual Attraction, and the Incest Taboo: A
   Chinese Case. American Anthropologist 68:883–898.

   1968   Adopt a Daughter-in-Law, Marry a Sister: A Chinese Solution to the
   Problem of the Incest Taboo. American Anthropologist 70:864–874.

   1970   Childhood Association and Sexual Attraction: A Further Test of the
   Westermarck Hypothesis. American Anthropologist 72:503–515.

   1976   Childhood Association, Sexual Attraction, and Fertility in Taiwan. *In*
   Demographic Anthropology: Quantitative Approaches. E. Zubrow, ed. pp.
   227–244. Albuquerque: University of New Mexico Press.

Wolf, Arthur P., and Chieh-shan Huang
   1980   Marriage and Adoption in China, 1845–1945. Stanford: Stanford University
   Press.

Wolfe, Linda D.
   1979   Behavioral Patterns of Estrous Females of the Arashiyama West Troop of
   Japanese Macaques (*Macaca fuscata*). Primates 20:525–534.

   1981a   Display Behavior of Three Troops of Japanese Monkeys (*Macaca fuscata*).
   Primates 22:24–32.

   1981b   A Case of Male Adoption in a Troop of Japanese Monkeys (*Macaca fuscata
   fuscata*). *In* Primate Behavior and Sociobiology. A. Chiarelli and R. Corruccini,
   eds. pp. 156–160. Berlin: Springer-Verlage.

   1983   Female Rank and Reproductive Success among Arashiyama B Japanese

Macaques (*Macaca fuscata*). To appear in International Journal of Primatology. (appeared in 1984, 5:133–143).

Wolfe, Linda D. and J. Patrick Gray
1981   Comment on Gaulin and Schlegel (1980). Ethology and Sociobiology 2:95–98.
1982a Latitude and Intersocietal Variation of Human Sexual Dimorphism of Stature. Human Ecology 10:409–416.
1982b A Cross-Cultural Investigation into the Sexual Dimorphism of Stature. *In* Sexual Dimorphism in *Homo sapiens:* A Question of Size. R. Hall, ed. pp. 197–230. New York: Praeger.

Wolpoff, Milford H.
1981   An Egg's Way. Reviews in Anthropology 8:1–8.

Wrangham, Richard W.
1975   The Behavioural Ecology of Chimpanzees in Gombe National Park, Tanzania. Ph.D. dissertation, Cambridge University.
1979   On the Evolution of Ape Social Systems. Social Science Information 18:335–386.
1980   An Ecological Model of Female-Bonded Primate Groups. Behaviour 75:262–299.
1981   Drinking Competition in Vervet Monkeys. Animal Behaviour 29:904–910.
1982   Mutualism, Kinship and Social Evolution. *In* Current Problems in Sociobiology. King's College Sociobiology Group. pp. 269–289. Cambridge: Cambridge University Press.

Wu, Hannah M. H., Warren G. Holmes, Steven R. Medina, and Gene P. Sackett
1980   Kin Preference in Infant *Macaca nemestrina*. Nature 285:225–227.

Wynne-Edwards, V. C.
1962   Animal Dispersion in Relation to Social Behavior. New York: Hafner.

Yengoyan, Aram A.
1981   Infanticide and Birth Order: An Empirical Analysis of Preferential Female Infanticide among Australian Aboriginal Populations. Anthropology UCLA 7:255–273.

Zahavi, A.
1975   Mate Selection—A Selection for a Handicap. Journal of Theoretical Biology 53:205–214.

Zeveloff, Samuel I., and Mark S. Boyce
1982   Why Neonates Are So Altricial. American Naturalist 120:537–542.

Zucker, E. L., and J. R. Kaplan
1981   Allomaternal Behavior in a Group of Free-Ranging Patas Monkeys. American Journal of Primatology 1:57–64.

Name Index

Subject Index

Society and Species Index